SQL
Fundamentals

SQL
Fundamentals

John J. Patrick

Prentice Hall PTR
Upper Saddle River, New Jersey 07458

Library of Congress Cataloging-in-Publication Data

Patrick, John J.
 SQL fundamentals / John J. Patrick
  p. cm.
 ISBN 0-13-096016-0
 1. SQL (Computer program language) I. Title.
QA76.73.S67P38 1999
005.75'65—dc21   99-24536
                   CIP

Editorial/Production Supervision: *Mary Sudul*
Acquisitions Editor: *Michael E. Meehan*
Editorial Assistant: *Bart Blanken*
Marketing Manager: *Bryan Gambrel*
Manufacturing Manager: *Pat Brown*
Cover Design Direction: *Jayne Conte*
Cover Design: *Bruce Kenselaar*

Prentice Hall books are widely used by corporations and government agencies for training, marketing, and resale.

The publisher offers discounts on this book when ordered in bulk quantities. For more information, contact Corporate Sales Department, Phone: 800-382-3419; fax: 201-236-714; email: corpsales@prenhall.com or write Corporate Sales Department, Prentice Hall PTR, One Lake Street, Upper Saddle River, NJ 07458.

Printed in the United States of America

10 9 8 7 6 5 4 3 2 1

ISBN 0-13-096016-0

Prentice-Hall International (UK) Limited, *London*
Prentice-Hall of Australia Pty. Limited, *Sydney*
Prentice-Hall Canada Inc., *Toronto*
Prentice-Hall Hispanoamericana, S.A., *Mexico*
Prentice-Hall of India Private Limited, *New Delhi*
Prentice-Hall of Japan, Inc., *Tokyo*
Simon & Schuster Asia Pte. Ltd., *Singapore*
Editora Prentice-Hall do Brasil, Ltda., *Rio de Janeiro*

Dedicated to four wonderful teachers

Seymour Hayden, who taught me mathematics
Stanley Sultan, who taught me Irish literature
Jim Seibolt, who taught me computers
Scot Stoney, who taught me databases

and to all my students

Table of Contents

Preface

SQL is quickly becoming one of the most important computer languages. It is now used in over one hundred software products, and new ones are being added frequently. This book explains how to use SQL to solve practical problems using actual SQL products. The products used in this book are Oracle and Access. They are two of the most widely used SQL products. They are also easily available and run on the personal computers many people have. By discussing these two products in detail, the door is opened to allow you to use any of the one hundred products based on SQL.

Every concept in this book is illustrated with an example of SQL code. In most cases, a task is set, then the SQL code is given to complete that task. The beginning and ending tables of data are also shown. There are more than 200 of these examples.

A web site will support this book to keep it up to date. New versions of Oracle or Access may be released. This may cause some of the examples to stop working. If that occurs, a new version of the example will be available from the web site.

In several places throughout this book, I have expressed opinions about computer technology, something that many technical books eschew. These opinions are my own and I take full responsibility for them. I also reserve the right to change my mind. If I do so, I will put my revised opinion on the web and the reasons that have caused me to change my thinking.

The web site for this book is:

`www.prenhall.com/divisions/ptr/`

Finally, I want to express my thanks and appreciation to all my students at UC Berkeley Extension. Your questions and insights contributed greatly to this book. Thanks also to Prentice Hall, particularly to my editor, Mike Meehan, and production manager, Mary Sudul.

Chapter 1

Storing Information in Tables

In Relational Databases all the data is stored in tables and all the results are expressed in tables. In this chapter we will examine tables in detail.

Introduction

What is SQL?

SQL is a computer language designed to get information from data that is stored in a Relational Database. I will discuss Relational Database in a moment. For now, you can think of it as one method of organizing a large amount of data on a computer. SQL allows you to find the information you want from a vast collection of data. The purpose of this book is to show you how to get the information you want from a database.

SQL is different from most other computer languages. With SQL, you describe the type of information you want. Then the computer determines the best procedure to use to obtain it and runs that procedure. This is called a "Declarative" computer language. The focus is on the result. You specify what the result should look like. The computer is allowed to use any method of processing as long as it obtains the correct result.

Most other computer languages are "Procedural." These are languages like C, Cobol, Java, Assembler, Fortran, Visual Basic—and many others. In these languages, you describe the procedure that will be applied to the data. You do not describe the result. The result is whatever emerges from applying the procedure to the data.

Let me use an analogy to compare these two approaches. Suppose I go to a coffee shop in the morning. With the Declarative approach, used by SQL, I can say WHAT I want—"I would like a cup of coffee and a donut." With the Procedural approach, I cannot say that. I have to say HOW the result can be obtained and give a specific procedure for it. That is, I have to say how to make a cup of coffee and how to make a donut. So, for the coffee, I have to say "Grind up some roasted coffee beans, add boiling water to them, allow the coffee to brew, pour it into a cup, and give it to me." For the donut, I will have to read from a cookbook. Clearly, the Declarative approach is much closer to the way we usually speak and it is much easier for most people to use.

The fact that SQL is relatively easy to use—relative to most other computer languages—is the main reason it is so popular and important. The claim is often made that anyone can learn SQL in a day or two. I think that claim is more a wish than it is reality. After all, SQL is a computer language, and computers are not as easy to use as a telephone—at least not yet.

Nonetheless, SQL is easy to use. With one day of training, most people can learn to obtain a lot of useful information. That includes people who are not programmers. People throughout an organization, from secretaries to vice presidents, can use SQL to obtain the information they need to make business decisions. At least, that is the hope and, to a large extent, it has been shown to be true.

Information is not powerful in itself. It only becomes powerful when it is available to most people throughout an organization—and at the time they need to use it. SQL is a tool for delivering that information.

About SQL:

- SQL is the language for getting information from a Relational Database.
- SQL says WHAT information to get, rather than HOW to get it.
- Basic SQL is easy to learn.
- SQL empowers people by giving them control over information.
- SQL allows people to handle information in new ways.
- SQL makes information powerful by bringing it to people at the time they need it.

Figure 1-1   What is SQL?

What Is a Relational Database and Why Would You Use One?

A Relational Database is one way to organize data in a computer. There are also many other ways to organize it. In this book, we will not discuss these other ways, except to say that each method has some strengths and some drawbacks. For now, we will look at the strengths that a Relational Database has to offer.

SQL is one of the main reasons to organize data into a Relational Database. Using SQL, information can be obtained from the data fairly easily by people throughout the organization. That is very important.

Another reason is that data in a Relational Database can be used by many people at the same time. Sometimes hundreds or thousands of people can all share the data in a database. All the people can see the data and all the people can change the data (if they have the authority to do so.) From a business perspective, it is a way to coordinate all the employees and have everybody working from the same body of information.

A third reason is that Relational Database is designed with the expectation that your information requirements may change over time. You may need to reorganize the information you have or add new pieces of information to it. Relational Databases are designed to make this type of change easy. Most other computer systems are difficult to change. They assume that you know what all the requirements will be, before you start to construct them. My experience is that people are not very good at predicting the future—even when they say they can. But, here I am showing my own bias toward using Relational Databases.

From the perspective of a computer programmer, the flexibility of a Relational Database and the availability of SQL make it possible to develop new computer applications much more rapidly than with traditional techniques. Some organizations take advantage of this. Others do not.

The ideas of a Relational Database were first developed in the early 1970's to handle very large amounts of data—millions of records. At first, the Relational Database was thought of as a "Back End Processor" that would provide information to a computer application written in a procedural language—such as C or Cobol. Even now, Relational Databases bear some of the birthmarks of that heritage.

Today, however, the ideas have been so successful that entire information systems are often constructed as Relational Databases, without much need for procedural code (except to support input forms.) That is, the ideas that were originally developed to have a supporting role for procedural code have now taken center stage. Much of the procedural code is no longer needed.

In Relational Databases all the data is kept in tables, which are two dimensional structures with columns and rows. I will describe tables in detail, later in this chapter. After you work with them for awhile, representing data in term of tables is a very nice data structure. It adapts easily to changes, it shares the data with all the users at the same time, and it runs SQL. Many people start thinking of their data in terms of tables. Tables become the metaphor of choice when working with data.

Today, many people use small personal databases to keep their address book, catalog their music tapes, organize their libraries, or track their finances. Many business applications are also built as Relational Databases. Many people prefer to have their data in a database—even if it has only a few records in it.

About Relational Databases—in the 1970s:

- Relational Databases were originally developed in the 1970's to organize a large amount of information in a consistent and coherent manner.

- They allowed thousands of people to work with the same information at the same time.

- They kept the information current and consistent at all times.

- They made information easily available to people at all levels of an organization - from secretaries to vice presidents. They used SQL, forms, standardized reports, and ad-hoc reports to deliver information to people in a timely manner.

- They empowered information by making it available when and where it could be used.

- They empowered people by making current information available to them at the time they needed to use it.

About Relational Databases—in the 1990s:

- There are also many smaller databases, used by a single person or shared by a few people.

- Databases have been so successful and are so ease to use that they are now employed for a wider range of application than they were originally designed for.

- Many people prefer to keep their data in databases.

Figure 1-2   What is a relational database and why would you use one?

Why Learn SQL?

SQL is used in over 100 software products. Once you learn SQL, you will be able to use all of these products. Of course, each one will require a little study of its special features, but you will soon feel at home with it and know how to use it. So, you can use this one set of skills over and over again.

There are reasons why SQL is used so much. One reason is that it is "relatively easy to learn"—relative to many other computer languages. Another reason is that it opens the door to Relational Databases and the many advantages they offer. Some people say that SQL is the best feature of Relational Databases and it is what makes them successful. Other people say that Relational Databases make SQL successful. But, most people agree that together they are a winning team.

SQL is the most successful Declarative computer language—a language where you say What you want rather than How to get it. There are some other Declarative languages and report generation tools, but most of them are much more limited in what they can do. SQL is more powerful and can be applied in more situations.

SQL can help you get information from a database that may not be available to people who do not know SQL. It can help you learn and understand the many products that are based on it.

Finally, (don't tell your boss) learning SQL can b enjoyable and fun. It can stretch your mind and give you new tools to think with. You might start to view some things from a new perspective.

Major SQL Products	**Other SQL Products** **(and products based on SQL)**
Oracle **MS Access** **DB2** **SQL Server** **Informix** **SQL Windows** **Sybase** **SAS sql procedure** **FoxPro** **dBase** **Tandom SQL**	SQLBase Cold Fusion SAP Business Objects ODBC Ingres Ocelot SQL OsloData PostgreSQL Rapid SQL XDB SQL/DS Mini SQL Empress Interbase Progress Supra SQL Report Writer Paradox Delphi VAX SQL Essbase Beagle SQL GNU SQL Server Just Logic/SQL PrimeBase Altera SQL Server Essentia Datascope PowerBuilder (and many more)

Figure 1-3   Why learn SQL?

What is in this book?

The subject of the book

This book shows you how to use SQL to get information from a Relational Database. It begins with simple queries that retrieve selected data from a single table. It progresses step by step to advanced queries that summarize the data, combine it with data from other tables, or display the data in specialized ways. It goes beyond the basics and shows you how to get the information you need from the database you have.

Who should read this book?

Everyone with an interest in getting information from a database can read this book. It can be a first book about databases for people who are new to the subject. You do not need to be a computer programmer. The discussion begins at the beginning. It does not assume any prior knowledge about databases. The only thing you need is the persistence to work through the examples and a little prior experience working with your own computer.

Professional programmers can also use .this book. The techniques shown here can help them find the solutions to many problems. Whether you are a novice or a professional, an end-user or a manager, the SQL skills you learn will be useful to you over and over again.

Organization of this book

This book discusses the practical realities of getting information from a database. A series of specific tasks are accomplished and discussed. Usually, the task and its solution are shown on the right-hand page. The left-hand page facing it discusses the theory and the details of the solution.

The tasks are designed and arranged to show the most important aspects of the subject. Each topic is discussed thoroughly and in an organized manner. All the major features and "surprising aspects" of each topic are shown.

Why compare two different implementations of SQL— Oracle and Access?

If a book that discusses only the theory of SQL, and no particular product that implements it, then the reader will be left with no practical skills. He or she will be able to think about things, but never be able to touch them.

If a book discusses only one implementation of SQL, then it is easy to get distracted by the quirks and special features it has. You also lose sight of the fact that SQL is used in many products, although in slightly different ways.

This book compares Oracle and Access because they are two of the most widely used SQL products and because they both run on a PC. They are somewhat different. You will see them side by side. Oracle is used mostly for larger business applications. Access is used mostly for personal databases applications and for smaller business applications.

Limitations of this book

Every book has some limitations. Some boundaries must be set to keep it focused and to limit its size. This section discusses the boundaries I set for this book. Many readers may prefer to skip this section and go on to the next topic.

This book is not intended to replace the technical manuals. It is a guide to the subject and tells you most of what you need to know. It presents examples of SQL commands and discusses many of their features. It shows the most useful options. However, it does not attempt to cover all the options or to discuss the detailed syntax of the commands. For that information, you will need to refer to the technical manuals or online help.

Oracle and Access are both very complex products and have many features. Each can run SQL in a variety of ways. To compare them, I had to pick a specific way to run each product. I tried to pick the method that is most commonly used by people who are seeking information from a database. For Oracle, I chose the Personal Oracle product running in the SQL Plus environment. For Access, I chose to enter SQL commands into the SQL window.

There are graphical techniques that are supposed to make SQL even easier. These are "one finger" report generation tools—"you just point and click." Most of them are based on the QBE grid (Query By Example.) I have not included them in this book because my purpose is to teach the SQL language in its character-based format. Also, these tools differ from product to product and each one has different limitation in what it can do.

The SQL language is used to build and administer databases in addition to getting information from them. These are important topics, but they require a book of their own. These topics and the SQL commands that support them are not discussed here.

This is a book about "interactive SQL." It does not cover "embedded SQL." With interactive SQL, a person writes SQL commands directly to the database, perhaps submitting queries to get information. With embedded SQL, the SQL commands are contained within a traditional computer program, which might be written in C or Cobol.

The SQL standard is not discussed in detail. There are two main SQL standards, SQL-89 and SQL-92. The SQL-89 standard, adopted in 1989, guides most of the SQL products available today. Most of the SQL features discussed in this book come from that standard. The SQL-92 standard was first adopted in 1992 and has been amended many times since then. Some of its features and orientations are still controversial. As of 1999, few commercial database products offer all of its features—or even desire to do so.

Instead of discussing the "official" SQL standard, I have chosen to discuss two of the most widely used implementations of SQL. To me, software that is actually being used sets the "de facto" SQL standard.

In this book I have chosen to emphasize the similarities between Oracle and Access SQL. I have not given as much weight to contrasting them and showing their differences. My purpose is to show the basic ideas of SQL and the techniques that will work in all the products that are based on it.

Figure 1-4   What is in this book?

The Parts of a Table

SQL always deals with data that is in tables. You probably understand tables already on an informal level. In this section we discuss the tables used in a Relational Database. We have to define what a table is and what its part are in order to use them on a computer. Computers need precise definitions.

Data is stored in tables

In a Relational Database, all the data is stored in tables. A table is a two dimensional structure that has "columns" and "rows." Using more traditional computer terminology, the columns are "fields" and the rows are "records." You can use either terminology.

Most people are familiar with seeing information in tables. Bus schedules are usually presented in tables. Newspapers use table to list the values of stocks. We all know how to use these tables. Tables are a good way to present a lot of information in a very condensed format. The tables in a Relational Database are very similar to these tables, which we all understand and use every day.

ALL the information in a Relational Database is kept in tables. There is no other type of container to keep it in—there are no other data structures. Even the most complex information is stored in tables. Someone once said that there are three types of data structures in a Relational Database—tables, and tables, and tables. In a Relational Database, we have nothing but tables—that means no numbers, no words, no letters, no dates—unless they are stored in a table.

Now, you might think that this restricts what a Relational Database can do and the data it can represent. Is it a limitation? The answer is NO. All data is capable of being represented in this format. Sometimes you have to do some work to put it in this format. It doesn't always just fall into this format by itself. But you can always succeed at putting data into tables, no matter how complex that data is. This has been proven in mathematics. (But I will not show you the proof here.)

Now let me talk to the computer programmers for a moment. Other readers can go to the next topic. In computer science, we study hierarchies, doubly linked lists, stacks, networks, and many other data structures. Can we really replace all of them with tables? Yes, we can. Usually, it is not as efficient to use tables—the computer does not run as fast. But anything you can do with any other data structure, can also be done using tables.

An abstract picture of a table

An example of a table: A table of information about children

First Name	Last Name	Age	Gender	Favorite Game
Nancy	Jones	1	F	Peek-a-boo
Paula	Jacobs	5	F	Acting
Deborah	Kahn	4	F	Dolls
Howard	Green	7	M	Baseball
Jack	Lee	5	M	Trucks
Cathy	Rider	6	F	Monsters

Each row contains information about one child.

Each column contains one type of information for all the children.

Notes
- In a Relational Database, all the data is stored in tables.
- A table has two dimensions called "Columns" and "Rows."
- Tables can hold even the most complex information.
- All operations begin with tables and end with tables. All the data is represented in tables.

Figure 1-5   Data is stored in tables

A row represents an object and the information about it

Each row of a table represents one object, event, or relationship. I will call them all objects for now, so I do not have to keep repeating the phrase "object, event, or relationship."

All the rows within a table represent the same type of object. If you have 100 doctors in a hospital, you might keep all the information about them in a single table. But, if you also want to keep information about 1000 patients who are in the hospital, usually you would use a different table for that information.

The tables in a Relational Database may contain hundreds or thousands of rows. Some tables even contain many millions of rows. In theory, there is no limit to the number of rows a table can have. In practice, your computer will limit the number of rows you can have. Today, business databases running on large computers sometimes reach 30,000,000 rows.

There are also some tables with only one row of data. You can even have an empty table with no rows of data in it. This is something like an empty box. Usually, a table is only empty when you first build it. After it is created, you start to put rows of data into it.

In a Relational Database, the rows of a table are considered to be in no particular order. They are an unordered set. This is different from the tables most people are familiar with. In a bus schedule, the rows are in a definite and logical order—they are not scrambled in a random order.

The reason for this difference is that the computer and the DBAs (DataBase Administers) who administer it are allowed to change the order of the rows in a table to make the computer more efficient. As a result, you, the end-user seeking information, cannot count on the rows being in some particular order.

An abstract picture of a row

Notes

- A row contains data for one object, event, or relationship.
- All the rows in a table contain data for similar objects, events, or relationships.
- A table may contain hundreds or thousands of rows.
- The rows of a table are not in a predictable order

Figure 1-6 A row represents an object and the information about it

A column represents one type of information

A column contains one particular type of information that is kept about all the rows in the table. A column cannot contain one type of information for one row and another type for another row. Each column usually contains a separate type of information.

Each column has a name, for instance "hair color." and a datatype. We will discuss datatypes in chapter 4, but for now let's keep it simple. There are three main datatypes—text, numbers, and dates. This means that there are three types of columns—columns containing text, columns containing numbers, and columns containing dates.

Some columns allow nulls, which are unknown values. Other columns do not allow them. If a column does not allow nulls, then data is required in the column for every row of the table. This means, it is a required field. When a column does allow nulls, the field is optional.

Most tables contain 5 to 40 columns. A table can contain more columns, 250 or more, depending on the Relational Database product you are using, but this is unusual.

Each column has a position within the table. That is, the columns are an ordered set. This contrasts with the rows, which have no fixed order.

Information about the columns—their names, datatypes, positions, and whether they accept nulls or not—is all considered to be part of the definition of the table itself. In contrast, information about the rows is not considered to be part of the definition of the table.

An abstract picture of a column

Notes

- A column contains one type of data about each row of the table.

- Each column has a name.

- Each column has a data type. The most important data types are:

    Text
    Numbers
    Dates and times

- Some columns accept nulls, others do not. A null is an unknown value.

- Each column has a position within the table. In contrast to rows, the columns of a table form an ordered set. There is a first column and a last column.

- Most tables have 40 columns or less.

Figure 1-7   A column represents one type of information

A cell is the smallest part of a table

A "cell" occurs where one row meets with one column. It is the smallest part of a table and it cannot be broken down into smaller parts of the table. A cell contains one single piece of data, a single unit of information.

A cell can contain:

> one word
> one letter
> one number
> one date (and time)
> a null

At least, this is the way you should begin to think about it. In practice, sometimes a cell can contain an entire sentence or paragraph or more.

A column is a collection of cells. They all have the same datatype and represent the same type of information.

A row is a collection of cells. Together, they represent information about the same object, event, or relationship.

An abstract picture of a cell

Notes

- A cell contains a single piece of data, a single unit of information.
- Usually a cell contains one of the following types of data:

  text—sometimes one word
  text—sometimes one letter (a code, such as M for male and F for female.)
  a number
  a date and time
  a null, which is an unknown value
- All the cells in a column contain the same type of information.
- All the cells in a row contain data about the same object, event, or relationship.

Figure 1-8   A cell is the smallest part of a table

Each cell should express just one thing

Each cell expresses just one thing—one piece of information. That is the intent of the theory of Relational Databases. In practice, it is not always clear what this means. The problem, partly, is that English and other spoken languages are not clear about it. Another part of the problem is that information does not always come in separate discrete units.

Let's examine one case in detail. A person, in America, usually has two names—a first name and a last name. Now that is a bit of a problem to me when I want to put information in the computer. There is one person, but there are two names. How should I identify the person? Should I put both names together in one cell? Or, should I put the names into two separate cells? The answer is not clear.

Both methods are valid. The designers of the database usually decide questions like this. If the database designers think that both names will always be used together, then they will usually put both names in a single cell.

But, if they think that we will sometimes use the names separately, then they will put each name in a separate cell.

The problem with this is that the way a database is used may change over time. So, even if a decision is correct when it is made, it may become incorrect later on.

Two ways to show the name of a person in a table

1. One column for the name.
    Both the first and last names are put in a single cell.

Full Name

| Susan Riley |

2. Two separate columns—one for the first name and another for the last name
    Each cell contains a single word.

First Name   Last Name

| Susan | Riley |

Notes

*   Both methods are equally valid.

*   The first method emphasizes that Susan Riley is one person, even though the English language uses two separate words to express her name. It implies that we will usually call her "Susan Riley," using both her names together as a single unit.

*   The second method emphasizes the English words. It implies that we will want to use several different variations of her name, calling her "Susan" or "Susan Riley" or "Miss Riley."

*   The database design intends each cell to be used in whole or not used at all. In theory, you should not need to subdivide the data in a cell. However in practice, that is sometimes required.

Figure 1-9   Each cell should express just one thing

Primary Key columns identify each row

Most tables contain a "primary key." This primary key identifies each row in the table and gives it a name. Each row must have its own identity. No two rows are allowed to have the same primary key.

The primary key consists of several columns of the table. By convention, these are usually the first columns in the table. The primary key may be one column or more than one. We say that there is only one primary key, even when it consists of several columns. So, it is the collection of these columns, taken as a single unit, that is the primary key and serves to identify each row.

The primary key is like a noun. It names the object of each row. The other columns are like adjectives. They give additional information about the object.

A table can only contain a single primary key, even if it consists of several columns. This makes sense because there is no point in identifying a row twice—those identities could conflict with each other. Suppose, for example, that we have a table of employees. Each employee can be identified by an employee number or by a social security number. The database designers would need to choose which column to make the primary key of the table. They could choose either one to be the primary key of the table, or they could choose to use both together to make a primary key. But, they are not allowed to say that each column by itself is a primary key.

The name of a column is considered to be part of he definition of the table. In contrast, the name of a row, which is the primary key of the row, is considered to be part of the data in the table.

There are two rules that regulate the columns of the primary key of a table:

1. None of the columns of the primary key can contain a null in any row. This makes sense because a null in an unknown value. So, a null in any part of the primary key would mean we do not know the identity of the object or the row. In databases, we do not want to enter information about unidentified rows.

2. Each row must have an identity that is different from every other row in the table. That is, no two rows can have the same identity—the same values in all the column of the primary key. The values of some of the columns can be the same, but there must be at least one column of the primary key where their values are different.

The first column is usually the primary key of the table

Primary
Key

A			
B			
C			
D			

But sometimes the primary key is the first several column of the table

Primary Key

A	1		
A	2		
B	1		
B	2		

Notes

* Most tables have primary keys.

* Usually, the primary key consists of the first column or the first several columns of the table.

* The primary key names the object, event, or relationship the row represents. In grammatical terms, it is a noun. It is the subject of all the information in the row.

* The other columns of the table make statements about the primary key. In grammatical terms, they are adjectives or adverbs that describe the object named by the primary key and give additional information about it.

Figure 1-10 Primary key columns identify each row

Most Tables are Tall and Thin

Many books on SQL give the impression that tables are usually square- that they have about the same number of row as they have columns. This false impression is left because the tables in most SQL books are approximately square. In any book, the tables must be kept small. In a book, when you run SQL code, you must be able to examine the results in full detail.

However, the tables that are used in real production systems usually have a different shape. They are tall and thin. They may have 30 columns, but 1,000,000 rows.

Not all tables have this shape, but most do. Some tables have only one row.

I suppose I am telling you this because I am one of the people who likes to visualize the data and the tables I am working with. If you like to visualize it too, then at least I have provided you with the correct picture. If you are not inclined to visualize these things, then do not worry about it, just go on to the next page.

Most tables have many more rows than columns

Figure 1-11   Most tables are tall and thin

Examples of tables

An example of a table in Oracle and Access

Up to now, we have discussed tables in theory. Now let's take a look at a real table. We will look at it in both Oracle and in Access. This is our first opportunity to examine how Oracle and Access compare with each other.

You will have to decide for yourself how similar they are and how different they are. To me, this example shows that they are about 90% similar and about 10% different. Of course, this is just one example. Ask yourself what numbers you would use to describe this.

Similarities between Oracle and Access

- Column names are printed at the top of the column. The column names are part of the structure of the table, they are not considered part of the data in the table.
- Columns containing text data are justified to the left.
- Columns containing numbers are justified to the right.
- Columns containing dates often display only the date and do not include the time. However, the data actually contains both the date and the time.

Differences between Oracle and Access

- DISPLAY FRAMEWORK. Oracle displays lines of character data. Access uses graphical techniques to display the data in a grid and color the borders of the grid.
- CASE. The Oracle table is shown in all upper case. The Access table uses upper case only for the first letter. It is a common convention to set the databases up this way. Mixed case data can be put into an Oracle table, but this makes the data more difficult to handle. So, Oracle data is usually either all upper case or all lower case. Access data is handled as if it is all upper case, although it is displayed in mixed case. This makes it look nicer, but sometimes it can also be deceiving.
- COLUMN HEADINGS. Oracle can use several lines for a column heading. Access displays the heading on a single line.
- DATE FORMATS. The dates are shown in different formats.
    Oracle date format: 29-JAN-98.
    Access date format: 01-29-1998
Actually both Oracle and Access can display dates in a variety of formats. These are the default formats which are used when no other format is specified. Oracle data contains a four-digit year even though it only displays the last two digits of the year.
- DATE ALIGNMENT. Oracle aligns date to the left. Access aligns them to the right.
- NULLS. We have set up Oracle to always display nulls as "(null)." This cannot be done in Access.
- CURSOR The Access table contains a cursor that points to a position on the screen. The Oracle table does not contain a cursor.
- THE LAST ROW. In Access, a blank row at the bottom of a table indicates that new rows of data can be entered into the table. This is not done in Oracle.

L_employees table—Oracle format

```
EMPLOYEE                          DEPT              CREDIT PHONE  MANAGER
      ID FIRST_NAME  LAST_NAME   CODE HIRE_DATE     LIMIT NUMBER      ID
-------- ----------  ----------  ---- ----------   ------- ------ -------
     201 SUSAN       BROWN       EXE  01-JUN-92    $30.00 3484   (null)
     202 JIM         KERN        SAL  15-AUG-95    $25.00 8722      201
     203 MARTHA      WOODS       SHP  01-FEB-97    $25.00 7591      201
     204 ELLEN       OWENS       SAL  01-JUL-96    $15.00 6830      202
     205 HENRY       PERKINS     SAL  01-MAR-98    $25.00 5286      202
     206 CAROL       ROSE        ACT  15-OCT-97    $15.00 3829      201
     207 DAN         SMITH       SHP  01-DEC-96    $25.00 2259      203
     208 FRED        CAMPBELL    SHP  01-APR-97    $25.00 1752      203
     209 PAULA       JACOBS      MKT  17-MAR-98    $15.00 3357      201
     210 NANCY       HOFFMAN     SAL  15-FEB-96    $25.00 2974      203
```

L_employees table—Access Format

Employee_id	First_name	Last_name	Dept_code	Hire_date	Credit_limit	Phone_number	Manager_id
201	Susan	Brown	Exe	06-01-1992	$30.00	3484	
202	Jim	Kern	Sal	08-15-1995	$25.00	8722	201
203	Martha	Woods	Shp	02-01-1997	$25.00	7591	201
204	Ellen	Owens	Sal	07-01-1996	$15.00	6830	202
205	Henry	Perkins	Sal	03-01-1998	$25.00	5286	202
206	Carol	Rose	Act	10-15-1997	$15.00	3829	201
207	Dan	Smith	Shp	12-01-1996	$25.00	2259	203
208	Fred	Campbell	Shp	04-01-1997	$25.00	1752	203
209	Paula	Jacobs	Mkt	03-17-1998	$15.00	3357	201
210	Nancy	Hoffman	Sal	02-15-1996	$25.00	2974	203
0					$0.00		0

Record: 11 of 11

Figure 1-12   An example of a table in Oracle and Access

Some database design decisions

The table we saw in the previous figure contained some design decisions that I want to point out to you because they reflect some common practices. Like all design decisions, they could have been made in other ways. This is not the only way to design the table. It may not even be the best way. But, it is a way you may encounter often and you need to be aware of it.

Decisions to be aware of

- The Phone Number column contains text data, not numbers. Although the data looks like numbers, and the column name says "numbers," it actually has a data type of "Text." You can tell this be its alignment, which is to the left. The reason the table is set up this way is that the Phone Number will be never be used for arithmetic. You never add two phone numbers together, or multiply them. You only use them the way they are, as a text field. So this table stores them as text.

- The Employee Id column contains numbers. You can tell this by its alignment, which is to the right. Now, we do not do arithmetic with Employee Ids, we never add them together, so why isn't this a text field too? The answer is that numbers are often used for primary key columns even when no arithmetic will be performed on them. This can make the computer handle the table more quickly.

- The Manager Id column contains numbers, but it is not a primary key column. So why doesn't it contain text? This column is intended to match with the Employee Id column, so it has been given the same data type as that column. This will improve the speed of matching the two columns.

- The name of the table, "L_employees" may seem strange. The "L" indicates that this table is part of a group of tables. The names of all the tables in the group start with the same letter(s). In this case it shows that the table is part of the "Lunches" database. (Here I am using the term "database" to mean a collection of related tables.)

L_employees table—Oracle format

```
EMPLOYEE                        DEPT                CREDIT PHONE   MANAGER
      ID FIRST_NAME LAST_NAME   CODE HIRE_DATE       LIMIT NUMBER      ID
-------- ---------- ----------  ---- ----------     ------- ------  -------
     201 SUSAN      BROWN       EXE  01-JUN-92       $30.00 3484    (null)
     202 JIM        KERN        SAL  15-AUG-95       $25.00 8722       201
     203 MARTHA     WOODS       SHP  01-FEB-97       $25.00 7591       201
     204 ELLEN      OWENS       SAL  01-JUL-96       $15.00 6830       202
     205 HENRY      PERKINS     SAL  01-MAR-98       $25.00 5286       202
     206 CAROL      ROSE        ACT  15-OCT-97       $15.00 3829       201
     207 DAN        SMITH       SHP  01-DEC-96       $25.00 2259       203
     208 FRED       CAMPBELL    SHP  01-APR-97       $25.00 1752       203
     209 PAULA      JACOBS      MKT  17-MAR-98       $15.00 3357       201
     210 NANCY      HOFFMAN     SAL  15-FEB-96       $25.00 2974       203
```

Figure 1-13   Some database design decisions

The Lunches database

Most of the examples of SQL code in this book are based on the Lunches database. Appendix B contains a complete listing of this database. To read this book, you will need to understand the story and the data. Here is the basic story.

There is a small company with ten employees. This company will serve lunch to its employees of three occasions. Each employee can attend as many of these lunches as his or her schedule permits. When an employee registers to attend a lunch, they get to pick what they want to eat. Ten foods are available for them to pick from. They can decide to have a single portion or a double portion of any of these foods. The Lunches database keeps track of all this information.

That is the story. Now let's look at the data. When I call this a "database," I mean that it is a collection of related tables. The set of tables, taken together, tell the story. There are six tables in this database:

Employees
Departments
Lunches
Foods
Suppliers
Lunch Items

To show that these tables are all related to each other and to distinguish them from other tables we may use, the names of these tables are all prefixed with the letter L. When there are multiple words, such as "Lunch Items," the spaces are replaced with underscore characters. This helps the computer understand that the two words together are a single name.

The "L_employees" table lists all the employees. Each employee can be identified by an Employee Id, which is a number assigned to them. This allows the company to hire new people without worrying that two people in the company might have the same name.

Each employee works for one department. The Department Code is shown in the Employees table. The full name of each department is shown in the "L_departments" table. These tables can be linked together by matching the "Dept_code" columns. For example, The Employees table shows us that employee 202, Jim Kern, has a Department Code of "SAL." The Departments table says that the "Sales" department uses the Department Code "SAL." So, this tells us that Jim Kern works in the sales department.

Each employee has a manager, who is also an employee of the company. The manager is identified by their Employee Id. For instance, the Manager Id column shows that Jim Kern is managed by employee 201. Employee 201 is Susan Brown.

Susan Brown is the only employee without a manager. You can tell this because there is a null in her Manager Id column. This is because she is the head of the company. The null in this case, does not mean that we do not know who her manager is. Rather it means that she does not have a manager.

The "L_lunches" table registers an employee to attend a lunch. It assigns a Lunch Id to each lunch that will be served. For example, employee 202, Jim Kern, will attend a lunch on November 16, 1998. His lunch is identified as Lunch Id = 2.

L_employees table

```
EMPLOYEE                         DEPT                CREDIT PHONE  MANAGER
      ID FIRST_NAME LAST_NAME   CODE HIRE_DATE       LIMIT NUMBER      ID
-------- ---------- ----------  ---- ----------      ------ ------ -------
     201 SUSAN      BROWN       EXE  01-JUN-92      $30.00 3484   (null)
     202 JIM        KERN        SAL  15-AUG-95      $25.00 8722      201
     203 MARTHA     WOODS       SHP  01-FEB-97      $25.00 7591      201
     204 ELLEN      OWENS       SAL  01-JUL-96      $15.00 6830      202
     205 HENRY      PERKINS     SAL  01-MAR-98      $25.00 5286      202
     206 CAROL      ROSE        ACT  15-OCT-97      $15.00 3829      201
     207 DAN        SMITH       SHP  01-DEC-96      $25.00 2259      203
     208 FRED       CAMPBELL    SHP  01-APR-97      $25.00 1752      203
     209 PAULA      JACOBS      MKT  17-MAR-98      $15.00 3357      201
     210 NANCY      HOFFMAN     SAL  15-FEB-96      $25.00 2974      203
```

L_departments table

```
DEPT
CODE DEPARTMENT_NAME
---- --------------------
ACT  ACCOUNTING
EXE  EXECUTIVE
MKT  MARKETING
PER  PERSONNEL
SAL  SALES
SHP  SHIPPING
```

L_lunches table

```
          LUNCH     EMPLOYEE
LUNCH_ID DATE            ID
-------- ---------- --------
       1 16-NOV-98      201
       2 16-NOV-98      202
       3 16-NOV-98      203
       4 16-NOV-98      207
       5 16-NOV-98      206
       6 16-NOV-98      210
       7 25-NOV-98      201
       8 25-NOV-98      205
       9 25-NOV-98      204
      10 25-NOV-98      207
      11 25-NOV-98      208
      12 04-DEC-98      201
      13 04-DEC-98      203
      14 04-DEC-98      205
      15 04-DEC-98      210
      16 04-DEC-98      208
```

Figure 1-14   The Lunches database (part 1 of 2)

The "L_foods" table lists the foods an employee can choose for their lunch. Each food is identified by a Supplier Id and a Product Code. The Product Codes belong to the suppliers. It is possible for two suppliers to use the same product code for different foods. In fact, the product code "AS" has two different meanings. Supplier JBR uses this product code to mean "soda," but supplier VSB uses it to mean "dessert."

The price increases are proposed, but are not yet in effect. The nulls in the Price Increase column mean that there will be price increase for this food item.

The "L_suppliers" table shows the full names for the suppliers of the foods. For example, the Foods table shows that the french fries will be obtained from Supplier Id FRV. And the Suppliers table shows that the full name of this supplier is "Frank Reed's Vegetables".

The "L_lunch_items" table shows which foods each employee has chosen for their lunch. It also shows whether they want a single or a double portion. For example, look at Lunch Id 2, which we already know to be Jim Kern's lunch on November 16. It consists of four items. The first item is identified as "ASP-SW," here I am putting the Supplier Id and the Product Code together separated by a dash. Looking in the Foods table, we find this is a sandwich. The Lunch Items table says he want two of them, which is shown in the Quantity column. See if you can figure out all the foods he wants for his lunch.

The correct answer is:

> 2 sandwiches
> 1 order of french fries
> 2 cups of coffee
> 1 dessert

If you understand this, that is all you need to know about this database.

L_foods table

```
SUPPLIER PRODUCT  MENU                                      PRICE
ID       CODE     ITEM DESCRIPTION           PRICE INCREASE
-------- -------  ----- -------------------- ------- --------

ASP      FS          1 FRESH SALAD           $2.00   $0.25
ASP      SP          2 SOUP OF THE DAY       $1.50  (null)
ASP      SW          3 SANDWICH              $3.50   $0.40
CBC      GS          4 GRILLED STEAK         $6.00   $0.70
CBC      HB          5 HAMBURGER             $2.50   $0.30
FRV      BR          6 BROCCOLI              $1.00   $0.05
FRV      FF          7 FRENCH FRIES          $1.50  (null)
JBR      AS          8 SODA                  $1.25   $0.25
JBR      VR          9 COFFEE                $0.85   $0.15
VSB      AS         10 DESSERT               $3.00   $0.50
```

L_suppliers table

```
SUPPLIER
ID       SUPPLIER_NAME
-------- -------------------------
ARR      ALICE & RAY'S RESTAURANT
ASP      A SOUP PLACE
CBC      CERTIFIED BEEF COMPANY
FRV      FRANK REED'S VEGETABLES
FSN      FRANK & SONS
JBR      JUST BEVERAGES
JPS      JIM PARKER'S SHOP
VSB      VIRGINIA STREET BAKERY
```

L_lunch_items table

```
                   SUPPLIER PRODUCT
LUNCH_ID ITEM_NUMBER ID      CODE    QUANTITY
-------- ----------- -------- ------- ---------

       1           1 ASP      FS             1
       1           2 ASP      SW             2
       1           3 JBR      VR             2
       2           1 ASP      SW             2
       2           2 FRV      FF             1
       2           3 JBR      VR             2
       2           4 VSB      AS             1
       3           1 ASP      FS             1
       3           2 CBC      GS             1
       3           3 FRV      FF             1
       3           4 JBR      VR             1
       3           5 JBR      AS             1


(and many more rows)
```

Figure 1-14   The Lunches database (part 2 of 2)

Oracle and Access

This section tells you how to obtain Oracle and Access. It also shows you how to use them with this book. In order to understand this book fully, you need to obtain one or both of these products. On a first reading, you can skim over this section to see what is here. Later, you will want to refer back to it when you need the details.

Obtaining Oracle and Access

Obtaining Oracle

This book uses a product called "Personal Oracle." It is also called "Oracle8 Personal Edition." You can obtain a trial copy of it on a CD-ROM for:

less than $5.00!

This trial copy is sufficient for everything you need to use with this book. You can also download it over the internet, which is free. I recommend you get the CD-ROM for $5.00 because it takes several hours to get it from the internet. You will get the CD-ROM within a few days. Later, if you want a fully licensed copy, for instance, to use for a business, you will need to buy it for about $400.00.

Personal Oracle can be run under the Windows operating systems—Windows 95, Windows 98, and Windows NT. There is also a version that can run under UNIX operating systems. At present. it does not run under Apple or other operating systems - but check the Oracle web site for current information. This book was written using version 8.0 of Oracle.

To order the CD-ROM, go to the Oracle web site:

www.oracle.com

Follow the links called "Try and Buy" You will get to a page called "Trial Software." You can order the Personal Oracle CD-ROM from that page.

Installing Oracle

Follow the instructions to install Personal Oracle. You should install the complete version with the standard options.

Obtaining Access

Many people already have Access. It come with the Microsoft Office package of products—if you get the Professional edition.

If you want to buy Access separately, it will cost you about $110.00 with the student discount. It will cost you about $300.00 without the student discount. Talk to your software dealers to find out how you can obtain the student discount. Often, you only need to register for one course at a local college or university.

Access works primarily with the Windows operating systems—95, 98, and NT. But, other versions may be available. This book was written using Access 97.

Figure 1-15   Obtaining Oracle and Access

Using Oracle

Starting the Oracle program

The first time you use Oracle, you must start the database engine. Look for "Personal Oracle8" on your startup menu. Then choose "Start Database."

You only need to do this the first time you use Oracle, unless you stop the database. Stopping the database can free up memory and other computer resources.

Once the database has been started, go to the "Oracle" menu item and choose "SQL Plus." "SQL Plus" is the environment that Personal Oracle runs in. You will be asked to log into the database and identify yourself. The screen will look like this:

When you install Oracle, the userids that are set up for you are:

User Name	Password	Notes
po8	po8	This is for an end_user
scott	tiger	This is for an end-user
demo	demo	This is for an end-user
system	manager	This is for a DBA (administrator)

At first, you should use po8/po8, because it is a blank userid. Scott/Tiger and Demo/Demo have demonstration tables on them you may want to look at. Later, you can set up your own users from the Systems/Manager userid. Leave the "Host String" blank. Press Enter. You will get a screen that looks like this:

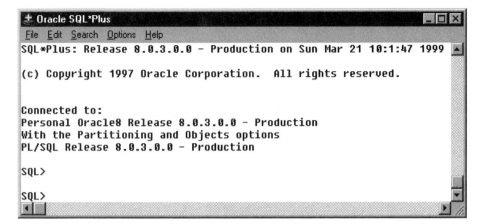

Now, you have started Personal Oracle. You need to do on more thing, if you want to use it with this book. Put the CD-ROM from this book into your drive. Then, enter the command:

    START Z:\ORACLE\CHAPTER1.SQL

Use the correct letter for your CD-ROM drive in place of Z. And use the number of the chapter you are reading in place of 1.

This cleans your userid and builds all the tables you will need for that chapter. (You have to press Enter to confirm that it is OK to clean your userid.) It also sets up a standard working environment. You will need to issue this command every time you log on to Oracle. Otherwise, the environment will not be set up correctly. The tables may still be there, but the database may be case sensitive. After you run this command, you will see a screen like:

```
± Oracle SQL*Plus                                              _ □ ×
 File  Edit  Search  Options  Help
.    *************************************************************
.    *                                                          *
.    *                 Chapter 1 is ready.                      *
.    *                                                          *
.    *            Set the Buffer Width to 300.                  *
.    *                                                          *
.    *************************************************************

SQL>
SQL>

SQL> |
```

Figure 1-16   Using Oracle (part 1 of 2)

The environment is set up as if it is a giant sheet of paper. In order to be able to scroll to the right, you will need to change the setting of your "Buffer Width." To do this, use the Options pull down menu, choose Environment, and set the Buffer Width to 300. (If it is already set to 300, then set it to 301. You need to change its value.)

Now you are ready to enter SQL commands. To test this, enter:

    SELECT * FROM L_EMPLOYEES;

You can enter this command in upper or lower case letters. Don't forget the semi-colon at the end of the command. It tells the SQL Plus environment that you are finished entering this command. You should now see the Employees table from the Lunches database. The screen should look like this:

```
EMPLOYEE                          DEPT                CREDIT PHONE   MANAGER
      ID FIRST_NAME LAST_NAME     CODE HIRE_DATE       LIMIT NUMBER       ID
-------- ---------- ----------    ---- ----------     ------- ------  -------
     201 SUSAN      BROWN         EXE  01-JUN-92      $30.00 3484     (null)
     202 JIM        KERN          SAL  15-AUG-95      $25.00 8722        201
     203 MARTHA     WOODS         SHP  01-FEB-97      $25.00 7591        201
     204 ELLEN      OWENS         SAL  01-JUL-96      $15.00 6830        202
     205 HENRY      PERKINS       SAL  01-MAR-98      $25.00 5286        202
     206 CAROL      ROSE          ACT  15-OCT-97      $15.00 3829        201
     207 DAN        SMITH         SHP  01-DEC-96      $25.00 2259        203
     208 FRED       CAMPBELL      SHP  01-APR-97      $25.00 1752        203
     209 PAULA      JACOBS        MKT  17-MAR-98      $15.00 3357        201
     210 NANCY      HOFFMAN       SAL  15-FEB-96      $25.00 2974        203
```

Making corrections to SQL commands in Oracle

At some time you might make a mistake while you are entering an SQL command into Oracle. There are several ways to make a correction. If the mistake is on the line you are currently typing, you can use the Backspace key to correct it.

One method to correct the code on a previous line is to use Copy and Paste. Highlight the code up to the mistake (and usually including the line the mistake is on.) Copy it using CTRL + C. Then paste it using CTRL + V. It will go to the correct location where new code can be entered. Correct the mistake. Then copy and paste the remaining part of the command.

The best method is to type the code into a separate file using Notepad or another editor. (Be sure to turn off the curly quotes. Only use straight quotes in SQL code.) Then copy the code and paste it into the SQL Plus environment. This is best because it gives you the most control over your code. You can use all the editing features your editor provides. Also, you can paste the same code into both Oracle and Access and run identical code in both environments.

Putting comments in Oracle SQL

All computer code should contain comments. SQL code is no exception. You can put comments in Oracle SQL and most other forms of SQL by beginning a line with two dashes.

-- This is a line comment.

This makes the entire line into a comment. If your comment continues onto the next line, you must begin that line with two dashes also.

In this book I am trying to write SQL code that works in both Oracle and in Access. Unfortunately, Access does not allow comments in its SQL code. So, I had to refrain from using comments in most of the code in this book.

Oracle Help and Technical Documentation

The Oracle technical documentation is on your CD-ROM. It is all there, but it can be hard to find what you are looking for. If you want a technical reference for Oracle, I recommend the book:

Oracle: The Complete Reference
by George Koch and Kevin Loney

Printing from Oracle

You may want to print your SQL code or the tables that result from running your code. In Oracle, there seems to be no way to do this. The easiest method is to use Copy and Paste. Highlight the things you want to print, copy them, paste them into a Notepad file or a Word file. Then use Notepad or Word to print them. (If you paste them into Wordpad, the columns headings will not stay aligned with the data.)

Spool files in Oracle

You may want to keep a record of all the work you have done in Oracle—the queries you have run and the responses you received. When you run the "Start" command to set up the tables for a chapter, a spool file is automatically started for you. It is created within the C:\TEMP directory and it is named SQL_1.LOG, where 1 is the number of the chapter. You must exit Oracle before you can see this file.

Exiting Oracle

To leave Oracle, enter the command: EXIT
You might also want to stop the database to free up the memory on your computer.

Figure 1-16   Using Oracle (part 2 of 2)

Using Access

Using the Access databases that come with this book

To enter SQL commands into an Access database, you must have "read and write" capability on that database. You have "read only" ability on the CD-ROM drive. So, before you use them, you must copy the Access databases from the CD-ROM drive onto your hard disk.

You also need to turn off the Read-only property on the database. See "How to Use the CD-ROM" for the instructions to do this. For each chapter of this book, there is a separate Access database containing the tables needed in that chapter.

Entering SQL commands into Access

Access is built on top of SQL, but it is covered with graphics. It can be a little difficult to find the SQL in it. So, here is a guide.

When Access starts it may look like this:

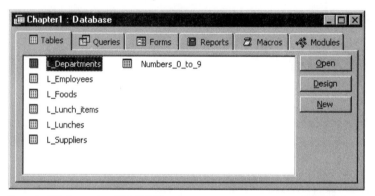

Step 1: Click on the QUERIES tab. Now the screen may look like:

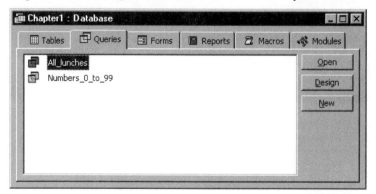

Step 2. Click on the NEW button. Now the screen may look like this:

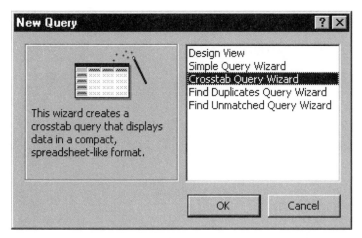

Step 3. Choose DESIGN VIEW and press the OK button. Now the screen may look like this:

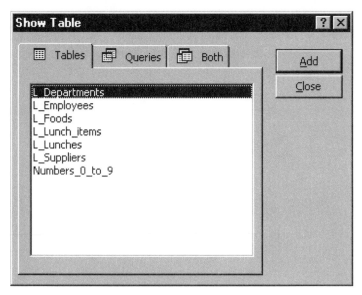

Figure 1-17   Using Access (part 1 of 3)

Step 4. Press the CLOSE button. Now the screen may look like:

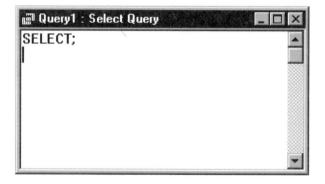

Step 5. Press the SQL button on the left side of the toolbar. Or use the VIEW pull-down menu and choose "SQL view." Now the screen may look like this:

Step 6. Now you can enter an SQL command:

```
Query1 : Select Query                    _ □ ✕

select * from l_employees;
```

Step 7. Press the RUN button on the toolbar. It is the button with the red exclamation mark (!). This runs the SQL command and shows the result:

Employee_id	First_name	Last_name	Dept_code	Hire_date	Credit_limit	Phone_number	Manager_id
201	Susan	Brown	Exe	06-01-1992	$30.00	3484	
202	Jim	Kern	Sal	08-15-1995	$25.00	8722	201
203	Martha	Woods	Shp	02-01-1997	$25.00	7591	201
204	Ellen	Owens	Sal	07-01-1996	$15.00	6830	202
205	Henry	Perkins	Sal	03-01-1998	$25.00	5286	202
206	Carol	Rose	Act	10-15-1997	$15.00	3829	201
207	Dan	Smith	Shp	12-01-1996	$25.00	2259	203
208	Fred	Campbell	Shp	04-01-1997	$25.00	1752	203
209	Paula	Jacobs	Mkt	03-17-1998	$15.00	3357	201
210	Nancy	Hoffman	Sal	02-15-1996	$25.00	2974	203
0					$0.00		0

Record: 1 of 10

Figure 1-17   Using Access (part 2 of 3)

It is best to keep your Access SQL in a separate file

You may not want to type your SQL code directly into the SQL window of Access, as we did above. It is often better to keep your code in a separate file that you control, such as a Notepad file. Then you can copy the code and paste it into the SQL window. (A Wordpad file or a Word file will also work, but make sure to turn off the curly quotes and use straight quotes instead. Notepad is safer to use because it always uses straight quotes.)

There are three reasons for this. This SQL window can only run one SQL command at a time. So if you want to run a series of SQL commands, you can put them all into a file, but copy them into the SQL window one at a time.

Another reason is that Access will rewrite your SQL commands if you save them in the Access environment. Access will often take good, readable SQL code and rewrite it in a way that makes it very difficult for any person to follow. It is code written only for a computer to understand.

Finally, the SQL window does not allow you to put comments in your code. Good code always contains comments, so that is why you should write your SQL code in a separate file.

Making corrections to SQL code in Access

This is simple to do. It is much easier than Oracle.

Printing SQL code and tables from Access

To print the SQL code, copy it and paste it into a Notepad file or Word file. Print it from Notepad or Word. To print the tables that the SQL code produce, use the File pull-down menu and choose Print.

Spool files in Access

Access does not have any way to create spool files.

Access Help and technical reference files

The help and reference files in Access are well organized and easy to use. Click the HELP pull-down menu and choose "Contents and Index." It is fairly easy to find whatever you are looking for.

Figure 1-17   Using Access (part 3 of 3)

Chapter 2

Getting Information from a Table

This chapter explains the basic technique of getting the information you want from a table when you do not want to make any changes to the data and when all the information is in one single table. The table may be very large, and you may want only a small amount of data from it.

The Select statement

In SQL, the Select statement is used to get information from a table. Much of this book is concerned with the Select statement. This chapter explains its four basic clauses and the options available for three of these clauses.

The goal: get a few columns and rows from a table

Our goal, at present, is to get the data we want from a table. The table may be large and contain a lot of data. We only want a small part of it and we do not want to change the data in any way. The Select statement will allow us to retrieve a few columns and a few rows of data from the table.

Let's put some numbers on this. The particular numbers are not important, but they will draw the picture more clearly. Suppose that printing all the data in the table would take a thousand pages. And suppose we want only two pages of data from it. The Select statement will allow us to get the two pages of data we want.

It is as if we want to read one particular article from an encyclopedia. We only want to see that one article. We do not want to read the entire encyclopedia from the beginning to the end. The Select statement will allow us to find the particular article we want to read.

Figure 2-1 shows a large table of data. A small amount of that data is being retrieved into the result of the Select statement. In this drawing, the columns and rows are rearranged so that the data is all in one place. More realistically, the data we want is scattered throughout the table. It is collected together by the Select statement.

Handling small tables of data

If the table of data is small, there may not be much reason to write a Select statement. For instance, if we can print the entire table in two pages, then why not print it completely and let people work to find the information they want? In many situations, this approach makes sense.

In this book, we will be using small tables as learning tools. With tables this size, there is not much reason to use Select statements. However, these tables are being used to show how the Select statement works when it is used with larger tables.

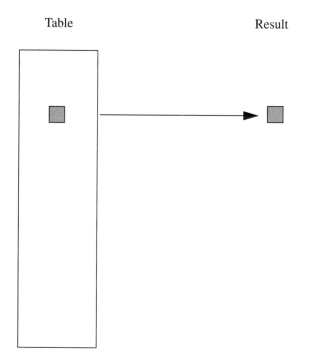

Figure 2-1   The goal: get a few columns and rows from a table

Overview of the Select statement

The Select statement is used to get some of the data from a table. It has four clauses:

SELECT	A list of the columns to get.
FROM	The name of the table that has the data.
WHERE	Which rows to get.
ORDER BY	The sort order for the rows.

The clauses must be written in this order. Two more clauses exist that are used in summarizing data. We examine them later.

This chapter discusses the options available for the Select, Where, and Order By clauses. For now, the From clause always lists only one table.

A Select statement is often called a "query." These two terms, "Select statement" and "query," are used interchangeably. The term "Select statement" emphasizes the syntax of the SQL command. The term "query" emphasizes the purpose of the command.

Figure 2-2

❶ The Select clause lists the columns you want to appear in the result table. They can be listed in any order. Their order in the Select clause determines their order within the result table. Note that a comma appears after each column name.

Also, note that the names of the columns do not contain spaces. The underscore character "_" is usually used instead of a space to separate the words in the name of each column. By writing "Last_name," with an underscore, you are telling the computer that this is the name of a single column. If you wrote "Last name," with a space, the computer would try to find a column named "Last," and it would do something else with the word "Name." This issue is discussed in more detail at the end of this chapter.

❷ The From clause names the table that the data comes from—the Employees table of the Lunches database. In the naming scheme used here, the "L_" indicates that the Employees table is part of the Lunches database. This table is shown in Figure 2-2 as the "Beginning table."

❸ The Where clause says which rows to show in the result table. The condition, "Credit_limit > 20.00," eliminates the rows for employees 204, 206, and 209 because they have a $15.00 credit limit.

Note that the dollar amount is written without the dollar sign. It must also be written without any commas. The decimal point is acceptable but not required. The condition could also be written as "Credit_limit > 20." In this statement, two zeroes are put after the decimal point to make it look more like a currency value.

❹ The Order By clause says to sort the rows of the result table in alphabetical order by the Last Name column. A semicolon marks the end of the SQL statement. The semicolon is required in Oracle; it is optional in Access. Since using a semicolon is valid within both products, I always use a semicolon at the end of every SQL statement.

Task

Show an example of a Select statement that uses all the clauses shown on the previous page.

Show the Employee Id, Last Name, and Credit Limit columns from the Employees Table of the Lunches database. Show only the employees who have a Credit Limit greater than $20.00. Sort the rows of the result by the Last Name of the employee.

Oracle & Access SQL

```
selectemployee_id,  ❶
      last_name,
      credit_limit
from l_employees ❷
where credit_limit > 20.00 ❸
order by last_name;  ❹
```

Beginning table (L_employees table)

EMPLOYEE ID	FIRST_NAME	LAST_NAME	DEPT CODE	HIRE_DATE	CREDIT LIMIT	PHONE NUMBER	MANAGER ID
201	SUSAN	BROWN	EXE	01-JUN-92	$30.00	3484	(null)
202	JIM	KERN	SAL	15-AUG-95	$25.00	8722	201
203	MARTHA	WOODS	SHP	01-FEB-97	$25.00	7591	201
204	ELLEN	OWENS	SAL	01-JUL-96	$15.00	6830	202
205	HENRY	PERKINS	SAL	01-MAR-98	$25.00	5286	202
206	CAROL	ROSE	ACT	15-OCT-97	$15.00	3829	201
207	DAN	SMITH	SHP	01-DEC-96	$25.00	2259	203
208	FRED	CAMPBELL	SHP	01-APR-97	$25.00	1752	203
209	PAULA	JACOBS	MKT	17-MAR-98	$15.00	3357	201
210	NANCY	HOFFMAN	SAL	15-FEB-96	$25.00	2974	203

Result table

EMPLOYEE ID	LAST_NAME	CREDIT LIMIT
201	BROWN	$30.00
208	CAMPBELL	$25.00
210	HOFFMAN	$25.00
202	KERN	$25.00
205	PERKINS	$25.00
207	SMITH	$25.00
203	WOODS	$25.00

Figure 2-2   Overview of the Select Statement

The Select clause

The Select clause is the first part of a query. The Select clause says which columns of information you want, what order you want them in, and what you want them to be called. Do not confuse the Select clause with the Select statement.

Overview of the Select clause

Figure 2-3 shows that there are three forms of the Select clause. The following pages show an example of each of these forms of the Select clause. The first form gets only the columns that are listed. It can rename these columns, giving them a "column alias." It also specifies the order in which the columns will be listed.

The second form gets all the columns of a table. This does not list the columns individually, so it cannot give the columns an alias or specify an order for the columns. The columns are listed in the order they appear in the table.

The third form is similar to the first, but it includes the word "Distinct." This eliminates all the duplicate rows from the result table. Two rows are duplicates if they have identical values in every column of the result table. If even one column is different, then they do not match and they are not duplicates.

The only required clauses are the Select clause and the From clause. You can write a Select statement with only these two clauses. The following query lists all the columns and all the rows of the Employees table.

```
select *
from l_employees;
```

Renaming a column

Any column name in the Select clause can be given a column alias. A "column alias" is a temporary name for a column. It is used only within a single Select statement and does not have any permanent effect on the table or the database.

A column alias lets you set the column headings of the Result table. Usually, they cannot be used to refer to the column in other clauses of the Select statement.

To assign a column alias, use the syntax:

Colunm_name AS alias_name

The word "AS" is optional, but I recommend that you use it because it makes the Select statement easier to read and understand.

Figure 2-3

❶   The column "Dept_code" is given the alias name "Department_abbreviation."

Forms of the Select clause

SELECT   *a list of columns*   Get only the columns listed.
                                       Put them in the order they are listed.
                                       You can rename them.

SELECT *
or   SELECT *table_name.* *   Get all the columns of the table.
                                       Put them in the same order they are in
                                       the table.
                                       You cannot rename them.

                                       The table name is required when any
                                       additional columns are listed, besides
                                       those of one table.

SELECT DISTINCT   *a list of columns* Get only the columns listed.
                                       Put them in the order they are listed.
                                       You can rename them.
                                       Eliminate duplicate rows from the
                                       result.

Example of renaming a column

Oracle & Access SQL

```
select dept_code as department_abbreviation ❶
from l_departments
where dept_code < 'n'
order by dept_code;
```

Beginning table (L_departments table)

```
DEPT
CODE DEPARTMENT_NAME
---- -------------------
ACT  ACCOUNTING
EXE  EXECUTIVE
MKT  MARKETING
PER  PERSONNEL
SAL  SALES
SHP  SHIPPING
```

Result table

```
DEPARTMENT_ABBREVIATION
-----------------------
ACT
EXE
MKT
```

Figure 2-3   Overview of the Select statement

Using the Select clause to get a list of columns

Figure 2-4 is an example of a Select clause that is used to get a list of columns. Only the columns listed in the Select clause appear in the result table. The other columns of the beginning table are omitted.

The order of the columns within the Select clause determines their order within the result table. This can be different than their order within the beginning table.

It is possible for the same column to be listed two or more times. This is sometimes useful when different formatting or functions are applied to the column.

Columns can be renamed by giving them a column alias. This changes the heading that appears in the result table.

Figure 2-4

❶   An underscore character is used in the alias to join the words "employee" and "number." This makes the column alias a single word, since it contains no spaces. The reason for doing this is that Oracle and Access SQL are the same as long as the column alias does not contain spaces.

Both Oracle and Access allow spaces in the column alias. However, the code is written with a slight difference. In Oracle, *double* quotes must be used around a column alias that contains a space. In Access, square brackets are used.

```
Oracle:     select employee_id as "employee number"

Access      select employee_id as [employee number]
```

❷   In Oracle, the width of a column is often determined by the data in that column. This can cause the heading of the column to be truncated, unless a command is issued to set the width of the column.

The Phone Number column in the figure would usually be four characters wide and have the heading "EXTE." To give it a width of ten characters, the command

```
        column extension format a10
```

was issued. This is an SQLplus command, not an SQL command. In Oracle, "SQLplus" is the environment in which SQL runs.

You did not need to issue this command because it was already issued for you by the "Chapter2.sql" script.

In Access, the width of the columns is controlled with the mouse, rather than by using commands.

Task

Get three columns from the Employees table:

       Employee_id
       Phone_number
       Last_name

Display them in that order. Change the name of the Employee Id column to Employee Number and the name of the Phone Number column to Extension.

Oracle & Access SQL

```
select employee_id as employee_number, ❶
       phone_number as extension, ❷
       last_name
from l_employees;
```

Beginning table (L_employees table)

```
EMPLOYEE                            DEPT            CREDIT PHONE   MANAGER
     ID FIRST_NAME LAST_NAME        CODE HIRE_DATE  LIMIT  NUMBER     ID
-------- ---------- ----------      ---- ---------- ------ ------ -------
    201 SUSAN      BROWN            EXE  01-JUN-92  $30.00 3484   (null)
    202 JIM        KERN             SAL  15-AUG-95  $25.00 8722      201
    203 MARTHA     WOODS            SHP  01-FEB-97  $25.00 7591      201
    204 ELLEN      OWENS            SAL  01-JUL-96  $15.00 6830      202
    205 HENRY      PERKINS          SAL  01-MAR-98  $25.00 5286      202
    206 CAROL      ROSE             ACT  15-OCT-97  $15.00 3829      201
    207 DAN        SMITH            SHP  01-DEC-96  $25.00 2259      203
    208 FRED       CAMPBELL         SHP  01-APR-97  $25.00 1752      203
    209 PAULA      JACOBS           MKT  17-MAR-98  $15.00 3357      201
    210 NANCY      HOFFMAN          SAL  15-FEB-96  $25.00 2974      203
```

Result Table

```
EMPLOYEE_NUMBER EXTENSION  LAST_NAME
--------------- ---------- ----------
            201 3484       BROWN
            202 8722       KERN
            203 7591       WOODS
            204 6830       OWENS
            205 5286       PERKINS
            206 3829       ROSE
            207 2259       SMITH
            208 1752       CAMPBELL
            209 3357       JACOBS
            210 2974       HOFFMAN
```

Figure 2-4   Using the Select statement to get a list of columns

Using the Select clause to get all the columns

Figure 2-5 is an example of a Select clause that gets all the columns of a table. In this example, no Where clause exists. So the result table contains all the columns and all the rows of the beginning table—the beginning table and the result table are identical.

This is the simplest Select statement that you can write. Both the Select clause and the From clause are required. All the other clauses are optional.

Variation 1: Adding a Where clause

If a Where clause is added to the Select statement, the result table can contain only some of the rows of the beginning table. For example, the following:

```
select   *
from l_employees
where manager_id is null;
```

lists only the row for employee 201.

Variation 2: Adding an Order By clause

If an Order By clause is added to the Select statement, the rows of the result table may be sorted in a different order. In Figure 2-5, the rows of the beginning table and the result table are arranged in the same order. However, since no Order By clause exists, the computer is allowed to list the rows of the result table in any order. To control the order, you need to write:

```
select   *
from l_employees
order by employee_id
```

Variation 3: Displaying the data in any table

If you know the name of any table, you can display all the data in it with the Select statement:

```
select *
from table_name;
```

If the table contains many rows and you want to stop the listing, you can use:

CTRL + C

or

File ➡ Cancel

Task

Get the entire Employees table, all the columns, and all the rows. Display all the columns in the same order they are defined in the table.

Oracle & Access SQL

```
select    *
from l_employees ;
```

Beginning table (L_employees table)

```
EMPLOYEE                           DEPT           CREDIT PHONE  MANAGER
      ID FIRST_NAME LAST_NAME      CODE HIRE_DATE  LIMIT  NUMBER      ID
-------- ---------- ----------     ---- ---------- ------ ------ -------
     201 SUSAN      BROWN          EXE  01-JUN-92  $30.00 3484   (null)
     202 JIM        KERN           SAL  15-AUG-95  $25.00 8722      201
     203 MARTHA     WOODS          SHP  01-FEB-97  $25.00 7591      201
     204 ELLEN      OWENS          SAL  01-JUL-96  $15.00 6830      202
     205 HENRY      PERKINS        SAL  01-MAR-98  $25.00 5286      202
     206 CAROL      ROSE           ACT  15-OCT-97  $15.00 3829      201
     207 DAN        SMITH          SHP  01-DEC-96  $25.00 2259      203
     208 FRED       CAMPBELL       SHP  01-APR-97  $25.00 1752      203
     209 PAULA      JACOBS         MKT  17-MAR-98  $15.00 3357      201
     210 NANCY      HOFFMAN        SAL  15-FEB-96  $25.00 2974      203
```

Result table

```
EMPLOYEE                           DEPT           CREDIT PHONE  MANAGER
      ID FIRST_NAME LAST_NAME      CODE HIRE_DATE  LIMIT  NUMBER      ID
-------- ---------- ----------     ---- ---------- ------ ------ -------
     201 SUSAN      BROWN          EXE  01-JUN-92  $30.00 3484   (null)
     202 JIM        KERN           SAL  15-AUG-95  $25.00 8722      201
     203 MARTHA     WOODS          SHP  01-FEB-97  $25.00 7591      201
     204 ELLEN      OWENS          SAL  01-JUL-96  $15.00 6830      202
     205 HENRY      PERKINS        SAL  01-MAR-98  $25.00 5286      202
     206 CAROL      ROSE           ACT  15-OCT-97  $15.00 3829      201
     207 DAN        SMITH          SHP  01-DEC-96  $25.00 2259      203
     208 FRED       CAMPBELL       SHP  01-APR-97  $25.00 1752      203
     209 PAULA      JACOBS         MKT  17-MAR-98  $15.00 3357      201
     210 NANCY      HOFFMAN        SAL  15-FEB-96  $25.00 2974      203
```

Figure 2-5   Using a Select statement to get all the columns

Using the Select statement to get the distinct values in one column

Figure 2-6 is an example of using "Select Distinct" on one column to find all of its values and to list each of them only once. In the figure, we apply Select Distinct to the Manager Id column. In the result table, manager id 201 is displayed only once, even though there are four rows of the beginning table with this value. The "duplicate" values are removed.

Notice that the null value does appear in the result table. If there were several nulls in the manager id column of the beginning table, the result table would still contain only a single null.

Variation 1: Adding a Where clause or Order By clause

Select Distinct may be used with a Where clause to limit the number of rows in the result table. Or it may be used with an Order By clause to sort the rows of the result table in either an ascending or a descending order.

Where nulls are placed in the sort order—a difference between Oracle and Access

In Oracle, nulls are placed at the bottom of the sort order. In Access they are placed at the top. This is not a big difference. It causes a slight difference in the appearance of the result, although the rows in the result are the same in both cases.

Everyone agrees on the sort order for the numbers "0" to "9" and for the letters "A" to "Z." However, there is no common agreement about how nulls fit into the sort order. In the absence of a common agreement, Oracle decided to resolve the issue one way, and Access decided to resolve it another way.

The result table shown in the figure shows the null at the bottom of the result table. This is the Oracle method. People using Access will find the null at the top. In Access, the null appears as a blank.

In this figure, one could argue that since the Select statement contains no Order By clause, the rows of the result table are allowed to be in any order. So, there is no significance to whether the null appears as the first or last row. To a certain extent, this is true. However, when Select Distinct is used, a sort is performed as part of the process of eliminating duplicates. So, the rows of the result table are presented in sorted order, even though no Order By clause is used. In this case, the sort is performed on the manager id column.

Variation 2: Eliminating the word "Distinct"

If the word "Distinct" is removed from the Select statement in Figure 2-6, then the result table will be the same as the manager id column of the beginning table. The value 201 will appear four times. No duplicate values will be removed. Nor will any sort occur. The rows might appear in the same order as in the beginning table, or they could appear in some completely different order.

Task

Get a list of all the different values in the Manager Id column of the Employees table.

Oracle & Access SQL

```
select distinct manager_id
from l_employees ;
```

Beginning table (L_employees table)

EMPLOYEE ID	FIRST_NAME	LAST_NAME	DEPT CODE	HIRE_DATE	CREDIT LIMIT	PHONE NUMBER	MANAGER ID
201	SUSAN	BROWN	EXE	01-JUN-92	$30.00	3484	(null)
202	JIM	KERN	SAL	15-AUG-95	$25.00	8722	201
203	MARTHA	WOODS	SHP	01-FEB-97	$25.00	7591	201
204	ELLEN	OWENS	SAL	01-JUL-96	$15.00	6830	202
205	HENRY	PERKINS	SAL	01-MAR-98	$25.00	5286	202
206	CAROL	ROSE	ACT	15-OCT-97	$15.00	3829	201
207	DAN	SMITH	SHP	01-DEC-96	$25.00	2259	203
208	FRED	CAMPBELL	SHP	01-APR-97	$25.00	1752	203
209	PAULA	JACOBS	MKT	17-MAR-98	$15.00	3357	201
210	NANCY	HOFFMAN	SAL	15-FEB-96	$25.00	2974	203

Result Table

MANAGER ID
201
202
203
(null)

Figure 2-6   Using the Select clause to get the distinct values in one column

Using the Select clause to get the distinct values of several columns

Figure 2-7 is an example of using Select Distinct with several columns. The logic is the same as in the previous example, "Using the Select clause to get the distinct values in one column." However, two features may seem surprising when you first see them.

What it means to "eliminate duplicate rows from the result"

The result table in Figure 2-7 contains two rows having a manager id of 201. In Figure 2-6, only one such row occurred. What is the difference?

In Figure 2-7, another column is in the result, the credit limit column. The two rows in which manager id equal to 201 have different values in the credit limit column, $15 and $25. Two *rows* of the result are distinct as long as they differ in at least one column. In Figure 2-6, the credit limit is not part of the result. So the difference between these rows is not in the result and, therefore, these two occurrences of 201 are condensed into a single row.

The beginning table contains four rows with Manager Id = 201. Two of them have a $25.00 credit limit and two have a $15.00 credit limit. The result table shows only one row for each of these combinations.

In the result table, each *row* is distinct. That is, the result table shows all the different combinations of all the columns listed in the Select clause taken together.

Task

Show how "Select Distinct" works when more than one column is listed. Get a list of all the different values in the Manager Id and Credit Limit columns of the Employees table.

Oracle & Access SQL

```
select distinct manager_id,
          credit_limit
from l_employees ;
```

Beginning table (L_employees table)

EMPLOYEE ID	FIRST_NAME	LAST_NAME	DEPT CODE	HIRE_DATE	CREDIT LIMIT	PHONE NUMBER	MANAGER ID
201	SUSAN	BROWN	EXE	01-JUN-92	$30.00	3484	(null)
202	JIM	KERN	SAL	15-AUG-95	$25.00	8722	201
203	MARTHA	WOODS	SHP	01-FEB-97	$25.00	7591	201
204	ELLEN	OWENS	SAL	01-JUL-96	$15.00	6830	202
205	HENRY	PERKINS	SAL	01-MAR-98	$25.00	5286	202
206	CAROL	ROSE	ACT	15-OCT-97	$15.00	3829	201
207	DAN	SMITH	SHP	01-DEC-96	$25.00	2259	203
208	FRED	CAMPBELL	SHP	01-APR-97	$25.00	1752	203
209	PAULA	JACOBS	MKT	17-MAR-98	$15.00	3357	201
210	NANCY	HOFFMAN	SAL	15-FEB-96	$25.00	2974	203

Result table

MANAGER ID	CREDIT LIMIT
201	$15.00
201	$25.00
202	$15.00
202	$25.00
203	$25.00
(null)	$30.00

Figure 2-7   Using a Select clause to ge the distinct values of several columns

The Where clause

The Where clause is used to choose which rows of data you want. Since a table can have thousands of rows, this clause must be flexible enough to specify many different conditions. There are many conditions that can be written in the Where clause. This makes it more complex than the other clauses we examine in this chapter.

Overview of the Where clause

The Where clause specifies a condition that is true for all the rows you want in the result table. For all other rows the condition is false or unknown.

Figure 2-8 lists the conditions you can use within a Where clause. The "Equal" condition can be used with numbers, text, or dates. Values of text and dates should be enclosed in single quotes.

The "Greater Than" condition and the "Less Than" condition also apply to numbers, text, and dates. Numbers are compared by their numeric value. Text is compared alphabetically. Dates are compared according to the calendar.

The "In" condition specifies set inclusion. It is used to check if the value is one of a set of values. All the possible values must be listed within parentheses. If the values are text or dates, then each value must be enclosed in single quotes.

The "Between" condition specifies a range of values. It includes the end points. The "Not Between" condition excludes the end points. Sometimes a "Between" condition can also be written as an "In" condition. For example,

$$\text{where integer\_column between 4 and 8}$$

means the same as

$$\text{where integer\_column in } (4, 5, 6, 7, 8)$$

if the column contains only integers. However, if it also contains other numbers, then the meanings are different. The number 6.5 would be included in the first condition, but not in the second one.

The "Like" condition specifies pattern matching. It applies only to text and the patterns are always alphabetic patterns. Numbers and dates can be converted to text and then this condition can be applied to them. The pattern should be enclosed in single quotes. Oracle patterns differ from Access patterns. This is explained in Figure 2-14.

The "Is Null" condition tests for nulls. This is the only condition that a null satisfies. Nulls are ignored by all the other conditions.

Each condition has both a positive form and a negative form. The negative form is always the exact opposite to the positive form. For example, the "Is Not Null" condition is true for every row where the "Is Null" condition is false.

Compound conditions can be formed using "And," "Or," and "Not."

In the Where clause, you must use the names of the columns as they are in the beginning table. Column alias names cannot be used.

Summary of the types of comparison conditions that can be in the Where clause

CONDITION	MEANING	EXAMPLES
=	equal	credit_limit = 25.00
		first_name = 'susan'
		hire_date = '01-jun-92'
<	less than	credit_limit < 25.00i
<=	less than or equal	first_name <= 'm'
>	greater than	hire_date > '01-jan-95'
>=	greater than or equal	
<>	not equal	
in	in a set	credit_limit in (15.00, 25.00)
not in	not in a set	dept_code not in ('exe', 'mkt', 'act')
between	in a range	credit_limit between 21.00 and 27.00
not between	not within a range	dept_code not between 'act' and 'sal'
like	matches a pattern	phone_number like '%48%'
not like	does not match a pattern	dept_code not like '%a%'
is null	is a null value	manager_id is null
is not null	is not a null value	manager_id is not null

Summary of the ways to form compound conditions by joining several of the conditions above—the Boolean connectors

and

or

not

Figure 2-8   Overview of the Where clause

Using an Equal condition in the Where clause

Figure 2-9 shows a query in which the Where clause uses an "Equal" condition. All the rows from the beginning table that have Manager_id = 203 are shown in the result table.

Note that the null is not shown. Employee 201 has a null in the Manager Id column. The null means that the value is missing in the database. It could be equal to 203, but we do not know if this is, so it is not in the result table.

Figure 2-9

❶ The Select clause lists four columns. The Result table shows these four columns.
❷ The Where clause contains only one condition. That condition is:

Manager_Id = 203

Three rows of the Beginning table satisfy this condition. The Result table shows all these rows.

Variation

Task

Include the row for employee 201, which has a null in the Manager_Id column.

Oracle & Access SQL

```
select employee_id,
       first_name,
       last_name,
       manager_id
from l_employees
where manager_id = 203
or manager_id is null;
```

Result table

EMPLOYEE_ID	FIRST_NAME	LAST_NAME	MANAGER_ID
201	SUSAN	BROWN	(null)
207	DAN	SMITH	203
208	FRED	CAMPBELL	203
210	NANCY	HOFFMAN	203

Task

For all employees who report to employee 203, Martha Woods, list:

> Employee_id,
> First_name
> Last_name
> Manager_id

Oracle & Access SQL

```
select employee_id, ❶
       first_name,
       last_name,
       manager_id
from l_employees
where manager_id = 203; ❷
```

Beginning table (L_employees table)

EMPLOYEE ID	FIRST_NAME	LAST_NAME	DEPT CODE	HIRE_DATE	CREDIT LIMIT	PHONE NUMBER	MANAGER ID
201	SUSAN	BROWN	EXE	01-JUN-92	$30.00	3484	(null)
202	JIM	KERN	SAL	15-AUG-95	$25.00	8722	201
203	MARTHA	WOODS	SHP	01-FEB-97	$25.00	7591	201
204	ELLEN	OWENS	SAL	01-JUL-96	$15.00	6830	202
205	HENRY	PERKINS	SAL	01-MAR-98	$25.00	5286	202
206	CAROL	ROSE	ACT	15-OCT-97	$15.00	3829	201
207	DAN	SMITH	SHP	01-DEC-96	$25.00	2259	203
208	FRED	CAMPBELL	SHP	01-APR-97	$25.00	1752	203
209	PAULA	JACOBS	MKT	17-MAR-98	$15.00	3357	201
210	NANCY	HOFFMAN	SAL	15-FEB-96	$25.00	2974	203

Result Table

EMPLOYEE ID	FIRST_NAME	LAST_NAME	MANAGER ID
207	DAN	SMITH	203
208	FRED	CAMPBELL	203
210	NANCY	HOFFMAN	203

Figure 2-9   Using an Equal condition in the Where clause

Using a Less Than condition in the Where clause

Figure 2-10 shows an example of a query that uses a "Less Than" condition in the Where clause. If there were rows with a null in the Credit Limit column, they would not be included in the result table.

Figure 2-10

❶   The Where clause contains only one condition. That condition is:

$$Credit\_Limit < 17.50$$

This condition uses the "less than" sign. The Beginning table has three rows that satisfy this condition. The Result table shows those three rows.

Variation

Task

Show another way to write this query, using the "greater than or equal to" sign and negating the condition with a Boolean "Not."

Oracle & Access SQL

```
select employee_id,
       first_name,
       last_name,
       credit_limit
from l_employees
where not (credit_limit >= 17.50);
```

Result table

Same as the one on the next page.

Task

List all employees who have a credit limit less than 17.50. Show the columns
> Employee_id,
> First_name
> Last_name
> Credit_limit

Oracle & Access SQL

```
select employee_id,
       first_name,
       last_name,
       credit_limit
from l_employees
where credit_limit < 17.50;  ❶
```

Beginning table (L_employees table)

EMPLOYEE ID	FIRST_NAME	LAST_NAME	DEPT CODE	HIRE_DATE	CREDIT LIMIT	PHONE NUMBER	MANAGER ID
201	SUSAN	BROWN	EXE	01-JUN-92	$30.00	3484	(null)
202	JIM	KERN	SAL	15-AUG-95	$25.00	8722	201
203	MARTHA	WOODS	SHP	01-FEB-97	$25.00	7591	201
204	ELLEN	OWENS	SAL	01-JUL-96	$15.00	6830	202
205	HENRY	PERKINS	SAL	01-MAR-98	$25.00	5286	202
206	CAROL	ROSE	ACT	15-OCT-97	$15.00	3829	201
207	DAN	SMITH	SHP	01-DEC-96	$25.00	2259	203
208	FRED	CAMPBELL	SHP	01-APR-97	$25.00	1752	203
209	PAULA	JACOBS	MKT	17-MAR-98	$15.00	3357	201
210	NANCY	HOFFMAN	SAL	15-FEB-96	$25.00	2974	203

Result Table

EMPLOYEE ID	FIRST_NAME	LAST_NAME	CREDIT LIMIT
204	ELLEN	OWENS	$15.00
206	CAROL	ROSE	$15.00
209	PAULA	JACOBS	$15.00

Figure 2-10   Using a Less Than condition in the Where clause

Using a Not Equal To condition in the Where clause

Figure 2-11 shows an example of a query that uses a "Not Equal" condition in its Where clause.

Most SQL products support several ways to write the "Not Equal" condition. Unfortunately, some of the ways that work in one product, may not work in another product. I prefer the method shown in figure 2-11 because it works in all products and it is easy for both people and computers to understand.

Figure 2-11

❶   The Boolean "Not" reverses the meaning of the condition that follows it. It only applies to that one condition.

SQL uses three valued logic

Note that the null value is not included in the result table. Employee 201 has a null in the Manager Id column. This row does not appear when the Where condition is

```
where manager_id = 203
```

nor does it appear when the Where condition is

```
where not (manager_id = 203)
```

It only appears when the Where condition is

```
where manager_id is null
```

Every row of the table satisfies one and only one of these three Where conditions. Together they divide the rows of the table into three groups that do not overlap.

Variations

Some other ways to write the "Not Equal" condition are:

```
where manager_id <> 203

where not manager_id = 203

where manager_id != 203

where manager_id ^= 203
```

Task

List all employees who do not report to employee 203, Martha Woods. Show the columns

> Employee_id,
> First_name
> Last_name
> Manager id

Oracle & Access SQL

```
select employee_id,
       first_name,
       last_name,
       manager_id
from l_employees
where not (manager_id = 203);  ❶
```

Beginning table (L_employees table)

EMPLOYEE ID	FIRST_NAME	LAST_NAME	DEPT CODE	HIRE_DATE	CREDIT LIMIT	PHONE NUMBER	MANAGER ID
201	SUSAN	BROWN	EXE	01-JUN-92	$30.00	3484	(null)
202	JIM	KERN	SAL	15-AUG-95	$25.00	8722	201
203	MARTHA	WOODS	SHP	01-FEB-97	$25.00	7591	201
204	ELLEN	OWENS	SAL	01-JUL-96	$15.00	6830	202
205	HENRY	PERKINS	SAL	01-MAR-98	$25.00	5286	202
206	CAROL	ROSE	ACT	15-OCT-97	$15.00	3829	201
207	DAN	SMITH	SHP	01-DEC-96	$25.00	2259	203
208	FRED	CAMPBELL	SHP	01-APR-97	$25.00	1752	203
209	PAULA	JACOBS	MKT	17-MAR-98	$15.00	3357	201
210	NANCY	HOFFMAN	SAL	15-FEB-96	$25.00	2974	203

Result Table

EMPLOYEE ID	FIRST_NAME	LAST_NAME	MANAGER ID
202	JIM	KERN	201
203	MARTHA	WOODS	201
204	ELLEN	OWENS	202
205	HENRY	PERKINS	202
206	CAROL	ROSE	201
209	PAULA	JACOBS	201

Figure 2-11   Using a Not Equal To condition in the Where clause

Using the In condition in the Where clause

Figure 2-12 is an example of a query that uses an "In" condition in its Where clause. The "In" condition is used to show membership in a set. It is used when there is a list of discrete values that satisfy the condition. The list of all these values is placed in parenthesis.

The values can be either numbers, text, or dates. All the values can be numbers, or they can all be text, or they can all be dates. It does not make sense to mix these categories.

Nor does not make sense to include Null in the list of valid values. The "In" condition is never satisfied by a null in the data.

Figure 2-12

❶   This condition means that the Manager_Id column is equal to either 202 or 203.

Variation

Task

Show another way to write the query in Figure 2-12. Use two "Equal" conditions combined together with a Boolean "Or."

Oracle & Access SQL

```
select employee_id,
       first_name,
       last_name,
       manager_id
from l_employees
where manager_id = 202
      or manager_id = 203;
```

Result table

Same as in figure 2-12.

Task

List all employees who report to employees 202 or 203, Jim Kern or Martha Woods. Show the columns

      Employee_id,
      First_name
      Last_name
      Manager id

Oracle & Access SQL

```
select employee_id,
       first_name,
       last_name,
       manager_id
from l_employees
where manager_id in (202, 203);  ❶
```

Beginning table (L_employees table)

```
EMPLOYEE                             DEPT                  CREDIT PHONE   MANAGER
      ID FIRST_NAME LAST_NAME      CODE HIRE_DATE     LIMIT NUMBER       ID
-------- ---------- ----------     ---- ----------   ------- ------   -------
     201 SUSAN      BROWN          EXE  01-JUN-92    $30.00 3484     (null)
     202 JIM        KERN           SAL  15-AUG-95    $25.00 8722        201
     203 MARTHA     WOODS          SHP  01-FEB-97    $25.00 7591        201
     204 ELLEN      OWENS          SAL  01-JUL-96    $15.00 6830        202
     205 HENRY      PERKINS        SAL  01-MAR-98    $25.00 5286        202
     206 CAROL      ROSE           ACT  15-OCT-97    $15.00 3829        201
     207 DAN        SMITH          SHP  01-DEC-96    $25.00 2259        203
     208 FRED       CAMPBELL       SHP  01-APR-97    $25.00 1752        203
     209 PAULA      JACOBS         MKT  17-MAR-98    $15.00 3357        201
     210 NANCY      HOFFMAN        SAL  15-FEB-96    $25.00 2974        203
```

Result Table

```
EMPLOYEE                           MANAGER
      ID FIRST_NAME LAST_NAME         ID
-------- ---------- ----------   -------
     204 ELLEN      OWENS            202
     205 HENRY      PERKINS          202
     207 DAN        SMITH            203
     208 FRED       CAMPBELL         203
     210 NANCY      HOFFMAN          203
```

Figure 2-12   Using the In condition in the Where clause

Using the Between condition in the Where clause

Figure 2-13 shows an example of a query that uses the "Between" condition in its Where clause. Note that the end points, April 1, 1997, and March 17, 1998, are both included in the result table.

The "Between" condition can be applied to numbers, text, and dates. In this example, it is applied to dates. In Oracle, dates must be enclosed in single quotes. In Access, they must be enclosed in pound signs, "#." This is the only difference between the Oracle SQL and the Access SQL.

Variation

Task

Write the query in Figure 2-13 with an "In" condition. In doing this, you would need to write about 350 dates:

Oracle SQL

```
select employee_id,
       first_name,
       last_name,
       hire_date
from l_employees
where hire_date in ('01-apr-97',
                    '02-apr-97',
                    '03-apr-97',


                    '15-mar-98',
                    '16-mar-98',
                    '17-mar-98');
```

Access SQL

```
select employee_id,
       first_name,
       last_name,
       hire_date
from l_employees
where hire_date in (#01-apr-97#,
                    #02-apr-97#,
                    #03-apr-97#,


                    #15-mar-98#,
                    #16-mar-98#,
                    #17-mar-98#);
```

Result table

Same as Figure 2-13.

Task

List all employees hired between April 1, 1997 and March 17, 1998. Show the columns
  Employee_id,
  First_name,
  Last_name,
  Hire_date.

Oracle SQL

```
select employee_id,
       first_name,
       last_name,
       hire_date
from l_employees
where hire_date between
    01-apr-97  and  17-mar-98 ;
```

Access SQL

```
select employee_id,
       first_name,
       last_name,
       hire_date
from l_employees
where hire_date between
    01-apr-97  and  17-mar-98 ;
```

Beginning table (L_employees table)

EMPLOYEE ID	FIRST_NAME	LAST_NAME	DEPT CODE	HIRE_DATE	CREDIT LIMIT	PHONE NUMBER	MANAGER ID
201	SUSAN	BROWN	EXE	01-JUN-92	$30.00	3484	(null)
202	JIM	KERN	SAL	15-AUG-95	$25.00	8722	201
203	MARTHA	WOODS	SHP	01-FEB-97	$25.00	7591	201
204	ELLEN	OWENS	SAL	01-JUL-96	$15.00	6830	202
205	HENRY	PERKINS	SAL	01-MAR-98	$25.00	5286	202
206	CAROL	ROSE	ACT	15-OCT-97	$15.00	3829	201
207	DAN	SMITH	SHP	01-DEC-96	$25.00	2259	203
208	FRED	CAMPBELL	SHP	01-APR-97	$25.00	1752	203
209	PAULA	JACOBS	MKT	17-MAR-98	$15.00	3357	201
210	NANCY	HOFFMAN	SAL	15-FEB-96	$25.00	2974	203

Result Table

EMPLOYEE ID	FIRST_NAME	LAST_NAME	HIRE_DATE
205	HENRY	PERKINS	01-MAR-98
206	CAROL	ROSE	15-OCT-97
208	FRED	CAMPBELL	01-APR-97
209	PAULA	JACOBS	17-MAR-98

Figure 2-13   Using the Between condition in the Where clause

Using the Like condition in the Where clause

Figure 2-14 shows an example of a query that uses the "Like" condition in its Where clause. The "Like" condition is used for finding patterns in text. It only works with text, not with numbers or dates.

In both Oracle and Access SQL, the pattern specification should be enclosed in single quotes.

Patterns are specified differently in Oracle than they are in Access. The wildcard characters are different. Access allows a greater variety of patterns than Oracle. These wildcard characters are

ORACLE	ACCESS	MEANING
% (percent sign)	* (asterisk)	A string of characters of any length, or possibly no characters at all (a zero-length string)
_ (underscore)	? (question mark)	One character
(not available)	# (pound sign)	One digit (numeric character)
(not available)	[a-m] (square brackets with a dash)	Range of characters
(not available)	[!a-m]	Outside a range of characters
(not available)	[*] or [?] or [#] (square brackets)	Special character. Putting a character in square brackets means to take it literally, rather than giving it a special meaning.

Some examples of patterns are:

PATTERN	ORACLE	ACCESS	EXAMPLES
String beginning with N	'n%'	'n*'	'none' 'Nancy' 'n123' 'no credit' 'n'
Four characters ending with E	'_ _ _ e'	'???e'	'none' '123e' '1 3e'
Starting with a letter between A and G, followed by two digits	(not available)	'[a-g]##'	'a47' 'b82' 'g05'

Task

List all employees who have the letter N in their last name. Show the columns
> Employee_id,
> First_name
> Last_name

Oracle SQL

```
select employee_id,
       first_name,
       last_name
from l_employees
where last_name like '%n%';
```

Access SQL

```
select employee_id,
       first_name,
       last_name
from l_employees
where last_name like '*n*';
```

Beginning table (L_employees table)

EMPLOYEE ID	FIRST_NAME	LAST_NAME	DEPT CODE	HIRE_DATE	CREDIT LIMIT	PHONE NUMBER	MANAGER ID
201	SUSAN	BROWN	EXE	01-JUN-92	$30.00	3484	(null)
202	JIM	KERN	SAL	15-AUG-95	$25.00	8722	201
203	MARTHA	WOODS	SHP	01-FEB-97	$25.00	7591	201
204	ELLEN	OWENS	SAL	01-JUL-96	$15.00	6830	202
205	HENRY	PERKINS	SAL	01-MAR-98	$25.00	5286	202
206	CAROL	ROSE	ACT	15-OCT-97	$15.00	3829	201
207	DAN	SMITH	SHP	01-DEC-96	$25.00	2259	203
208	FRED	CAMPBELL	SHP	01-APR-97	$25.00	1752	203
209	PAULA	JACOBS	MKT	17-MAR-98	$15.00	3357	201
210	NANCY	HOFFMAN	SAL	15-FEB-96	$25.00	2974	203

Result Table

EMPLOYEE ID	FIRST_NAME	LAST_NAME
201	SUSAN	BROWN
202	JIM	KERN
204	ELLEN	OWENS
205	HENRY	PERKINS
210	NANCY	HOFFMAN

Figure 2-14   Using the Like condition in the Where clause

Using the Is Null condition in the Where clause

Figure 2-15 shows an example of a query that uses an "Is Null" condition in its Where clause. A null is used to show where data is missing in the database tables.

Note that you must write this condition "IS null," not "= null." This is to remind you that a null is missing data and it is not like any other value in the table. It does not have a particular value.

Before nulls were invented, computer systems often used spaces or special values, such as 99, to designate that data was missing. These caused two problems.

One problem was a lack of uniformity. Each computer system used different values to designate missing data. Often a single application used three of these special values—one for numbers, one for text, and one for date fields.

The special values for numbers were often all 9s. But one application might use 999, while another used 999999. Sometimes the various fields within a single application would use different numbers of digits.

The special values for text were often spaces. However, some applications used a single space. Others would fill the field with spaces. The computer would not always consider these to be equal. Some applications even used a "zero length string," which just confused things even more.

For date fields, January 1, 1900, often designated missing data. But some applications used other dates.

The other problem was that these special data values were sometimes processed as if they were actual data. This could lead to errors that were difficult to detect, particularly if some calculation was done that changed the values of these fields.

To solve these problems, nulls were created to designate missing data. A rigid distinction is made between nulls and other types of data. Nulls do not have datatypes, meaning that no distinction exists between a null in a numeric column and one in a text column or date column.

Nulls receive special treatment in several situations within a database. Throughout this book, I point out when they are treated differently from other data.

Task

List all employees who have a null in the Manager id column. Show these columns:
 Employee_id,
 First_name
 Last_name
 Manager_id

Oracle & Access SQL

```
select employee_id,
       first_name,
       last_name,
       manager_id
from l_employees
where manager_id is null;
```

Beginning table (L_employees table)

```
EMPLOYEE                        DEPT              CREDIT PHONE  MANAGER
      ID FIRST_NAME LAST_NAME  CODE HIRE_DATE    LIMIT NUMBER      ID
-------- ---------- ---------- ---- ---------- ------- ------ -------
     201 SUSAN      BROWN      EXE  01-JUN-92  $30.00 3484   (null)
     202 JIM        KERN       SAL  15-AUG-95  $25.00 8722      201
     203 MARTHA     WOODS      SHP  01-FEB-97  $25.00 7591      201
     204 ELLEN      OWENS      SAL  01-JUL-96  $15.00 6830      202
     205 HENRY      PERKINS    SAL  01-MAR-98  $25.00 5286      202
     206 CAROL      ROSE       ACT  15-OCT-97  $15.00 3829      201
     207 DAN        SMITH      SHP  01-DEC-96  $25.00 2259      203
     208 FRED       CAMPBELL   SHP  01-APR-97  $25.00 1752      203
     209 PAULA      JACOBS     MKT  17-MAR-98  $15.00 3357      201
     210 NANCY      HOFFMAN    SAL  15-FEB-96  $25.00 2974      203
```

Result table

```
EMPLOYEE                       MANAGER
      ID FIRST_NAME LAST_NAME      ID
-------- ---------- ---------- -------
     201 SUSAN      BROWN      (null)
```

Figure 2-15   Using the Is Null condition in the Where clause

Using a compound condition in the Where clause

Figure 2-16 shows an example of a query that has a Where clause that uses a compound condition. It shows how to include the null values when using a "Not Equal" condition. You must explicitly ask for the nulls, if you want them to appear in the result table.

Compound conditions can be formed using the following Boolean connectors:

    AND
    OR
    NOT

"And" and "Or" combine two conditions to form a single compound condition. They can be applied repeatedly, thus combining many conditions into one compound condition. "Not" is applied to a single condition and reverses the condition's meaning.

Parentheses should be used to make the statement easy for humans to read and understand.

Figure 2-16

❶   "Not" is used to reverse the meaning of "Manager_id = 203" to create the meaning "Manager Id is not equal to 203." The parentheses are optional; I use them here to make the meaning more clear to people who read the SQL code.

❷   "Or" is used to combine the two conditions:

        "Not (manager_id = 203)"

and

        "Manager_id is null"

form a single compound condition:

        "Not (manager_id = 203) or manager_id is null"

Task

List all employees who do not report to employee 203, Martha Woods. Include rows with a null in the manager id column. Show these columns:

> Employee_id,
> First_name
> Last_name
> Manager id

Oracle & Access SQL

```
select employee_id,
       first_name,
       last_name,
       manager_id
from l_employees
where not (manager_id = 203)  ❶
   or manager_id is null;  ❷
```

Beginning table (L_employees table)

```
EMPLOYEE                        DEPT                 CREDIT PHONE   MANAGER
      ID FIRST_NAME LAST_NAME   CODE HIRE_DATE        LIMIT NUMBER      ID
-------- ---------- ----------  ---- ----------      ------- ------ -------
     201 SUSAN      BROWN       EXE  01-JUN-92       $30.00 3484   (null)
     202 JIM        KERN        SAL  15-AUG-95       $25.00 8722      201
     203 MARTHA     WOODS       SHP  01-FEB-97       $25.00 7591      201
     204 ELLEN      OWENS       SAL  01-JUL-96       $15.00 6830      202
     205 HENRY      PERKINS     SAL  01-MAR-98       $25.00 5286      202
     206 CAROL      ROSE        ACT  15-OCT-97       $15.00 3829      201
     207 DAN        SMITH       SHP  01-DEC-96       $25.00 2259      203
     208 FRED       CAMPBELL    SHP  01-APR-97       $25.00 1752      203
     209 PAULA      JACOBS      MKT  17-MAR-98       $15.00 3357      201
     210 NANCY      HOFFMAN     SAL  15-FEB-96       $25.00 2974      203
```

Result table

```
EMPLOYEE                        MANAGER
      ID FIRST_NAME LAST_NAME       ID
-------- ---------- ----------  -------
     201 SUSAN      BROWN       (null)
     202 JIM        KERN           201
     203 MARTHA     WOODS          201
     204 ELLEN      OWENS          202
     205 HENRY      PERKINS        202
     206 CAROL      ROSE           201
     209 PAULA      JACOBS         201
```

Figure 2-16 Using a compound condition in the Where clause

Using a complex compound condition in the Where clause

Figure 2-17 shows an example of a query with a very complex compound condition in its Where clause. The purpose of this example is to show how such a condition can be organized. All complex conditions can be written in this format, although to put them in this form often takes some effort.

This format is easy for people to read and understand, and simple to manipulate. Using it can prevent many errors that can occur in conditions that are in a more complex format. The three connectors And, Or, and Not are strictly controlled.

"Not" is applied only to simple conditions. It is not applied to compound conditions that include an And or Or.

"And" is used to combine simple conditions and conditions involving Not. None of these conditions are allowed to contain an Or. Many conditions can be combined together with And. No parentheses are needed to show a particular order for the Ands to be applied. Each of these compound conditions is usually enclosed in parentheses.

"Or" is the top-level connector. It combines all the compound conditions using And and Not. No parentheses are needed to apply the Ors in a particular order.

Figure 2-17

❶   Figure 2-17 shows only the Oracle SQL. The Access SQL is similar, except that the dates must be enclosed in pound signs (#) instead of single quotes. The discussion about the structure of compound conditions applies to Access as well as to Oracle.

❷   This line and the next two lines are a compound condition joined together with And. The parentheses enclosing these three lines are optional but make the condition easier to read.

❸   This is an Or joining together the compound conditions formed with And.

❹   This shows a Not applied to a Between condition. The "And" on this line is part of the Between condition. It is not the Boolean "And" connector.

❺   This line and the next two lines are a compound condition joined together with And.

Task

Show an example of a Where clause using a compound condition with many clauses.

Oracle SQL ❶

```
select employee_id,
       first_name,
       last_name
from l_employees
where (manager_id is null ❷
       and first_name = 'susan'
       and credit_limit = 30.00)
    or ❸
       (not (hire_date between '01-jan-91' and '25-jun-94') ❹❺
       and last_name in ('smith', 'jacobs', 'patrick')
       and not dept_code = 'shp')
    or
       (credit_limit > 22.00
       and hire_date = '01-mar-98')
    or
       (employee_id > 700
       and dept_code in ('sal', 'mkt')
       and manager_id = 400);
```

Beginning table (L_employees table)

EMPLOYEE ID	FIRST_NAME	LAST_NAME	DEPT CODE	HIRE_DATE	CREDIT LIMIT	PHONE NUMBER	MANAGER ID
201	SUSAN	BROWN	EXE	01-JUN-92	$30.00	3484	(null)
202	JIM	KERN	SAL	15-AUG-95	$25.00	8722	201
203	MARTHA	WOODS	SHP	01-FEB-97	$25.00	7591	201
204	ELLEN	OWENS	SAL	01-JUL-96	$15.00	6830	202
205	HENRY	PERKINS	SAL	01-MAR-98	$25.00	5286	202
206	CAROL	ROSE	ACT	15-OCT-97	$15.00	3829	201
207	DAN	SMITH	SHP	01-DEC-96	$25.00	2259	203
208	FRED	CAMPBELL	SHP	01-APR-97	$25.00	1752	203
209	PAULA	JACOBS	MKT	17-MAR-98	$15.00	3357	201
210	NANCY	HOFFMAN	SAL	15-FEB-96	$25.00	2974	203

Result table

EMPLOYEE ID	FIRST_NAME	LAST_NAME
201	SUSAN	BROWN
205	HENRY	PERKINS
209	PAULA	JACOBS

Figure 2-17   Using a very complex compound condition in the Where clause

Using **NOT** with **IN**, **BETWEEN**, **LIKE**, and **IS NULL**

Figure 2-18 shows that the word "Not" can be used in two different ways with the conditions In, Between, Like, and Is Null. Fortunately, the meanings are the same.

Version 1 shows the word "Not" used as part of the condition test. One condition test is called "In," and another one is called "Not In." The same applies to all these conditions:

IN	NOT IN
BETWEEN	NOT BETWEEN
LIKE	NOT LIKE
IS NULL	IS NOT NULL

Version 2 shows the word "Not" used as a Boolean connector modifying an entire condition. In the first line of the Where clause, "Not" is applied to the condition:

"dept_code in ('act', 'mkt')"

Another set of parentheses can make this more clear:

"not (dept_code in ('act', 'mkt'))"

instead of

"not dept_code in ('act', 'mkt')"

Here is version 2 written with the extra parentheses on each line:

```
select employee_id,
       first_name,
       last_name,
       manager_id
from l_employees
where not (dept_code in ('act', 'mkt'))
  and not (last_name between
       'v' and 'z')
  and not (last_name like '%s')
  and not (manager_id is null);
```

Task

List all the employees whose:

      Department Code is not "Act" or "Mkt"

      Last Name does not begin with a "V" or any letter after "V"

      Last Name does not end with "S"

      Manager Id is not a null

Show the Employee Id, First Name, Last Name, and Manager Id of these employees.

Oracle & Access SQL
Version 1

```
select employee_id,
       first_name,
       last_name,
       manager_id
from l_employees
where dept_code not in ('act', 'mkt')
   and last_name not between
       'v' and 'z'
   and last_name not like '%s'
   and manager_id is not null;
```

Version 2

```
select employee_id,
       first_name,
       last_name,
       manager_id
from l_employees
where not dept_code in ('act', 'mkt')
   and not last_name between
       'v' and 'z'
   and not last_name like '%s'
   and not manager_id is null;
```

Beginning table (L_employees table)

```
EMPLOYEE                          DEPT            CREDIT PHONE  MANAGER
      ID FIRST_NAME LAST_NAME     CODE HIRE_DATE   LIMIT NUMBER     ID
-------- ---------- ----------    ---- ---------- ------- ------ -------
     201 SUSAN      BROWN         EXE  01-JUN-92  $30.00 3484   (null)
     202 JIM        KERN          SAL  15-AUG-95  $25.00 8722      201
     203 MARTHA     WOODS         SHP  01-FEB-97  $25.00 7591      201
     204 ELLEN      OWENS         SAL  01-JUL-96  $15.00 6830      202
     205 HENRY      PERKINS       SAL  01-MAR-98  $25.00 5286      202
     206 CAROL      ROSE          ACT  15-OCT-97  $15.00 3829      201
     207 DAN        SMITH         SHP  01-DEC-96  $25.00 2259      203
     208 FRED       CAMPBELL      SHP  01-APR-97  $25.00 1752      203
     209 PAULA      JACOBS        MKT  17-MAR-98  $15.00 3357      201
     210 NANCY      HOFFMAN       SAL  15-FEB-96  $25.00 2974      203
```

Result table

```
EMPLOYEE                          MANAGER
      ID FIRST_NAME LAST_NAME          ID
-------- ---------- ----------    -------
     202 JIM        KERN              201
     207 DAN        SMITH             203
     208 FRED       CAMPBELL          203
     210 NANCY      HOFFMAN           203
```

Figure 2-18   Using NOT, with IN, BETWEEN, LIKE, and IS NULL

The Order By clause

The Order By clause determines how the rows of the result table will be sorted when they are printed in the result table or displayed on the screen. If you leave out the Order By clause, you are telling the computer that you do not care about this order and you are giving the computer permission to display the rows of the result in any order.

Overview of the Order By clause

In working with most of the tables in this book, you can get acceptable results even if you do not write an Order By clause, because most of the tables are small. They contain only a few rows. However, when you work with larger tables, you need to use an Order By clause.

Figure 2-19 shows the syntax of this clause and a few examples of it. The clause contains a list of columns and a specification for each of these columns to sort them in either ascending order or descending order.

The first column listed in the Order By clause is the primary sort order. The columns that are listed after the first one are used only when two rows have identical values in the first column.

This rule applies to all the columns. For example, the third column is used only to sort the rows that have identical values in the first two columns of the Order By clause.

Ascending order is the default; it is often not specified. To sort on a column in descending order, "Desc" must always be specified.

Columns are usually specified by their names. Another method is to specify a number—this is the number of the column within the Select clause. This is an older method and it is being phased out. Some brands of SQL, including Oracle, allow you to use a column alias in an Order By clause.

A column can sometimes be listed in the Order By clause without listing it in the Select clause. However, a good programming practice is usually to list in the Select clause all the columns used in the Order By clause.

In Oracle, nulls are sorted at the bottom. In Access, they are sorted at the top. Other slight differences in the sort order can occur, depending on a variety of factors such as:

- which SQL product you are using
- whether you are using a small computer or a large computer
- whether you are using a special alphabet
- options set by your DBA (Database Administrator)

Syntax of the Order By clause

Order By   *list of column names followed by the sort order for each column*

Order By   *list of numbers followed by the sort order for each column*

Sort order options for each column

Asc	ascending order (default)
Desc	descending order

Examples

```
order by employee_id


order by last_name, first_name


order by hire_date desc,
            last_name,
            first_name
```

Figure 2-19   Overview of the Order By clause

Sorting the rows of several columns in ascending order

Figure 2-20 shows a query with two columns in its Order By clause. Both of these columns are sorted in ascending order.

Figure 2-20

❶   The rows of the result table are sorted first and primarily on the Department Code. For instance, all four rows with a Department Code of "SAL" are sorted before the three rows with "SHP."

❷   The rows with identical values in the Department Code column are then sorted on the Last Name column. Within the "SAL" department code, the last names are put in ascending alphabetic order. Within the "SHP" department code is a separate alphabetic order based on the Last Name column.

Task

List the department codes and last names of all the employees, except for employee 209. Sort the rows of the result table on both columns in ascending order.

Oracle & Access SQL

```
select dept_code,
       last_name
from l_employees
where not (employee_id = 209)
order by dept_code, ❶
         last_name; ❷
```

Beginning table (L_employees table)

EMPLOYEE ID	FIRST_NAME	LAST_NAME	DEPT CODE	HIRE_DATE	CREDIT LIMIT	PHONE NUMBER	MANAGER ID
201	SUSAN	BROWN	EXE	01-JUN-92	$30.00	3484	(null)
202	JIM	KERN	SAL	15-AUG-95	$25.00	8722	201
203	MARTHA	WOODS	SHP	01-FEB-97	$25.00	7591	201
204	ELLEN	OWENS	SAL	01-JUL-96	$15.00	6830	202
205	HENRY	PERKINS	SAL	01-MAR-98	$25.00	5286	202
206	CAROL	ROSE	ACT	15-OCT-97	$15.00	3829	201
207	DAN	SMITH	SHP	01-DEC-96	$25.00	2259	203
208	FRED	CAMPBELL	SHP	01-APR-97	$25.00	1752	203
209	PAULA	JACOBS	MKT	17-MAR-98	$15.00	3357	201
210	NANCY	HOFFMAN	SAL	15-FEB-96	$25.00	2974	203

Result table

DEPT CODE	LAST_NAME
ACT	ROSE
EXE	BROWN
SAL	HOFFMAN
SAL	KERN
SAL	OWENS
SAL	PERKINS
SHP	CAMPBELL
SHP	SMITH
SHP	WOODS

Figure 2-20   Sorting the rows on several columns in ascending order

Sorting the rows of several columns with some in ascending order and others in descending order

Figure 2-21 shows the same query as in Figure 2-20, except that the sort on the Last Name column is in descending order. The contrast with the result table in Figure 2-20 shows the difference this makes.

Figure 2-21

❶ The rows of the result table are sorted first and primarily on the Department Code column.

❷ All the rows with the same value in the Department Code column are sorted on the Last Name column in descending order. This sort is applied twice, once with the "SAL" Department Codes and again with the "SHP" ones.

Task

List the department codes and last names of all the employees, except for employee 209. Sort the rows of the result table in ascending order on the department code column and in descending order on the Last Name column.

Oracle & Access SQL

```
select dept_code,
       last_name
from l_employees
where not (employee_id = 209)
order by dept_code, ❶
         last_name desc; ❷
```

Beginning table (L_employees table)

```
EMPLOYEE                          DEPT               CREDIT PHONE   MANAGER
      ID FIRST_NAME LAST_NAME     CODE HIRE_DATE     LIMIT  NUMBER       ID
-------- ---------- ----------    ---- ----------    ------ ------  -------

     201 SUSAN      BROWN         EXE  01-JUN-92     $30.00 3484    (null)
     202 JIM        KERN          SAL  15-AUG-95     $25.00 8722       201
     203 MARTHA     WOODS         SHP  01-FEB-97     $25.00 7591       201
     204 ELLEN      OWENS         SAL  01-JUL-96     $15.00 6830       202
     205 HENRY      PERKINS       SAL  01-MAR-98     $25.00 5286       202
     206 CAROL      ROSE          ACT  15-OCT-97     $15.00 3829       201
     207 DAN        SMITH         SHP  01-DEC-96     $25.00 2259       203
     208 FRED       CAMPBELL      SHP  01-APR-97     $25.00 1752       203
     209 PAULA      JACOBS        MKT  17-MAR-98     $15.00 3357       201
     210 NANCY      HOFFMAN       SAL  15-FEB-96     $25.00 2974       203
```

Result table

```
DEPT
CODE LAST_NAME
---- ----------
ACT  ROSE
EXE  BROWN
SAL  PERKINS
SAL  OWENS
SAL  KERN
SAL  HOFFMAN
SHP  WOODS
SHP  SMITH
SHP  CAMPBELL
```

Figure 2-21   Sorting the rows on several columns with some in ascending order and others in descending order

Other techniques

Often, tables contain codes. The meanings of these codes are contained in other tables.

Using a lookup table to find the meanings of codes

Figure 2-22

❶ The Select clause contains the "Department_name" column. This is a column from the Departments table. The Employees table does not have a column with this name.

❷ The From clause lists both the Employees table and the Departments table. A comma appears between the names of these two tables.

❸ This condition is the join condition. It relates one table to the other table. These tables are related through a column called "Dept_code." For example, the first row of the Employees table shows that Susan Brown has Department Code "EXE." The second row of the Departments table shows that the Department Code "EXE" is associated with the Department Name "Executive." Putting these two pieces together, we find that Susan Brown has the Department Name "Executive." In effect, this looks up the meaning of the "EXE" code.

The Employees table contains a column named "Dept_code," and the Departments table contains a different column that has the same name. To distinguish these columns, the table name is written before the column name and a period is placed between the name of the table and the name of the column. The lookup procedure finds the value of the Dept_code column in the Employees table and then finds the same value in the Dept_code column of the Departments table. In SQL, this procedure is written as follows:

> l_employees.dept_code = l_departments.dept_code

The order of the two columns before and after the equal sign does not matter. This condition could also be written like this:

> l_departments.dept_code = l_employees.dept_code

❹ The Where clause serves two purposes. This line shows that it can contain additional conditions on the data. This is a separate purpose from that shown on the previous line, where the condition related one table to another table.

Task

List all the employees and the names of their departments. Use the Departments table to get the full name of the department from the department code. List these columns:
    Employee_id
    First_name
    Last_name
    Department name
Sort the row by the employee_id.

Oracle & Access SQL

```
select employee_id, first_name, last_name, department_name ❶
from l_employees, l_departments ❷
where l_employees.dept_code = l_departments.dept_code ❸
    and not (last_name = 'woods') ❹
order by employee_id;
```

Beginning table 1(L_employees table)

```
EMPLOYEE                         DEPT                  CREDIT PHONE   MANAGER
      ID FIRST_NAME LAST_NAME   CODE HIRE_DATE          LIMIT NUMBER      ID
-------- ---------- ----------  ---- ----------        ------- ------ -------
     201 SUSAN      BROWN       EXE  01-JUN-92         $30.00 3484   (null)
     202 JIM        KERN        SAL  15-AUG-95         $25.00 8722      201
     203 MARTHA     WOODS       SHP  01-FEB-97         $25.00 7591      201
     204 ELLEN      OWENS       SAL  01-JUL-96         $15.00 6830      202
     205 HENRY      PERKINS     SAL  01-MAR-98         $25.00 5286      202
     206 CAROL      ROSE        ACT  15-OCT-97         $15.00 3829      201
     207 DAN        SMITH       SHP  01-DEC-96         $25.00 2259      203
     208 FRED       CAMPBELL    SHP  01-APR-97         $25.00 1752      203
     209 PAULA      JACOBS      MKT  17-MAR-98         $15.00 3357      201
     210 NANCY      HOFFMAN     SAL  15-FEB-96         $25.00 2974      203
```

Beginning table 2(L_departments table)

```
DEPT
CODE DEPARTMENT_NAME
---- -----------------
ACT  ACCOUNTING
EXE  EXECUTIVE
MKT  MARKETING
PER  PERSONNEL
SAL  SALES
SHP  SHIPPING
```

Result table

```
EMPLOYEE
      ID FIRST_NAME LAST_NAME   DEPARTMENT_NAME
-------- ---------- ----------  -----------------
     201 SUSAN      BROWN       EXECUTIVE
     202 JIM        KERN        SALES
     204 ELLEN      OWENS       SALES
     205 HENRY      PERKINS     SALES
     206 CAROL      ROSE        ACCOUNTING
     207 DAN        SMITH       SHIPPING
     208 FRED       CAMPBELL    SHIPPING
     209 PAULA      JACOBS      MARKETING
     210 NANCY      HOFFMAN     SALES
```

Figure 2-22   Using a lookup table to find the meanings of codes

The Whole Process

This section contains a quick summary of the process an SQL statement describes.

The whole process—so far

1. The FROM clause chooses the beginning table of data.

2. The WHERE clause chooses which rows of data you want from this table.

3. The SELECT clause chooses the columns of data you want, puts them in the desired order, and can rename them.

4. The ORDER BY clause sorts the rows of the result.

The Whole Process (so far)

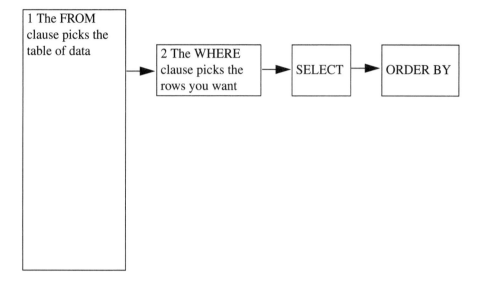

Figure 2-23   The whole process—so far

Punctuation matters

To talk in detail about punctuation is almost embarrassing . We usually expect the punctuation to be easy. Yet punctuation is very important to a computer. Any mistake in punctuation can completely confuse the computer. More than half the errors most people make while learning SQL are errors in punctuation.

This matter is made more difficult because punctuation has additional meanings in SQL that it does not have in English or any other natural language. Also, Oracle and Access use punctuation somewhat differently.

You may want to skim this section for now and refer to it in more detail later.

Spaces in names

In general, the name of any database object should not contain any spaces, including column names, table names, column aliases, and several more types of objects I have not discussed yet. An exception to this general rule is explained below, but for now, I want to show you how spaces are usually avoided. As an example, "Hire Date" is not a good name for a column because it contains a space between "Hire" and "Date."

Two methods are often used to solve this problem. One method replaces all spaces with the underline character. I picked that method to use in this book. It is the method most often used with SQL because it does not need to distinguish between uppercase and lowercase letters. So "Hire Date" is written as:

```
hire_date
```
or
```
HIRE_DATE.
```

The other method uses mostly lowercase letters, except that each word begins with one uppercase letter, and the spaces are removed. With this method, you write the following:

```
HireDate
```

In Oracle, you are sometimes allowed to use spaces in a name, if you enclose the name in double quotes:

```
"hire date"
```

In Access, you are sometimes allowed to use spaces in a name, if you enclose the name in square brackets:

```
[hire date]
```

Access allows spaces in more names than Oracle does.

I suggest that you should avoid ever using spaces in names, even though both Oracle and Access may allow it.

SQL can be written in free format

Most of the SQL in this book is written in a highly structured way. I recommend using this format. However, the formatting is not required. The code can all be written on one line. Or you can get creative and write it in some fancy shape.

The clauses of the Select statement must always be written in a specified order. However, you can run the lines together in any way you wish. You can write any of the following:

```
select *
from l_employees;
```

or

```
select * from l_employees;
```

or

```
select
      *      from
      l_employees
   ;
```

Two exceptions to this flexibility. Oracle does not allow any completely blank lines in the middle of an SQL statement. Access allows blank lines, but it does not allow any characters after the semicolon that marks the end of the SQL statement.

Commas

Commas separate the items of a list. No comma must be at the end of the list. If the last item of a list is removed, the comma preceding it must also be removed. ❶ shows a common error:

```
select  first_name,
        last_name, ❶
from l_employees;
```

Do not use commas or dollar signs when entering numbers. Decimal points are the only punctuation allowed within numbers.

Double dash (comment line)

In Oracle and most other SQL products, any text written after two dashes is a comment. The dashes can be written at the beginning of the line or in the middle:

```
-- This is a comment line
```

or

```
select first_name, last_name -- this is a comment
```

Access does not allow comments in the SQL window. So when I write SQL for both Oracle and Access, I cannot put comments into it.

Single quotes

Single quotes or double quotes must surround character strings. Numbers do not have quotes around them. In Oracle, dates must also be enclosed in quotes. In Access, dates are enclosed in pound signs.

In Access, single quotes and double quotes have the same meaning. In Oracle, the meanings are different. In Oracle, you should always use single quotes, except in two special situations, outlined in the sections "Double quotes" and "Apostrophe."

Double quotes

Access uses double quotes and single quotes to mean the same thing. In Oracle, double quotes are used around a column alias that contains special characters or a space. They are also used to put text into date formats, which I discuss later. Here is an example in Oracle:

```
select  first_name as "first name"
from l_employees
order by "first name";
```

Apostrophe

An apostrophe can be written as two single quotes next to each other. To find the names of all the suppliers with an apostrophe in their names, you can write in Oracle:

```
select *
from l_suppliers
where supplier_name like '%''%';
```

Between the two percent signs are two single quotes. This method also works in Access, except that an asterisk replaces the percent sign in the pattern:

```
where supplier_name like '*''*'
```

An easier method to write an apostrophe in Access encloses a single apostrophe in a pair of double quotes:

```
where supplier_name like "*'*"
```

Semicolon

A semicolon marks the end of an SQL statement. This tells the computer that the statement is complete and may now be processed. Oracle requires a semicolon to end a statement (although Oracle also accepts some other methods of statement termination). In Access, the semicolon is optional.

Pound sign

Access uses the pound sign to enclose dates. For example:

```
select *
from l_employees
where hire_date = #15-feb-96#;
```

Oracle encloses dates in single quotes:

```
where hire_date = '15-feb-96';
```

Period (and exclamation mark)

A period is often used between a table name and a column name to say that the column is part of that particular table:

```
select l_employees.first_name
from l_employees;
```

In Access, an exclamation mark is sometimes used to mean the same:

```
select l_employees!first_name
from l_employees;
```

Access cannot include a period in a column alias.

Ampersand

In Oracle, the ampersand is often used to indicate a variable. For instance, "&fox" could be a variable. If you want to use an ampersand as an ordinary character, you will want to turn this feature off. To do so, run the following command:

```
set define off
```

This is an SQLplus command, not an SQL command. It sets the environment in which SQL runs in Oracle.

Double bar

The double bar is the uppercase symbol above the backslash. The key usually shows two short lines, one above the other. However, many printers display it as a single line. This symbol is used for the concatenation function. Oracle also uses it to make two or more lines in a column heading within the "Column" command. For example:

```
column first_name heading 'FIRST | NAME'
```

Figure 2-24   Punctuation matters

Summary

In this chapter, you learned to get information from a table using a Select statement. You learned the four main clauses of the Select statement:

Select
From
Where
Order By

and many details about them. You learned how to use a lookup table to find the meaning of codes in the data. Along the way, I have discussed nulls, a standard way to write compound Boolean conditions, and punctuation.

You also saw that most of the time, the same SQL code that works in Oracle also works in Access.

Exercises

Objective

Get data from a single table. Display only a subset of the columns and a subset of the rows.

Directions

For each set of problems,
1. Type in part A.
2. Look at the listing of the full table in the Lunches database and make sure you understand the result.
3. Write the select statement for part B OR part C OR both. You can decide how much you want to do.

There are several methods you can use to enter SQL commands. The recommended way is to type your commands into Notepad, then copy the whole command and paste it into Oracle SQL*Plus. Another way is to type you commands directly into SQL*Plus. You can use cut and paste to make corrections.

1. Goal: Get all the columns and all the rows of a table.

1A. List all the columns and rows of the employees table.

Oracle & Access SQL

```
select *
from l_employees;
```

1B. List all the columns and rows of the foods table.

1C. List all the columns and rows of the lunches table.

2. Goal: Get a subset of the columns, and all the rows of a table.

2A. List the last name and phone number columns of the employees table.

Oracle & Access SQL

```
select last_name,
phone_number
from l_employees;
```

2B. List the description and price columns of the foods table.

2C. Use the lunches table. Get the lunch id and lunch date columns.

3. Goal: Sort the rows to put them in order.

3A. Sort the rows of problem 2A by the last name in ascending order.

Oracle & Access SQL

```
select last_name,
phone_number
from l_employees
order by last_name;
```

3B. Sort the rows of problem 2B by the description.

3C. Sort the rows of problem 2C by the lunch date.

4. Goal: Sort the rows in descending order.

4A. Sort the rows of problem 2A by the last name in descending order.

Oracle & Access SQL

```
select last_name,
phone_number
from l_employees
order by last_name desc;
```

4B. Sort the rows of problem 2B by the description in descending order.

4C. Sort the rows of problem 2C by the lunch date in descending order.

5. Goal: Sort the rows on more than one column. Put the columns in a particular order.

5A. Using the employees table, list the columns:
>   dept_code
>   credit_limit
>   last_name
>   first_name

Place the columns in that order. Sort the rows by:
>   dept_code in ascending order
>   credit_limit in descending order
>   last_name in ascending order

Oracle & Access SQL

```
select dept_code,
credit_limit,
last_name,
first_name
from l_employees
order by dept_code,
credit_limit desc,
last_name;
```

Note: The first column of the sort, on dept_code, is the primary sort order. Then, within records which all have the same dept_code, those records are sorted by credit_limit in descending order. Then, for records that have the same dept_code and also the same credit_limit, those records are sorted by last_name.

6. Goal: Get one specific row with a Where condition that uses equality ("=").

6A. From the employees table, get the row for Susan.

Oracle & Access SQL

```
select   *
from l_employees
where first_name = 'susan';
```

Notes:
1.   Use single quotes around the first name, Susan.
2.   The text inside the quotes may be case sensitive. This depends on the profile and how the database is set up.

6B. From the foods table, get the price of a grilled steak.

6C. From the employees table, get the hire date and phone number for Paula Jacobs.

7. Goal: Get several specific rows with a Where condition that uses < and >.

7A. List the first name, last name, and credit limits of the employees with a credit limit over $20.00. Sort them by the size of the credit limit.

Oracle & Access SQL

```
select first_name,
last_name,
credit_limit
from l_employees
where credit_limit > 20
order by credit_limit;
```

Note: Do not put a comma or a dollar sign in the credit limit.

7B. List the foods costing less than $2.00. Sort them by the description of the food.

7C. List the employees hired before 1997.

8. Goal: Get specific rows, using IN - for a set of values

8A. List the credit limits for the employees:

      Brown

      Woods

      Owens

Oracle & Access SQL

```
select first_name,
last_name,
credit_limit
from l_employees
where last_name in ('brown', 'woods', 'owens')
order by last_name;
```

Notes:
1. Single quotes are used for character string data and dates.
2. Quotes are not used with numbers.

8B. List the prices of the foods:

      Hamburger

      French Fries

      Soda

8C. List the department name of the departments:

      mkt

      sal

9. Goal: Get specific rows, using BETWEEN - for a range of values

9A. List the employees hired in 1996.

Oracle SQL

```
select employee_id,
first_name,
last_name,
hire_date
from l_employees
where hire_date between '01-jan-96' and '31-dec-96'
order by hire_date;
```

Access SQL

```
select employee_id,
first_name,
last_name,
hire_date
from l_employees
where hire_date between #01-jan-96# and #31-dec-96#
order by hire_date;
```

Note: The end points are included in the range.

9B. List the foods priced between $1.00 and $2.00.

9C. List the employees with last names starting with H through P. (This is a little tricky.)

10. Goal: Get several specific rows. Use a LIKE condition in the Where clause for pattern matching.

10A. List the employees that have the letter 'N' in their last names.

Oracle SQL   Access SQL

`select last_name`
`from l_employees`
`where last_name like '%n%'`
`order by last_name;`
	`select last_name`
	`from l_employees`
	`where last_name like '*n*'`
	`order by last_name;`

Notes:
1.   % (percent sign) is a wildcard meaning a string of any number of characters, possibly 0 characters.
2.   _ (underline) is a wildcard meaning exactly one character.

10B. List the foods that have 'fresh' in their descriptions.

10C. List the employees that have a phone number ending with 4.

11. Goal: Get specific rows, using IS NULL

11A. List the employees who do not have a manager.

```
select first_name,
last_name
from l_employees
where manager_id is null;
```

Notes:
1. NULL means:
    there is no value
    or the value is unknown
    or the value is not in the database
2. NULLs are treated differently from other data. To keep you aware of this differ-
    ence, you must write IS NULL. You will get an error if you write = NULL.

12. Goal: Get specific rows, using:
    NOT IN
    NOT BETWEEN
    NOT LIKE
    IS NOT NULL
    ^=

12A. If you saved your work for the previous exercises (you should have saved it), go
back and add a NOT or ^.

Notes:
1. ^ is the uppercase 6 on most keyboards.
2. You will get an error if you write 'NOT =.'

13. Goal: Get specific rows, using AND, OR, NOT, (,) to combine several conditions together.

13A. List the employees in the 'sal' or 'mkt' departments who were hired in 1998.

Oracle SQL   Access SQL

| ```
select first_name,
last_name
from  l_employees
where (dept_code = 'sal'
or dept_code = 'mkt')
and hire_date >= '01-jan-98'
and hire_date <= '31-dec-98'
order by last_name ;
``` | ```
select first_name,
last_name
from  l_employees
where (dept_code = 'sal'
or dept_code = 'mkt')
and hire_date >= #01-jan-98#
and hire_date <= #31-dec-98#
order by last_name ;
``` |

Note: You can combine any number of conditions together. Many complex Select statements have ten conditions or more.

13B. List the rows of the lunch_items table having Supplier id = 'cbc' and product_code = 'gs.'

Chapter 3

Saving Your Results

The table of results of a query has columns and rows. It is a table and it can be handled like any other table. This chapter shows you how to save the results of a query in a new table and make modifications to the data. It also shows you how to use the Data Dictionary to find all the tables and views you have created.

Saving Your Results in a New Table or View

All the queries you have written so far display their results on the screen. After the computer is turned off, the results are gone. This section shows how to save the results in a table. Alternatively, they can be saved in a view, which is similar to a table.

Creating a new table from the results of a Select statement

Figure 3-1 shows how to create a new table from the results of a Select statement. Both Oracle and Access can do this operation, but they specify it with different syntax. Oracle follows the SQL standard, but Access has created its own non-standard expression.

In both Oracle and Access the name of the new table must be a new name that is not already used. Each table must have a unique name. If the name is already being used, you will receive an error message and your SQL statement will not be processed.

You are the owner of the new table and have complete control over it. You are the only person who can use it, unless you decide to share it with other people. You can modify the data in this table by adding new rows, deleting rows, or changing the values of individual columns.

Figure 3-1

❶   You can begin with any Select statement like the ones you have written. It displays its results on the computer screen, but it does not save the results This example shows all the features you have used so far. It includes the four main clauses of the Select statement - the Select, From, Where, and Order By clauses.

❷   The Order By clause must be removed for now. You can restore it later. Recall that a table does not keep its rows in any particular order. You are now going to create a new table. If you used an Order By clause, you would be specifying an order for the rows of the new table. That is why the Order By clause must be deleted. (Actually, Access allows you to keep this clause. Access does allow you to specify an order for the rows of a table. But this is non-standard feature of Access, so I will not discuss it any further.)

❸   In Oracle, you add a new clause before the Select clause. It says "Create table." Then it gives the name of the new table. Then it shows the word "As."

❹   In Access, you add a new clause after the end of the Select clause and before the From clause. It says "Into." Then it gives the name of the new table.

❺   After you create a new table, you can write any Select statement using the data from the new table. The From clause here names the new table.

❻   The Select statement using the new table can have an Order By clause. This can specify as order for the rows of the result table. It can restore the order deleted at ❷.

Task

Save the result table of a Select statement by creating a new permanent table. Show how to change a Select statement so that the result is saved in a new table, instead of being displayed on the screen. The new table created here is named "Sales staff."

Beginning SELECT Statement—does not save the results

```
select employee_id, ❶
       first_name,
       last_name,
       dept_code
from l_employees
where dept_code = 'sal'
order by employee_id; ❷
```

Modified SELECT Statement—saves the results in a table

Oracle SQL

```
create table sales_staff as ❸
select employee_id,
       first_name,
       last_name,
       dept_code
from l_employees
where dept_code = 'sal';
```

Access SQL

```
select employee_id,
       first_name,
       last_name,
       dept_code
into sales_staff ❹
from l_employees
where dept_code = 'sal';
```

Display the new table—and show the rows in a specific order
Oracle & Access SQL

```
select *
from sales_staff ❺
order by employee_id; ❻
```

Figure 3-1   Creating a new table from the results of a Select statement

Creating a new view from the results of a Select statement

Figure 3-2 shows an example of saving the result of a Select statement in a view. A view is very much like a table. The next figure discusses the difference between a view and a table, but for now, you can think of a view as a special type of table. Often, when we use the word "table," we really mean "table or view."

Access uses the term "saved query" instead of the term "view." However, they both mean the same thing. In this book we will use the term "view," because Standard SQL calls it a view.

Figure 3-2

❶ The beginning Select statement is the same one used in the Figure 3-1. It lists the employee id, first name, last name, and department code for all employees in the sales department. You might ask, "Why should we list the department code, when we know it will always say the person is in the sale's department?" When this query becomes public, then the "department code" column will be deleted. Here is it included to help make sure the query is running correctly—as an aid to debugging the SQL.

❷ The Order By clause must be removed, for the same reason as in Figure 3-1.

❸ In Oracle, the modification of the SQL is the same as in Figure 3-1, except here you say "Create view" instead of "Create table." The name for the new view is different here than in Figure 3-1 because you cannot use the same name for both a table and a view.

❹ Access does not have an SQL command to create a view, at least not the SQL window level. (Access can also run SQL at other levels, but that is outside the current discussion.). Instead, it uses the graphics on the screen to create a "saved query." This type of method uses the Graphical User Interface or "GUI." which is pronounced "gooey."

The new view

After the new view is created, it can be used like a table. It can be used in the From clause of any Select statement.

You are the owner of this view and have complete control over it. You are the only person who can use it, unless you decide to share it with other people.

As in figure 3-1, you can display the new view and restore the Order By clause you removed in ❷.

Task

Same as Figure 3-1, except save the results in a view instead of a table. In this example, name the new view "Sales staff view."

Beginning SELECT Statement—does not save the results

```
select employee_id, ❶
       first_name,
       last_name,
       dept_code
from l_employees
where dept_code = 'sal'
order by employee_id; ❷
```

Modified SELECT statement—saves the results in a view

Oracle SQL   ### Access SQL

```
create view sales_staff_view as ❸
select employee_id,
       first_name,
       last_name,
       dept_code
from l_employees
where dept_code = 'sal';
```

(This is not available in Access as an SQL command.)

Access method ❹

Step 1: Enter the Select statement in the SQL window and omit the Order By clause.
Step 2: Save the query using on of these methods:

With the mouse and the toolbar	Click the Save button
With the mouse and pull-down menus	File → Save
From the keyboard	CTRL + S

Step 3: Enter a name for the query.

Figure 3-2   Creating a new view from the results of a Select statement

The similarities and differences between a table and a view

When you create and run a query, you can save the "result table" it produces. It can be saved as a table or as a view. Here is how these two structures compare with each other.

The similarities

Tables and views are very similar. They look alike. They both are two-dimensional structures that contain data. They both have columns and rows. They can both be used as a source of data in the From clause of a Select statement.

Most of the time there is no need to distinguish between them. Views are based on tables. In fact, they are "views of tables." Often, when we use the word "table," we mean "a view or a table." When we want to differentiate a table from a view, we usually call the table a "base table" or a "data table."

The differences

A table stores data directly on the disk. It stores data. A view stores a Select statement, a "saved query." It does not store any data. For a view to appear as data, it must run the Select statement. The result table of this Select statement is the data of the view.

The disk space requirements are different. A table may require a substantial amount of disk space to store its data. It may contain thousands or even millions of rows. A view needs very little disk space to store the Select statement. Tables require more disk space.

The processing requirements are different. When a table is used as a source of data in the From clause of a Select statement, the computer must read the table from the disk. This may require a lot of I/O processing, but very little CPU processing or memory usage. However, when a view is used as a source of data, the CPU and memory may be used substantially. Since the view depends on some base tables, I/O processing is also required. So views require more processing.

Tables are static, but views are dynamic. The data in a table does not change by itself, but the data in a view is updated automatically. The data in a table changes only when a change is made explicitly to it. A row can be added or deleted. The data in any cell can be changed. However, the commands to make these changes must name the table directly. These commands directly address the table. They say "make this change to this table."

In contrast, the data in a view changes whenever a change is made to any of the base tables it is built upon. When a view is used, the Select statement is run that defines the view. The data is drawn from the underlying tables at that time. So, the data in a view can change when no commands have been issued to explicitly change it.

In some circumstances, this means that the data in a table can become old and out of date, but the data in a view will always be current. In other circumstances, it means that the data in a table is stable and predictable, but the data in a view can change without warning and is not stable.

Similarities

Both tables and views:

*   Are two-dimensional structures that contain data

*   Have columns, rows, and cells

*   Can contain the same types of data

*   Can be used in the From clause of Select statements

Differences

Table	View
Stores the data in the database.	Stores the Select statement in the database.
Uses a lot of disk space for a large table. Most users are only allowed to create tables that are of limited size.	Uses very little disk space.
The data can be changed without affecting any other table.	A view has no data of it's own. The data belongs to the tables in the From clause of the Select statement. The data in most views cannot be changed. For the few views that do allow the data to be changed, when the data is changed, it is really the data in the underlying table that is being changed.
The data in a table is stable and does not change by itself. It does not change when other tables are changed.	A view is changing and dynamic. The Select statement is run every time the view is used. If the underlying tables have changed, then the view contains different data.
The data is a table may become out of date.	The data in a view is always current.

Which one should you use?
It depends on what you want to have.

Table	View
You want the data to be stable	You want the data to stay current
You have a small amount of data that requires a lot of processing to produce	You have a large amount of data
You will need to make changes to the data	You will not need to make changes to the data

Figure 3-3   The similarities and differences between a table and a view

Deleting a table or a view

Now that you know how to create new tables and views, you also need to know how to delete them. Otherwise, you will eventually have more of them than you want.

Deleting a table:
Method 1—using an SQL command

In both Oracle and Access, you can delete a table with an SQL command. "Drop table" is followed by the name of the table. This gets rid of the table entirely. The data in the table, the table structure, the definitions of the columns, and the name of the table are all deleted.

Method 2—using the graphics on the screen.

In Access, you can also use a GUI method to delete a table:

1. Click the Tables tab.
2. Select and highlight the name of the table you want to delete
3. Press the Delete key, or use the mouse to choose   Edit → Delete.

In Oracle, the SQL Plus environment does not support any GUI methods. Oracle does have some GUI tools, but they are packaged separately from the SQL Plus environment.

Task

Delete the table named "Sales Staff."

Method 1—using an SQL command
Oracle & Access SQL

```
drop table sales_staff;
```

Method 2—using the graphics on the screen (GUI)
Oracle   Access

(None.) | Highlight the name of the table and press the Delete key

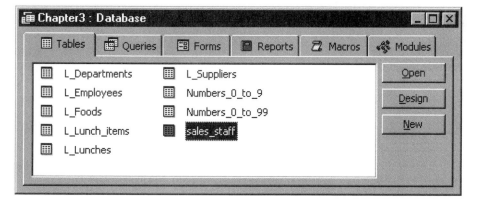

Beginning table

```
EMPLOYEE                          DEPT
      ID FIRST_NAME LAST_NAME     CODE
-------- ---------- ----------    ----
     202 JIM        KERN          SAL
     204 ELLEN      OWENS         SAL
     205 HENRY      PERKINS       SAL
     210 NANCY      HOFFMAN       SAL
```

Result

(The table has been deleted entirely. All the rows of data have been deleted. Also, the table itself has been deleted. This includes the name of the table, the names of the columns, and their datatypes and sequence. The name of the table is no longer reserved and another table or view can now use it.)

Figure 3-4   Deleting a table or a view (part 1 of 2)

Deleting a view

Method 1—using an SQL command

In Oracle , you can delete a view with an SQL command. "Drop view" is followed by the name of the view. This deletes the Select statement that defines the view and the name of the view.

In Access, there is no SQL command to drop a view, which Access calls a saved query.

Method 2—using the graphics on the screen

In Access, to drop a view you must use a GUI method. The steps of the GUI method are:

1. Click the Queries tab.
2. Select and highlight the name of the saved query you want to delete.
3. Press the Delete key, or use the mouse to choose   Edit → Delete.

In Oracle, GUI methods are not supported in the SQL Plus environment.

Perspective

In Oracle, you must use an SQL command to create a view. You must also use an SQL command to delete a view.

In Access, you must use the GUI to create a view. You must also use the GUI to delete a view.

Task

Delete the view named "Sales_Staff_View."

Method 1—using an SQL command
Oracle SQL   **Access SQL**

```
drop view sales_staff_view; | (None.)
```

Method 2—using the graphics on the screen (GUI)
Oracle   **Access**

(None.) | Highlight the name of the saved query and press the Delete key.

Beginning view

```
EMPLOYEE                          DEPT
      ID FIRST_NAME LAST_NAME  CODE
-------- ---------- ---------- ----
     202 JIM        KERN       SAL
     204 ELLEN      OWENS      SAL
     205 HENRY      PERKINS    SAL
     210 NANCY      HOFFMAN    SAL
```

Result

(The view has been deleted. The name of the view is no longer reserved and it can be used by a new table or view. The Select statement that defined the view is no longer stored within the database.)

Figure 3-4   Deleting a table or view (part 2 of 2)

One view can be built on top of another view

A view can be defined from another view. This is similar to defining a view from a base table. In the Select statement that defines a view, the From clause can name either a base table or another view.

Why would you want to do this? Why not just define each view directly from base tables? There are two reasons. One reason is to control complexity. A view defined on other views using a series of simple queries can sometime replace one defined by a very complex query. This can result in code that is easier for people to understand. The code can be verified and debugged more easily. It is more likely to be correct.

The other reason is to coordinate two parts of a computer application. This can tie the parts together. So if one part is changed, the other part will be changed automatically to maintain a specific relationship with the first part.

In Figure 3-5, the Slaes_Staff_2 view could have been defined directly from the base table, L_employees. The figure is intended to show an example of the process of building one view on top of another view. In this case, the view is so simple that there is no particular reason to define it in two steps.

Figure 3-5

❶ This shows how the view, "Sales_staff_1," is created. In the Select statement that defines this view, the From clause refers to a base table, L_employees.

❷ This shows how the view, "Sales_staff_2," is created. It is built "on top of" the Sales_staff_1 view.

❸ The From clause refers to the first view, Sales_staff_1, rather than to a base table.

There are layers of views

Circular definitions are not allowed. When one view is built from another view, care must be taken to ensure that there are no "circles" in the definition. A "circle" would occur if view_1 depended on view_2 and view_2 depended on view_1. The computer must be able to find the base tables for every view. It could not do this if circle were allowed in the definitions.

Because of this, the views can be thought of as being organized into layers. Views built directly from base tables are the first layer. Views built from these are the second layer, and so on.

What happens when an underlying base table or view is deleted?

If the view sales_staff_1 is deleted, then the view sales_staff_2 becomes invalid and cannot work. However, in both Oracle and Access, the Select statement defining sales_staff_2 is retained. If the underlying view, sales_staff_1, is restored, then the sales_staff_2 view will work again.

In some other SQL products, all the views are deleted that are built on top of a base table or view that is being deleted. This is a cascaded delete. So dropping a base table or view can automatically trigger the dropping of many other views that are built on top of them. In this situation, you must be cautious before you drop any base table or view.

Task

Create a view, "sales_staff_2." Build it on top of the view, "sales_staff_1."

Step 1—Create the first view from a base table ❶

Oracle SQL

```
create view sales_staff_1 as
select employee_id,
       first_name,
       last_name,
       dept_code
from l_employees
where dept_code = 'sal';
```

Access GUI method

(Enter this query into the SQL window:)

```
select employee_id,
       first_name,
       last_name,
       dept_code
from l_employees
where dept_code = 'sal';
```

(Save the query. Name it "sales_staff_1")

Step 2—Create a second view from the first one ❷

Oracle SQL

```
create view sales_staff_2 as
select employee_id,
       first_name,
       last_name
from sales_staff_view_1 .
where employee_id < 209;
```

Access GUI method

(Enter this query into the SQL window:)

```
select employee_id,
       first_name,
       last_name
from sales_staff_view_1
where employee_id < 209;
```

(Save the query. Name it "sales_staff_2")

Result of step 1—Sales_staff_1 view

```
EMPLOYEE                           DEPT
      ID FIRST_NAME LAST_NAME     CODE
-------- ---------- ----------    ----
     202 JIM        KERN          SAL
     204 ELLEN      OWENS         SAL
     205 HENRY      PERKINS       SAL
     210 NANCY      HOFFMAN       SAL
```

Result of step 2—Sales_staff_2 view

```
EMPLOYEE
      ID FIRST_NAME LAST_NAME
-------- ---------- ----------
     202 JIM        KERN
     204 ELLEN      OWENS
     205 HENRY      PERKINS
```

Figure 3-5   One view can be built on top of another view

Preventative deletes

Each table and view must have a name within the database. Each database object must have a name that identifies it. Two different objects cannot both use the same name. Most of the time, this works well.

However, there are times when you are creating a new table or view and you need to try several versions of the code before you get it correct. The problem here is that the new version does not automatically replace the old one. When you try to create the second version of the table or view, you are prevented from creating it because the name is already being used by the first version. You will get an error message and the table or view will not be created.

What is a preventative delete?

A "preventative delete" drops the previous version of a table or view before it creates the new version. This ensures that the name will be available within the database. People use this common practice when they are developing new code.

It is called a "preventative delete" because it prevents an error from occurring if the name is already being used by a previous version. Sometimes, we do not expect that anything will actually be deleted. There may be no such object to delete. The delete is done to prevent a possible problem.

Coding a preventative delete

A preventative delete can be coded by putting a Drop statement before a Create statement. This is usually done within a script file, where several commands are run as a single unit. The script will continue to run if the Drop command fails, which can occur if the object has not yet been created. Oracle supports scripts, but the SQL window in Access can only accept one command at a time. So we will discuss this technique only for Oracle.

For views, Oracle also has a special option to support preventative deletes. You can say "Create or replace view," instead of "Create view." This is not part of standard SQL. It is an extension to the standard that is special to Oracle. Oracle does not have a similar feature for tables. This is probably because it would be "too dangerous" to encourage the use of preventative deletes with tables.

Figure 3-6 shows some ways to code a preventative delete in Oracle.

Figure 3-6

❶ This "Drop Table" statement is a preventative delete. It is placed directly before the table is created.

❷ This "Drop View" statement is a preventative delete.

❸ "Create Or Replace View" is a special feature available in Oracle to support preventative deletes.

A preventative delete for a table

Oracle SQL	Access

```
drop table sales_staff; ❶
create table sales_staff as
select employee_id,
       first_name,
       last_name,
       dept_code
from l_employees
where dept_code = 'sal';
```

(Access issues a warning message if you try to use the same name twice in the database.)

A preventative delete for a view
Method 1—using standard SQL

Oracle SQL	Access

```
drop view sales_staff_view; ❷
create view sales_staff_view as
select employee_id,
       first_name,
       last_name,
       department_code
from l_employees
where department_code = 'sal';
```

(Access issues a warning message if you try to use the same name twice in the database.)

Method 2—using a special feature in Oracle

Oracle SQL	Access

```
create or replace view sales_staff_view as ❸
select employee_id,
       first_name,
       last_name,
       department_code
from l_employees
where department_code = 'sal';
```

(This feature is not available in Access.)

Figure 3-6   Preventative deletes

Modifying the Data in a Table

After you have created a new table, you may want to put some rows of data in it. For tables that already contain data, you may want to add new rows, change the data in a few columns of an existing row, or delete rows entirely. This section shows you how to do these things.

Adding one new row to a table

Figure 3-7 shows how to add a single new row to a table. There are two methods to do this. One method specifies a value for each column of the table. The values must be listed in the same order as the columns of the table. The columns of a table always have a specific order. The information in the table is not affected by the order of the columns, However, the order of the columns does affect the syntax of some SQL statements, such as this one.

The other method puts values in only some of the columns of the table. These columns are listed after the name of the table in the SQL command. Nulls are placed in all the columns that are not listed. The list of values must contain an entry for each column in the list. The values must be listed in the same order as the columns.

When you use this method, you must include every column of the primary key in the list of columns. Otherwise, nulls would be entered in the columns of the primary key, which is not allowed. You will receive an error message if you forget to list any of the columns of the primary key.

Figure 3-7

❶   There is no list of columns following the table name. This means that values will be entered in all the columns of the table.

❷   The value in each column must be compatible with the type of data already in that column. The main types of data are text, number, and date/time. Text is also called "character string" data. The data types must match. For example, you cannot put text into a column of numbers or a column of dates.

If you want to put nulls in the data, you can use the word "null" for the value, without the quotation marks. This works with any type of column—text, number, and date/time. With the quotation marks, "null" becomes a text value containing the four letters N, U, L, L.

❸   The three columns listed after the table name are the only columns in which data can be entered. All other columns will be null.

❹   The values must be listed in the same order as the columns in ❸.

❺   The first Insert statement, using method 1 added this row.

❻   The second Insert statement, using method 2, added this row.

Task

Add two new rows to the Foods table of the Lunches database.

Method 1—putting data in all the columns
Oracle & Access SQL

```
insert into l_foods ❶
values ('arr', 'ap', 11,  'apple pie', 1.50, null); ❷
```

Method 2—putting data in only some of the columns
Oracle & Access SQL

```
insert into l_foods (product_code, description, supplier_id) ❸
values ('bp', 'blueberry pie', 'arr'); ❹
```

Beginning table (L_foods table)

```
SUPPLIER PRODUCT   MENU                                      PRICE
ID       CODE      ITEM DESCRIPTION              PRICE INCREASE
-------- -------   -------  --------------------   --------  --------
ASP      FS          1 FRESH SALAD                $2.00    $0.25
ASP      SP          2 SOUP OF THE DAY            $1.50  (null)
ASP      SW          3 SANDWICH                   $3.50    $0.40
CBC      GS          4 GRILLED STEAK              $6.00    $0.70
CBC      HB          5 HAMBURGER                  $2.50    $0.30
FRV      BR          6 BROCCOLI                   $1.00    $0.05
FRV      FF          7 FRENCH FRIES               $1.50  (null)
JBR      AS          8 SODA                       $1.25    $0.25
JBR      VR          9 COFFEE                     $0.85    $0.15
VSB      AS         10 DESSERT                    $3.00    $0.50
```

Result table

```
SUPPLIER PRODUCT   MENU                                      PRICE
ID       CODE      ITEM DESCRIPTION              PRICE INCREASE
-------- -------   -------  --------------------   --------  --------
ASP      FS          1 FRESH SALAD                $2.00    $0.25
ASP      SP          2 SOUP OF THE DAY            $1.50  (null)
ASP      SW          3 SANDWICH                   $3.50    $0.40
CBC      GS          4 GRILLED STEAK              $6.00    $0.70
CBC      HB          5 HAMBURGER                  $2.50    $0.30
FRV      BR          6 BROCCOLI                   $1.00    $0.05
FRV      FF          7 FRENCH FRIES               $1.50  (null)
JBR      AS          8 SODA                       $1.25    $0.25
JBR      VR          9 COFFEE                     $0.85    $0.15
VSB      AS         10 DESSERT                    $3.00    $0.50
ARR      AP         11 APPLE PIE                  $1.50  (null)    ❺
ARR      BP     (null)  BLUEBERRY PIE           (null)  (null)    ❻
```

Figure 3-7   Adding one new row to a table

Adding many new rows to a table with a Select statement

Figure 3-8 shows how to add several new rows to a table by using a Select statement. This can only be done when the data is already in the database in some form. You cannot enter data that is completely new using this method.

This is another variation on the command to enter a single row of data. The SQL syntax is:

> INSERT INTO table_name
> select_statement;

or

> INSERT INTO table_name (list_of_columns)
> select_statement;

The Select statement must not contain an Order By clause. An Order By clause would place the rows in a specific order, which would not make sense in this context. The rows of the table, after the new rows are added, are in no particular order.

Figure 3-8

❶   The L_foods table will receive the new rows of data. Since no columns are listed after the table name, the Select statement must create a value for every column of the table.

❷   There are six columns in the table receiving the data, so there must be six columns listed in the Select clause. Note that the last two columns are explicitly coded as "null." The columns of the Select clause must be in the same order as the columns of the receiving table. The datatype of each column in the Select clause must match the datatype in the receiving table.

❸   The data will be gotten from the L_foods table. This is the same table that is receiving the new rows of data. This is an unusual situation, however it works without any problems.

❹   The Where clause limits the data that is taken from the table named in the From clause in ❸.

❺   The Select statement does not contain an Order By clause.

❻   There is a list of columns after the name of the table receiving the data. These are the only columns that can receive data. All the other columns will be null.

❼   Four columns are listed after the table name in ❻, so the Select clause must contain four columns in the same order.

❽   These three rows have been added to the table by a single Insert statement. Either the Method 1 SQL statement or the Method 2 SQL statement can add all three of these rows.

Task

Use the Foods table, duplicate all the rows from supplier ASP and change the supplier to ARR. Put nulls in the price and price increase columns of the new rows.

Method 1—putting data in all the columns
Oracle SQL

```
insert into l_foods  ❶
select 'arr',  ❷
          product_code,
          menu_item,
          description,
          null,
          null
from l_foods  ❸
where supplier_id = 'asp';  ❹
❺
```

Access SQL

(Access does not support this syntax.
Use variation 2 instead.)

Method 2—putting data in only some of the columns
Oracle & Access SQL

```
insert into l_foods (supplier_id, product_code, menu_item, description)  ❻
select 'arr',  ❼
        product_code,
        menu_item,
        description
from l_foods
where supplier_id = 'asp';
```

Result table

SUPPLIER ID	PRODUCT CODE	MENU ITEM	DESCRIPTION	PRICE	PRICE INCREASE	
ASP	FS	1	FRESH SALAD	$2.00	$0.25	
ASP	SP	2	SOUP OF THE DAY	$1.50	(null)	
ASP	SW	3	SANDWICH	$3.50	$0.40	
CBC	GS	4	GRILLED STEAK	$6.00	$0.70	
CBC	HB	5	HAMBURGER	$2.50	$0.30	
FRV	BR	6	BROCCOLI	$1.00	$0.05	
FRV	FF	7	FRENCH FRIES	$1.50	(null)	
JBR	AS	8	SODA	$1.25	$0.25	
JBR	VR	9	COFFEE	$0.85	$0.15	
VSB	AS	10	DESSERT	$3.00	$0.50	
ARR	FS	1	FRESH SALAD	(null)	(null)	❽
ARR	SP	2	SOUP OF THE DAY	(null)	(null)	❽
ARR	SW	3	SANDWICH	(null)	(null)	❽

Figure 3-8   Adding many new rows to a table with a Select statement

Changing data in the rows already in a table

Figure 3-9 shows how to change data in rows that are already in the table. You can modify the values in one column or several columns. Usually, only a few columns are modified at a time. If you want to modify the data in all the columns, an easier approach might be to add a new row to the table and delete the old row.

The syntax of the SQL statement is:

```
UPDATE table_name
SET column_1 = value_1,
        column_2 = value_2
WHERE condition;
```

The values on any number of columns can be changed in one statement.

The syntax here is easier to read and work with than in the Insert command. The name of the column is aligned with its value. You do not need to correlate two separate lists. However, this break comes with a price. The names of the columns must be stated explicitly in each Update statement.

The value can be a fixed value or it can be a function, as in this example. It can even be a subquery. In later chapters, I discuss row functions and subqueries in detail.

The Where clause is critical. The Where clause says which rows of the table should be changed. Without it, all the rows of the table are changed. It sets a condition. This condition can be like any of the conditions I used in the Where clause of a Select statement. Data is changed only in the rows where the condition is true.

You must keep careful control of the Where clause, if you want to change the values in a single row. The default is to change all the row of the table. The best way to limit the change to a single row is to write the Where condition using the primary key of the table.

Figure 3-9

❶ The data will be changed in the L_foods table.

❷ Ten cents is added to the Price column, and then the result is placed back in the Price column. The comma at the end of the line shows that the value of another column will be changed.

❸ Ten cents is added to the Price Increase column, and then the result is placed in the Price Increase column. To give a column a fixed value, place that value after the "=" sign.

Since no comma is at the end of this line, no more columns are being changed. Also note that no From clause exists.

❹ The Where clause limits the rows that are changed. Only two rows satisfy the condition

```
supplier_id = 'jbr'
```

These are the only rows that are changed.

Task

Add 10 cents to the both the price and the price increases for all the foods supplied by JBR.

Oracle & Access SQL

```
update l_foods ❶
set price = price + 0.10, ❷
     price_increase = price_increase + 0.10 ❸
where supplier_id = 'jbr'; ❹
```

Beginning table (L_foods table)

SUPPLIER ID	PRODUCT CODE	MENU ITEM	DESCRIPTION	PRICE	PRICE INCREASE
ASP	FS	1	FRESH SALAD	$2.00	$0.25
ASP	SP	2	SOUP OF THE DAY	$1.50	(null)
ASP	SW	3	SANDWICH	$3.50	$0.40
CBC	GS	4	GRILLED STEAK	$6.00	$0.70
CBC	HB	5	HAMBURGER	$2.50	$0.30
FRV	BR	6	BROCCOLI	$1.00	$0.05
FRV	FF	7	FRENCH FRIES	$1.50	(null)
JBR	AS	8	SODA	$1.25	$0.25
JBR	VR	9	COFFEE	$0.85	$0.15
VSB	AS	10	DESSERT	$3.00	$0.50

Ending table

SUPPLIER ID	PRODUCT CODE	MENU ITEM	DESCRIPTION	PRICE	PRICE INCREASE
ASP	FS	1	FRESH SALAD	$2.00	$0.25
ASP	SP	2	SOUP OF THE DAY	$1.50	(null)
ASP	SW	3	SANDWICH	$3.50	$0.40
CBC	GS	4	GRILLED STEAK	$6.00	$0.70
CBC	HB	5	HAMBURGER	$2.50	$0.30
FRV	BR	6	BROCCOLI	$1.00	$0.05
FRV	FF	7	FRENCH FRIES	$1.50	(null)
JBR	AS	8	SODA	$1.35	$0.35
JBR	VR	9	COFFEE	$0.95	$0.25
VSB	AS	10	DESSERT	$3.00	$0.50

Figure 3-9   Changing data in the rows already in a table

Deleting rows from a table

Figure 3-10 shows how to delete rows from a table. You can delete one row or several rows. The SQL syntax is:

```
DELETE FROM table_name
WHERE condition;
```

The Where condition is critical here, as in the Update statement. Without it, all the rows of the table will be deleted. The table structure will remain, and the table itself will still exist. But it will have no data in it.

The Where clause controls which rows will be deleted. It sets a condition. This condition can be like any of the ones we used in the Where clause of a Select statement. All the rows for which the condition is true will be deleted.

Figure 3-10
❶   Rows of data will be deleted from the L_foods table.
❷   Delete all the rows where the Supplier Id is "cbc" or "jbr."

Deleting all the duplicate rows from a table
Sometimes people ask how to delete the duplicate rows from a table. The problem is that writing a Where condition that deletes only the duplicate rows is difficult.

You have several ways to do this. Here is one of them. This method uses only the things you have already learned: Create a new table using Select Distinct. This gets rid of all the duplicate rows. Here is the code to do this:

Oracle SQL
```
CREATE TABLE new_table_name AS
SELECT DISTINCT *
FROM table_with_duplicate_rows;
```

Access SQL
```
SELECT DISTINCT *
INTO new_table_name
FROM table_with_duplicate_rows;
```

Task

Delete all the rows with supplier id CBC and JBR from the Foods table.

Oracle & Access SQL

```
delete from l_foods ❶
where supplier_id in ('cbc', 'jbr'); ❷
```

Beginning table (L_foods table)

SUPPLIER ID	PRODUCT CODE	MENU ITEM	DESCRIPTION	PRICE	PRICE INCREASE
ASP	FS	1	FRESH SALAD	$2.00	$0.25
ASP	SP	2	SOUP OF THE DAY	$1.50	(null)
ASP	SW	3	SANDWICH	$3.50	$0.40
CBC	GS	4	GRILLED STEAK	$6.00	$0.70
CBC	HB	5	HAMBURGER	$2.50	$0.30
FRV	BR	6	BROCCOLI	$1.00	$0.05
FRV	FF	7	FRENCH FRIES	$1.50	(null)
JBR	AS	8	SODA	$1.25	$0.25
JBR	VR	9	COFFEE	$0.85	$0.15
VSB	AS	10	DESSERT	$3.00	$0.50

Ending table

SUPPLIER ID	PRODUCT CODE	MENU ITEM	DESCRIPTION	PRICE	PRICE INCREASE
ASP	FS	1	FRESH SALAD	$2.00	$0.25
ASP	SP	2	SOUP OF THE DAY	$1.50	(null)
ASP	SW	3	SANDWICH	$3.50	$0.40
FRV	BR	6	BROCCOLI	$1.00	$0.05
FRV	FF	7	FRENCH FRIES	$1.50	(null)
VSB	AS	10	DESSERT	$3.00	$0.50

Figure 3-10   Deleting rows from a table

Using the GUI environment to change the table data in Access

Access is oriented to using the GUI environment to change the data in a table. The Insert, Update, and Delete commands work in Access, but the GUI environment is the easiest way to work with the data.

Beginning table

Supplier_id	Supplier_name
Arr	Alice & Ray's Restaurant
Asp	A Soup Place
Cbc	Certified Beef Company
Frv	Frank Reed's Vegetables
Fsn	Frank & Sons
Jbr	Just Beverages
Jps	Jim Parker's Shop
Vsb	Virginia Street Bakery

Record: 1 of 8

Inserting new rows

To add new rows, type the data into the blank row at the bottom of the table, the one with the asterisk beside it. As soon as you start to enter data in one new row, another blank row will be added at the bottom of the table.

Supplier_id	Supplier_name
Arr	Alice & Ray's Restaurant
Asp	A Soup Place
Cbc	Certified Beef Company
Frv	Frank Reed's Vegetables
Fsn	Frank & Sons
Jbr	Just Beverages
Jps	Jim Parker's Shop
Vsb	Virginia Street Bakery
NEW	ROW

Record: 9 of 9

Updating the data

To change data in rows already in the table, type over the value that is there.

Deleting rows

To delete a row of data, highlight the row by clicking on the left margin, and then press the Delete key.

Figure 3-11 Using the GUI environment to change the table data in Access

Modifying Data through a View

You can apply the Insert, Update, and Delete commands to a view of the table in order to modify the data in a table, instead of applying them directly to the table itself. Only a special type of view can be used to modify the data. Most views are unable to do this modification.

Changing data through a view

Why change the data through a view?

If you are the only person using a database, you will probably change the data directly in the tables. That way is simpler. However, a common practice is to change the data through a view when you are working with a larger database, which many people are using at the same time.

This is partly a matter of how large databases are managed and administered. Usually, only the Database Administrators, DBAs, are allowed to work directly with the tables. Everyone else must use views to use the database.

The main purpose of this rule is to allow the DBAs to make changes to the database while other people are working with it. This rule provides a separation between the DBAs and the other users, so that they have a minimal impact on each other.

Another reason is that views can be used for database security and to restrict the changes that can be made to the data. They can limit the columns and rows of data that a particular user is able to see and change.

What types of views can change the data?

Views that can change the data in a table are called "updateable views." In general, only a few very simple views are updateable. A view is updateable when:

*   It contains data from only one table.
*   It contains some or all of the columns and rows from the table.
*   It does not summarize the data or condense it by using Select Distinct, so that the data in each cell of the view comes from the data in only one cell of the table.

Some SQL products are able to allow a few more views to be updateable. However, this list is the usual set of updateable views within most products.

In Access, you can tell easily whether if a view is updateable. If it is, a blank row is shown at the bottom of the view where you can enter new rows of data.

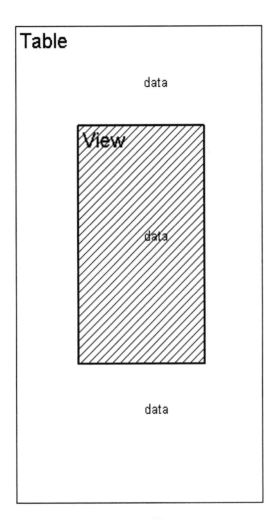

- The view here is like a "window" that allows us to see some of the data in a table in an unaltered state. This is a special type of view.
- The data *belongs to* the table. Some of it can be *seen through* the view.
- The Select statement that defines the view specifies the "window frame." It determines which data can be seen through the view and which cannot.
- When data is changed through the view, the changes actually occur in the table.

Figure 3-12   Changing data through a view

Example of changing data through a view

Figure 3-13 shows an example of changing the data in a table, using a process that changes it through a view. Part 1 shows all the components of this process. Parts 2 and 3 show data actually being changed.

This looks more complicated than changing the data directly in the table. However, from the user's perspective, the difference is very small. The user issues the same Insert, Update, and Delete commands. The only difference is that these commands name a view instead of naming a base table.

The components of the process

1. The first component, shown in part 1 of Figure 3-13, is the beginning table. This is where the data is stored.
2. The second component is the beginning view. This is derived from the beginning table by applying the Select statement that defines the view. The view definition is not shown separately in this diagram.
3. The data is changed through the view using an Insert, Update, or Delete command. Only the data that appears in the beginning view can be changed. The Update command cannot change the data in any column or row that does not appear in the beginning view. The Delete command can delete only rows that appear in this view.

    In contrast, changes can be made to the data whether or not they will appear in the ending view. The Insert commands can add new rows to the table, even if they do not appear in the ending view. The update command can change the value in a column in a way that makes the row disappear from the ending view.

    Figure 3-13 shows an example of this situation. When Dan Smith is changed from the shipping department to the marketing department, his row disappears from the ending view, because the view shows only people who are in the shipping department.

    When a new row is inserted into the database through a view, all the columns not shown in the view are set to null.
4. The fourth component is the ending view. This is shown here from the user's perspective. From the computer's perspective, the changes are made directly to the result table. Then the ending view is derived from the result table.

    In Access, if you are changing the data using the GUI environment, the ending view does not appear immediately. To see the ending view, you must close the view and then open it again. Access keeps showing you the beginning view while you are making changes to the data. This provides a stable working environment for making the changes. So the row for Dan Smith does not immediately disappear after he is changed to the marketing department. Inserts and Updates performed with the GUI are retained until the view is closed and reopened.
5. The last component is the result table. This shows all the changes made to the data, whether or not they appear in the ending view.

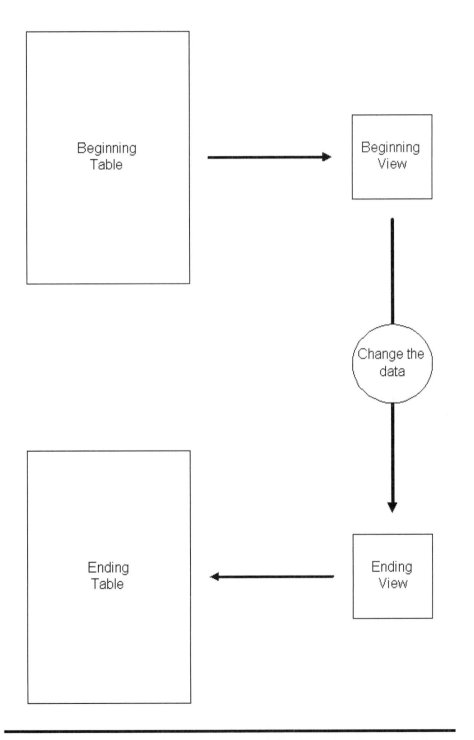

Figure 3-13   Example of changing data through a view (part 1 of 3)

Beginning table (L_employees table)

```
EMPLOYEE                         DEPT                CREDIT PHONE   MANAGER
      ID FIRST_NAME LAST_NAME    CODE HIRE_DATE      LIMIT NUMBER       ID
-------- ---------- ----------   ---- ----------    ------- ------  -------
     201 SUSAN      BROWN        EXE  01-JUN-92     $30.00 3484    (null)
     202 JIM        KERN         SAL  15-AUG-95     $25.00 8722       201
     203 MARTHA     WOODS        SHP  01-FEB-97     $25.00 7591       201
     204 ELLEN      OWENS        SAL  01-JUL-96     $15.00 6830       202
     205 HENRY      PERKINS      SAL  01-MAR-98     $25.00 5286       202
     206 CAROL      ROSE         ACT  15-OCT-97     $15.00 3829       201
     207 DAN        SMITH        SHP  01-DEC-96     $25.00 2259       203 ❶
     208 FRED       CAMPBELL     SHP  01-APR-97     $25.00 1752       203
     209 PAULA      JACOBS       MKT  17-MAR-98     $15.00 3357       201
     210 NANCY      HOFFMAN      SAL  15-FEB-96     $25.00 2974       203
```

Task

Transfer Dan Smith to the marketing department. Because the Employees table is part of a large database used by many people at the same time, you are required to make this change by updating a view.

Notes

❶   In the beginning table, Dan Smith is in the shipping department.

❷   Dan Smith appears in the Shipping Department View.

❸   Since you can see Dan Smith's record in the view, you decide to change it.

❹   This update statement changes the Shipping Department view. It does not change the Employees table.

❺   After you change his department, Dan Smith's record disappears from the Shipping Department View. So, you cannot verify that the change was made correctly.

❻   The data in the Employees table has been changed.

Ending table (L_employees table)

```
EMPLOYEE                         DEPT                CREDIT PHONE   MANAGER
      ID FIRST_NAME LAST_NAME    CODE HIRE_DATE      LIMIT NUMBER       ID
-------- ---------- ----------   ---- ----------    ------- ------  -------
     201 SUSAN      BROWN        EXE  01-JUN-92     $30.00 3484    (null)
     202 JIM        KERN         SAL  15-AUG-95     $25.00 8722       201
     203 MARTHA     WOODS        SHP  01-FEB-97     $25.00 7591       201
     204 ELLEN      OWENS        SAL  01-JUL-96     $15.00 6830       202
     205 HENRY      PERKINS      SAL  01-MAR-98     $25.00 5286       202
     206 CAROL      ROSE         ACT  15-OCT-97     $15.00 3829       201
     207 DAN        SMITH        MKT  01-DEC-96     $25.00 2259       203 ❻
     208 FRED       CAMPBELL     SHP  01-APR-97     $25.00 1752       203
     209 PAULA      JACOBS       MKT  17-MAR-98     $15.00 3357       201
     210 NANCY      HOFFMAN      SAL  15-FEB-96     $25.00 2974       203
```

Beginning view (Shipping_dept view)

```
EMPLOYEE                       DEPT   CREDIT
     ID FIRST_NAME LAST_NAME   CODE   LIMIT
-------- ---------- ---------- ----  -------
    203 MARTHA      WOODS       SHP   $25.00
    207 DAN         SMITH       SHP   $25.00   ❷
    208 FRED        CAMPBELL    SHP   $25.00
```

Transfer Dan Smith to another department
Oracle & Access SQL—change the data through
the view ❸

```
update shipping_dept ❹
set dept_code = 'mkt'
where employee_id = 207;
```

Ending view (Shipping_dept view) ❺

```
EMPLOYEE                       DEPT   CREDIT
     ID FIRST_NAME LAST_NAME   CODE   LIMIT
-------- ---------- ---------- ----  -------
    203 MARTHA      WOODS       SHP   $25.00
    208 FRED        CAMPBELL    SHP   $25.00
```

Figure 3-13   Example of changing data through a view (part 2 of 3)

Beginning table (L_employees table) ❶

```
EMPLOYEE                          DEPT                CREDIT PHONE  MANAGER
      ID FIRST_NAME LAST_NAME     CODE HIRE_DATE      LIMIT NUMBER      ID
-------- ---------- ----------    ---- ----------    ------- ------  -------
     201 SUSAN      BROWN         EXE  01-JUN-92     $30.00 3484    (null)
     202 JIM        KERN          SAL  15-AUG-95     $25.00 8722       201
     203 MARTHA     WOODS         SHP  01-FEB-97     $25.00 7591       201
     204 ELLEN      OWENS         SAL  01-JUL-96     $15.00 6830       202
     205 HENRY      PERKINS       SAL  01-MAR-98     $25.00 5286       202
     206 CAROL      ROSE          ACT  15-OCT-97     $15.00 3829       201
     207 DAN        SMITH         SHP  01-DEC-96     $25.00 2259       203
     208 FRED       CAMPBELL      SHP  01-APR-97     $25.00 1752       203
     209 PAULA      JACOBS        MKT  17-MAR-98     $15.00 3357       201
     210 NANCY      HOFFMAN       SAL  15-FEB-96     $25.00 2974       203
```

Task

Add a new employee, John Green, to the Shipping department.. Because the Employees table is part of a large database used by many people at the same time, you are required to make this change by updating a view.

Notes

❶   In the beginning table, there is no record for John Green.

❷   At first, John Green does not appear in the Shipping Department View.

❸   John Green will be added to the Employee table by adding his record to the Shipping Department view.

❹   This insert statement puts the record into the Shipping Department view. It does not put it into the Employees table.

❺   After you add John Green's record to the view, you can see it in the view.

❻   The data in the Employees table has been changed.

Ending table (L_employees table)

```
EMPLOYEE                          DEPT                CREDIT PHONE  MANAGER
      ID FIRST_NAME LAST_NAME     CODE HIRE_DATE      LIMIT NUMBER      ID
-------- ---------- ----------    ---- ----------    ------- ------  -------
     201 SUSAN      BROWN         EXE  01-JUN-92     $30.00 3484    (null)
     202 JIM        KERN          SAL  15-AUG-95     $25.00 8722       201
     203 MARTHA     WOODS         SHP  01-FEB-97     $25.00 7591       201
     204 ELLEN      OWENS         SAL  01-JUL-96     $15.00 6830       202
     205 HENRY      PERKINS       SAL  01-MAR-98     $25.00 5286       202
     206 CAROL      ROSE          ACT  15-OCT-97     $15.00 3829       201
     207 DAN        SMITH         MKT  01-DEC-96     $25.00 2259       203
     208 FRED       CAMPBELL      SHP  01-APR-97     $25.00 1752       203
     209 PAULA      JACOBS        MKT  17-MAR-98     $15.00 3357       201
     210 NANCY      HOFFMAN       SAL  15-FEB-96     $25.00 2974       203
     999 JOHN       GREEN         SHP  (null)        $25.00 (null)  (null)  ❻
```

Beginning view (Shipping_dept view) ❷

```
EMPLOYEE                         DEPT   CREDIT
      ID FIRST_NAME LAST_NAME    CODE   LIMIT
-------- ---------- ----------   ----   -------
     203 MARTHA     WOODS        SHP    $25.00
     207 DAN        SMITH        SHP    $25.00
     208 FRED       CAMPBELL     SHP    $25.00
```

Add John Smith to the shipping department
Oracle & Access SQL—change the data through
the view ❸

```
insert into shipping_dept ❹
values (999, 'john', 'green', 'shp', 25.00);
```

Ending view (Shipping_dept view)

```
EMPLOYEE                         DEPT   CREDIT
      ID FIRST_NAME LAST_NAME    CODE   LIMIT
-------- ---------- ----------   ----   -------
     203 MARTHA     WOODS        SHP    $25.00
     208 FRED       CAMPBELL     SHP    $25.00
     999 JOHN       GREEN        SHP    $25.00   ❺
```

Figure 3-13   Example of changing data through a view (part 3 of 3)

Views Using With Check Option

In Figure 3-13, you saw that Inserts and Updates can be made to the data in the beginning view, even if the row will not appear in the ending view. For instance, I was able to change Dan Smith from the shipping department to the marketing department, even though the row for Dan Smith would not appear in the ending view.

Sometimes this result is what we want and sometimes it is not. Sometimes we want to allow only changes that will appear in the ending view. This restriction can be done by adding the phrase "With Check Option" at the end of the definition of the view.

Figure 3-14 shows the Oracle SQL to create the view used in Figure 3-13. It then shows the same statement with the addition of With Check Option.

Access does not support With Check Option.

The effect of With Check Option

When With Check Option is used, an Insert or Update fails unless the changed row appears in the ending view. In the example of Figure 3-13, I could not change the department for Dan Smith. Nor could I add a new employee who was not in the shipping department.

In effect, this option is a way to validate the changes that are made to the data. It places restrictions on what changes can be made. It can be used to enforce business rules and also to support database security.

Create the view used in Figure 3-13

Oracle SQL	Access GUI method
```create view shipping_dept as select employee_id, first_name, last_name, dept_code, credit_limit from l_employees where dept_code = 'shp';```	1. Enter in the SQL window: ```select employee_id, first_name, last_name, dept_code, credit_limit from l_employees where dept_code = 'shp';``` 2. Save the query giving it the name "shipping_dept."

Create the view using With Check Option

Oracle SQL	Access
```create view shipping_dept as select employee_id, first_name, last_name, dept_code, credit_limit from l_employees where dept_code = 'shp' with check option;```	(Access does not support this option.)

Figure 3-14   Views using With Check Option

Finding Information about Tables and Views

This section describes how to find information about the tables and views in a database. The database needs to keep track of all the tables and views for its own processing. This information is available to everyone who uses the database.

The Data Dictionary

The "Data Dictionary" is a set of tables that contains all the information about the structure of the database. It contains the names of all the tables, their columns, their primary keys, the names of the views, the Select statements that define the views, and much more. The Data Dictionary is sometimes called the "System Catalog." Most SQL products have a Data Dictionary.

This set of tables is created and maintained by the database system itself. It contains all the information the database system needs to support its own processing, its "self-knowledge." Since this information is stored in tables, you can use Select statements to get information from them. These tables are like any other tables. This may seem natural, but it is actually a big step forward. Often in software, the "inner knowledge" is in a completely different format from the "outer knowledge."

The details of the Data Dictionary differ for each SQL product. They even differ slightly from one version of a product to the next. The differences are in the names of the data dictionary tables, what columns they contain, and what codes are used.

These details are tied very closely to the inner workings of the database engine itself, the DBMS. When new capabilities are added to the DBMS, new information is often added to the data dictionary. Much of this information is meant only for the database administrators and can be ignored by other people. However, you can also use a lot of information. Almost anything you might want to know about the database is contained in the data dictionary.

Oracle has a Data Dictionary; Access does not

Oracle has a Data Dictionary. For now, I focus on obtaining information about tables and views from it.

Access does not have a Data Dictionary. This fact is somewhat unusual for an SQL product. However, Access presents much of this information using the GUI.

The Oracle Data Dictionary—information about tables and views

Information to get	Data Dictionary table	Data Dictionary columns
table names	user_tables	table_name
view names	user_views	view_name
view definition	user_views	text
columns of tables and views	user_tab_columns	column_name
primary keys of tables	user_cons_columns	(see Figure 3-20)

- "All" can replace "User" in the table names. For example:

    all_tables
    all_views
    all_tab_columns
    all_constraints
    all_cons_columns

- "User" tables are limited to information about the database objects that you own.

- "All" tables may also include information about database objects that are owned by other people, but only if they have decided to share them with you.

Figure 3-15   The Data Dictionary

How to find the names of all the tables

In working with any database, the first thing you want to know is the names of the tables. All the data is contained in tables. They are the basic building blocks for everything else in the database. Once you know the name of a table, you can examine its data by using the command

```
SELECT *
FROM table_name;
```

This works with most tables. Unfortunately, it does not work well with the tables of the Oracle Data Dictionary. It used to work well with version 7 of Oracle. But changes have been made to the Data Dictionary in version 8, so that often the tables are too complex for this command to work well. Perhaps this will be fixed in the future. For now, you often need to know in advance which columns of the Data Dictionary table you want to use.

Figure 3-16

❶　Only the "Table_name" column is selected from this table, which has a large number of columns, making it difficult to read if all the columns are displayed.

❷　In Oracle, the table named "User_tables" contains information about all your tables, including the names of these tables. These are the tables that are on your own userid and that you own.

If you have permission to use other people's tables and you want the names of all the tables you are allowed to use, then refer to the table named "All_tables."

In Oracle, these Data Dictionary tables do not contain the names of views. In some other SQL products, the information about the tables and views is kept together in a single table.

Task

Find the names of all your tables.

Oracle SQL

```
select table_name ❶
from user_tables; ❷
```

Oracle result table

```
TABLE_NAME
------------------
L_DEPARTMENTS
L_EMPLOYEES
L_FOODS
L_LUNCHES
L_LUNCH_ITEMS
L_SUPPLIERS
NUMBERS_0_TO_9
NUMBERS_0_TO_99
```

Access GUI Method

Click the Tables tab with the mouse.

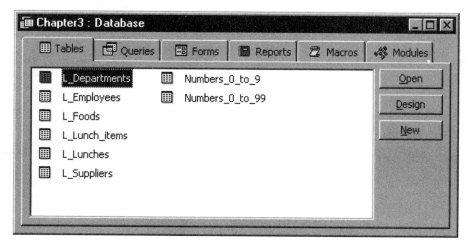

Figure 3-16   How to find the names of all the tables

How to find the names of all the views

Views are another important part of a database. Figure 3-17 shows how to find the names of all your views.

Figure 3-17

❶   The "View_name" column is the only one you need.

❷   In Oracle, information about all the views that you own and that are on your use-rid is kept in the table named "User_views."

Task

Find the names of all your views.

Oracle SQL

```
select view_name ❶
from user_views; ❷
```

Oracle result table

```
VIEW_NAME
--------------
SHIPPING_DEPT
```

Access GUI method

Click the Queries tab with the mouse.

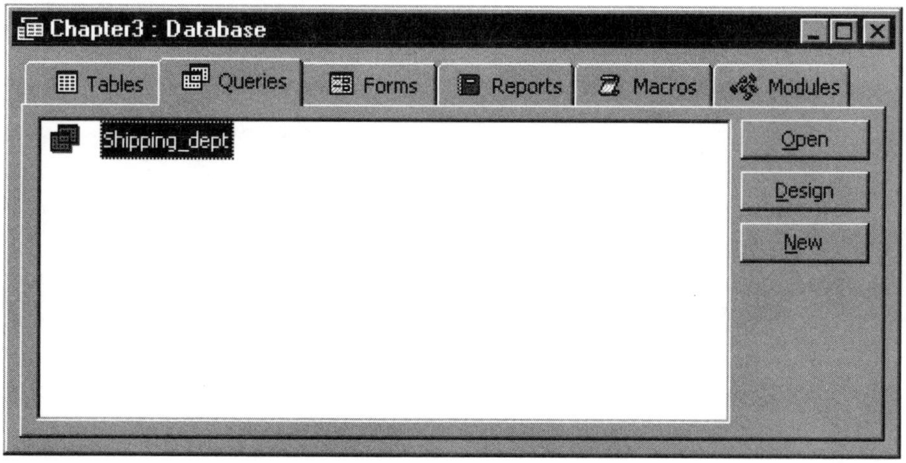

Figure 3-17   How to find the names of all the views

How to find the Select statement that defines a view

A Select statement defines each view. Figure 3-18 shows how to find the Select statement for any view.

Figure 3-18

❶ These are the columns you want:

View_name is the name of the view.

Text_length is the number of characters in the Select statement that defines the view.

Text is the Select statement that defines the view. Usually, Oracle preserves the Select statement exactly the way you wrote it, with all the formatting you used.

❷ In Oracle, the Data Dictionary table with information about your views is named "User_views."

❸ This Where clause limits the information to a single view. Without this clause, the definitions of all your views would be shown, which might be more information than you want to have.

❹ Access does not retain the format you used to enter the Select statement. It uses its own formatting. Sometimes it rewrites the Select statement entirely. In this example, the format is easy to read. But sometimes the format is terrible. It is difficult to understand because it is written for computers and not humans.

Task

Find the Select statement that defines the "Shipping_dept" view.

Oracle SQL

```
select view_name, ❶
        text_length,
        text
from user_views ❷
where view_name = 'shipping_dept'; ❸
```

Oracle result table

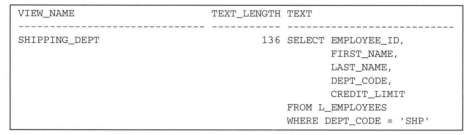

```
VIEW_NAME                        TEXT_LENGTH TEXT
------------------------------   ----------- --------------------------
SHIPPING_DEPT                           136 SELECT  EMPLOYEE_ID,
                                                    FIRST_NAME,
                                                    LAST_NAME,
                                                    DEPT_CODE,
                                                    CREDIT_LIMIT
                                             FROM L_EMPLOYEES
                                             WHERE DEPT_CODE = 'SHP'
```

Access GUI method ❹

1. Click the Queries tab.
2. Click once on the name of the query (view) about which you want information.
    This action highlights the name of the query.
3. Click the Design button.

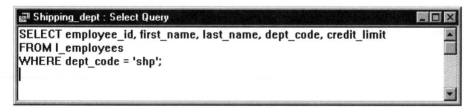

```
Shipping_dept : Select Query
SELECT employee_id, first_name, last_name, dept_code, credit_limit
FROM l_employees
WHERE dept_code = 'shp';
```

Figure 3-18   How to find the Select statement that defines a view

How to find the names of the columns in a table or view

When you look at a table, the column names seem to be displayed above each column. These names are meant to help a person read and understand the table, but they are not always the actual names you need to use to write a Select statement. They can be truncated or they can be changed entirely by the SQLplus environment. Figure 3-18 shows how to get the names to use in coding a Select statement.

Figure 3-19

❶   The "column_name" column is the only column you need.

❷   In Oracle, the Data Dictionary table named "User_tab_columns" contains information about the columns of both tables and views. The name of this table should be pronounced "User Table Columns." In the spelling, the word "Table" is truncated.

❸   This Where clause is needed to limit the result to the columns of a single table or view. Otherwise, the result will include the names of all the columns of all your tables and views.

❹   The "field names" are the names of the columns. Access is able to show the names of the columns for tables, but not for views.

Oracle method using the SQLplus environment

The method below uses the DESCRIBE command from SQLplus, which is the environment for running SQL in Oracle. It has several commands of its own; this is one of them.

Oracle command to the SQLplus environment

```
describe l_employees
```

Oracle result

Name	Null?	Type
EMPLOYEE_ID	NOT NULL	NUMBER(3)
FIRST_NAME		VARCHAR2(10)
LAST_NAME		VARCHAR2(10)
DEPT_CODE		VARCHAR2(3)
HIRE_DATE		DATE
CREDIT_LIMIT		NUMBER(4,2)
PHONE_NUMBER		VARCHAR2(4)
MANAGER_ID		NUMBER(3)

Task

Find the names of the columns of the L_employees table.

Oracle SQL—column name of tables and views

```
select column_name ❶
from user_tab_columns ❷
where table_name = 'l_employees'; ❸
```

Oracle result table

```
COLUMN_NAME
-----------------
EMPLOYEE_ID
FIRST_NAME
LAST_NAME
DEPT_CODE
HIRE_DATE
CREDIT_LIMIT
PHONE_NUMBER
MANAGER_ID
```

Access GUI method—column names for tables, but not views ❹

1.   Click the Tables tab.
2.   Click once on the name of the table you choose. The table name will be high-lighted.
3.   Click the Design button.

Figure 3-19   How to find the names of the columns in a table or view

How to find the primary key of a table

Figure 3-20 shows how to find the primary key of a table. The primary key can consist of several columns. Views do not have primary keys.

Figure 3-20

❶   You can list all the columns of this table.

❷   In Oracle, the Data Dictionary table named "User_cons_columns" contains information about the primary keys. The name of this table is pronounced "User Constraint Columns." In the spelling, the word "Constraint" has become truncated.

A constraint is any rule that restricts the data that can be entered into a column. Nulls are not allowed in primary key columns and the value in each primary key must be unique. So, a primary key is one type of constraint. Thus, information about them is kept in this table.

❸   This Where clause limits the result to the constraints on one table. This is what you want. Otherwise the result can become confusing to read.

❹   The result table shows that the primary key of the L_food table consists of two columns—Supplier_id and Product_code.

❺   In Access, the columns of the primary key are shown with the "key" symbol to the left of the column names.

Task

Find all the columns in the primary key of the L_foods table.

Oracle SQL

```
select * ❶
from user_cons_columns ❷
where table_name = 'l_foods'; ❸
```

Oracle result ❹

OWNER	CONSTRAINT_NAME	TABLE_NAME	COLUMN_NAME	POSITION
STUDENT	PK_L_FOODS	L_FOODS	SUPPLIER_ID	1
STUDENT	PK_L_FOODS	L_FOODS	PRODUCT_CODE	2

Access GUI method ❺

1. Click the Tables tab.
2. Click once on the name of the table you choose. The table name will become highlighted.
3. Click on the Design button.

	Field Name	Data Type	Description
🔑	Supplier_id	Text	
🔑	Product_code	Text	
	Menu_item	Number	
	Description	Text	
	Price	Currency	
	Price_increase	Currency	

Field Properties

General | Lookup

A field name can be up to 64 characters long, including spaces. Press F1 for help on field names.

Figure 3-20   How to find the primary key of a table

Summary

In this chapter, you learned:

- How to create a new table using a Select statement.
- How to create a view.
- The contrast between a table and a view.
- How to control the data in a table by Inserting new rows, Updating columns, and Deleting rows.
- How to control the data in a table by changing it through a view.
- How to use the Data Dictionary to find information about tables and views.

In later chapters, you will use this ability to solve problems in a series of steps. The first step will create a new table or view. Then the next step(s) will be Select statements that operate on the new tables or views. Many problems that would be complex to solve with a single Select statement can be solved easily by using a series of Select statements.

You can now create many of your own tables and control the data in them. In Chapter 4, you will learn about tables in even more detail.

Exercises

1. Goal: Create a new table by saving the results of a Select statement.

1A. Create a new table using the Select statement in problem 13A of chapter 2.

Oracle SQL | Access SQL

```
create table exercise_1a as
select first_name,
last_name
from  l_employees
where (dept_code = 'sal'
or dept_code = 'mkt')
and hire_date >= '01-jan-98'
and hire_date <= '31-dec-98';
```

```
select first_name,
last_name
into exercise_1a
from  l_employees
where (dept_code = 'sal'
or dept_code = 'mkt')
and hire_date >= #01-jan-98#
and hire_date <= #31-dec-98#;
```

Note: The Order By clause has been removed.

1B. Create a new table from the L_employees table having the columns:
       employee_id
       hire_date
       first_name
       last_name
       dept_code
in this order. Rename the "dept_code" column to "department_code." Include only the rows for employees in the shipping and sales departments.

2. Goal: Create a new view.

2A. Create a view similar to the table created in exercise 1A.

Oracle SQL	Access SQL
| ```
create view exercise_2a as
select first_name,
last_name
from  l_employees
where (dept_code = 'sal'
or dept_code = 'mkt')
and hire_date >= '01-jan-98'
and hire_date <= '31-dec-98';
``` | (Enter this query in the SQL window.)<br><br>```
select first_name,
last_name
from  l_employees
where (dept_code = 'sal'
or dept_code = 'mkt')
and hire_date >= #01-jan-98#
and hire_date <= #31-dec-98#;
```<br><br>(Save the query. Name it "exercise_2a.") |

Note: A view is always create with a Select statement. There is no other way to create a view.

2B. Create a view similar to the table created in exercise 1B.

3. Goal: Show that you can use the new table and view to write queries.

3A. List the last name and first name of people in the shipping department hired in 1997. Sort this list on the last name.

Oracle SQL

```
select last_name,
first_name
from exercise_1b
where hire_date between '01-jan-97' and '31-dec-97'
 and department_code = 'shp'
order by last_name;
```

Access SQL

```
select last_name,
first_name
from exercise_1b
where hire_date between #01-jan-97# and #31-dec-97#
 and department_code = 'shp'
order by last_name;
```

3B. Use the table you created in exercise 1B to list the hire date, employee id, first name, and last name of all the employees in the shipping and sales departments hired in 1996 or 1997.

3C. Same as 3B, except use the view you created in exercise 2B.

4. Goal: Show the difference between a table and a view.

4A. Add a new row to the L_employees table. Add yourself to the sales department. Then observe the effect of this change on the L_employees table, the exercise_1B table, and the exercise_2B view. Predict what you are going to see, then see if you are correct. (Use your own name here.)

Oracle SQL—part 1

```
insert into l_employees
values(999, 'john', 'patrick', 'sal', '20-nov-98', 24.51, null, 210);
```

Access SQL—part 1

```
insert into l_employees
values(999, 'john', 'patrick', 'sal', #20-nov-98#, 24.51, null, 210);
```

Oracle & Access SQL—part 2

```
select * from l_employees;
select * from exercise_1b;
select * from exercise_2b;
```

4B. Make a change to the L_employees table. Change yourself to the shipping department. Observe the effect of this as in 4A.

4C. Make a change to the exercise_2B view. Change your hire date. Observe the effect.

4D. Make a change to the exercise_2B view. Change yourself to the accounting department. Observe the effect

4E. Delete a row from the exercise_1B table. Delete employee 205. Observe the effect.

5. Goal: Find information about the new table and view in the Data Dictionary

5A. Find the name of the new tables in the list of all the tables.

Oracle SQL   Access SQL

`select table_name` `from user_tables;`

(Access does not have a data dictionary.)

5B. Find the name of the new views and the Select statements that define them.

5C. Find the names of all the columns in one of the table or views.

6. Goal: Find information about the primary key columns in the Data Dictionary.

6A. Find the primary key column of all the tables.

Oracle SQL   Access SQL

`select *` `from user_cons_columns;`

(Access does not have a data dictionary.)

6B. Identify the primary key columns of each table. Which tables have a single column in their primary key? Which table have two or more column? Which tables do not have a primary key? Do the new tables and views have primary keys?

7. Goal: Create a view with the check option and show the difference this makes. (Access can create the view, but cannot use "with check option.")

7A. Create a view of all the foods that cost less than two dollars. Add "with check option" to this view. Demonstrate what "with check option" does.

Oracle SQL	Access SQL
```create view exercise_7a as select * from 1_foods where price < 2.00 with check option;```	(Enter this code in the SQL window.) ```select * from 1_foods where price < 2.00;``` (Save the query. Name it "exercise_7a")
This works. ```update exercise_7a set price = 1.75 where menu_item = 2;```	
This does not work. ``` update exercise_7a set price = 2.50 where menu_item = 2;```	

7B. Create a new view, similar to exercise 2B, except add "with check option." Demonstrate the difference "with check option" makes.

Show an example of an insert, update, or delete command that does NOT work because of With Check Option. Also show one that does work.

(You can only do this in Oracle.)

8. Goal: Build one view on top of another view.

8A. Create a new view on top of the view in 7A that only includes the foods other than coffee.

Oracle SQL	Access SQL
| ```
create view exercise 8a as
select *
from exercise_7A
where description <> 'coffee';
``` | (Enter this query in the SQL window.)<br><br>```
select *
from exercise_7A
where description <> 'coffee';
```<br><br>(Save the query. Name it "exercise_8a." |

8B. Create a new view on top of the view you created in 2B that includes only the employees in the sales department.

Chapter 4

Creating Your Own Tables

In this chapter, you learn how to create your own tables in a way that gives maximum control over every aspect of the table. In Chapter 3, tables were created with Select statements. Here they are created with commands and they use the basic building blocks of the database system.

Creating tables

A table can be created with an SQL command. This gives you precise control over every part of the table.

The Create Table command

The CREATE TABLE statement creates a new table. When it is first created, this table will not have any rows of data in it. This command has the format:

CREATE TABLE *table_name*
(*column_name_1data_type_1,*
column_name_2data_type_2,
...*);*

This is the simplest form of the command. Many other options that can be specified in this command or can be added later. All the columns of the table must be listed.

This method allows the greatest control over all the elements of a table. It shows what a table consists of:

a table name
names of the columns
data types of the columns
a sequence to the columns

People sometimes think of a table as consisting of data, but this is incorrect. The table is a container, like a box. The data is held in a table.

The list of datatypes in Oracle is a little different than the one for Access. Each SQL product supports datatypes that differ slightly from other SQL products. Since the datatypes are named in this command, the SQL statement for Oracle is different than the one for Access.

Primary keys and many other options can be specified when the table is first created or they can be specified after it is already built. They can even be specified after the table has data in it. The ALTER TABLE statement used to add a primary key to a table after it has been created.

In figure 4-1, the Create Table statements are the same for Oracle and Access, except for the names of the datatypes.

Task

Create the Employees table using the method of defining its columns with a "Create Table" statement.

Oracle SQL

```
create table l_employees
  (employee_id number(3),
   first_name  varchar2(10),
   last_name   varchar2(10),
   dept_code   varchar2(3),
   hire_date   date,
   credit_limit number(4,2),
   phone_number varchar2(4),
   manager_id number(3));
```

Access SQL

```
create table l_employees
  (employee_id byte,
   first_name  text(10),
   last_name   text(10),
   dept_code   text(3),
   hire_date   datetime,
   credit_limit currency,
   phone_number text(4),
   manager_id byte);
```

(When a table is created, at first it does not contain any data. So, you can not see it, unless you want to look at it in the Data Dictionary.)

Figure 4-1   The Create Table command

Datatypes in Oracle and Access

Data is represented inside the computer as a pattern of 1s and 0s. Only certain patterns are meaningful, all others are nonsense. These meaningful patterns are called "datatypes."

Oracle uses a different set of meaningful patterns than Access does. For instance, both Oracle and Access have ways of representing the date "January 1, 2000." However, they use different patterns of 1s and 0s to represent it. The meaning of the data is the same, but the binary representation of it is different. In short, they use different datatypes. Each SQL product has its own set of datatypes. Each one assigns meanings slightly differently to patterns of binary digits.

For the most part, the meanings are the same, even though they are represented differently on a binary level. The differences show up only at the extremes. Consider dates. Both Oracle and Access can handle dates between 100 AD and 4712 AD. Most of the dates that people actually use in databases are in this range.

However, Oracle dates and Access dates do have some differences because of the different patterns of 1s and 0s which represent them. In particular, Oracle can also handle dates between 4712 BC and 100 AD, whereas Access can handle dates between 4712 AD and 9999 AD.

The main point here is that the datatypes for Oracle and Access are very similar, but they differ in the small details. The names of these datatypes are different. So, the Create Table statements are different.

Figure 4-2 shows the similarities and differences between the datatype used in Oracle and Access. The data types for text, date/time, and storage are very similar. Access has a one bit data type for Yes/No and True/False, which Oracle does not have. Oracle might use an entire byte of data to represent this. Usually, this is acceptable.

Another difference is the numbers. Access uses many data types for numbers. This is the traditional approach and most computer products follow it. Oracle combines decimal numbers and floating point numbers together in a single datatype.

The datatypes for storage are used for binary data such as pictures, sound clips, video clips, and compiled programs. These are not active elements within the database—you cannot search or sort on them or apply functions to them. We will not be concerned with them very much in this book.

The use of storage datatypes in databases is currently in the process of change. It is changing in two opposite directions at the same time. From one perspective, their use is being phased out in favor of storing files within the operating system, rather than in a database. From another perspective, their use is increasing to support Object Oriented concepts. Object Oriented databases are a hot topic, which is currently being developed.

The names of the datatypes given here are the "internal" names. That is, the names used when discussing he internals of the database engine. For Access they are the names used by the JET engine. The GUI graphical presentation layer of Access sometimes uses slightly different names.

Many of these datatypes also have synonyms or "external" names. These are intended to make one SQL product compatible with another. This attempts to map the datatypes of one product to the datatypes of another.

ORACLE	ACCESS	
CHARACTER DATA TYPES		
char(size)	not available	Fixed length character strings. The maximum length is "size." From 1 to 255 bytes long.
varchar2(size)	text(size)	Variable length character string. The maximum length is "size." Oracle: size: from 0 to 2000 bytes long. Access size: from 0 to 255 bytes long. In Oracle, columns more than 255 bytes long are "long strings" are have restricted capabilities.
DATE/TIME DATA TYPES		
date	datetime	A date and time. Oracle: from 4712 BC to 4712 AD Access: from 100 AD to 9999 AD
NUMERIC DATA TYPES		
integer		Integer with a standard size.
num- ber(size,d)		Number. Either regular numbers or scientific nota- tion (floating point) numbers. "Size" is the total number of digits. "D" is the number of digits after the decimal point.
	byte	Integer, from 0 to 255.
	short	Integer, from about -32,000 to +32,000.
	long	Integer, from about -2,000,000,000 to +2,000,000,000.
	currency	Integer and 4 decimal places. Plus or minus about 900,000,000,000,000 Automatically formatted as currency.
	single	Floating point number. (Positive or negative.) From about 3.4E38 to 1.4E-45.
	double	Floating point number. (Positive or negative.) From about 1.8E308 to 4.9E-324.
BINARY DATA TYPES		
	bit	Any binary choice. Yes or No. True or False.
STORAGE DATA TYPES		
long	longtext	Character data. Oracle: up to 2 gigabytes long. Access: up to 1.2 gigabytes long.
raw(size) LOB	binary	Binary data. Oracle: up to 255 bytes long.
longraw LOB	longbinary	Binary data. Oracle: up to 2 gigabytes long. Access: up to 1.2 gigabytes long

Figure 4-2   Datatypes in Oracle and Access

Sequences

A SEQUENCE is used to generate numbers sequentially. The idea is that each row will be given a different number. This can be used to put the rows in a specific order or to make sure that no two rows are identical. Sometimes a sequence is used as a "meaningless" primary key for a table. It is up to the application to determine what meaning this order has.

In the Lunches database, a sequence is used as the primary key of the L_lunches table. In this case, each time a person signs up to attend a lunch, that lunch is assigned the next number. So far, the numbers 1 to 16 have been used. The next row in this table will be assigned the number 17.

A sequence is not a datatype, although Access and many other SQL products sometimes list it with the datatypes. The data that is put in the table is a number and has the datatype of a number. The sequence is a way of assigning these numbers.

Once a number is placed in a row, it is ordinary numeric data. It does not change or get updated automatically. Usually, you can assign any number you want in a column that contains a sequence of numbers. If you assign a value, then that is what the value will be.

Oracle and Access have different ways of implementing sequences. Oracle sets up a database structure, similar to a table, which keeps track of the last number assigned and the next number to be assigned. You need to know which sequence applies to which column and refer to it directly when you create a new row for a table.

Access has a "datatype" called "Counter" that automatically assigns the sequential numbers to new rows, unless you assign a value to the column. If a new column is added to a table and that column is given the datatype "Counter," then all the rows currently in the table are assigned sequential numbers. Access assigns numbers automatically to new rows.

In Access, on the graphical (GUI) level, the word "Counter" is replaced by the word "AutoNumber." However, on the JET engine level, which processes the SQL, this datatype is called "Counter." Access is a complex product. We are dealing with it on one particular level in this book.

Figure 4-3

❶   In Oracle, you use a Sequence by referring either to its current value or its next value. These are written:

        Sequence_name.CURRVAL
and
        Sequence_name.NEXTVAL

In this statement, when a new row is inserted into the Lunches table, the first column is set to the next value of the sequence.

Oracle SQL—sequence commands

```
-- create a new sequence
create sequence seq_lunch_id
increment by 1
start with 17;


-- use the sequence to create a new row
insert into l_lunches
values (seq_lunch_id.nextval, '04-dec-98', 204); ¶


-- delete a sequence
drop sequence seq_lunch_id;
```

Access method

Figure 4-3   Sequences

Changing tables

The structure of a table is not cast in concrete and fixed forever. Tables can be changed in many ways, even after they contain data.

Adding a primary key to a table

Figure 4-4 shows how to add a primary key to a table, even after the table contains many rows of data. You can do this with an "Alter Table" statement. The syntax is:

> ALTER TABLE *table_name*
> ADD CONSTRAINT *name_of_the_constraint*
>   PRIMARY KEY (*list_of_columns_in_the_primary_key*);

The Alter Table statement can perform many functions. This is only one of them.

A "constraint" is any limitation on the data that can be put into a table. The primary key must be unique for each row, and none of its columns can be null. Therefore, a primary key is a type of constraint.

Figure 4-4
❶   The Foods table will be changed by this command.

❷   This gives a name to the constraint. Here the name is "Pk_l_foods." It combines "PK," meaning "Primary Key," with the name of the table. This is my own naming convention. You can name it something else.

The name of the constraint is used mostly in error messages and in a few operations such as deleting the constraint or temporarily disabling it. It is not referred to directly in any Select statement. The name should suggest the purpose of the constraint.

❸   The words "Primary key" say that this is a primary key constraint. The list of columns that follows contains the columns that will form the primary key. This list can contain any number of columns, even all the columns in the table. However, it is usually limited to one or two columns.

If data is already in the table, it must already conform to the restrictions of a primary key. Otherwise, this command will fail and you will receive an error message. A primary key cannot be put on a table that has duplicate values in the primary key or any nulls in any column of the primary key.

A table is allowed to have only one primary key, although this key may consist of a combination of several columns.

Task

Add a primary key to the Foods table of the Lunches database.

Oracle & Access SQL—add a primary key to a table

```
alter table l_foods ❶
     add constraint pk_l_foods ❷
     primary key (supplier_id, product_code); ❸
```

Figure 4-4   Adding a primary key to a table

Deleting a primary key from a table

Figure 4-5 shows how to delete a primary key from a table. A table can have only one primary key. The main reason to delete a primary key from a table is to prepare to put a new primary key on that table. The new primary key might include additional columns.

Figure 4-5

❶   On this line, "Pk_1_foods" is the name of the constraint. The name of a constraint is easy to forget. You might need to find the name of the constraint in the Data Dictionary, in order to delete the primary key.

❷   Using this syntax, you do not need to know the name of the constraint in order to delete the primary key.

Task

Delete the primary key from the Foods table of the Lunches database.

Method 1
Oracle SQL & Access SQL

```
alter table l_foods
drop constraint pk_l_foods;  ❶
```

Method 2
Oracle SQL   Access

```
alter table l_foods
drop primary key;  ❷
```

(Access does not support this syntax.)

Figure 4-5   Deleting a primary key from a table

Adding a new column to a table

Figure 4-6 shows how to add a new column to a table that has already been defined and that may already have rows of data in it. Oracle and Access must use their own datatypes in this command. The Alter Table command is used to add a new column.

Figure 4-6

❶   In Oracle, the Department_number column is given the Oracle datatype "Number(4)" of a four-digit number. Notice that the word "Add" is followed by the column name. The implication is that a new column is being added.

❷   In Access, the Department_number column is given the Access datatype "Short." Notice that the word "Add" is followed by the word "Column."

❸   Initially, the new column contains nulls. After you define this column, you need to put data into it. The new column is always the last column in the table. Within most SQL products, you have no control over the placement of the column.

Task

Add a new column to the Departments table of the Lunches database. Name the new column "Department_number."

Oracle SQL

```
alter table l_departments
add department_number   number(4);  ❶
```

Access SQL

```
alter table l_departments
add column department_number short;  ❷
```

Beginning table (L_departments table)

```
DEPARTMENT
CODE        DEPARTMENT_NAME
----------  ------------------------------
ACT         ACCOUNTING
EXE         EXECUTIVE
MKT         MARKETING
PER         PERSONNEL
SAL         SALES
SHP         SHIPPING
```

Ending table ❸

```
DEPARTMENT
CODE        DEPARTMENT_NAME                  DEPARTMENT_NUMBER
----------  ------------------------------   -----------------
ACT         ACCOUNTING                       (null)
EXE         EXECUTIVE                        (null)
MKT         MARKETING                        (null)
PER         PERSONNEL                        (null)
SAL         SALES                            (null)
SHP         SHIPPING                         (null)
```

Figure 4-6   Adding a new column to a table

Deleting a column from a table

Figure 4-7 shows how to delete a column from a table, using the Alter Table command. This can not be done in Oracle or in Standard SQL, but it can be done in Access. It is a special feature, an extension, that Access has added to Standard SQL.

The reason that Oracle and most other SQL products do not support this feature is that they are tuned to work efficiently with large databases (several million rows), whereas Access is tuned to work with smaller ones. The Alter Table command is usually tuned so that it can change large tables efficiently. That is, the Alter Table command is usually optimized for efficiency rather than for flexibility.

You may need to add a new column to a table quickly or change its primary key. But, deleting a column of data is less urgent. It can be done using other commands. In the next figure you will see a method of changing tables that is optimized for flexibility rather than efficiency.

Task

Delete the Phone Number column from the Employees table of the Lunches database. Do this using Access and the Alter Table command.

Oracle SQL

(Oracle does not support this operation.)

Access SQL

```
alter table l_employees
drop column phone_number;
```

Beginning table (L_employees table)

Employee_id	First_name	Last_name	Dept_code	Hire_date	Credit_limit	Phone_number	Manager_id
201	Susan	Brown	Exe	06-01-1992	$30.00	3484	
202	Jim	Kern	Sal	08-15-1995	$25.00	8722	201
203	Martha	Woods	Shp	02-01-1997	$25.00	7591	201
204	Ellen	Owens	Sal	07-01-1996	$15.00	6830	202
205	Henry	Perkins	Sal	03-01-1998	$25.00	5286	202
206	Carol	Rose	Act	10-15-1997	$15.00	3829	201
207	Dan	Smith	Shp	12-01-1996	$25.00	2259	203
208	Fred	Campbell	Shp	04-01-1997	$25.00	1752	203
209	Paula	Jacobs	Mkt	03-17-1998	$15.00	3357	201
210	Nancy	Hoffman	Sal	02-15-1996	$25.00	2974	203
0					$0.00		0

Record: 1 of 10

Ending table

Employee_id	First_name	Last_name	Dept_code	Hire_date	Credit_limit	Manager_id
201	Susan	Brown	Exe	06-01-1992	$30.00	
202	Jim	Kern	Sal	08-15-1995	$25.00	201
203	Martha	Woods	Shp	02-01-1997	$25.00	201
204	Ellen	Owens	Sal	07-01-1996	$15.00	202
205	Henry	Perkins	Sal	03-01-1998	$25.00	202
206	Carol	Rose	Act	10-15-1997	$15.00	201
207	Dan	Smith	Shp	12-01-1996	$25.00	203
208	Fred	Campbell	Shp	04-01-1997	$25.00	203
209	Paula	Jacobs	Mkt	03-17-1998	$15.00	201
210	Nancy	Hoffman	Sal	02-15-1996	$25.00	203
0					$0.00	0

Record: 1 of 10

Figure 4-7   Deleting a column from a table

Making other changes to tables

Figure 4-8 shows a method of making changes to a table that does not use the Alter Table command. You already know this method, but I want to remind you of it here, in the context of the present discussion. This method can make almost any change you can imagine. It is very flexible, but it is less efficient than the Alter Table command. This is usually important only when you are working with very large tables.

Following are some of the changes you can make to any table:

- Add new columns
- Delete columns
- Delete rows
- Rename columns
- Change the data in columns
- Change the data type of columns
- Reorder columns
- elete a primary key

These give you nearly total control over every aspect of a table.

The technique is to use a Create Table statement with a Select statement, as in Figure 4-8. You used this same technique in Figures 3-1 and 3-2.

Figure 4-8

❶ In Oracle, the SQL statements, the Create Table command, and the Update command can be run as one unit as a single script.

❷ In Access, each SQL command must be run separately.

❸ This adds a new column to the table and names it "Notes."

❹ In the Update statement, the Phone Number must be referred to by its new name, "Ext."

❺ Here is the procedure to follow if you want to name this new table "L_employees," so that it would replace the beginning table:

```
1.  DROP TABLE L_EMPLOYEES;

2.  CREATE TABLE L_EMPLOYEES AS
    SELECT * FROM PHONE_LIST;
```

Task

Create a Phone List table from the Employees table. Include the columns Last Name, First Name, and Phone Number. Make major changes to the beginning table:

> Rename the Phone Number column to Ext
>
> Change the order of the First Name and Last Name columns
>
> Delete many columns from the beginning table
>
> Add a new column for Notes—leave it blank
>
> Change the phone number for Woods to 9408

Oracle SQL ❶

```
create table phone_list as
select last_name,
    first_name,
    phone_number as ext,
    '             ' as notes  ❸
from l_employees
where employee_id between
              203 and 206;


update phone_list
set ext = '9408'  ❹
where last_name = 'woods';
```

Access SQL ❷

```
select last_name,
    first_name,
    phone_number as ext,
    '             ' as notes
into phone_list
from l_employees
where employee_id between
              203 and 206;


update phone_list
set ext = '9408'
where last_name = 'woods';
```

Beginning table (L_employees table)

```
EMPLOYEE                       DEPT          CREDIT PHONE   MANAGER
      ID FIRST_NAME LAST_NAME  CODE HIRE_DATE LIMIT NUMBER      ID
-------- ---------- ---------- ---- --------- ------- ------ -------
     201 SUSAN      BROWN      EXE  01-JUN-92 $30.00 3484   (null)
     202 JIM        KERN       SAL  15-AUG-95 $25.00 8722      201
     203 MARTHA     WOODS      SHP  01-FEB-97 $25.00 7591      201
     204 ELLEN      OWENS      SAL  01-JUL-96 $15.00 6830      202
     205 HENRY      PERKINS    SAL  01-MAR-98 $25.00 5286      202
     206 CAROL      ROSE       ACT  15-OCT-97 $15.00 3829      201
     207 DAN        SMITH      SHP  01-DEC-96 $25.00 2259      203
     208 FRED       CAMPBELL   SHP  01-APR-97 $25.00 1752      203
     209 PAULA      JACOBS     MKT  17-MAR-98 $15.00 3357      201
     210 NANCY      HOFFMAN    SAL  15-FEB-96 $25.00 2974      203
```

New table (Phone_list table) ❺

```
LAST_NAME  FIRST_NAME EXT  NOTES
---------- ---------- ---- -------------
WOODS      MARTHA     9408
OWENS      ELLEN      6830
PERKINS    HENRY      5286
ROSE       CAROL      3829
```

Figure 4-8   Making other changes to tables

Tables with duplicate rows

- Tables are allowed to have duplicate rows:
  - In Relational Database, tables are allowed to contain duplicate rows.
  - Two rows are duplicates when they have the same values in every column.
  - If a table has a primary key, it cannot contain any duplicate rows.
- The problem is what the duplicate rows mean.
  - Two different interpretations are possible.
    - Each row may represent a distinct object.
    - All the duplicate rows may represent the same object.

- Example in which each duplicate row is a distinct object.

You are using a database to track your expenses. On Monday, you buy a hamburger for $1.00 and eat it. On Tuesday, you buy another hamburger for $1.00 and eat it. If you are entering data only for the object you bought and the price, then you have two rows showing you bought a hamburger for $1.00. These are duplicate rows. Together, they mean that you bought two hamburgers and spent $2.00.

(Of course, if you also entered the date, then the rows would not be duplicates. So they are only duplicates because you have not recorded all the data.)

- Example in which duplicate rows all represent the same object.

You are running an advertising campaign and you buy copies of several mailing lists. Some people appear on more than one list. The names and addresses are identical. These are duplicate rows. But you want to send the mailing only once to each person.

- The best approach is to avoid having tables with duplicate rows.
  - Sometimes, you can do this by adding more columns of data to the table.
  - Sometimes, you can use Select Distinct or Union to get rid of the duplicate rows.
- To get rid of all the duplicate rows in a table, create a new table using:

```
CREATE TABLE new_table_name AS
SELECT DISTINCT *
FROM table_name;
```

```
┌─────────────────────────────────────────────────────┐
│                 Avoid Confusion                      │
│          Avoid Tables with Duplicate Rows            │
└─────────────────────────────────────────────────────┘
```

One interpretation
Each row is a separate event
Two duplicate rows are two different events

```
object bought       price
----------------    ------
newspaper             .50
coffee                .85
hamburger            1.00
flowers              5.00
hamburger            1.00
book                 8.95
movie ticket         5.00
```

Another interpretation
Duplicate rows are redundant
They contain the same information
A duplicate row gives no additional meaning

```
First Name    Last_Name    Address
----------    ---------    --------------------
Susan         Brown        512 Elm Street
Jim           Kern         837-9th Avenue
Martha        Woods        169 Park Avenue
Susan         Brown        512 Elm Street
Ellen         Owens        418 Henry Street
```

Figure 4-9   Tables with duplicate rows

Finding more information about tables in the Data Dictionary

Here are some more techniques for getting information for the Oracle Data Dictionary.

Finding information about columns

Figure 4-10 shows how to find detailed information in the Oracle Data Dictionary about the columns of a table or view.

Figure 4-10

❶   This is a comment line. It may be omitted. Comment lines begin with two dashes.

❷   These are the columns you want to list.

❸   The data is obtained from the "User_tab_columns" table.

❹   This Where clause limits the result to showing the columns of a single table.

❺   This Order By clause sorts the columns into the same order they have within the Employees table.

❻   The meaning of some of the columns is:

Data_length:
The maximum number of bytes the column requires.

Number columns	always 22
Date columns	always 7
Text column	the maximum length of the column

Data_precision:
Used only with number columns. This is the maximum number of digits allowed for the number—both the digits before the decimal point and those after it.

Data_scale:
Used only with number columns. This is the number of digits after the decimal point.

Nullable:
Indicates whether can be null or not. For this table, the only the Employee_id column cannot contain nulls. The reason it cannot contain nulls is because it is the primary key.

Task

Find the information that gives the datatypes of all the columns of a table or view.

Oracle SQL

```
-- Find information from the Oracle Data Dictionary about
-- columns in your tables and views. ❶
select column_id, ❷
       column_name,
       data_type,
       data_length,
       data_precision,
       data_scale,
       nullable
from user_tab_columns ❸
where table_name = 'l_employees' ❹
order by column_id; ❺
```

Result table ❻

COLUMN_ID	COLUMN_NAME	DATA_TYPE	DATA_LENGTH	DATA_PRECISION	DATA_SCALE	N
1	EMPLOYEE_ID	NUMBER	22	3	0	N
2	FIRST_NAME	VARCHAR2	10	(null)	(null)	Y
3	LAST_NAME	VARCHAR2	10	(null)	(null)	Y
4	DEPT_CODE	VARCHAR2	3	(null)	(null)	Y
5	HIRE_DATE	DATE	7	(null)	(null)	Y
6	CREDIT_LIMIT	NUMBER	22	4	2	Y
7	PHONE_NUMBER	VARCHAR2	4	(null)	(null)	Y
8	MANAGER_ID	NUMBER	22	3	0	Y

Figure 4-10   Finding information about columns

Finding information about sequences

You can find information about your Oracle sequences in the Oracle Data Dictionary. The table to look in is called "User_Sequences." The columns of this table are:

Sequence_name	The name of the sequence.
Min_value	The minimum value of the sequence.
Max_value	The maximum value of the sequence.
Increment_by	The amount to add for the next value of the sequence.
Cycle_flag	Should the sequence return to the minimum value after the maximum value has been reached?
Last_number	The last number used.

This table has a few more columns.

Task

Find information about your sequences in Oracle.

Oracle SQL

```
select *
from user_sequences;
```

Result table

```
SEQUENCE_NAME   MIN_VALUE MAX_VALUE INCREMENT_BY C O CACHE_SIZE LAST_NUM
----------------- -------- -------- ---------- - - ---------- --------
SEQ_LUNCH_ID            1 1.000E+27          1 N N         20       17
```

Figure 4-11   Finding information about sequences

Finding information about your database objects

You can list all the database objects you own by using the table "User_objects." The columns of this table are:

Object_name	The name of the object.
Object_id	A number Oracle assigns to the object.
Object_type	The type of database object (Table, View, Sequence, etc.)
Created	The date and time that the object was created.
Last_DDL_time	The last date and time that the object was changed.
Timestamp	Same as Created, but stored in a different format.
Status	"Valid" or "Invalid"

Task

Find information about all your database objects in Oracle.

Oracle SQL

```
select object_name,
       object_type,
       created,
       status
from user_objects;
```

Result table

```
OBJECT_NAME        OBJECT_TYPE   CREATED   STATUS
----------------   -----------   -------   -------
L_DEPARTMENTS      TABLE         21-SEP-98 VALID
L_EMPLOYEES        TABLE         21-SEP-98 VALID
L_FOODS            TABLE         21-SEP-98 VALID
L_LUNCHES          TABLE         21-SEP-98 VALID
L_LUNCH_ITEMS      TABLE         21-SEP-98 VALID
L_SUPPLIERS        TABLE         21-SEP-98 VALID
NUMBERS_0_TO_9     TABLE         21-SEP-98 VALID
NUMBERS_0_TO_99    TABLE         21-SEP-98 VALID
PK_L_DEPARTMENTS   INDEX         21-SEP-98 VALID
PK_L_EMPLOYEES     INDEX         21-SEP-98 VALID
PK_L_FOODS         INDEX         21-SEP-98 VALID
PK_L_LUNCHES       INDEX         21-SEP-98 VALID
PK_L_LUNCH_ITEMS   INDEX         21-SEP-98 VALID
PK_L_SUPPLIERS     INDEX         21-SEP-98 VALID
SEQ_LUNCH_ID       SEQUENCE      23-SEP-98 VALID
TEMP_EMPLOYEES     VIEW          23-SEP-98 VALID
```

Figure 4-12   Finding information about your database objects

Finding where to find things in the Data Dictionary

The key to the Data Dictionary is contained in two of its tables. They are called "Dictionary" and "Dict_columns." When you want to find some type of information, these tables can help you find it.

The columns of the "Dictionary" table are:

    Table_name
    Comments

The columns of the "Dict_columns" table are:

    Table_name
    Column_name
    Comments

Both of the Comments fields are very long. Before you use these tables, limit the amount of data that will be printed to 40 characters with the command

    column comments format a40 word_wrap

When there are more than 40 characters of data in the comment field, the information will be wrapped to the next lines. When this occurs, the new line will start with a whole word, instead of the remainder of the word that would not fit on the previous line.

Task

Find information about all the tables in the Oracle Data Dictionary.

Oracle SQL

```
column comments format a40 word_wrap;
select *
from dictionary;
```

Result table

TABLE_NAME	COMMENTS
ALL_ALL_TABLES	Description of all object and relational tables accessible to the user
ALL_ARGUMENTS	Arguments in object accessible to the user
ALL_CATALOG	All tables, views, synonyms, sequences accessible to the user
ALL_CLUSTERS	Description of clusters accessible to the user
ALL_CLUSTER_HASH_EXPRESSIONS	Hash functions for all accessible clusters

Task

Find information about all the columns from all the tables in the Oracle Data Dictionary.

Oracle SQL

```
column comments format a40 word_wrap;
select *
from dict_columns
where table_name = 'user_views';
```

Result table

TABLE_NAME	COLUMN_NAME	COMMENTS
USER_VIEWS	VIEW_NAME	Name of the view
USER_VIEWS	TEXT_LENGTH	Length of the view text
USER_VIEWS	TEXT	View text

Figure 4-13   Finding where to find things in the Data Dictionary

Formats

A format refers to the way a value is presented. For instance "01-jan-00" and "January 1, 2000" are two formats for the same date. Formats are different from functions. Functions make a change to the value. Formats only change the way the value is presented.

Date formats

In both Oracle and Access, dates and times are stored together within a single datatype. Whenever you see a date, there is always a time stored with it. Whenever you see a time, there is always a date stored with it.

Dates and times are stored in an internal format. You never see or deal with them directly. All dates and times are formatted when you see them or when you enter them into a table.

Figure 4-14 shows some of the most useful date formats. These can be combined together in any way you wish. These are used both for displaying dates and entering dates into tables.

In Oracle, there is one default format for dates. It is usually set to "dd-mon-yy," which shows dates in the format '20-jan-99.' If you want to display or enter dates in any other format, you must explicitly state what that format is. In Oracle, dates and times are enclosed in single quotes. This is similar to text strings.

In Access, dates are enclosed in pound signs (#). This sets them apart from text strings. When you enter a date, Access knows it is a date by the pound signs. Access will attempt to automatically determine what format this date is in. Access can accept dates in many formats.

Oracle Format	Access Format	Result
YEAR		
yyyy	yyyy	1998 (Four digit year)
yy	yy	98 (Two digit year)
MONTH		
month	mmmm	October (Full name of the month)
mon	mmm	Oct (Abbreviated name of the month)
mm	mm	10 (Nunber of the month, 01 to 12)
DAY		
dd	dd	18 (Date of the month, 01 to 31)
day	dddd	Friday (Full name of the day)
dy	ddd	Fri (Abbreviated name of the day)
d	w	6 (Numeric day of the week, (1 is Sunday, 7 is Saturday)
	y	350 (Julian day of the year, 1 to 366)
TIME		
hh24	hh	14 (24 hour time, 00 to 23)
hh12	hh am/pm	02 (12-hour time, 00 to 11)
hh	hh am/pm	02 (12 hour time, 00 to 11)
mi	nn	30 (Minute after the hour, 00 to 59)
ss	ss	59 (Second, 00 to 59)
OTHER		
q	q	4 (Quarter of the year, 1 to 4)
ww	ww	45 (Week of the year,1 to 54)
JULIAN AND NEARLY JULIAN		
j		Number of Julian days since Dec 31, 4713 BC. Used to reliably calculate with dates.
sssss		Number of seconds since midnight. Used to calculate with times.

Some combinations

mm-dd-yyyy hh:mi:ss am	mm-dd-yyyy hh:nn:ss am/pm	10-18-1998 05:36:45 PM
mm-dd-yyyy hh:mi am	mm-dd-yyyy hh:nn am/pm	10-18-1998 05:36 PM
day, month dd, yyyy	dddd, mmmm dd, yyyy	Sunday, October 18, 1998
dd-mon-yy	dd-mmm-yy	18-Oct-98
mm-dd-yyyy	mm-dd-yyyy	10-18-1998
hh:mi:ss am	hh:nn:ss am/pm	05:36:45 PM
hh:mi am	hh:nn am/pm	05:36 PM

Figure 4-14   Date formats

Displaying formatted dates

In Oracle, the "To_char" function is used to specify the format to use when displaying a date. "To_char" means that we are converting a date datatype to a character datatype.

This function has two parameters. The first is the name of the column containing the dates. The second is the format to be used in displaying the date. The format specification must be enclosed in single quotes. You can add text to the format, such as "In the year of our Lord." This text must be enclosed in double quotes.

In Access, the "Format" function is used the same way.

Figure 4-15

❶   This is an SQLplus command that sets the formats of the "Formatted_date" column in Oracle. It sets the width of the column to 20 characters.

❷   In Oracle, the "To_char" function is used to control the format in which a date will be displayed. The second parameter is the Oracle date format you want to use—enclosed in single quotes.

The "To_char" function is used, and not the "To_date" function. When the date is stored in the database, it has a datatype of "Date." You want to change the format to a text datatype, so that it can be displayed.

❸   In Access, the "Format" function is used to control the format in which a date will be displayed. The second parameter is the Access date format you want to use—enclosed in single quotes.

❹   The data in the table shows that all the Formatted Dates have 12:00 AM (midnight) as their time. This default time is set in Oracle when no specific time is entered.

Task

From the employees table, list the employee id, first name, and hire date of all the employees. Add another column showing the hire date formatted in the form: "mm-dd-yyyy followed by the time." Sort the rows of the result by the employee id.

Oracle SQL

```
column formatted_date format a20;  ❶
select employee_id, first_name, hire_date,
       to_char(hire_date, 'mm-dd-yyyy hh:mi am') as formatted_date  ❷
from l_employees
order by employee_id;
```

Access SQL

```
select employee_id, first_name, hire_date,
       format(hire_date, 'mm-dd-yyyy hh:nn am/pm') as formatted_date  ❸
from l_employees
order by employee_id;
```

Beginning table (L_employees table)

EMPLOYEE ID	FIRST_NAME	LAST_NAME	DEPT CODE	HIRE_DATE	CREDIT LIMIT	PHONE NUMBER	MANAGER ID
201	SUSAN	BROWN	EXE	01-JUN-92	$30.00	3484	(null)
202	JIM	KERN	SAL	15-AUG-95	$25.00	8722	201
203	MARTHA	WOODS	SHP	01-FEB-97	$25.00	7591	201
204	ELLEN	OWENS	SAL	01-JUL-96	$15.00	6830	202
205	HENRY	PERKINS	SAL	01-MAR-98	$25.00	5286	202
206	CAROL	ROSE	ACT	15-OCT-97	$15.00	3829	201
207	DAN	SMITH	SHP	01-DEC-96	$25.00	2259	203
208	FRED	CAMPBELL	SHP	01-APR-97	$25.00	1752	203
209	PAULA	JACOBS	MKT	17-MAR-98	$15.00	3357	201
210	NANCY	HOFFMAN	SAL	15-FEB-96	$25.00	2974	203

Result table ❹

EMPLOYEE ID	FIRST_NAME	HIRE_DATE	FORMATTED_DATE
201	SUSAN	01-JUN-92	06-01-1992 12:00 AM
202	JIM	15-AUG-95	08-15-1995 12:00 AM
203	MARTHA	01-FEB-97	02-01-1997 12:00 AM
204	ELLEN	01-JUL-96	07-01-1996 12:00 AM
205	HENRY	01-MAR-98	03-01-1998 12:00 AM
206	CAROL	15-OCT-97	10-15-1997 12:00 AM
207	DAN	01-DEC-96	12-01-1996 12:00 AM
208	FRED	01-APR-97	04-01-1997 12:00 AM
209	PAULA	17-MAR-98	03-17-1998 12:00 AM
210	NANCY	15-FEB-96	02-15-1996 12:00 AM

Figure 4-15   Displaying formatted dates

Entering formatted dates

Figure 4-16 shows how to enter a date into a table when the date is formatted in a special way, such as including a time.

Figure 4-16

❶   In Oracle, dates can be entered into tables by using the "To_date" function. This tells Oracle to create a date datatype from the text datatype of the data that is entered.

In Oracle, dates can be entered in any format, but the specific format of the text data must be explicitly specified. A time can be entered along with a date, if the format includes a time.

If a time is entered, it will be permanently stored in the table. However, it will only be displayed when it is asked for explicitly. Dates containing times can cause errors to occur if the users are not aware that the times are contained in the data.

❷   In Access, a date is surrounded by pound signs (#). This says to Access that you want to enter a date. Most date formats are recognized automatically by Access. Their format does not need to be explicitly declared.

It is best to avoid ambiguous date formats. For example, does #7/4/99# mean April 7 or July 4? The meaning in America is different than the meaning in Europe.

❸   The time, 11:30 am, is present in the data, even though it is not displayed.

Task

Insert a new row into the Lunches table. Use the data:

> Lunch_id = 17
> Lunch_date = December 9, 1998 at 11:30 AM
> Employee_id = 201

Use a date format, if needed, to enter the date.

Oracle SQL

```
insert into l_lunches values
(17, to_date('12-09-1998 11:30 am', 'mm-dd-yyyy hh:mi am'), 201); ❶
```

Access SQL

```
insert into l_lunches
values (17, #dec 9 1998 11:30 am#, 201); ❷
```

Beginning table (L_Lunches table)

```
          LUNCH         EMPLOYEE
LUNCH_ID  DATE                ID
--------- ---------- ---------
        1 16-NOV-98        201
        2 16-NOV-98        202
        3 16-NOV-98        203
        4 16-NOV-98        207
        5 16-NOV-98        206
        6 16-NOV-98        210
        7 25-NOV-98        201
        8 25-NOV-98        205
        9 25-NOV-98        204
       10 25-NOV-98        207
       11 25-NOV-98        208
       12 04-DEC-98        201
       13 04-DEC-98        203
       14 04-DEC-98        205
       15 04-DEC-98        210
       16 04-DEC-98        208
```

New row ❸

```
       17 09-DEC-98        201
```

Figure 4-16   Entering formatted dates

Summary

In this chapter, you learned to create tables with the Create Table command. You learned about datatypes, sequences, and date formats. You also learned more about the Oracle Data Dictionary.

In this chapter, you dealt with many of the internal details of Oracle and Access. You learned that they are very similar to each other, although they differ in some small details.

Exercises

1. Goal: Create a table, use several data types including a sequence, put some data in it.

1A. Create the following table.
Use a sequence to assign the Lunch Number.
Make the first column the primary key.
Display the table with a Select statement.

MY_LUNCHES TABLE

Lunch_number	Lunch_time	Restaurant	Cost
1	Monday, Sept 21, 1999 11:30	The Paris Cafe	$12.52
2	Tuesday, Sept 22, 1999 1:00	The Healthy Kitchen	$8.39
3	Wednesday, Sept 23, 1999 1:30	Jack In The Box	$4.75
4	Thursday, Sept 24, 1999 12:15	A Soup Place	$6.73
5	Friday, Sept 25, 1999 12:45	Burger King	$4.25

Oracle SQL   Access SQL

Oracle SQL	Access SQL
| ```
create table my_lunches
   (lunch_number    integer,
   lunch_time       date,
   restaurant       varchar2(30),
   cost             number(4,2));
``` | ```
create table my_lunches
   (lunch_number    long,
   lunch_time       datetime,
   restaurant       text(30),
   cost             currency);
``` |
| ```
alter table my_lunches
add constraint pk_my_lunches
primary key (lunch_number);
``` | (Same as Oracle.) |
| ```
create sequence lunch_seq
start with 1
increment by 1;
``` | (Click on the Table tab. Click on the Design button. Change the Datatype of the Lunch_Number field to AutoNumber.) |
| ```
insert into my_lunches
values (lunch_seq.nextval,
to_date('09-21-1999 11:30 am',
'mm-dd-yyyy hh:mi am'),
'the paris cafe', 12.52);
``` | ```
insert into my_lunches
(lunch_time, restaurant, cost)
values (#09-21-1999 11:30 am#,
'the paris cafe', 12.52);
``` |
| (Add the other rows using copy and paste.) | (Add the other rows using copy and paste.) |
| ```
column lunch_time format a30
column restaurant format a20
column cost format $99.99
``` | (Access does not need to set column formats.) |
```

Oracle SQL

```
select  lunch_number,
to_char(lunch_time, 'day, mon dd, yyyy hh:mi') as lunch_time,
restaurant,
cost
from my_lunches;
```

Access SQL

```
select  lunch_number,
format(my_lunches.lunch_time, 'dddd, mmm dd, yyyy hh:nn') as
lunch_time,
restaurant,
cost
from my_lunches;
```

1B. Find out what day of the week you were born on. Also, find the day of the week for other significant dates in your life. Create a table, similar to exercise 1A. Include a sequence and use it when you Insert rows of data. Include text, a date with times, and a number. Add a primary key to the table. Display your table with a Select statement. Format the dates in a way that shows the day of the week.

2. Goal: Get rid of duplicate rows, then add a primary key to a table

2A. Display the table EX4_2A. Then fix it by getting rid of the duplicate rows and adding a primary key to the table which includes the first two columns. Find this primary key in the Data Dictionary.

Oracle SQL	Access SQL
| ```
select *
from ex4_2a;
``` | (Same as Oracle.) |
| ```
create table ex4_2a_new as
select distinct *
from ex4_2a;
``` | ```
select distinct *
into ex4_2a_new
from ex4_2a;
``` |
| ```
select *
from ex4_2a_new;
``` | (Same as Oracle.) |
| ```
alter table ex4_2a_new
add constraint pk_ex4_2a_new
primary key (first_col,
second_col);
``` | (Same as Oracle.) |
| ```
select *
from user_cons_columns;
``` | Using the GUI, look at the Table in Design view.) |

2B. Modify the table you created in exercise 1B.
Try adding a duplicate row. (The primary key will prevent you from doing this.)
Drop the primary key.
Now add the duplicate row.
Next, fix your table, as in exercise 2A.

3. Goal: Add a new column to a table

3A. Add a new column to the My_lunches table. Call it "Companion." Make it a variable length text column with a maximum length of 20 characters. Use the Alter Table command to do this.

Then add the following data to the table in this column:

LUNCH_NUMBER	COMPANION
1	Fred Swentson
4	Jill Donner

Then display the table.

Oracle SQL   Access SQL

Oracle SQL	Access SQL
`alter table my_lunches` `add companion varchar2(20);`	`alter table my_lunches` `add column companion text(20);`

`update my_lunches`
`set companion = 'fred swentson'`
`where lunch_number = 1;`
	(Same as Oracle.)

`update my_lunches`
`set companion = 'jill donner'`
`where lunch_number = 4;`
	(Same as Oracle.)

`select *` `from my_lunches;`	(Same as Oracle.)

3B. Add a new column to the table you created in exercise 1B.
Put some data in it.

4. Goal: Make several changes to a table by using a Select statement to create a new table from it. Add a primary key to this new table.

4A. Make the following changes to the My_Lunches table:

Delete the Lunch_number column.

Change the name of the Lunch_time column to "Lunch_date" and make it the primary key.

Make the Companion column the second column of the table. Rename it to "Companion_1."

Add a new column to the table called "Companion_2."

Put the Cost column next and the Restaurant column last.

Oracle SQL	Access SQL
```-- There is a trick here that sets the -- length of the Companion_2 column. -- You could use any text of the -- desired length. create table temp_1 as select lunch_time as lunch_date, companion as companion_1, '12345678901234567890' as companion_2, cost, restaurant from my_lunches;```	```select lunch_time as lunch_date, companion as companion_1, '12345678901234567890' as companion_2, cost, restaurant into temp_1 from my_lunches;```
```-- this automatically drops the -- primary key drop table my_lunches;```	```drop table my_lunches;```
```create table my_lunches as select * from temp_1;```	```select * into my_lunches from temp_1;```
```update my_lunches set companion_2 = null;```	(Same as Oracle.)
```drop table temp_1;```	(Same as Oracle.)
```alter table my_lunches add constraint pk_my_lunches primary key (lunch_date);```	(Same as Oracle.)
```select * from my_lunches;```	(Same as Oracle.)

4B. Make some changes to the table you created in exercise 1B.

5. Find column information in the data dictionary.

5A. Find information about the columns of the My_lunches table.

Oracle SQL	Access SQL
| ```
select column_id,
       column_name,
       data_type,
       data_length,
       data_precision,
       data_scale,
       nullable
from user_tab_columns
where table_name = 'my_lunches'
order by column_id;
``` | (Access uses the GUI to do this.) |

5B. Find the column information about the table you created in exercise 1B.

6. Goal: Find information about Oracle sequences in the Data Dictionary.

6A. Find information about the lunches_seq sequence.

Oracle SQL	Access SQL
| ```
select *
from user_sequences
``` | (All sequences in Access begin with one and increment by one.) |

6B. Find information about the sequence you created in exercise 1B.

7. Goal: Find information about all the database objects on your userid from the Data Dictionary. Identify all the object you have created.

Oracle SQL	Access SQL
| ```
select *
from user_objects;
``` | (Use Tools => Analyze =>Documenter.) |
```

8. Goal: use the index to the Oracle Data Dictionary.

8A. Find the information about sequences in the Data Dictionary.

Oracle SQL

```
column comments format a40 word_wrap

select *
from dictionary
where table_name like '%seq%';


select *
from dict_columns
where table_name = 'user_sequences';
```

8B. Find the information about views in the Data Dictionary.

9. Use the online documentation. Read the entry on data types.

Chapter 5

Row Functions

In all the Select statements we have written so far, the data in the result was an exact copy of the data in some cell of the beginning table. In this chapter, we remove that limitation. Row functions can create new values that do not exist in the original table.

Introduction to row functions

Row functions calculate a new value based on the data in one single row of the table. The value can be based on the data in one column or in several different columns. Some row functions operate on numbers; others operate on text or dates.

Getting data directly from the beginning table

In all the SQL we have done so far, the data in the result table came directly from the data in the original table. More specifically, the value in each cell of the result table was copied from some cell of the original table. No change at all was made to the value in the cell.

Figure 5-1 shows this process. Data from a few rows and columns of the beginning table are gathered together to form the result table. All the other data in the beginning table is ignored.

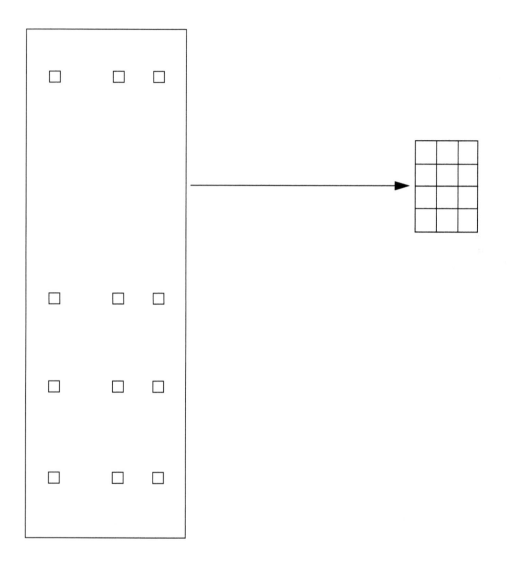

Figure 5-1   Getting data directly from the beginning table

Understanding a row function

Row functions calculate or construct a new value that is not in the beginning table. This new value is constructed from the values in one or more cells of the original table. All these cells must be part of a single row within the table.

The top part of Figure 5-2 shows a single new value constructed from all the values within one row of the beginning table.

The bottom part of Figure 5-2 shows the effect this has when every row of the table applies the function and creates a new value. In effect, this action adds a new column of data to the beginning table. Then the techniques you have learned already are applied to this enhanced table to create a final report from some of the rows and some of the columns.

The new values may appear in the result table, they may be used to pick rows from the beginning table, or they may be used to sort the rows of the result table. That is, the row function may be used in the Select clause, the Where clause, or the Order By clause of a Select statement.

The new column of information is not stored on the disk with the other data of the table. It does not become a permanent part of the table itself. Rather, it is held in memory while the Select statement is being processed. Then the memory is released after the Select statement has finished processing. So the new column of data exists only while one Select statement is being processed.

More precisely, the processing of the Select statement occurs *as if* the new values were all stored in memory. Actually, the computer is allowed to take shortcuts as long as it obtains the correct result. So the new values may be calculated for only a few of the rows, if they are sufficient to obtain the result table.

Of course, you can create a new table that stores the new column as data on the disk by using the Create Table statement you learned in Chapter 3.

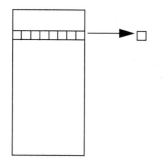

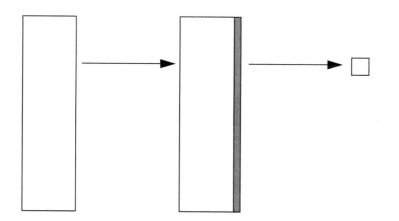

Figure 5-2   Understanding a row function

An example of a row function

Figure 5-3 shows an example of a row function. In this case, the function adds ten dollars to the credit limit. This is a function because a new value is obtained. If a row of the beginning table has a credit limit of $25, then the function produces a value of $35. This function uses only one column, credit limit, from the row. Other row functions can use multiple columns.

In Figure 5-3, the row function is used in three clauses of the Select statement—the Select clause, the Where clause, and the Order By clause. In each of these clauses, the function is written out explicitly. The row function can be specified in any one of these clauses or in several of them at the same time.

Figure 5-3

❶   In Oracle, this command to the SQLplus environment formats the New Credit Limit column. The "New Limit" column is given a format that displays it as a currency value, with a dollar sign, a decimal point, and two decimal places. In Access, this format is not needed.

❷   In the Select clause, the value of the row function is given a new name, "New Limit." We'd like for this new name to be used in the Where clause and the Order By clause, but it cannot be used there. In Figure 5-4, you learn a technique that allows you to use this name in those clauses.

Actually, Oracle does allow you to use this new name in the Order By clause, but not in the Where clause. Access and most other SQL products do not allow it to be used in either clause. However, instead of trying to remember these complex rules, you are best off using the technique of Figure 5-4 when the same function is used in several clauses.

❸   In the Where clause, the function is shown surrounded by parentheses. These are optional, but they do make the code easier to read and understand. So their use is recommended. In writing the row function itself, the two zeros after the decimal point are optional. They are written here to make the ten dollars look like a currency value, rather than just some abstract number.

In the Where clause, the test "< 37.50" is applied to the row function. Again, all numbers, even currency, must be written without dollar signs or commas. The Where clause could have used any of the conditions you learned in Chapter 2.

❹   The Order By clause says to sort the rows of the result table on the value of the row function. By default, this means to sort them in ascending order. When two rows have the same value, their order is determined by the Employee Id. If you check the result table, you will see that this is the order of the rows. The Order By clause could have sorted the row function in descending order.

Task

List the employees and their new credit limits. Add $10.00 to all the current credit limits, but do not allow them to exceed $37.00. Sort the results by the size of the new credit limit and then by the employee_id.

Oracle column formatting

```
column new_limit format $99.99  ❶
```

Oracle & Access SQL

```
select employee_id,
       first_name,
       last_name,
       credit_limit + 10.00 as new_limit  ❷
from l_employees
where (credit_limit + 10.00) < 37.50  ❸
order by (credit_limit + 10.00),  ❹
         employee_id;
```

Beginning table (L_employees table)

EMPLOYEE ID	FIRST_NAME	LAST_NAME	DEPT CODE	HIRE_DATE	CREDIT LIMIT	PHONE NUMBER	MANAGER ID
201	SUSAN	BROWN	EXE	01-JUN-92	$30.00	3484	(null)
202	JIM	KERN	SAL	15-AUG-95	$25.00	8722	201
203	MARTHA	WOODS	SHP	01-FEB-97	$25.00	7591	201
204	ELLEN	OWENS	SAL	01-JUL-96	$15.00	6830	202
205	HENRY	PERKINS	SAL	01-MAR-98	$25.00	5286	202
206	CAROL	ROSE	ACT	15-OCT-97	$15.00	3829	201
207	DAN	SMITH	SHP	01-DEC-96	$25.00	2259	203
208	FRED	CAMPBELL	SHP	01-APR-97	$25.00	1752	203
209	PAULA	JACOBS	MKT	17-MAR-98	$15.00	3357	201
210	NANCY	HOFFMAN	SAL	15-FEB-96	$25.00	2974	203

Result table

EMPLOYEE ID	FIRST_NAME	LAST_NAME	NEW_LIMIT
204	ELLEN	OWENS	$25.00
206	CAROL	ROSE	$25.00
209	PAULA	JACOBS	$25.00
202	JIM	KERN	$35.00
203	MARTHA	WOODS	$35.00
205	HENRY	PERKINS	$35.00
207	DAN	SMITH	$35.00
208	FRED	CAMPBELL	$35.00
210	NANCY	HOFFMAN	$35.00

Figure 5-3   An example of a row function

Using a series of steps with a row function

Figure 5-4 shows a technique that can be used when the same row function is used in several different clauses of a Select statement. When this was done in Figure 5-3, the function was written several times. We had no guarantee that the function was exactly the same each time it was used. A typing error could make one instance slightly different from another.

This technique prevents such an error from occurring. It also makes the code easier to write and understand. If the row function is complex, it assures that all references to the function are defined in exactly the same way.

Figure 5-4

❶　The first step of this technique creates a view that defines the row function and gives a name to the column it creates. In Figure 5-4, the row function is "credit_limit + 10.00," and the name of the new column is "New_limit." Oracle and Access use slightly different techniques to create a view, as you learned in Chapter 3. Step 1 could have created a table instead of a view, but using a view is usually more efficient.

Note that the row function is written only once with the new technique. It had to be written several times with the previous technique.

❷　The second step is the same as the original Select statement, except that the name of the new column, "New_limit," is used instead of writing out the explicit definition of the function itself, "Credit_limit + 10.00."

❸　Here, the New Limit column occurs in the Select clause.

❹　Note that the From clause refers to the view created in step 1.

❺　Here, the New Limit column occurs in the Where clause.

❻　Here, the New Limit column occurs in the Order By clause.

PREVIOUS TECHNIQUE

The previous Select statement
Oracle & Access SQL

```
select employee_id,
       first_name,
       last_name,
       credit_limit + 10.00 as new_limit
from l_employees
where (credit_limit + 10.00) < 37.50
order by (credit_limit + 10.00),
         employee_id;
```

NEW TECHNIQUE

Step 1—create a view ❶
Oracle SQL

```
create view step_1 as
select employee_id,
       first_name,
       last_name,
       credit_limit + 10 as new_limit
from l_employees;
```

Access method

1. Enter this in the SQL window:

```
select employee_id,
       first_name,
       last_name,
       credit_limit + 10 as new_limit
from l_employees;
```

2. Save the query. Name it "Step_1."

Step 2—use the new view ❷
Oracle & Access SQL

```
select employee_id,
       first_name,
       last_name,
       new_limit ❸
from step_1 ❹
where new_limit < 37.50 ❺
order by new_limit, ❻
         employee_id;
```

Figure 5-4   Using a series of steps with a row function

Number functions

Some row functions perform arithmetic on numbers. Others round or truncate numbers. These row functions often seem to produce entirely new data in the table.

Functions on numbers

The row functions for arithmetic do exactly what you expect them to do. An asterisk is used for the multiplication sign, as it is in most computer languages. Null does not mean zero; it means an unknown value. So any row function that operates on a null produces a null as the result.

Access has the Integer Division function, which Oracle does not have. Oracle has more rounding and truncation functions than Access. But these "missing" functions, or their equivalents, can all be constructed as is shown below, in "Examples of constructing the 'missing' functions."

The table on the next page shows some of the most frequently used functions on numbers. I omitted from this list the trigonometry functions and logarithms. Both Oracle and Access have them. Other, more specialized functions can be found in the technical reference.

Examples of constructing the "missing" functions
Getting Integer Division in Oracle:

In Access, you have $13\backslash3 = 4$

In Oracle, you have $((13 - mod(13,3)) / 3) = 4$

Getting CEIL in Access:

In Oracle, you have $ceil(3.1) = 4$

In Access, you have $int(3.1 + .99) = 4$

(Yes, this does need to be adjusted for the precision of the numbers with which you are dealing.)

Getting ROUND in Access:

In Oracle, you have $round(3.4567,2) = 3.46$

In Access, you have $int(3.4567 * (10 \wedge 2) + .5) / (10\wedge2) = 3.46$

Getting TRUNC in Access:

In Oracle, you have $trunc(3.4567,2) = 3.45$

In Access, you have $int(3.4567 * (10\wedge2)) / (10\wedge2) = 3.45$

Oracle	Access	Description and Examples
ARITHMETIC		
+	+	Addition Oracle & Access: 3 + 2 = 5 Oracle & Access: 3 + null = null
-	-	Subtraction Oracle & Access: 3 – 2 = 1 Oracle & Access: 3 – null = null
*	*	Multiplication Oracle & Access: 3 * 2 = 6 Oracle & Access: 3 * null = null
/	/	Division Oracle & Access: 10 / 3 = 3.3333 Oracle & Access: 10 / null = null
power	^	Value raised to an exponent Oracle: power(5,2) = 25 Access: 5^2 = 25
sqrt	sqr	Square root Oracle: sqrt (25) = 5 Access: sqr(25) = 5
(can be made)	\	Integer Division Access: 10 \ 3 = 3 Access: 10 \ null = null
mod	mod	Remainder after division Oracle: mod (10,3) = 1 Access: 10 mod 3 = 1
SIGN, ROUNDING, AND TRUNCATION		
sign	sgn	Sign indicator (1 if positive, –1 if negative, 0 if zero) Oracle: sign(–8) = –1 Access: sgn(–8) = –1
abs	abs	Absolute value Oracle & Access: abs (–8) = 8
ceil	(can be made)	Smallest integer larger than or equal to a value Oracle: ceil (3.5) = 4
floor	int	Largest integer less than or equal to a value Oracle: floor (3.5) = 3 Access: int(3.5) = 3
round	(can be made)	Round to a specified precision Oracle: round (3.4567, 2) = 3.46
trunc	(can be made)	Truncate to a specified precision Oracle: trunc (3.4567, 2) = 3.45

Figure 5-5   Functions on numbers

Testing row functions

Figure 5-6 shows three techniques for testing a row function. They are a way to discover what a row function does by using it to calculate some values.

The "problem" with doing calculations in SQL is that everything in SQL must be done in terms of tables. You must begin with a table and end with a table. So how can you multiply two numbers?

You have to start with a table—any table, no matter what data is in the table.

Figure 5-6

❶   Method 1 uses the row function in the Select clause. No column from the beginning table is needed in this clause. So no data from the beginning table will be displayed. The From clause names a table, any table. The Where clause adds a condition that only one row will satisfy. Without this Where clause, the value of the row function would be displayed once for every row of the beginning table.

❷   Method 2 is similar to method 1, except that instead of a Where clause, it uses Select Distinct to obtain a single row in the result table.

❸   Method 3 uses a special table that Oracle constructs called "Dual." The Dual table has only one row and one column. The data in it is unimportant. It is a placeholder, or "dummy table." It is used when a table is required by SQL but no particular table is needed. It is perfect for performing calculations or testing row functions.

To use this technique in Access, you need to create your own "Dual" table. This is not difficult, but Access has not already done it for you. You might even be able to find a better name for this table.

Task

Show how to test row functions in Oracle and Access. As an example, show 3 * 4 = 12.

Method 1 ❶
Oracle & Access SQL

```
select 3 * 4
from l_employees
where employee_id = 201;
```

Method 2 ❷
Oracle & Access SQL

```
select distinct 3 * 4
from l_employees;
```

Method 3 ❸
Oracle & Access SQL

```
select 3 * 4
from dual;
```

Beginning table (L_employees table)

```
EMPLOYEE                        DEPT            CREDIT PHONE   MANAGER
      ID FIRST_NAME LAST_NAME   CODE HIRE_DATE  LIMIT NUMBER       ID
-------- ---------- ----------  ---- ---------  ------ ------ -------
     201 SUSAN      BROWN       EXE  01-JUN-92  $30.00 3484   (null)
     202 JIM        KERN        SAL  15-AUG-95  $25.00 8722      201
     203 MARTHA     WOODS       SHP  01-FEB-97  $25.00 7591      201
     204 ELLEN      OWENS       SAL  01-JUL-96  $15.00 6830      202
     205 HENRY      PERKINS     SAL  01-MAR-98  $25.00 5286      202
     206 CAROL      ROSE        ACT  15-OCT-97  $15.00 3829      201
     207 DAN        SMITH       SHP  01-DEC-96  $25.00 2259      203
     208 FRED       CAMPBELL    SHP  01-APR-97  $25.00 1752      203
     209 PAULA      JACOBS      MKT  17-MAR-98  $15.00 3357      201
     210 NANCY      HOFFMAN     SAL  15-FEB-96  $25.00 2974      203
```

Beginning table (Dual table)

```
D
-
X
```

Result table

```
     3*4
---------
      12
```

Figure 5-6   Testing row functions

Text functions

Some row functions operate on text. Most of them produce text as output, but a few of them produce numbers.

Functions on text

Figure 5-7 shows the most frequently used functions on text. Others can be found in the technical manuals. These row functions operate on both fixed-length and variable-length strings of characters.

Concatenation puts two strings of text together and creates a single string. The second string begins right after the first string ends. If the first string is fixed-length, you may want to trim off the spaces on the right before you concatenate it.

Substring is the opposite of concatenation. It goes into the middle of the string, beginning at a starting position and continuing for a specified length.

SOUNDEX is used to compare the sounds of two words, in order to find words that sound alike but are spelled differently. It is used mostly to find people's names when you are not sure how to spell them. The U.S. census bureau originally developed this function. It is available in Oracle, but not in Access. It is usually used in the Where clause, on both sides of an equal sign.

UPPER puts all the letters in uppercase or lowercase. LOWER puts them all in lowercase. INITCAP capitalizes the first letter of each word and puts all the other letters in lowercase.

LTRIM deletes all the blank spaces on the left, up to the first non-blank character. RTRIM does the same on the right. TRIM deletes all the blank spaces on both the left and the right. It is available only in Access. However, Oracle can get the same result by combining the LTRIM and RTRIM functions. These functions are seldom needed when you are working with variable-length character strings. They are used mostly when you are working with fixed-length character strings.

LENGTH gives the total number of characters in the string. For fixed-length strings, it gives the maximum number of characters the string can hold, which is the length of the fixed-length string. When working with fixed-length strings, you may want to trim the beginning and ending blanks from them before taking their lengths.

INSTR tests to see whether one string is part of another string. If the first string contains the second string, then the starting position is the result. If the first string does not contain the second string, then a zero is the result.

Oracle	Access	Description and Examples
FUNCTIONS THAT RESULT IN TEXT		

concat or ‖	&	Concatenation
		    Oracle: concat('sun', 'flower') = 'sunflower'
		    Oracle: 'sun' ‖ 'flower' = 'sunflower'
		    Access: 'sun' & 'flower' = 'sunflower'

substr	mid	Substring
		    Oracle: substr ('sunflower', 4, 3) = 'flo'
		    Access: mid('sunflower', 4, 3) = 'flo'
		        (starting position = 4, length = 3)

soundex	(not available)	Used to compare names that sound similar Oracle: where soundex('John') = soundex ('Jon')
FUNCTIONS THAT CONTROL CAPITALIZATION		

upper	ucase
	or
	StrConv(,1)
		Uppercase
		    Oracle: upper ('sunflower') = 'SUNFLOWER'
		    Access: ucase('sunflower') = 'SUNFLOWER'
		    Access: StrConv('sunflower,1) = 'SUNFLOWER'

lower	lcase
	or
	StrConv(,2)
		Lowercase
		    Oracle: lower ('SUNFLOWER') = 'sunflower'
		    Access: lcase('SUNFLOWER') = 'sunflower'
		    Access: StrConv('SUNFLOWER',2) = 'sunflower'

initcap	StrConv(,3)	Capitalizes the first letter of one or more words.
		Puts the other letters in lowercase.
		    Oracle: initcap ('sunflower') = 'Sunflower'
		    Access: StrConv('sunflower,3) = 'Sunflower'

FUNCTIONS THAT CONTROL BLANK SPACES		
ltrim	ltrim	Left trim—remove the spaces on the left ltrim(' hello world ') = 'hello world '
rtrim	rtrim	Right trim—remove the spaces on the right rtrim(' hello world ') = ' hello world'
(can be made)	trim	Trim on both the left and right Access: trim(' hello world ') = 'hello world'
FUNCTIONS THAT RESULT IN NUMBERS		

length	Len	Number of characters in a string of text
		    Oracle: length ('sunflower') = 9
		    Access: len('sunflower') = 9

instr	InStr	Starting position of one string occurring in another
		    Oracle: instr ('sunflower', 'low') = 5
		    Oracle: instr ('sunflower', 'zzz') = 0
		        zero means that the second string does not
		        occur in the first string.
		    Access: InStr('sunflower', 'low') = 5

Figure 5-7   Functions on text

Combining the first and last names

Figure 5-8 shows how to combine the first name and the last name in a single column. A single space is placed between the two names.

First, the trailing spaces are deleted after the first name. This step is required if the first name is a fixed-length character string. It is optional if the first name is a variable-length character string.

The first name is concatenated to a single space; in Figure 5-8, you see a single space between the two single quotes. Then this is concatenated to the last name. Sometimes you may want to trim the spaces from the last name.

Oracle and Access use different signs for concatenation, but they mean the same thing. On most keyboards, the sign used in Oracle is the double bar, on the same key as the backslash. Two of these are used together.

Variation of this technique can be used to put the name in other formats such as:

Susan W. Brown
Ms. Brown
Brown, Susan W.

Figure 5-8

❶   In Oracle, the concatenation operator is ||, where | is the uppercase symbol on the backslash key. In the middle of the concatenation is:

single quote – space – single quote

❷   In Access, the concatenation operator is &.

Task

List the employee id and the full name of each employee. Combine the first and last names to form the full name.

Oracle SQL

```
select employee_id,
       rtrim(first_name) || ' ' || last_name as full_name ❶
from l_employees;
```

Access SQL

```
select employee_id,
       trim(first_name) & ' ' & last_name as full_name ❷
from l_employees;
```

Beginning table (l_employees table)

EMPLOYEE ID	FIRST_NAME	LAST_NAME	DEPT CODE	HIRE_DATE	CREDIT LIMIT	PHONE NUMBER	MANAGER ID
201	SUSAN	BROWN	EXE	01-JUN-92	$30.00	3484	(null)
202	JIM	KERN	SAL	15-AUG-95	$25.00	8722	201
203	MARTHA	WOODS	SHP	01-FEB-97	$25.00	7591	201
204	ELLEN	OWENS	SAL	01-JUL-96	$15.00	6830	202
205	HENRY	PERKINS	SAL	01-MAR-98	$25.00	5286	202
206	CAROL	ROSE	ACT	15-OCT-97	$15.00	3829	201
207	DAN	SMITH	SHP	01-DEC-96	$25.00	2259	203
208	FRED	CAMPBELL	SHP	01-APR-97	$25.00	1752	203
209	PAULA	JACOBS	MKT	17-MAR-98	$15.00	3357	201
210	NANCY	HOFFMAN	SAL	15-FEB-96	$25.00	2974	203

Result table

EMPLOYEE ID	FULL_NAME
201	SUSAN BROWN
202	JIM KERN
203	MARTHA WOODS
204	ELLEN OWENS
205	HENRY PERKINS
206	CAROL ROSE
207	DAN SMITH
208	FRED CAMPBELL
209	PAULA JACOBS
210	NANCY HOFFMAN

Figure 5-8   Combining the first and last names

Capitalization

Capitalization is an issue in both Oracle and Access. However, they deal with it differently. You can have two different goals.

One goal is to not have case sensitivity when searching for data or sorting the results. When you have case-sensitivity, an uppercase letter is considered different from a lowercase letter. So "JOHN," "John," and "john" are all different. Usually, this difference causes more confusion than it is worth. Hence, case sensitivity is avoided.

The other goal is to have the text look nice when it is printed. Most people agree that the best look is when the first letter of each word is capitalized and the other letters are in lowercase.

Oracle solution

Usually, Oracle databases turn off case sensitivity by storing all the data in uppercase letters.

Oracle allows mixed-case data, but then the searches are case-sensitive. To search for "John," the Where clause needs to say WHERE FIRST_NAME = 'John'

The text within the single quotes is case-sensitive. It will not find any matches if the case of any letter does not exactly match the case of the data in the table.

If all the data is in uppercase, then Oracle can further reduce the case sensitivity with the SQLplus command SET SQLCASE UPPER. This changes all the SQL commands to uppercase before they are processed. All the text within quotation marks is also changed automatically to uppercase. SQL plus is the environment in which Oracle is usually run.

Figure 5-9 shows how the second objective can be met in Oracle. The INITCAP function can be applied to the data to make it look more pleasing. Unfortunately, it must be applied individually to each column of data. It cannot be applied globally to all the columns. It is available, but it is often ignored.

To put the column headings in mixed case, the Column command is used. This SQLplus command supports mixed case and is applied after the SQL process is finished. At the end of the SQL processing, the first column is named "description." Then SQLplus applies the heading "Food Item" to it.

Access solution

Access achieves the first goal by never using case sensitivity when it searches for data or when it sorts the data. It acts internally as if all the data is in a single case. A way to make Access case-sensitive may exist, but this is not the default.

Access achieves the second goal by preserving the data in the form that you type it. If you begin each word with a capital letter when you enter the data, then Access will always present it that way. Figure 5-9 shows that Access has a row function that capitalizes the first letter of every word. However, this function is seldom needed.Column headings in Access are displayed in the same case used in the Select clause of the query. The capital "P" in "Price" within the Select clause causes the same capitalization in the column name of the result table. The column alias "Food Item" contains a space, so it must be enclosed in square brackets.

Task

List the foods and their prices. Improve the appearance of the descriptions of the foods by capitalizing the first letter of each word and making all the other letters lowercase. Use the same case for the column headings. Sort the result by the Menu Item column.

Oracle SQL

Access SQL

column description heading 'Food Item'
column price heading 'Price'
 	
select initcap(description) as description,
      price
from l_foods
order by menu_item;
	select strconv(description,3)
	                    as [Food Item],
	      Price
	from l_foods
	order by menu_item;

Beginning table (L_Foods table)

```
SUPPLIER PRODUCT   MENU                                     PRICE
ID       CODE      ITEM DESCRIPTION            PRICE INCREASE
-------- -------   ------- -------------------- -------- --------

ASP      FS           1 FRESH SALAD            $2.00   $0.25
ASP      SP           2 SOUP OF THE DAY        $1.50   (null)
ASP      SW           3 SANDWICH               $3.50   $0.40
CBC      GS           4 GRILLED STEAK          $6.00   $0.70
CBC      HB           5 HAMBURGER              $2.50   $0.30
FRV      BR           6 BROCCOLI               $1.00   $0.05
FRV      FF           7 FRENCH FRIES           $1.50   (null)
JBR      AS           8 SODA                   $1.25   $0.25
JBR      VR           9 COFFEE                 $0.85   $0.15
VSB      AS          10 DESSERT                $3.00   $0.50
```

Result table

```
Food Item            Price
-------------------- --------

Fresh Salad          $2.00
Soup Of The Day      $1.50
Sandwich             $3.50
Grilled Steak        $6.00
Hamburger            $2.50
Broccoli             $1.00
French Fries         $1.50
Soda                 $1.25
Coffee               $0.85
Dessert              $3.00
```

Figure 5-9   Capitalization

Date Functions

Some row functions operate on dates. Functions on dates are different from the date formats you learned in Chapter 4. Date formats change the appearance of the date, without changing its value. Date functions change the value of the data to another date.

Functions on dates

Figure 5-10 shows the date functions that are used most often. Date calculations are usually made in terms of the number of days, rather than months or years. The reason is that the number of days in a month or year can vary.

Both Oracle and Access can add a number of days to a date. They can both subtract a number of days from a date. They can both find the number of days between two dates.

Using the table of numbers from 0 to 99, you can add these numbers to any date and create a calendar that is 100 days long.

When you are working with dates, be sure to remember that each date also has a time, even if the time is not being displayed. A fraction can be added to a date to change the time.

Oracle	Access	Result
+ number	+ number or DateAdd	Add a number of days to a date. Oracle: '20-jan-99' + 3 = '23-jan-99' Access: #01-20-1999# + 3 = #01-23-1999# Access: DateAdd('d',3,#01-20-1999#) = #01-23-1999#
– number	– number or DateAdd	Subtract a number of days from a date. Oracle: '20-jan-99' – 3 = '17-jan-99' Access: #01-20-1999# – 3 = #01-17-1999# Access: DateAdd('d',-3,#01-20-1999#) = #01-17-1999#
add_months	DateAdd	Adds months to a date. The number of months must be an integer. Oracle: add_months('20-jan-99', 3) = '20-apr-99' Access: DateAdd('m',3,#01-20-1999#) = #04-20-1999#
(can be constructed)	DateDiff	The number of days between two dates. Oracle: '23-jan-99' – '20-jan-99' = 3 Access: DateDiff('d',#01-20-1999#,#01-23-1999#) = 3
last_day	(can be constructed)	Date of the last day of the month. Oracle: last_day ('20-feb-96') = '29-feb-96' Oracle: last_day('20-feb-98') = '28-feb-98'
next_day	(can be constructed)	Date of the next specified weekday. Oracle: next_day ('20-jan-98', 'mon') = '26-jan-98' Oracle: next_day ('28-feb-98', 'wed') = '04-mar-98'
trunc	(can be constructed)	Sets the date/time to 12 am midnight, the beginning of the day. Optionally, you may set the date/time to a different starting point such as the beginning of the hour, week, or century. Oracle: trunc('20-jan-98') = '20-jan-98' The first date might be at 6:00 pm. The second date is at 12:00 am, 18 hours earlier.
round	(can be constructed)	Rounds the date/time to 12 am midnight, the beginning of the day or optionally to another starting point. Oracle: round('20-jan-98') = '21-jan-98' The first date might be at 6:00 pm. The second date is at 12:00 am, 6 hours later.
months_betw een	DateDiff(	Number of months between two dates. Oracle: months_between('01-apr-99', '01-jan-99') = 3 Oracle: months_between('01-jan-99','01-apr-99') = –3 Access: DateDiff('m',#01-01-99#,#04-01-99#) = 3

- The Oracle dates shown here are assumed to already be in date format. This assumption works when they are in a column that has a Date datatype. If you are writing these dates directly into a Select statement, the TO_DATE function must be used to convert the text string within quotes to a Date datatype.

Figure 5-10   Functions on dates

An example of a date function

Figure 5-11 shows an example of a date function. This function calculates the number of months each employee has worked for the company as of January 1, 1999. A month is not counted until a full month has been worked.

The Oracle version of this function seems to be different from the Access version. This example shows that the date functions work a bit differently, even though they can produce the same results. This shows some of the subtleties of working with months. If we worked with days, the two products would be much more alike.

Figure 5-11

❶   In Oracle, the MONTHS_BETWEEN function produces an integer and a decimal. This is a number. The decimal part of this number must be truncated to avoid counting partial months worked. It is truncated to zero decimal places, which is why the number 0 appears at the end of the line of code. This particular function is the truncation function that works with numbers, not the truncation function that works with dates.

❷   In Access, the DATEDIFF function with the 'M' option calculates the number of months, but rounds it up to the nearest integer. To keep this rounding process under control, we need to add 27 days to the hire date, saying in a way that the person was hired 27 days later than they were actually hired. (February has 28 days, so you have to add a number smaller than 28.) For the data in this example, the result is exactly the same in Access as it is in Oracle. However, other data could show some differences of one month, caused by a difference in rounding.

Note that in Oracle, January 1 is the first parameter of the MONTHS_BETWEEN function. In Access, it is the second parameter of the DATEDIFF function. The order of the parameters is reversed.

Task

List all the employees, their hire dates, and the number of months each person will have worked for the company as of January 1, 1999.

Oracle SQL

```
select first_name, last_name,
       hire_date,
       trunc(months_between('01-jan-99', hire_date),0)   ❶
            as months_with_the_company
from l_employees;
```

Access SQL

```
select first_name, last_name,
       hire_date,
       DateDiff('m', hire_date + 27, #01-jan-99#)   ❷
            as months_with_the_company
from l_employees;
```

Beginning table (L_employees table)

EMPLOYEE ID	FIRST_NAME	LAST_NAME	DEPT CODE	HIRE_DATE	CREDIT LIMIT	PHONE NUMBER	MANAGER ID
201	SUSAN	BROWN	EXE	01-JUN-92	$30.00	3484	(null)
202	JIM	KERN	SAL	15-AUG-95	$25.00	8722	201
203	MARTHA	WOODS	SHP	01-FEB-97	$25.00	7591	201
204	ELLEN	OWENS	SAL	01-JUL-96	$15.00	6830	202
205	HENRY	PERKINS	SAL	01-MAR-98	$25.00	5286	202
206	CAROL	ROSE	ACT	15-OCT-97	$15.00	3829	201
207	DAN	SMITH	SHP	01-DEC-96	$25.00	2259	203
208	FRED	CAMPBELL	SHP	01-APR-97	$25.00	1752	203
209	PAULA	JACOBS	MKT	17-MAR-98	$15.00	3357	201
210	NANCY	HOFFMAN	SAL	15-FEB-96	$25.00	2974	203

Result table

FIRST_NAME	LAST_NAME	HIRE_DATE	MONTHS_WITH_THE_COMPANY
SUSAN	BROWN	01-JUN-92	79
JIM	KERN	15-AUG-95	40
MARTHA	WOODS	01-FEB-97	23
ELLEN	OWENS	01-JUL-96	30
HENRY	PERKINS	01-MAR-98	10
CAROL	ROSE	15-OCT-97	14
DAN	SMITH	01-DEC-96	25
FRED	CAMPBELL	01-APR-97	21
PAULA	JACOBS	17-MAR-98	9
NANCY	HOFFMAN	15-FEB-96	34

Figure 5-11   An example of a date function

Other functions

A few other row functions also have special purposes.

Other functions

Figure 5-12 shows five other types of row functions. The first two types are discussed here. The others are discussed in the next few pages.

Functions to use in debugging

In Oracle, the DUMP function allows you to look into the internals of the software and see the internal representation of your data. Sometimes this can help you solve a problem or understand why the computer is behaving in some unexpected fashion.

The example in Figure 5-12 examines the character string 'ab' using hexadecimal notation. The internal representation has a datatype of 96. The string has a length of 2. The internal codes for the two characters are 41 and 42.

I once solved a problem with this function. Data that I thought was a variable-length character string turned out instead to be a fixed-length character string. I could tell the difference simply by looking at the length of the internal strings.

Functions to enter non-printable values

In Oracle and Access, the CHR function can be used to control special features on your printer or other hardware. For instance, if you have a long report, it can tell your printer where you want to begin printing on a new page.

This technique is advanced and should be used sparingly. To use it fully, you will need the technical manual for your printer. The good part is that it allows you to use the full capabilities of your printer. The bad part is that it can limit your code so that it requires a particular type of printer.

Whenever you use something like this technique, be sure to document it carefully. Say what you are doing and why you are doing it. Be kind to the people who will work on the code after you are finished with it.

Oracle	Access	Description and Examples
FUNCTIONS TO USE IN DEBUGGING		
dump(,16)	asc	Shows the internal format of a number or text. Oracle: dump('ab', 16) = 'Typ=96 Len=2: 41,42' Access: asc('a') = 97
FUNCTIONS TO ENTER NON-PRINTABLE VALUES		
chr	chr	ASCII character codes Oracle & Access use this function the same. printer control characters (your printer may differ) chr(10) causes the printer to skip a line chr(12) causes the printer to start a new page
FUNCTIONS TO CHANGE THE DATATYPE		
to_char	CStr	Converts a number to a character string (text). Also used to control the formats of dates in Oracle. Oracle: to_char(7) = '7' Access: CStr(7) = '7'
to_date	CDate	Converts a number or character string to a date. Also used to control the input of dates with a specified format in Oracle. Oracle: to_date(1, 'j') = '01-jan-12' (4712 BC) Oracle: to_date('03/99', 'mm/yy') = '01-mar-99' Access: CDate(1) = #12-31-1899# Access: CDate('Jan 20, 1999') = #01-20-1999#
to_number	CInt CDbl (others)	Converts a character string to a number. Oracle: to_number('8') = 8 Access: CInt('8') = 8
FUNCTIONS TO CHANGE NULLS TO OTHER VALUES		
nvl	nz	Converts nulls to another value. Oracle: nvl(col_1,0) = 0 if col_1 is null. Oracle: nvl(col_1,0) = col_1 if col_1 is not null. Access: nz(col_1,0) = '0' if col_1 is null Access: nz(col_1,0) = 'col_1' if col_1 is not null
FUNCTIONS TO IDENTIFY THE USER AND THE DATE		
user	CurrentUser()	Name of the userid for the current session. Oracle: user = 'JPATRICK' Access: CurrentUser() = 'Admin'
sysdate	Now()	The current date and time. Oracle: sysdate = '20-dec-99' Access: Now() = '12-20-1999 10:30:25 AM"

Figure 5-12   Other functions

Using functions to change the datatype

Functions to change datatypes keep the "outer meaning" of the data the same while changing the "inner representation," the datatype, of the data. For instance, '8' as a character string differs from '8' as a number. They both mean '8,' but if you could see the patterns of 1s and 0s inside the computer, you would see one binary pattern for the number and a different binary pattern for the character string.

Why should you care about this difference? One reason is that row functions work only with data that has certain datatypes. For example, consider addition. Addition is defined on numbers, but not on character strings. When '8' and '4' are numbers, then '8' + '4' makes sense, and is equal to the number '12.' However, when '8' and '4' are character strings, '8' + '4' does not make sense. It is not equal to anything, and will give you an error message if you use it. At least, so says the theory. Things work a bit differently in practice, as you will see.

Oracle, Access, and most other SQL products do a certain amount of "automatic datatype conversion." Differing products do different amounts of this. The idea is to make things easier for the user. A novice user might become confused and enraged if the database refuses to add '8' and '4.' An error message about the datatypes might not calm him. So to make things work more smoothly, the '8' and '4' are automatically converted into numbers and then added together. This addition happens silently, behind the scenes. No information message says that this is occurring.

Figure 5-13 shows that automatic datatpye conversion is used by both Oracle and Access to perform arithmetic on text strings. In this case, Oracle performs all the operations correctly. Access performs subtraction, multiplication, and division correctly, but it has a slight flaw when it performs addition. Access says that '8' + '4' = 84. Clearly, it is doing concatenation, instead of addition in this case. To obtain the correct result, you need to convert the text datatype to an integer datatype, using the CINT function. The mistake occurs only when you rely on automatic datatype conversion. If you do the conversion yourself, everything works correctly.

Figure 5-13

❶   This prints out the primary key and the two text items, so you can show them in the result table. Why does a primary key exist? It does not do anything in this example; however, every table should have a primary key.

❷   The next lines add, subtract, multiply, and divide the two text items. For these operations to make sense, the text must be automatically converted into numbers before the arithmetic can be done.

❸   The CInt (Convert into Integer) function is used to convert the text into integers. Then Access can add them, giving 8 + 4 = 12.

There is a reason why Access says that '8' + '4' = '84'. In many computer languages for the PC, the plus sign is used with text strings to mean concatenation. For example,

"sun" + "flower" = "sunflower"

So a reason for it exists, but some people think that it is a bad reason.

Task

Show the effects of automatic datatype conversion. Perform arithmetic on numbers that are in columns having a datatype of text.

Oracle & Access SQL

```
select pkey, text_1, text_2, ❶
       text_1 + text_2 as text_add, ❷
       text_1 - text_2 as text_subtract,
       text_1 * text_2 as text_multiply,
       text_1 / text_2 as text_divide
from fig5_13;
```

Beginning table (Fig5_13 table)

```
PKEY TEXT_1 TEXT_2
---- ------ ------
A    8      4
B    33     11
```

Oracle result table—correct

```
PKEY TEXT_1 TEXT_2  TEXT_ADD TEXT_SUBTRACT TEXT_MULTIPLY TEXT_DIVIDE
---- ------ ------  -------- ------------- ------------- -----------
A    8      4            12             4            32           2
B    33     11           44            22           363           3
```

Access result table—addition is incorrect

pkey	text_1	text_2	text_add	text_subtract	text_multiply	text_divide
A	8	4	84	4	32	2
B	33	11	3311	22	363	3

Query2 : Select Query — Record: 3 of 3

Access SQL—correction

```
select pkey, text_1, text_2,
       CInt(text_1) + CInt(text_2) as text_add, .
       text_1 - text_2 as text_subtract,
       text_1 * text_2 as text_multiply,
       text_1 / text_2 as text_divide
from fig5_13;
```

Figure 5-13   Using functions to change the datatype

Using functions to change nulls to other values

The NVL function in Oracle and the NZ function in Access change the nulls in some columns to another value, such as zero. When the original value in the column is not null, no change is made and the value stays the same. The column can have any datatype—number, text, or date.

In Oracle, the NVL function ("null value function") does not change the datatype of the column. So the datatype of the replacement value must be the same as that which the column originally has. This restriction means that nulls in a numeric column can be changed to zero or some other number, but not to text or a date. The nulls in a text column must be replaced with text, or possibly with a string of blanks. The nulls in a date column can be changed only to a date.

In Access, the NZ function always changes the column to a text datatype. Any data, including numbers and dates, can be always be represented as text. The replacement value, which will be substituted for nulls, can be any datatype. However, it will be changed to text when it is output from the NZ function.

Figure 5-14 shows how to replace nulls with other values in columns that have number, text, and date datatypes. Oracle and Access are very similar, except that Oracle uses the NVL function whereas Access uses the NZ function. The only other difference in this example is the replacement value for the date column. In Oracle, dates are enclosed in single quotes; in Access, they are enclosed in pound signs.

Figure 5-14

❶ In method 1, each null is replaced by a value that has the same datatype as the column that contains the null.

❷ In this example, Oracle uses the NVL function, which uses zero to replace the nulls in a column of numbers. It uses "zilch," a text string, to replace the nulls in a column of text. And it uses January 1, 1930, a date, to replace the nulls in a column of dates.

The datatype of the original column is not changed. A column of numbers remains a column of numbers. A column of dates remains a column of dates.

❸ In Access, the NZ function can use the same values as Oracle to replace the nulls. The difference in the syntax is in the name of the function and in the characters enclosing the date. The difference in the result is that the NZ function in Access converts all the columns to text, whereas in Oracle, the NVL function leaves the datatype of the column unchanged.

❹ In method 2, each null is replaced by text.

❺ Oracle does not support this method.

❻ In Access, nulls can always be replaced with text strings.

Task

Show how to replace nulls with other values. Show this procedure with a number column, a text column, and a date column.

Method 1 ❶
Oracle SQL

```
select pkey,
       nvl(num_col,0),  ❷
       nvl(text_col, 'zilch'),
       nvl(date_col, '01-jan-30')
from fig5_14;
```

Access SQL

```
select pkey,
       nz(num_col,0),  ❸
       nz(text_col, 'zilch'),
       nz(date_col, #01-jan-30#)
from fig5_14;
```

Method 2 ❹
Oracle SQL

(This is not available in Oracle.) ❺

Access SQL

```
select pkey,
       nz(num_col, 'no number'),  ❻
       nz(text_col, 'no text'),
       nz(date_col, 'no date')
from fig5_14;
```

Beginning table (Fig5_14 table)

```
PKEY    NUM_COL TEXT_COL DATE_COL
-----   --------- -------- ---------
A             1 M          (null)
B             2 (null)   20-JAN-99
C        (null)   N       21-JAN-99
```

Result table—method 1

```
PKEY   NVL(NUM_COL,0) NVL(TEXT NVL(DATE_
-----  -------------- -------- ---------
A             1 M          01-JAN-30
B             2 ZILCH    20-JAN-99
C             0 N        21-JAN-99
```

Result table—method 2

pkey	Expr1001	Expr1002	Expr1003
A	1	M	no date
B	2	no text	01-20-1999
C	no number	N	01-21-1999

Record: 1 of 3

Figure 5-14   Using functions to change nulls to other values

Using functions to identify the user and the date

Figure 5-15 shows how to use functions to identify the user, the date, and the time. The technique is similar in Oracle and Access, although the details are quite different.

The name of the userid, in Oracle, is obtained from the USER function. This is the name you use when you log onto Oracle. In Access, it is obtained from the CURREN-TUSER() function. Unless you have set up special security for Access, this is the name you use to log onto your operating system.

The date and time, in Oracle, are obtained from the SYSDATE function. In Access, they are obtained from the NOW() function. They are formatted, in Oracle, with the TO_CHAR function. In Access, they are formatted with the FORMAT function. You learned the details of the date formats in Chapter 4.

The other difference between Oracle and Access is in the From and Where clauses. Oracle can use the DUAL table, which is a special table Oracle always sets up. Access needs to use some other table; any table will do. Access also needs to use a Where clause to obtain only a single row. This technique is the same we used for testing row functions in Figure 5-6.

Task

Show how to identify the user, the date, and the time.

Oracle SQL

```
select user,
       to_char(sysdate, 'day month dd, yyyy hh:mi am') as
date_time
from dual;
```

Oracle result table

```
USER                             DATE_TIME
------------------------------   --------------------------------------
JPATRICK                         WEDNESDAY SEPTEMBER 30, 1998 08:47 AM
```

Access SQL

```
select CurrentUser() as user,
       format(Now(),'dddd mmmm dd, yyyy hh:nn am/pm') as date_time
from l_employees
where employee_id = 201;
```

Access result table

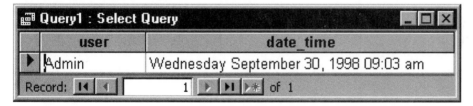

Figure 5-15   Using functions to identify the user and the date

Starting Expression Builder in Access

In Access, the row functions are organized in the Expression Builder. This is where you can find all the functions you need.

To start the Expression Builder (refer to Figure 5-16):

1. Click the Queries tab.
2. Click the New button.
3. Highlight Design View.
4. Click the OK button.
5. Click the Close button.
6. Right-click on a Field cell or a Criteria cell.
7. Click on Build.

In contrast, in Oracle, you usually use the printed documentation or the online documentation to find the right row function.

Expression Builder

Figure 5-16   Starting Expression Builder in Access

Creating Patterns of Numbers and Dates

Row functions can be used to create patterns of numbers or dates. These are useful in creating a variety of reports. They are particularly useful for finding data that is missing or that is an exception to the pattern. When you create these patterns, the beginning table is usually a table of numbers.

Listing the multiples of three

Figure 5-17 shows how to list all the multiples of three between 50 and 300. The purpose of this is to show you how to create patterns of numbers. The particular patterns you may need will vary. There is no particular significance to this pattern, except it is easy to create.

The beginning table is the table of numbers from 0 to 99. I have created this table for you already. In Chapter 9, you will discover how to generate a table like this with as many numbers as you want. For now, 100 numbers are enough to handle.

To get the multiples of three, you multiply all the numbers in the table by three. This function is used in the Select clause, the Where clause, and the Order By clause. Figure 5-4 shows an alternative method to use in writing this statement, so that the function does not have to be written out each time.

To create other patterns, you could multiply the numbers in the beginning table by any number, M. Then you could add another number, A. If the numbers in the table are called T, this creates a table of numbers of the form $(T * M) + A$. You can also take any section from this table by setting a starting point and an ending point.

Of course, any series of number you can list, you can also save in a new table or view.

Figure 5-17

❶   This multiplies each number by three and names the column "Multiples_of_3."

❷   The beginning table is a table of consecutive numbers. It has already been created for you.

❸❹   The row function must be written out completely in the Where clause and in the Order By clause. As an alternative, you could first create a view. Figure 5-3 explains this technique.

❺   The rows of this table are shown in their logical order, so that this example is easy to understand. But of course, the rows in any table are in no particular order. If you display this table without an Order By clause, the rows will probably be in a different order. To see them in this order, you must include "Order By N."

Task

Beginning with the table of numbers from 0 to 99, list all the numbers that are multiples of three that are greater than 50 and less than 300.

Oracle & Access SQL

```
select 3 * n as multiple_of_3 ❶
from numbers_0_to_99 ❷
where (3 * n) between 50 and 300 ❸
order by (3 * n); ❹
```

Beginning table (Numbers_0_to_99 table) ❺

```
        N
---------
        0
        1
        2
        3
        4
        5


       97
       98
       99
```

Result table

```
MULTIPLE_OF_3
-------------
           51
           54
           57
           60


          291
          294
          297
```

Figure 5-17   Listing the multiples of three

Listing the prime numbers

Figure 5-17 created a simple pattern of number. Now, I want to show you that you can create some very complex patterns of numbers. The prime numbers are one of the most complex sequences. So I use them as an example.

Figure 5-18 shows how to list the prime numbers between 10 and 99. You need to find the numbers that cannot be evenly divided by 2, 3, 5, or 7. You do so in the Where clause. The MOD function shows the remainder after division. If you write "MOD(X, Y) = 0," this means that Y divides evenly into X. You want the opposite of that. So you want

$$\text{not } (\text{mod}(N, 2) = 0)$$

This gives you the numbers that are not divisible by 2. Similar logic is used with 3, 5, and 7.

In Access, this condition is written

$$\text{not } ((N \text{ mod } 2) = 0)$$

Task

List all the prime numbers that are greater than 10 and less than 100.

Oracle SQL

```
select n as prime_number
from numbers_0_to_99
where n > 10
    and not (mod(n, 2) = 0)
    and not (mod(n, 3) = 0)
    and not (mod(n, 5) = 0)
    and not (mod(n, 7) = 0)
order by n;
```

Access SQL

```
select n as prime_number
from numbers_0_to_99
where n > 10
    and not ((n mod 2) = 0)
    and not ((n mod 3) = 0)
    and not ((n mod 5) = 0)
    and not ((n mod 7) = 0)
order by n;
```

Beginning table (Numbers_0_to_99 table)

```
        N
---------
        0
        1
        2


       98
       99
```

Result table

```
PRIME_NUMBER
------------
          11
          13
          17
          19
          23


          83
          89
          97
```

Figure 5-18   Listing the prime numbers

Listing all the days of one week

Figure 5-19 shows how to list all the days of one week. The purpose is to show you that you can create patterns of dates, just like you can create patterns of numbers. In fact, any pattern of numbers you can create can also be made into a pattern of dates.

Since Oracle and Access handle dates differently, the Select statements here are different, but the basic idea is the same. You begin with a date, and you can add integers to it to get the dates of other days. Before you add integers to it, you must ensure that the date has the datatype of a date, not a text datatype.

We will code this example in two different ways. The first way of coding it has the advantage of being a single Select statement. The disadvantages are that it is complex, some sections of the code are repeated several times, and it is difficult to modify.

The second method of coding uses three different steps. Each step is simple and easy to understand. No code needs to be repeated. And it is easy to modify and adapt to other purposes.

Figure 5-19—part 1

❶ This Column command sets the width of the Abbreviated_day column to 20 characters. The next line does the same for the Full_day column.

In Oracle, the width of columns is set by Column commands. These are SQLplus commands, i.e., commands to the environment in which Oracle SQL runs. They are not SQL commands.

In Access, the width of the columns can be adjusted with the mouse. This action is also adjusting the environment, not the SQL. The difference is that Oracle operates in a command environment, whereas Access operates in a GUI (graphical) environment.

❷ The To_date function is used to convert the text string "24-feb-99" into a date, i.e., to give it a date datatype. This conversion must take place in order to add a number to it. You cannot add a number to "24-feb-99" when it is a text string, but you can add a number to it when it has the datatype of a date.

❸ This line and the next apply the To_char function to the date created on line ❷. This function displays the date in a specified format. The format for this line is "DY," which tells Oracle to format the date as "Mon" for Monday, "Tue" for Tuesday, etc. The format for the next line is "DAY," which tells Oracle to format the date as "Monday" for Monday, "Tuesday" for Tuesday, etc.

The syntax may seem confusing, because it contains both the To_char function and the To_date function. Here is the explanation. First, the To_date function is applied to the text string "24-feb-99." This action changes the datatype to a date. A number is added to the date, resulting in another date.

Then the To_char function is applied to the date. This formats it as a text string and displays the date in the format you specify.

❹ This causes these dates to be listed in their usual order. It could also be written "Order by to_date('24-feb-99') + digit." However, that approach is more complex.

❺ In Access, the pound signs say that "24-feb-99" is a date and should be given the datatype of a date. So Access does not need to use a function, such as To_date.

❻ In Access, the Format function is used to display dates in a specified format. Note that the Access formats must be used—"DDD" and "DDDD."

Task

List all the days for one week beginning February 24, 1999. For each date, also list the day of the week in both abbreviated form and fully spelled out.

Oracle SQL

```
column abbreviated_day format a20 ❶
column full_day format a20
select to_date('24-feb-99') + digit as days, ❷
       to_char(to_date('24-feb-99') + digit,'dy') as abbreviated_day, ❸
        to_char(to_date('24-feb-99') + digit,'day') as full_day
from numbers_0_to_9
where digit < 7
order by digit; ❹
```

Access SQL

```
select #24-feb-99# + digit as days, ❺
       format(#24-feb-99# + digit,'ddd') as abbreviated_day, ❻
       format(#24-feb-99# + digit,'dddd') as full_day
from numbers_0_to_9
where digit < 7
order by digit;
```

Beginning table (Numbers_0_to_9 table)

```
    DIGIT
---------
        0
        1
        2
        3
        4
        5
        6
        7
        8
        9
```

Result table

```
DAYS        ABBREVIATED_DAY         FULL_DAY
---------   --------------------    --------------------
24-FEB-99   WED                     WEDNESDAY
25-FEB-99   THU                     THURSDAY
26-FEB-99   FRI                     FRIDAY
27-FEB-99   SAT                     SATURDAY
28-FEB-99   SUN                     SUNDAY
01-MAR-99   MON                     MONDAY
02-MAR-99   TUE                     TUESDAY
```

Figure 5-19   Listing all the days of one week (part 1 of 3)

Another method for writing the SQL code

Part 2 of Figure 5-19 shows another way to write the SQL code to list the days of one week. This method also creates a table containing all the dates, so they will be available if you need them in the future.

Figure 5-19—part 2

❶ Step 1 creates two tables. One is to hold the starting date. The other will contain all the dates of the calendar. Each table has a single column with a date datatype. Oracle and Access are different here only because the datatypes are spelled differently. The beginning date is entered.

❷ In Oracle, all three SQL statements can be run at once. Oracle can run a series of commands. Alternatively, each SQL statement can be run separately.

❸ In Access, each SQL must be run separately. The SQL window in Access can process only a single SQL statement.

❹ Step 2 generates all the dates for one week. It uses the Insert command with a Select statement.

❺ The Begin_date already has a datatype of Date, because the Begin_date column of the Date_constants table has a datatype of Date. Hence, no conversion function is needed here, such as To_date, in contrast with the previous coding technique.

❻ You need to list both tables in the From clause.

Task

Show another way to write the code to list all the days of one week.

Step 1 ❶
Oracle SQL ❷   ## Access SQL ❸

```
create table date_constants        create table date_constants
(begin_date        date);          (begin_date        datetime);

create table one_week              create table one_week
(week_days         date);          (week_days         datetime);

insert into date_constants         insert into date_constants
values ('24-feb-99');              values (#24-feb-99#);
```

Result table—step 1 (Date_constants table)

```
BEGIN_DATE
----------
24-FEB-99
```

Step 2 ❹
Oracle & Access SQL

```
insert into one_week
select begin_date + digit  ❺
from numbers_0_to_9, date_constants  ❻
where digit < 7;
```

Result table—step 2 (One_week table)

```
WEEK_DAYS
---------
24-FEB-99
25-FEB-99
26-FEB-99
27-FEB-99
28-FEB-99
01-MAR-99
02-MAR-99
```

Figure 5-19   Listing all the days of one week (part 2 of 3)

Figure 5-19 - part 3

❶   Step 3 applies date formats to the dates and creates the three columns of the final listing.

❷❸   The Week_days column already has a datatype of Date. Also, it already contains data for all the days of the week. These dates are formatted using the To_char function in Oracle and the Format function in Access.

This avoids the complexity of the previous coding technique. Here, only a single function is used at a time. In the previous code, one function had to be embedded within another.

❹   The data is taken from the One_week table, which you created in the previous step.

❺   The Order By clause can sort the days in date order. This code is easier to understand than the previous code, which said "Order By digit."

This method is longer than the previous method, in that it has more code and more steps. However, each individual step is simpler and easier to code. In this example, the benefits of the second method may not be apparent. But when a problem is very complex, the second method can be checked and debugged much more easily than the first. Often, you will get the correct result much more quickly using the longer method.

Step 3 ❶

Oracle SQL

```
select week_days,
       to_char(week_days, 'dy') ❷
              as abbreviated_day,
       to_char(week_days, 'day')
              as full_day
from one_week ❹
order by week_days; ❺
```

Access SQL

```
select week_days,
       format(week_days, 'ddd') ❸
              as abbreviated_day,
       format(week_days, 'dddd')
              as full_day
from one_week
order by week_days;
```

Result table

```
DAYS        ABBREVIATED_DAY       FULL_DAY
---------   --------------------  --------------------
24-FEB-99   WED                   WEDNESDAY
25-FEB-99   THU                   THURSDAY
26-FEB-99   FRI                   FRIDAY
27-FEB-99   SAT                   SATURDAY
28-FEB-99   SUN                   SUNDAY
01-MAR-99   MON                   MONDAY
02-MAR-99   TUE                   TUESDAY
```

Figure 5-19   Listing all the days of one week (part 3 of 3)

Summary

In this chapter, you learned how to use row functions to create values that are not in the original table. You learned that a wide variety of row functions exists, as well as many more in the technical manuals that we did not have time to examine. You also learned to create patterns by using row functions along with a table of integers.

Exercises

1. Goal: Test some row functions with specific values to see what they do.

(Suggestion for people using Access: Create a table with one row and one column. Name the table DUAL. Put in any data you like, such as an A. Then you can use this to test the row functions.)

1A. Test addition by adding 12 and 34.

Oracle & Access SQL

```
select 12 + 34 from dual;
```

1B. Test the following row functions. The Oracle and Access versions do the same things

Purpose	Oracle	Access
nulls in arithmetic	12 + null	12 + null
concatenation	'first' || 'second'	'first' & 'second'
substring	substr('abcdefghij',3,4)	mid('abcdefghij',3,4)
	before the next exercises: 1. set sqlcase mixed 2. select ('AbCd') from dual	
upper case	upper('abcd')	ucase('abcd')
lower case	lower('ABCD')	lcase('ABCD')
initial capital	initcap('ABC DEF')	StrConv('ABC DEF', 3)
	now reset your userid: 1. set sqlcase upper	
length of text	length('abcdefg')	Len('abcdefg')
starting position, when the second string is part of the first	instr('abcdefg', 'cd')	InStr('abcdefg','cd')
starting position, when it is not	instr('abcdefg','zz')	InStr('abcdefg','zz')
add days to a date	to_date('07-mar-99') + 2	#07-mar-99# + 2
add months to a date	add_months (to_date('07-mar-99'),2)	DateAdd('m',2,#07-mar-99#)
add years to a date	add_months (to_date('07-mar-99'),24)	DateAdd('y',2,#07-mar-99#)
find the number of days between two dates	to_date('27-mar-99') - to_date('07-mar-99)	#27-mar-99# - #07-mar-99#

2. Test the row functions on numbers using the table of numbers from 0 to 9.

2A. Test division by dividing all the numbers from 0 to9 by 3. List both the number being divided and the answer.

Oracle & Access SQL

```
select digit,
       digit / 3 as answer
from numbers_0_to_9;
```

2B. Test the following functions.

Purpose	Oracle	Access
addition	digit + 100	digit + 100
subtraction	5 - digit	5 - digit
multiplication	25 * digit	25 * digit
division	10 / (digit + 1)	10 / (digit + 1)
exponents	power(2, digit)	2^digit
square root	sqrt(digit)	sqr(digit)
integer division	(skip this one) or see figure 5-5	digit \ 3
remainder after division	mod(digit,3)	(skip this one) or see figure 5-5
sign	sign(digit - 5)	sgn(digit - 5)
absolute value	abs(digit - 5)	abs(digit - 5)

3. Goal: Use SQL to solve an equation in algebra. This uses "numeric methods" to find the solution to any equation - with as much precision as you want to have.

3A. Find a solution to the following equation between 0 and 99. Make your solution accurate to two decimal places.

$$4X3 - 100X2 + 2X - 20500 = 0$$

solution:

Step 1. Calculate the function for every integer between 0 and 99.
Oracle & Access SQL

```
select n,
       4 * n * n * n - 100 * n * n + 2 * n - 20500 as value_of_function
from numbers_0_to_99
order by n;
```

Step 2. Find the places where the value of the function crosses zero - where it goes from positive to negative or vice versa. These are the solutions to the equation (to within a certain precision). In this case, it crosses zero between 30 and 31

Step 3. Construct a table with the numbers with two decimal places between 30 and 31.

Oracle SQL	Access SQL
```create table numbers_30_to_31 as select 30 + (n / 100) as x from numbers_0_to_99;```	```select 30 + (n / 100) as x into numbers_30_to_31 from numbers_0_to_99;```

Step 4. Look at the table to make sure it is correct.
Oracle & Access SQL

```
select *
from numbers_30_to_31
order by x;
```

Step 5. Calculate the function for all the numbers with two decimal places between 30 and 31.
Oracle & Access SQL

```
select x,
       (4 * x * x * x) - (100 * x * x) + 2 * x - 20500 as value_of_function
from numbers_30_to_31
order by x;
```

Step 6. Find the place where the function crosses zero. This gives the solution to the equation with a greater level of precision. In this case, the solution to the equation is between 30.49 and 30.50.

3B. Find a solution to the following equation between 0 an 99. Find the solution accurate to one decimal place.

$$5X2 - 208X - 125 = 0$$

4. Goal: Create a calendar of dates with some special features. (Use a method similar to figure 5-19, part 2)

4A. Create a calendar showing the workdays, Monday through Friday, for March, April, and May of 2001. List the day of the week in one column and the date in the format MM/DD/YYYY in the next column. Leave one blank line between the weeks.

Solution
Step 1. Create a table to hold the starting and ending dates. Put data in this table. Look at it to make sure it is correct.

Oracle SQL

Access SQL

Oracle SQL	Access SQL
| ```
create table boundaries
(start_date        date,
end_date          date);
``` | ```
create table boundaries
(start_date        datetime,
end_date          datetime);
``` |
| ```
insert into boundaries values
(to_date('01-03-2001',
        'dd-mm-yyyy'),
to_date('31-05-2001',
        'dd-mm-yyyy'));
``` | ```
insert into boundaries values
(#01-mar-2001#, #31-may-2001#);
``` |
| ```
select * from boundaries;
``` | (Same as Oracle.) |
```

Step 2. Create a calendar table with one column for numbers and another for the dates. The numbers will be needed to position the blank lines in the correct places, Put data into the calendar, using the table of numbers from 0 to 99. Then look at this data to make sure it is correct.

Oracle SQL   Access SQL

Oracle SQL	Access SQL

```create table calendar```
 ```(num_1 integer,```
 ```date_1 date);```
	```create table calendar```
	 ```(num_1 short,```
	 ```date_1 datetime);```

```insert into calendar```
 ```select n,```
 ```   start_date + n```
 ```from numbers_0_to_99,```
 ```   boundaries```
 ```where start_date + n <= end_date;```
	```insert into calendar```
	 ```(num_1,date_1)```
	 ```select n,```
	 ``` start_date + n```
	 ```from numbers_0_to_99,```
	 ``` boundaries```
	 ```where start_date + n <= end_date;```

```select *```
 ```from calendar```
 ```order by num_1;```
	```select *```
	 ```from calendar```
	 ```order by num_1;```

Step 3. Delete the rows for Sundays from the calendar table. Change the Saturdays to nulls. They will become the blank rows.

Oracle SQL   Access SQL

Oracle SQL	Access SQL
```delete from calendar``` ```where to_char(date_1, 'dy') = 'sun';```	```delete from calendar``` ```where format(date_1, 'ddd') = 'sun';```

```update calendar```
 ``` set date_1 = null```
 ```where to_char(date_1, 'dy') = 'sat';```
	```update calendar```
	 ``` set date_1 = null```
	 ```where format(date_1, 'ddd') = 'sat';```

Step 4. In Oracle, make the nulls appear as blanks. This is an SQLplus command.

Oracle SQL   Access SQL

Oracle SQL	Access SQL
```set null ' '```	(In Access, nulls already appear as blanks.)

Step 5. List the dates as specified, putting a blank line between the weeks. The date is listed twice, in two different columns, but with different formatting.

Oracle SQL

```
column day_of_the_week format a15;
select to_char(date_1, 'day') as day_of_the_week,
       to_char(date_1, 'mm/dd/yyyy') as work_day
from calendar
order by num_1;
```

Access SQL

```
select format(date_1, 'dddd') as day_of_the_week,
       format(date_1, 'mm/dd/yyyy') as work_day
from calendar
order by num_1;
```

Step 6 In Oracle, reset SQLplus to show the nulls.

Oracle SQL	Access SQL
`set null '(null)'`	(This step is not needed.)

4B. Create a calendar showing all the weekends, Saturday and Sunday, for a two month period after your next birthday. List these dates in a format like 'June 5, 1999.' In a second column, put the abbreviation on the day, 'Sat' or 'Sun.' Put one blank line between the weeks.

4C. Create a table that is a calendar for all the days of your life. Start with the day you were born and enter a row with the date for every day that you plan to be alive. If you plan to live about 110 years, then there will be about 40,000 rows in the table.

Only 40,000 rows! That is almost nothing! Database tables often contain millions of rows. Any table with less than 100,000 rows is often considered to be small—almost trivial. No wonder we do not get much done in our lives—we live for such a very short amount of time.

5. Separate the first name from the last name when they are both in the same column.

5A. The table EX5_5 contains one column that contains both the first and last name of several people. Add a new column to the table that contains only the first names.

Solution.
Step 1. Add a new column to the table.

Oracle SQL   Access SQL

`alter table ex5_5` `add first_name  varchar2(15);`	`alter table ex5_5` `add column first_name  text(15);`
`select * from ex5_5;`	(Same as Oracle.)

Step 2. (This shows the thought process. You might be able to solve the problem without it.) List the full names and the position of the space between the first and last name.

Oracle & Access SQL

```
select full_name,
       instr(full_name, ' ')
from ex5_5;
```

Step 3. (This shows the thought process. You might be able to solve the problem without it.) List the full names and then just the first name. Remove the blank space from the end of the first name.

Oracle SQL

```
select full_name,
       substr(full_name, 1, instr(full_name, ' ') - 1) as first_name
from ex5_5;
```

Access SQL

```
select full_name,
       mid(full_name, 1, instr(full_name, ' ') - 1) as first_name
from ex5_5;
```

Step 4. Put the first names in the new column.

Oracle SQL

```
update ex5_5
  set first_name = substr(full_name, 1, instr(full_name, ' ') - 1);
```

Access SQL

```
update ex5_5
  set first_name = mid(full_name, 1, instr(full_name, ' ') - 1);
```

Step 5. Look at the final result.

Oracle & Access SQL

```
select * from ex5_5;
```

5B. Add a new column to the table EX5_5 and put the last names in it.
(Hint: If no length is given to the SUBSTR function, it goes to the end of the text string.)

6A. Find out how many days old you are.

Solution 1—Enter your birthdate directly. In Oracle, since you are entering it as a character string, you must convert it to a date before you can calculate on it.

Oracle SQL   Access SQL

```
select sysdate - to_date('20-sep-71')  | select now() - #20-sep-71#
from dual;                             | from dual;
```

Solution 2—Create a table that contains your birthdate. Since the data is already a date within the table, it is not necessary to convert it to a date.

Oracke SQL   Access SQL

`create table my_info`
`(birth_date date);`
 	
`insert into my_info`
`values ('20-sep-71');`
 	
`select sysdate - birth_date`
`from my_info;`
	`create table my_info`
	`(birth_date datetime);`
	
	`insert into my_info`
	`values (#20-sep-71#);`
	
	`select now() - birth_date`
	`from my_info;`

6B. Find out the date when you will be 15,000 days old.
(Hint: Add 15000 to your birthdate.)

Chapter 6

Summarizing Data

In the previous chapters, the data in the result table came directly from the beginning table or was a function of a single row of that table. In this chapter, the data in the result table can summarize the data in an entire column of the beginning table.

Introduction to the Column Functions

The data in a table is summarized using column functions. These functions examine all the data in a column, and every row of the table is involved. You can control the level of summarization. You can create one summary for the entire table or you can divide the table into groups of rows and get a summary for each group.

Summary of all the data in a column

Figure 6-1 is a conceptual drawing that shows the way a column function works when it is applied to the whole table. All the data in a single column is summarized and produces one result. For example, the result might be the sum of all the numbers in the column.

The column can be a row function as well as a column of data stored on the disk. Any of the row functions you studied in Chapter 5 can create a new column. A column function can then operate on it.

This summary extends over all the rows in the entire table, which may be hundreds, thousands, or even millions of rows. The data in all these rows is condensed into a single number, text string, or date.

Several different column functions exist. Each one summarizes the data in a different way. One gets the maximum value, one gets the average, and one gets the minimum. There are several others; Figure 6-3 lists all of them.

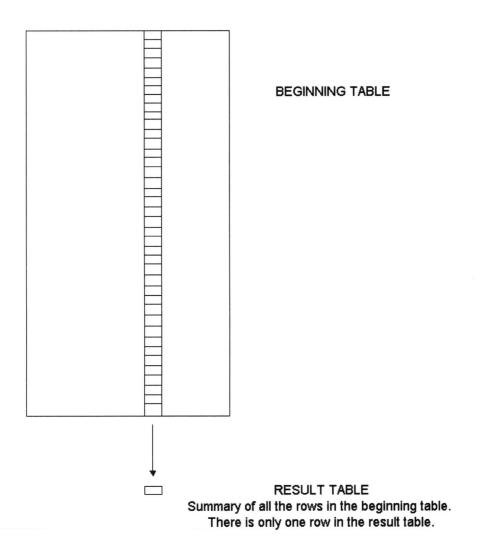

BEGINNING TABLE

RESULT TABLE
Summary of all the rows in the beginning table.
There is only one row in the result table.

Figure 6-1   Summary of all the data in a column

Summary of groups of data within a column

Figure 6-2 is a conceptual drawing that shows the way a column function works when it is applied to groups of rows within a table. Each row of the table is assigned to a group. Each row can be part of only a single group.

The column function produces a summary of each group of rows. This summary is a single value for each group. So the result of the column function has one row for every group of rows in the beginning table.

Hence, the number of groups in the beginning table determines the level of summarization, how detailed and fine-grained it is. At one extreme, each row of the beginning table can be a separate group. Then no summarization occurs. At the other extreme, all the rows of the beginning table can be put into a single group. This is the case when we summarize the entire table, as in Figure 6-1. Then all the data within the column is condensed down to a single entry—a single number, text item, or date.

BEGINNING TABLE

RESULT TABLE
Summary of each group of rows.
There is one row in the result for
every group of rows in the beginning
table.

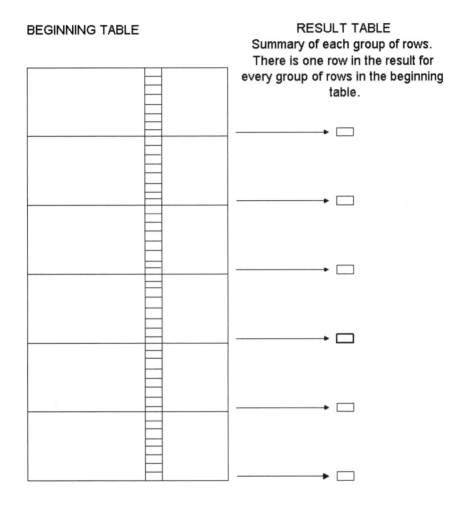

Figure 6-2   Summary of groups of data within a column

A list of the column functions

Figure 6-3 lists the column functions. Each one produces a different type of summarization. They are explained in detail in the next few pages. Column functions are also called "aggregate functions" or "group functions."

Compared to the row functions, only a few column functions exist—only seven main ones, to be exact, not counting the Standard Deviation or Variance functions, which are mostly used in statistics. This total also does not count two-column functions that are seldom used, the sum, and average of the distinct values within a column.

Of course, some SQL products extend this list and define other column functions for special purposes.

Nulls are ignored by all the column functions—except one

The column functions ignore nulls in the data. Nulls are treated as if they did not exist. The one exception is the COUNT(*) function, which does count nulls and treats them like any other type of data.

The reason that nulls are treated this way is that it is the way that summarization usually deals with unknown values. SQL has not created any new rules here. It has only followed the standard way that summarization is done.

Column Functions

Oracle SQL	Access SQL	Meaning
Column functions for text, number, and date columns		
Max	Max	Maximum value in the column.
Min	Min	Minimum value in the column.
Count (*)	Count(*)	Total number of rows in the table.
Count (column)	Count(column)	Number of rows in the column that are not Null.
Count (distinct column)	Not available as a column function, but the same result can be achieved by another method	Number of distinct values in the column.
Column functions for numeric columns only		
Sum	Sum	Sum of all the values in a column.
Avg	Avg	Average of all the values in a column.
Stddev—(two Ds)	Stdev—(one D)	Standard deviation
Variance	Var	Variance

Examples

Column Function	Text	Number	Date
(Data)	Apple	1	25-jan-55
	Banana	2	null
	Cherry	null	21-jan-33
	null	2	17-jan-99
	Peach	3	19-jan-82
Minimum	Apple	1	21-jan-33
Maximum	Peach	3	17-jan-99
Sum	n/a	8	n/a
Average	n/a	8/4 = 2	n/a
Count(*)	5	5	5
Count(column)	4	4	4
Count(Distinct column)	4	3	4

Figure 6-3   A list of the column functions

Finding the maximum and minimum values

Figure 6-4 shows how to use a column function. It uses the Minimum and Maximum column functions, showing them applied to three columns. These columns have datatypes of Text, Numbers, and Dates.

The result of a column function is always a single value. Note that the result table in this example contains only a single row. This single value summarizes all the values in the entire column within all the rows of the table.

When the query does not contain a Where clause, the column function applies to all the rows in the table. Figure 6-5 shows the effect of a Where clause.

Nulls and column functions

Column functions ignore nulls. So where nulls are placed in the sort order doesn't matter—whether they come first, as in Access, or last, as in Oracle. The maximum or minimum value will not be affected by any nulls the column may contain. The maximum and minimum are never a null, unless the entire column is null.

A few people get upset about this fact. They argue that if a column contains even one null, which is an unknown value, then the maximum or minimum is unknown. So it should be a null. For those people, I want to make the following points:

1. Summarization always deals with the known data and ignores the unknown data. This approach is part of the process of summarization. It is not a feature that is unique to SQL.
2. If summarization handled nulls in the way they suggest, then almost all summarized values would be nulls. A single null would be more important than thousands of known values. Then summarization itself would be ineffective. So the process of summarization cannot treat nulls in the way they suggest.

A person can object to all summarization, but that is another matter.

3. The result of every SQL query is based on the data as it is right now. We can never obtain some "ultimately perfect" database. We almost never can know every detail we would like to know about any topic.
4. If you really want the null to dominate all the known values, you can do that. (You will need to substitute an extreme value for the null.)

Figure 6-4

❶   The Minimum function is applied to the Credit Limit column, a numeric column. The numeric order is used to decide the minimum value.

❷   The Maximum function is applied to the Last Name column, a text column. The alphabetic order is used to decide the maximum value.

❸   The Maximum function is applied to the Hire Date column, a date column. The date order is used to decide the maximum value.

❹   The result table contains only one row. Note that in Oracle the column headings for the text and date columns are truncated.

Task

Find the following:

> The minimum Credit Limit given to any employee.
> The maximum Credit Limit given to any employee.
> The Last Name for any employee that comes at the end of an alphabetical listing.
> The latest date when any of the employees was hired.

Oracle & Access SQL

```
select min(credit_limit), ❶
       max(credit_limit),
       max(last_name), ❷
       max(hire_date) ❸
from l_employees;
```

Beginning table (L_employees table)

```
EMPLOYEE                          DEPT            CREDIT PHONE   MANAGER
      ID FIRST_NAME LAST_NAME     CODE HIRE_DATE  LIMIT NUMBER      ID
-------- ---------- ----------    ---- ---------- ------ ------ -------
     201 SUSAN      BROWN         EXE  01-JUN-92  $30.00 3484   (null)
     202 JIM        KERN          SAL  15-AUG-95  $25.00 8722      201
     203 MARTHA     WOODS         SHP  01-FEB-97  $25.00 7591      201
     204 ELLEN      OWENS         SAL  01-JUL-96  $15.00 6830      202
     205 HENRY      PERKINS       SAL  01-MAR-98  $25.00 5286      202
     206 CAROL      ROSE          ACT  15-OCT-97  $15.00 3829      201
     207 DAN        SMITH         SHP  01-DEC-96  $25.00 2259      203
     208 FRED       CAMPBELL      SHP  01-APR-97  $25.00 1752      203
     209 PAULA      JACOBS        MKT  17-MAR-98  $15.00 3357      201
     210 NANCY      HOFFMAN       SAL  15-FEB-96  $25.00 2974      203
```

Result table ❹

```
MIN(CREDIT_LIMIT) MAX(CREDIT_LIMIT) MAX(LAST_N MAX(HIRE_
----------------- ----------------- ---------- ---------
               15                30 WOODS      17-MAR-98
```

Figure 6-4   Finding the maximum and minimum values

Using a Where clause with a column function

When a Where clause is used in a query that contains a column function, the Where clause is applied first. The column function is applied only to the rows that satisfy the Where condition—not to all the rows of the table.

Figure 6-5 shows the same query used in Figure 6-6, with the addition of a Where clause. This changes some of the values in the result table.

Figure 6-5
❶   The Where clause limits the scope of the column functions to consider only employees 202 to 206.
❷   The Where clause is applied first. In effect, this reduces the number of rows in the beginning table.

Task

Same task as for Figure 6-4, but only for some of the rows of the table.
Find the following:

> The minimum Credit Limit given to any employee.
> The maximum Credit Limit given to any employee.
> The Last Name for any employee that comes at the end of an alphabetical listing.
> The latest date when any of the employees was hired.

Limit this to employees 202 to 206.

Oracle & Access SQL

```
select min(credit_limit),
       max(credit_limit),
       max(last_name),
       max(hire_date)
from l_employees
where employee_id between 202 and 206; ❶
```

Beginning table (L_employees table)

```
EMPLOYEE                         DEPT            CREDIT PHONE  MANAGER
      ID FIRST_NAME LAST_NAME    CODE HIRE_DATE   LIMIT NUMBER      ID
-------- ---------- ----------   ---- ---------- ------ ------ -------
     201 SUSAN      BROWN        EXE  01-JUN-92  $30.00 3484   (null)
     202 JIM        KERN         SAL  15-AUG-95  $25.00 8722      201
     203 MARTHA     WOODS        SHP  01-FEB-97  $25.00 7591      201
     204 ELLEN      OWENS        SAL  01-JUL-96  $15.00 6830      202
     205 HENRY      PERKINS      SAL  01-MAR-98  $25.00 5286      202
     206 CAROL      ROSE         ACT  15-OCT-97  $15.00 3829      201
     207 DAN        SMITH        SHP  01-DEC-96  $25.00 2259      203
     208 FRED       CAMPBELL     SHP  01-APR-97  $25.00 1752      203
     209 PAULA      JACOBS       MKT  17-MAR-98  $15.00 3357      201
     210 NANCY      HOFFMAN      SAL  15-FEB-96  $25.00 2974      203
```

Rows of the table after the Where clause is applied ❷

```
EMPLOYEE                         DEPT            CREDIT PHONE  MANAGER
      ID FIRST_NAME LAST_NAME    CODE HIRE_DATE   LIMIT NUMBER      ID
-------- ---------- ----------   ---- ---------- ------ ------ -------
     202 JIM        KERN         SAL  15-AUG-95  $25.00 8722      201
     203 MARTHA     WOODS        SHP  01-FEB-97  $25.00 7591      201
     204 ELLEN      OWENS        SAL  01-JUL-96  $15.00 6830      202
     205 HENRY      PERKINS      SAL  01-MAR-98  $25.00 5286      202
     206 CAROL      ROSE         ACT  15-OCT-97  $15.00 3829      201
```

Result table

```
MIN(CREDIT_LIMIT) MAX(CREDIT_LIMIT) MAX(LAST_N MAX(HIRE_
----------------- ----------------- ---------- ---------
               15                25 WOODS      01-MAR-98
```

Figure 6-5   Using a Where clause with a column function

Finding the rows that have the maximum or minimum value

Often, finding the maximum or minimum value in a column is not enough. You want to find out more information about the row or rows where the maximum or minimum value occurs. Figure 6-6 shows two techniques to achieve this goal.

Be sure to remember that several rows may all have the minimum or maximum value. In the Employees table, only one row has the maximum value. So asking "Which row has the maximum value?" is okay. However, three rows have the minimum value. So the question "Which row has the minimum value?" contains an incorrect assumption that only one such row exists.

Incidentally, you can see that no column function is able to display the additional information that Figure 6-6 requires. The result table of a column function is always one single row. But in Figure 6-6, the result table contains three rows.

These two methods are very similar. The difference is that the first one relies on you to enter the value 15.00. The second one uses an inner Select statement to calculate the 15.00 and substitute it into the outer query.

Figure 6-6

❶   In the first method, you run two separate queries. The first one finds the correct value of the maximum or minimum. In this example, you want to find the minimum, which is 15. You take this value and use it in the Where clause of the second query. This method relies on you to transfer the information from the result table of the first query to the SQL code of the second query.

❷   This finds the smallest Credit Limit that any of the employees has. The result is $15.00.

❸   A second query gets additional information about the employees who have the minimum Credit Limit.

❹   The value "15.00" is obtained from the result of the first query. The dollar sign is dropped. Numbers within SQL code may not contain dollar signs or commas.

The decimal point and two zeros are optional. They are written here to show that this value is a currency value. It could also be written as "15"—without the decimal point and zeros.

❺   The second method uses a subquery to get the minimum value. A subquery is a Select statement embedded within another Select statement. I discuss them further in Chapter 9. In this case, the inner Select statement is evaluated first. It obtains the minimum value for the credit limit, which is 15.00. The computer substitutes this result in the outer Select statement, replacing the inner Select statement. Then the outer query is evaluated, giving the result table.

The benefit of this method is that it uses only one query. Also, it does not rely on you to transfer data from one query to another.

❻   This is the subquery.

Task

Find the employees that have the minimum credit limit.

Method 1 ❶
Oracle & Access SQL—step 1 ❷

```
select min(credit_limit)
from l_employees;
```

Oracle & Access SQL—step 2 ❸

```
select employee_id, first_name, last_name, credit_limit
from l_employees
where credit_limit = 15.00 ❹
order by employee_id;
```

Method 2 ❺
Oracle & Access SQL

```
select employee_id, first_name, last_name, credit_limit
from l_employees
where credit_limit = (select min(credit_limit) ❻
                      from l_employees)
order by employee_id;
```

Beginning table (L_employees table)

EMPLOYEE ID	FIRST_NAME	LAST_NAME	DEPT CODE	HIRE_DATE	CREDIT LIMIT	PHONE NUMBER	MANAGER ID
201	SUSAN	BROWN	EXE	01-JUN-92	$30.00	3484	(null)
202	JIM	KERN	SAL	15-AUG-95	$25.00	8722	201
203	MARTHA	WOODS	SHP	01-FEB-97	$25.00	7591	201
204	ELLEN	OWENS	SAL	01-JUL-96	$15.00	6830	202
205	HENRY	PERKINS	SAL	01-MAR-98	$25.00	5286	202
206	CAROL	ROSE	ACT	15-OCT-97	$15.00	3829	201
207	DAN	SMITH	SHP	01-DEC-96	$25.00	2259	203
208	FRED	CAMPBELL	SHP	01-APR-97	$25.00	1752	203
209	PAULA	JACOBS	MKT	17-MAR-98	$15.00	3357	201
210	NANCY	HOFFMAN	SAL	15-FEB-96	$25.00	2974	203

Result table

EMPLOYEE ID	FIRST_NAME	LAST_NAME	CREDIT LIMIT
204	ELLEN	OWENS	$15.00
206	CAROL	ROSE	$15.00
209	PAULA	JACOBS	$15.00

Figure 6-6   Finding the rows with the maximum or minimum value

Two types of counting: counting rows and counting data

SQL has two different methods of counting the values in a column. They differ in how they count nulls. Also, a third method counts the number of different values in the column. In Figure 6-9, I discuss that type of counting.

Figure 6-7 shows the two varieties of the COUNT column functions. It shows COUNT(*), and it shows that COUNT(column) can be applied to columns that are numbers, text, and dates. It also shows that nulls are not counted by the COUNT(column) function.

Counting all the rows in a table

The COUNT(*) function counts all the rows in the table. The result is the same as if all the values in any column were counted, including the nulls. This is the only column function that treats nulls the same way that it treats other values.

You can think of this function in two ways. If you think of it as counting all the rows in a table, then any nulls in the table do not get involved in this.

If you think of it as counting all the values in a column, then all the nulls are included in the count. No matter which column is counted, the result is the same for every column. You are free to think about the function in either way.

Counting all the values in a column, excluding nulls

The COUNT(column) function counts all the values in the specified column that are not nulls. It tells you how much data is entered in the column. Clearly, each column can have a different count. The column can have any datatype—text, number, or date.

Figure 6-7

❶   Count(*) finds the number of rows in the table.

❷   This applies the Count(column) function to a text column.

❸   This applies the Count(column) function to a date column.

❹   This applies the Count(column) function to a column of numbers. The result is 9 because one null is in this column.

❺   The result table contains only one row.

Task

Count the number of rows in the Employee table. Also, count the number of non-null values in these three columns:

Last Name

Hire Date

Manager Id

Oracle & Access SQL

```
select count(*),  ❶
       count(last_name),  ❷
       count(hire_date),  ❸
       count(manager_id)  ❹
from l_employees;
```

Beginning table (L_Employees table)

```
EMPLOYEE                       DEPT              CREDIT PHONE   MANAGER
      ID FIRST_NAME LAST_NAME  CODE HIRE_DATE    LIMIT  NUMBER      ID
-------- ---------- ---------- ---- ----------   ------ ------ -------
     201 SUSAN      BROWN      EXE  01-JUN-92    $30.00 3484   (null)
     202 JIM        KERN       SAL  15-AUG-95    $25.00 8722      201
     203 MARTHA     WOODS      SHP  01-FEB-97    $25.00 7591      201
     204 ELLEN      OWENS      SAL  01-JUL-96    $15.00 6830      202
     205 HENRY      PERKINS    SAL  01-MAR-98    $25.00 5286      202
     206 CAROL      ROSE       ACT  15-OCT-97    $15.00 3829      201
     207 DAN        SMITH      SHP  01-DEC-96    $25.00 2259      203
     208 FRED       CAMPBELL   SHP  01-APR-97    $25.00 1752      203
     209 PAULA      JACOBS     MKT  17-MAR-98    $15.00 3357      201
     210 NANCY      HOFFMAN    SAL  15-FEB-96    $25.00 2974      203
```

Result table ❺

```
 COUNT(*)  COUNT(LAST_NAME)  COUNT(HIRE_DATE)  COUNT(MANAGER_ID)
--------- ---------------- ---------------- -----------------
      10               10               10                 9
```

Figure 6-7   Two types of counting: counting rows and counting data

Counting to zero

Figure 6-8 shows that when the Count(column) function is applied to a column of nulls, the result is zero. When you want zeros to appear in your result, usually you must use the Count(column) function and not the function Count(*).

You will see this feature used later in this chapter, in "Dividing a table into groups of rows and summarizing each group." If you want to show a zero for groups without data in some column, then you usually use the column function Count(column).

Figure 6-8

❶   The Count(*) function counts all five rows in the table.

❷   The Count(column) function, on the column Col_2, counts the number of rows that are not null. If all the rows are null, then it produces a zero.

Task

Count the number of rows in the table below. Also, count the amount of data in Col_2 and show a zero as the result.

Oracle & Access SQL

```
select count(*), ❶
     count(col_2) ❷
from figure6_8;
```

Beginning table (Figure6_8 table)

```
PK_1 COL_2
---- ------
A    (null)
B    (null)
C    (null)
D    (null)
E    (null)
```

Result table

```
COUNT(*)  COUNT(COL_2)
--------- ------------
       5            0
```

Figure 6-8   Counting to zero

Counting the number of distinct values in a column

Figure 6-9 shows how to count the number of different values in a column. Nulls are not counted as values. You can use this technique to find out how many different codes are in a column.

In Oracle, the function COUNT(DISTINCT column) produces this result.

In Access, you must use two steps. Access supports SELECT DISTINCT, but it does not support the use of Distinct within column functions.

The first step creates a table or a view containing all the distinct values within the column. The null is included in this list. The second step counts the values in this table, without counting the null. This gives the correct result.

Figure 6-9

❶   In Oracle, you can use the Count(Distinct column) function.

❷   In Access, you must write two separate queries. You must run each one separately.

❸   In Access, the first query creates a table containing all the different values, including the null. If several nulls were in the Manager Id column of the beginning table, still only one null would be in the temporary table. That is, Select Distinct treats all nulls as though they have the same value, even though they are all unknown values.

The term "Temporary Table" is a bit of a contradiction. All tables are permanent within the database. This one is called temporary, because we intend to delete it after the result has been obtained. To delete it, you can use the command:

```
Drop table temp_manager;
```

❹   In Access, the second query uses the function Count(column).

Task

Find the number of different values in the Manager Id column of the Employees table.

Oracle SQL ❶

```
select count(distinct manager_id)
from l_employees;
```

Access SQL ❷

```
select distinct manager_id ❸
into temp_manager
from l_employees;

select count(manager_id) ❹
from temp_manager;
```

Beginning table (L_employees table)

```
EMPLOYEE                        DEPT                 CREDIT PHONE  MANAGER
      ID FIRST_NAME LAST_NAME   CODE HIRE_DATE        LIMIT NUMBER      ID
-------- ---------- ----------  ---- ----------     ------- ------ -------
     201 SUSAN      BROWN       EXE  01-JUN-92      $30.00 3484   (null)
     202 JIM        KERN        SAL  15-AUG-95      $25.00 8722      201
     203 MARTHA     WOODS       SHP  01-FEB-97      $25.00 7591      201
     204 ELLEN      OWENS       SAL  01-JUL-96      $15.00 6830      202
     205 HENRY      PERKINS     SAL  01-MAR-98      $25.00 5286      202
     206 CAROL      ROSE        ACT  15-OCT-97      $15.00 3829      201
     207 DAN        SMITH       SHP  01-DEC-96      $25.00 2259      203
     208 FRED       CAMPBELL    SHP  01-APR-97      $25.00 1752      203
     209 PAULA      JACOBS      MKT  17-MAR-98      $15.00 3357      201
     210 NANCY      HOFFMAN     SAL  15-FEB-96      $25.00 2974      203
```

Temporary table created in Access

Result table

```
COUNT(DISTINCTMANAGER_ID)
-------------------------
                        3
```

Figure 6-9   Counting the number of distinct values in a column

The Sum and Average functions

Figure 6-10 shows an example using the Sum and Average column functions. These functions can be applied only to a column of numbers. Text and date columns are not allowed.

Nulls are ignored by both of these functions. Figure 6-11 shows how this fact can sometimes cause a problem for the Sum function. For the Average function, nulls are ignored both in adding up the column and in counting the number of items to set the divisor.

Figure 6-10

❶   This is an example of the Sum(column) function.

❷   This is an example of the Avg(column) function. It finds the average of the numbers.

❸   The result table contains only one row.

Task

Find the sum and average of all the credit limits in the Employees table.

Oracle & Access SQL

```
select sum(credit_limit), ❶
       avg(credit_limit) ❷
from l_employees;
```

Beginning table (L_employees table)

EMPLOYEE ID	FIRST_NAME	LAST_NAME	DEPT CODE	HIRE_DATE	CREDIT LIMIT	PHONE NUMBER	MANAGER ID
201	SUSAN	BROWN	EXE	01-JUN-92	$30.00	3484	(null)
202	JIM	KERN	SAL	15-AUG-95	$25.00	8722	201
203	MARTHA	WOODS	SHP	01-FEB-97	$25.00	7591	201
204	ELLEN	OWENS	SAL	01-JUL-96	$15.00	6830	202
205	HENRY	PERKINS	SAL	01-MAR-98	$25.00	5286	202
206	CAROL	ROSE	ACT	15-OCT-97	$15.00	3829	201
207	DAN	SMITH	SHP	01-DEC-96	$25.00	2259	203
208	FRED	CAMPBELL	SHP	01-APR-97	$25.00	1752	203
209	PAULA	JACOBS	MKT	17-MAR-98	$15.00	3357	201
210	NANCY	HOFFMAN	SAL	15-FEB-96	$25.00	2974	203

Result table ❸

SUM(CREDIT_LIMIT)	AVG(CREDIT_LIMIT)
225	22.5

Figure 6-10   The Sum and Average functions

The problem with addition and how to solve it

SQL has a problem with addition when:

- Two or more columns are added together.
- Nulls are in some of those columns

One of the properties of addition is that the order in which you add the numbers does not matter. The sum is always the same. Part 1 of Figure 6-11 shows that SQL sometimes violates this property.

The problem is that SQL has two kinds of addition, row addition and column addition. They have different ways of handling nulls.

Row addition adds numbers within one row. It is a row function. Row addition handles a null as an unknown value. So, for example:

```
3 + null = null
```

Column addition adds numbers within one column. It is one of the functions used for summarization. All summarization functions ignore nulls. So, for example:

```
    3
+ null
-------
    3
```

Part 1 of Figure 6-11 shows two columns of numbers, and these columns contain some nulls. When the numbers are added together, the result depends upon the order in which the addition is performed.

When the columns are added first, using column addition, you get the result that the sums of the columns are 6 and 15. Adding these together with row addition, you get

```
6 + 15 = 21.
```

When the rows are added first, using row addition, you get the result that the sums of the rows are 5, null, 8, and null. Adding these together with column addition, you get

```
   5
null
   8
null
----
  13
```

Figure 6-11, part 1

❶ This line adds the columns first.
❷ This line adds the rows first.

The Problem

Task

Add all the number in columns 2 and 3 of the beginning table.

Show that in SQL you get two different answers, depending on the order in which you add the numbers.

If you add each of the columns first, you get one answer.

If you add across the rows first, you get a different answer.

Oracle & Access SQL

```
select sum(col_2) + sum(col_3) as columns_added_first, ❶
       sum(col_2 + col_3) as rows_added_first ❷
from figure6_11;
```

Beginning table (Figure6_11 table)

```
PK_1        COL_2      COL_3
------ --------- ---------
A              1          4
B         (null)          5
C              2          6
D              3 (null)
```

Result table—without changing the nulls to zeros

```
COLUMNS_ADDED_FIRST ROWS_ADDED_FIRST
------------------- ----------------
                 21               13
```

Explanation

Pk_1	Col_2	Col_3		Col_2 + Col_3
A	1	4		5
B	null	5		null
C	2	6		8
D	3	null		null
	------	-----		-----
	6	15	= 21	13

Figure 6-11   The problem with addition and how to solve it (part 1 of 2)

The Solution

Changing the nulls into a numeric value can solve the problem with addition. Usually, the nulls are changed into zeros. In Oracle, the NVL ("null value") function can be used to change the nulls. In Access, you use the NZ function. The nulls must be changed in every column where they occur.

When no nulls exist, row addition and column addition produce the same sums. The order in which the numbers are added does not matter.

Part 2 of Figure 6-11 shows that the problem has been solved. The sum is always 21, whether the columns are added first or the rows are added first.

Figure 6-11, part 2

❶   In Oracle, the NVL function is applied to both columns.
❷   In Access, the NZ function is applied to both columns.

The Solution

Task

Add all the numbers in columns 2 and 3 of the beginning table.

Show that when you change the nulls to zeros, the problem with addition is solved. Then you get the same result whether you add the columns first or the rows first.

Addition—with the nulls changed to zeros
Oracle SQL

```
select sum(nvl(col_2, 0)) + sum(nvl(col_3, 0)) as columns_added_first, ❶
    sum(nvl(col_2, 0) + nvl(col_3, 0)) as rows_added_first
from figure6_11;
```

Access SQL

```
select sum(nz(col_2, 0)) + sum(nz(col_3, 0)) as columns_added_first, ❷
    sum(nz(col_2, 0) + nz(col_3, 0)) as rows_added_first
from figure6_11;
```

Beginning table (Figure6_11 table)

```
PK_1        COL_2      COL_3
------ --------- ---------
A             1          4
B         (null)         5
C             2          6
D             3  (null)
```

Result table—with the nulls changed to zeros

```
COLUMNS_ADDED_FIRST ROWS_ADDED_FIRST
------------------- ----------------
                 21               21
```

Explanation

Pk_1	Col_2	Col_3		Col_2 + Col_3
A	1	4		5
B	0	5		5
C	2	6		8
D	3	0		3
	------	-----		-----
	6	15	= 21	21

Figure 6-11   The problem with addition and how to solve it (part 2 of 2)

A practical example

Figure 6-12 shows an example of giving nulls numeric values to ensure that addition works correctly. In this example, a store has received orders for merchandise, which it will ship to the customers. The store wants to know the total value of all the invoices, where each invoice is calculated with the formula:

(Price * Quantity) + Tax + Shipping = Invoice

The problem is that sometimes the Tax or Shipping columns contain nulls, meaning that the amount is an unknown. In this situation, you need to carefully control how the calculation is performed and how the rows that contain nulls are counted.

You have three choices:

Choice 1

Bill all the amounts we know and estimate an amount for the nulls. To do so:

* change the null in the tax column to an estimate of the tax

* change the nulls in the shipping column to an estimate of the shipping charge

Figure 6-12 shows this solution.

Choice 2

Bill all the amounts we know and nothing for the nulls. To do so, change all the nulls to zeros. This approach is similar to the code in Figure 6-12, except that the second parameter of the NVL and NZ functions is 0. So in Oracle, you have

Oracle SQL

```
select sum((price * quantity)
            + nvl(tax, 0)
            + nvl(shipping, 0))
                as total_invoices
from figure6_12;
```

Access SQL

```
select sum((price * quantity)
            + nz(tax, 0)
            + nz(shipping, 0))
                as total_invoices
from figure6_12;
```

Choice 3

Ignore any invoice with incomplete data. To do so, you do not need to change the nulls at all. Just calculate the invoices first using row addition. Then add the column of invoices.

Oracle & Access SQL

```
select sum((price * quantity) + tax + shipping) as
total_invoices
from figure6_12;
```

Task

Find the total for all the invoices in the table below. Calculate an invoice as:

(Price * Quantity) + Tax + Shipping = Invoice

Estimate values for the nulls that occur in the tax and shipping columns by applying the rules:

- A null in the TAX column is replaced with   0.07 * price * quantity
- A null in the SHIPPING column is replaced with   0.12 * price * quantity

Oracle SQL

```
column total_invoices format $999,990.99
select sum((price * quantity)
          + nvl(tax, 0.07 * price * quantity)
          + nvl(shipping, 0.12 * price * quantity)) as
total_invoices
from figure6_12;
```

Access SQL

```
select sum((price * quantity)
          + nz(tax, 0.07 * price * quantity)
          + nz(shipping, 0.12 * price * quantity)) as
total_invoices
from figure6_12;
```

Beginning table (Figure6_12 table)

PK_1	PRICE	QUANTITY	TAX	SHIPPING
A	$211.00	3	$48.00	$63.00
B	$138.00	7	(null)	$72.00
C	$592.00	1	$51.00	$76.00
D	$329.00	2	$54.00	(null)

Result table

TOTAL_INVOICES
$3,359.58

Figure 6-12   A practical example

Dividing a Table into Groups of Rows and Summarizing Each Group

You can divide the rows of a table into separate groups. The Group By clause in a Select statement can do this division. Then the column functions summarize each group. This approach allows you to control the level of summarization and detail.

The Group By clause

Figure 6-13 shows an example that uses a Group By clause. This divides the rows of the table into groups and controls the level of summarization performed by the column functions.

Figure 6-13

❶   First, the Where clause is applied to the beginning table. It eliminates the rows of all the employees in the Accounting department. Employee 206 is deleted from processing by this Select statement.

❷   Second, the remaining rows of the table are divided into groups by their value in the Manager Id column. This step creates four groups:

> The 3 rows with a manager id of 201.
> The 2 rows with a manager id of 202.
> The 3 rows with a manager id of 203.
> The 1 row with a null in the manager id column.

After this, the column functions summarize the data in each of the groups. They produce one row in the result table for each of the groups.

The result table is usually structured to identify each group and then give summary information about that group. It does not need to be structured this way, but usually that is the most logical way to present the data.

To achieve this result, the Select clause lists the grouping column(s) first, followed by column functions. The Select clause here is organized that way.

❸   Last, the Order By clause sorts the rows of the result table into a logical order. Usually you will list the same columns in the Order By clause that you listed in the Group By clause.

❹   The null value forms a group of its own. Oracle sorts the null at the bottom; Access sorts it at the top.

Task

For each manager, list the number of people they supervise, and the minimum and maximum credit limits of their employees. Omit employees that work in the accounting department.

Oracle & Access SQL

```
select manager_id,
       count(employee_id) as number_of_employees,
       min(credit_limit) as minimum_credit,
       max(credit_limit) as maximum_credit
from l_employees
where not (dept_code = 'act')   ❶
group by manager_id   ❷
order by manager_id;   ❸
```

Beginning table (L_Employees table)

EMPLOYEE ID	FIRST_NAME	LAST_NAME	DEPT CODE	HIRE_DATE	CREDIT LIMIT	PHONE NUMBER	MANAGER ID
201	SUSAN	BROWN	EXE	01-JUN-92	$30.00	3484	(null)
202	JIM	KERN	SAL	15-AUG-95	$25.00	8722	201
203	MARTHA	WOODS	SHP	01-FEB-97	$25.00	7591	201
204	ELLEN	OWENS	SAL	01-JUL-96	$15.00	6830	202
205	HENRY	PERKINS	SAL	01-MAR-98	$25.00	5286	202
206	CAROL	ROSE	ACT	15-OCT-97	$15.00	3829	201
207	DAN	SMITH	SHP	01-DEC-96	$25.00	2259	203
208	FRED	CAMPBELL	SHP	01-APR-97	$25.00	1752	203
209	PAULA	JACOBS	MKT	17-MAR-98	$15.00	3357	201
210	NANCY	HOFFMAN	SAL	15-FEB-96	$25.00	2974	203

Beginning table divided into groups on the Manager Id column

EMPLOYEE ID	FIRST_NAME	LAST_NAME	DEPT CODE	HIRE_DATE	CREDIT LIMIT	PHONE NUMBER	MANAGER ID
202	JIM	KERN	SAL	15-AUG-95	$25.00	8722	201
203	MARTHA	WOODS	SHP	01-FEB-97	$25.00	7591	201
209	PAULA	JACOBS	MKT	17-MAR-98	$15.00	3357	201
204	ELLEN	OWENS	SAL	01-JUL-96	$15.00	6830	202
205	HENRY	PERKINS	SAL	01-MAR-98	$25.00	5286	202
207	DAN	SMITH	SHP	01-DEC-96	$25.00	2259	203
208	FRED	CAMPBELL	SHP	01-APR-97	$25.00	1752	203
210	NANCY	HOFFMAN	SAL	15-FEB-96	$25.00	2974	203
201	SUSAN	BROWN	EXE	01-JUN-92	$30.00	3484	(null)

Result table ❹

MANAGER ID	NUMBER_OF_EMPLOYEES	MINIMUM_CREDIT	MAXIMUM_CREDIT
201	3	15	25
202	2	15	25
203	3	25	25
(null)	1	30	30

Figure 6-13   The Group By clause

Groups formed on two or more columns

Figure 6-14 shows a Group By clause that contains a list of two columns. All the rows that have identical values in both these columns form a group. If two rows have different values in either of these columns, then they belong to different groups.

A Group By clause can list any number of columns. In general, whenever a new column is added to the Group By clause, each prior group splits into one or more new groups. The groups are the same, regardless of the order in which the columns are listed in the Group By clause.

Figure 6-14

❶   Since the Group By clause lists both the Manager Id and Credit Limit columns, including the columns in the Select clause makes sense. The other column in the Select clause is a column function.

❷   The Where clause is applied first. It eliminates a row from the beginning table before the remaining rows are formed into groups.

❸   Groups of rows are formed that have identical values in both the Manager Id and Credit Limit columns.

Then the column functions in the Select clause are evaluated separately for each group. The result table contains one row for each group.

❹   As a last step, the rows of the result table are sorted on the two columns used to create the groups. Though the order of these columns does not matter in the Group By clause, it does matter in the Order By clause. Since the Manager Id is listed first in the Order By clause, the primary sort is done on that column.

Task

For each manager, list the number of people they supervise who have each Credit Limit. Do not include employees who work in the accounting department.

Oracle & Access SQL

```
select manager_id, credit_limit, ❶
       count(employee_id) as number_of_employees
from l_employees
where not (dept_code = 'act') ❷
group by manager_id, credit_limit ❸
order by manager_id, credit_limit; ❹
```

Beginning table (L_Employees table)

EMPLOYEE ID	FIRST_NAME	LAST_NAME	DEPT CODE	HIRE_DATE	CREDIT LIMIT	PHONE NUMBER	MANAGER ID
201	SUSAN	BROWN	EXE	01-JUN-92	$30.00	3484	(null)
202	JIM	KERN	SAL	15-AUG-95	$25.00	8722	201
203	MARTHA	WOODS	SHP	01-FEB-97	$25.00	7591	201
204	ELLEN	OWENS	SAL	01-JUL-96	$15.00	6830	202
205	HENRY	PERKINS	SAL	01-MAR-98	$25.00	5286	202
206	CAROL	ROSE	ACT	15-OCT-97	$15.00	3829	201
207	DAN	SMITH	SHP	01-DEC-96	$25.00	2259	203
208	FRED	CAMPBELL	SHP	01-APR-97	$25.00	1752	203
209	PAULA	JACOBS	MKT	17-MAR-98	$15.00	3357	201
210	NANCY	HOFFMAN	SAL	15-FEB-96	$25.00	2974	203

Table with the rows grouped by Manager Id and Credit Limit

EMPLOYEE ID	FIRST_NAME	LAST_NAME	DEPT CODE	HIRE_DATE	CREDIT LIMIT	PHONE NUMBER	MANAGER ID
209	PAULA	JACOBS	MKT	17-MAR-98	$15.00	3357	201
202	JIM	KERN	SAL	15-AUG-95	$25.00	8722	201
203	MARTHA	WOODS	SHP	01-FEB-97	$25.00	7591	201
204	ELLEN	OWENS	SAL	01-JUL-96	$15.00	6830	202
205	HENRY	PERKINS	SAL	01-MAR-98	$25.00	5286	202
207	DAN	SMITH	SHP	01-DEC-96	$25.00	2259	203
208	FRED	CAMPBELL	SHP	01-APR-97	$25.00	1752	203
210	NANCY	HOFFMAN	SAL	15-FEB-96	$25.00	2974	203
201	SUSAN	BROWN	EXE	01-JUN-92	$30.00	3484	(null)

Result table

MANAGER ID	CREDIT LIMIT	NUMBER_OF_EMPLOYEES
201	$15.00	1
201	$25.00	2
202	$15.00	1
202	$25.00	1
203	$25.00	3
(null)	$30.00	1

Figure 6-14   Groups formed on two or more columns

Summarized data cannot mix with non-summarized data in the same Select statement

A Select statement cannot list both of the following:

- Summarized data
- Detail data, which is not summarized

The reason is that the output of a Select statement must be a table. I have been calling this the "Result table." It must have columns and rows, like any other table.

Why is this a reason? It is a reason because of the number of rows in the result table and the meaning of these rows. Consider the example in Figure 6-15, part 1.

The first two columns of the Select clause are First Name and Last Name. No column functions are applied to theses columns, nor are they listed in the Group By clause, because no Group By clause exists. So these columns list detail data. If the Select clause listed only these columns, the result table would have 10 rows.

Each row of the result table would come from a single row in the beginning table. The result table would be similar to:

```
FIRST_NAME     LAST_NAME
----------     ---------

(10 rows of detail data)
```

The third column uses the Maximum column function, so it is summarized data. If the Select clause listed only this column, the result table would have one row. That row would come from an entire group of rows in the beginning table. In this case, no Group By clause exists, so all the rows of the beginning table are placed into one single group. Thus the one row of the result table is a summary of all the rows of the beginning table.

The result table would be similar to:

```
MAX(CREDIT_LIMIT)
-----------------

(1 row of summarized data)
```

These two tables cannot be combined together to form a single table. For this reason, you are not allowed to mix summarized data and detail data in the same Select statement.

Figure 6-15, part 1

❶   First Name and Last Name are detail data, which is not summarized.

❷   The Maximum Credit Limit is summarized data, because it applies a column function.

❸   In Oracle, the message "Not a single-group group function" refers to the problem discussed in Figure 6-15, part 1. You will probably get this message and wonder what it means.

❹   In Access, the error message is a little better. But it still can be confusing.

Task

Show the error that occurs when a summarized column and a non-summarized column are mixed within the same Select statement.

Oracle & Access SQL—this contains an error

```
select first_name, ❶
       last_name,
       max(credit_limit) ❷
from l_employees;
```

Beginning table (L_employees table)

```
EMPLOYEE                       DEPT             CREDIT PHONE  MANAGER
      ID FIRST_NAME LAST_NAME  CODE HIRE_DATE   LIMIT  NUMBER      ID
-------- ---------- ---------- ---- ----------  ------ ------ -------
     201 SUSAN      BROWN      EXE  01-JUN-92   $30.00 3484   (null)
     202 JIM        KERN       SAL  15-AUG-95   $25.00 8722      201
     203 MARTHA     WOODS      SHP  01-FEB-97   $25.00 7591      201
     204 ELLEN      OWENS      SAL  01-JUL-96   $15.00 6830      202
     205 HENRY      PERKINS    SAL  01-MAR-98   $25.00 5286      202
     206 CAROL      ROSE       ACT  15-OCT-97   $15.00 3829      201
     207 DAN        SMITH      SHP  01-DEC-96   $25.00 2259      203
     208 FRED       CAMPBELL   SHP  01-APR-97   $25.00 1752      203
     209 PAULA      JACOBS     MKT  17-MAR-98   $15.00 3357      201
     210 NANCY      HOFFMAN    SAL  15-FEB-96   $25.00 2974      203
```

Oracle error message—not very helpful

```
SELECT FIRST_NAME,
       *
ERROR at line 1:
ORA-00937: not a single-group group function ❸
```

Access error message—a little better ❹

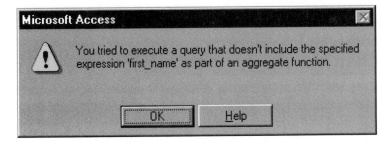

Microsoft Access

You tried to execute a query that doesn't include the specified expression 'first_name' as part of an aggregate function.

[OK]   [Help]

Figure 6-15   Summarized data cannot mix with non-summarized data
in the same Select statement (part 1 of 3)

How to solve the problem

At times, you will attempt to mix summarized data with detail data. It happens to everyone. You will receive the error messages shown in Figure 6-15, part 1. The question is "How do you move on and solve the problem?"

Several techniques are available. Which one you choose depends on what you are trying to do. Here are some things to try and think about how they may relate to your goals:

Figure 6-15, part 2

❶❷   Create two Select statements.

1.   Put all the detail columns in one.
2.   Put all the summarized columns in the other. The summarized columns are the ones that use a column function or are listed in the Group By clause.

This approach helps you see the various kinds of information your query is requesting. It separates the summarized data from the detail data.

❸   Apply a column function to the columns that have detail data. Any column function can get the query to run and produce a result. Sometimes this solution is correct (see Chapter 10 for an example). In this case, it creates a new person, Carol Brown, who is not in the beginning table.

Task

Show some techniques for working with a Select statement that mixes summarized data with detail data.

Oracle & Access SQL ❶

```
select  max(credit_limit)
from l_employees;
```

Result table for ❶

```
MAX(CREDIT_LIMIT)
-----------------
               30
```

Oracle & Access SQL ❷

```
select first_name,
       last_name
from l_employees;
```

Result table for ❷

```
FIRST_NAME LAST_NAME
---------- ----------
SUSAN      BROWN
JIM        KERN
MARTHA     WOODS
ELLEN      OWENS
HENRY      PERKINS
CAROL      ROSE
DAN        SMITH
FRED       CAMPBELL
PAULA      JACOBS
NANCY      HOFFMAN
```

Oracle & Access SQL ❸

```
select min(first_name),
       min(last_name),
       max(credit_limit)
from l_employees;
```

Result table for ,

```
MIN(FIRST_ MIN(LAST_N MAX(CREDIT_LIMIT)
---------- ---------- -----------------
CAROL      BROWN                     30
```

Figure 6-15   Summarized data cannot mix with non-summarized data in the same Select statement (part 2 of 3)

Figure 6-15, part 3

❹   Add the detail columns to the Group By clause. This step creates many new groups.

❺   Substitute a literal value for the summarized columns. Here, I wanted to give the same credit limit to all the employees. I wanted to give them all the maximum credit limit currently in the table.

From ❶, I knew that the maximum credit limit is $30.00. So I placed that amount as a literal value in the Select statement. (A subquery cannot be used to put the maximum value in the Select clause—at least, not until the newer SQL standard is implemented.)

Oracle & Access SQL ❹

```
select first_name,
       last_name,
       max(credit_limit)
from l_employees
group by first_name,
         last_name;
```

Result table for ❹

```
FIRST_NAME LAST_NAME  MAX(CREDIT_LIMIT)
---------- ---------- -----------------
CAROL      ROSE                     15
DAN        SMITH                    25
ELLEN      OWENS                    15
FRED       CAMPBELL                 25
HENRY      PERKINS                  25
JIM        KERN                     25
MARTHA     WOODS                    25
NANCY      HOFFMAN                  25
PAULA      JACOBS                   15
SUSAN      BROWN                    30
```

Oracle & Access SQL ❺

```
select first_name,
       last_name,
       '$30.00' as credit_limit
from l_employees;
```

Result table for ❺

```
                      CREDIT
FIRST_NAME LAST_NAME  LIMIT
---------- ---------- ------
SUSAN      BROWN      $30.00
JIM        KERN       $30.00
MARTHA     WOODS      $30.00
ELLEN      OWENS      $30.00
HENRY      PERKINS    $30.00
CAROL      ROSE       $30.00
DAN        SMITH      $30.00
FRED       CAMPBELL   $30.00
PAULA      JACOBS     $30.00
NANCY      HOFFMAN    $30.00
```

Figure 6-15   Summarized data cannot mix with non-summarized data
in the same Select statement (part 3 of 3)

Null groups in a single grouping column

Figure 6-16 shows that when a grouping column contains nulls, all the nulls are placed into a single group, which is called a "Null group." This shows how nulls are handled in the summarization process when they occur in a column that is used to divide the rows of the beginning table into groups. Nulls are ignored when they occur in a column that is being summarized by a column function, but they are formed into a "null group" when they occur in a grouping column.

The null group is similar to the "Other" category that is often used when data is summarized. It represents the data that does not fit into any of the categories associated with a specific value. It is a "Miscellaneous" category.

Nulls may appear to be handled as if they all have the same value. Indeed, if all the nulls in column 2 are changed to the value "C," then the groups remain the same—they contain the same rows of the beginning table. To handle nulls this way would be incorrect. Nulls represent missing data or unknown values. We should never conclude that two nulls are equal to each other simply because they are both nulls.

"Null = Null" is incorrect

Fortunately, this is only an appearance. It comes about by confusing a category that has a specific value with the "Miscellaneous" category.

The problem with primary keys in the result table

We often say that every table should have a primary key, although we allow a few exceptions. In the result table, the column that identifies the groups is almost a primary key. It does not contain any duplicate values. However, it may contain nulls, and nulls are not allowed in a primary key.

One possible solution is to change the nulls to another value. However, this can cause other problems.

Figure 6-16

❶   In Figure 6-16, the data is grouped on only one column, Col_2.

❷   The Group By clause lists only one column, Col_2.

❸   The result table contains a null group in Col_2. The last column, which contains zeros, is meant to remind you that the Count(column) function is able to result in zero.

Task

Group the table below on the Col_2 column. For each group of rows, calculate:
1.   the number of rows in the group
2.   the number of rows that have data in column Col_4
3.   the number of rows that have data in column Col_5

Oracle & Access SQL

```
select col_2, ❶
       count(*),
       count(col_4),
       count(col_5)
from figure6_16
group by col_2 ❷
order by col_2;
```

Beginning table (Figure6_16 table)

```
    PK_1 COL_2   COL_3   COL_4   COL_5
--------- ------  ------  ------  ------
       1 A       Y       M       (null)
       2 A       Y       (null)  (null)
       3 A       Z       M       (null)
       4 A       Z       (null)  (null)
       5 A       (null)  M       (null)
       6 A       (null)  (null)  (null)

       7 B       Y       M       (null)
       8 B       Y       (null)  (null)
       9 B       Z       M       (null)
      10 B       Z       (null)  (null)
      11 B       (null)  M       (null)
      12 B       (null)  (null)  (null)

      13 (null)  Y       M       (null)
      14 (null)  Y       (null)  (null)
      15 (null)  Z       M       (null)
      16 (null)  Z       (null)  (null)
      17 (null)  (null)  M       (null)
      18 (null)  (null)  (null)  (null)
```

Result table ❸

COL_2	COUNT(*)	COUNT(COL_4)	COUNT(COL_5)
A	6	3	0
B	6	3	0
(null)	6	3	0

Figure 6-16   Null groups in a single grouping column

Null groups in two or more grouping columns

Figure 6-17 is similar to Figure 6-16, except that the data is grouped on two columns instead of one. In this situation, the nulls form separate null groups in the two columns. The nulls in one column are not mixed with the nulls in the other column.

In the result table, this approach creates the five separate null groups highlighted in Figure 6-17. They are not combined to form a single group.

Figure 6-17

❶   The two columns Col_2 and Col_3 are used to group the data from the beginning table.

❷   The Group By clause lists both Col_2 and Col_3.

❸   The result table has five separate null groups.

Task

Group the table below on the two columns Col_2 and Col_3. For each group of rows, calculate:

1. the number of rows in the group
2. the number of rows that have data in column Col_4
3. the number of rows that have data in column Col_5

Oracle & Access SQL

```
select col_2, col_3, ❶
       count(*), count(col_4), count(col_5)
from figure6_16
group by col_2, col_3 ❷
order by col_2, col_3;
```

Beginning table (Figure6_16 table)

PK_1	COL_2	COL_3	COL_4	COL_5
1	A	Y	M	(null)
2	A	Y	(null)	(null)
3	A	Z	M	(null)
4	A	Z	(null)	(null)
5	A	(null)	M	(null)
6	A	(null)	(null)	(null)
7	B	Y	M	(null)
8	B	Y	(null)	(null)
9	B	Z	M	(null)
10	B	Z	(null)	(null)
11	B	(null)	M	(null)
12	B	(null)	(null)	(null)
13	(null)	Y	M	(null)
14	(null)	Y	(null)	(null)
15	(null)	Z	M	(null)
16	(null)	Z	(null)	(null)
17	(null)	(null)	M	(null)
18	(null)	(null)	(null)	(null)

Result table ❸

COL_2	COL_3	COUNT(*)	COUNT(COL_4)	COUNT(COL_5)
A	Y	2	1	0
A	Z	2	1	0
A	(null)	2	1	0
B	Y	2	1	0
B	Z	2	1	0
B	(null)	2	1	0
(null)	Y	2	1	0
(null)	Z	2	1	0
(null)	(null)	2	1	0

Figure 6-17   Null groups in two or more grouping columns

An example

Figure 6-18 shows the number of lunches each employee will attend. This shows three things. One thing it shows is that the Count(column) function is able to place a zero by the names of any employees who are not attending any lunches. In the beginning view, the null in the Lunch Date column expresses the fact that Paula Jacobs is not attending any of the lunches. In the result table, this is shown as a zero.

If the Count(*) function was used instead of the Count(column) function, the result would show a one instead of a zero. This mistake is an easy one to make.

Another thing that Figure 6-17 shows is that the Group By clause must list three columns—the Employee Id, First Name, and Last Name. This requirement might not seem logical. You might think that the Employee Id is the primary key of the Employees table, and therefore it can have only one name associated with it. You might ask, "Why do we need to put the First Name and the Last Name in the Group By clause?"

The reason is that SQL is not intelligent enough to figure out which columns are required in the Group By clause and which columns are not. No attempt has been made to build that kind of intelligence into SQL. You must explicitly name every column that participates in the grouping.

Figure 6-15 showed that you cannot mix summarized data with detail data. One column in the Select clause is summarized, using the Count(column) function. So all the columns must be summarized. That means that every column in the Select clause must be either:

* Summarized by a column function
* Summarized by the Group By clause

Figure 6-18 also introduces the Having clause, which is the subject of Figure 6-19. This shows the query before the Having clause is applied.

Figure 6-18

❶ The three columns on this line do not have column functions applied to them. So they must all be listed in the Group By clause.

❷ The Count(column) function is used on this line. So the result will be summarized data, and all the columns of the Select clause must be summarized.

❸ Figure 6-18 is a view, instead of a table. It can still be used in a From clause, as a source of data for a Select statement.

❹ The Group By clause lists all three columns of the Select clause that do not involve column functions.

❺ The zero in the last column is produced by the Count(column) function.

Task

List the number of lunches each employee will attend. If an employee is not attending any lunches, show a zero. Identify each employee by their Employee Id, First Name, and Last Name.

Oracle & Access SQL

```
select employee_id, first_name, last_name, ❶
       count(lunch_date) ❷
from figure6_18 ❸
group by employee_id, first_name, last_name ❹
order by employee_id; ❺
```

Beginning view (Figure 6-18 view)

```
EMPLOYEE                            LUNCH
      ID FIRST_NAME  LAST_NAME      DATE
-------- ----------  ----------     ----------
     201 SUSAN       BROWN          16-NOV-98
     201 SUSAN       BROWN          25-NOV-98
     201 SUSAN       BROWN          04-DEC-98
     202 JIM         KERN           16-NOV-98
     203 MARTHA      WOODS          16-NOV-98
     203 MARTHA      WOODS          04-DEC-98
     204 ELLEN       OWENS          25-NOV-98
     205 HENRY       PERKINS        25-NOV-98
     205 HENRY       PERKINS        04-DEC-98
     206 CAROL       ROSE           16-NOV-98
     207 DAN         SMITH          16-NOV-98
     207 DAN         SMITH          25-NOV-98
     208 FRED        CAMPBELL       25-NOV-98
     208 FRED        CAMPBELL       04-DEC-98
     209 PAULA       JACOBS         (null)
     210 NANCY       HOFFMAN        16-NOV-98
     210 NANCY       HOFFMAN        04-DEC-98
```

Result table ❻

```
EMPLOYEE
      ID FIRST_NAME  LAST_NAME    COUNT(LUNCH_DATE)
-------- ----------  ----------   -----------------
     201 SUSAN       BROWN                        3
     202 JIM         KERN                         1
     203 MARTHA      WOODS                        2
     204 ELLEN       OWENS                        1
     205 HENRY       PERKINS                      2
     206 CAROL       ROSE                         1
     207 DAN         SMITH                        2
     208 FRED        CAMPBELL                     2
     209 PAULA       JACOBS                       0
     210 NANCY       HOFFMAN                      2
```

Figure 6-18   An example

The Having clause

When the result table contains data that is grouped and summarized, the Having clause can eliminate some of the groups. The groups are still formed. All the calculations and summarization are done. But some of the groups are not displayed or printed in the result table. They are eliminated at the end of the process.

Figure 6-19 shows the same query as Figure 6-20, except that a Having clause is added after the Group By clause. This addition eliminates the employees who are having fewer than two lunches.

For the data shown here, only a few rows are eliminated from the result table. The Having clause is usually used with a larger amount of data. For instance, out of 100 employees, most of them would attend only one lunch. Then the Having clause would help you find the few people who are attending two or more lunches. The Having clause is often used this way—to find exceptions in the data.

The Having clause is always used with a Group By clause. However, a Group By clause is often used without a Having clause. Once the data is grouped, usually you have few enough groups that they can all be displayed or printed. The Having clause is most useful when you have so many groups that to look at them all at once is confusing.

As Figure 6-19 shows, the Having clause is written directly after the Group By clause and before the Order By clause. The Having clause can be compared and contrasted to the Where clause.

Ways that the Having clause is similar to the WHERE clause
- They both set conditions that some data will pass and other data will not pass.
- A null can never satisfy the condition in either a Having clause or a Where clause, except for the Is Null condition.
- They both eliminate data from the result table.

Ways that the Having clause is different from the Where clause
- The Where clause eliminates rows from the beginning table, before any other processing occurs.
- The Having clause eliminates groups of data, after most of the processing has already taken place.
- The Where clause cannot use column functions in the conditions it sets.
- The Having clause can use column functions in its conditions.

Figure 6-19
❶   This is the Having clause. It usually involves a column function.
❷   The rows of the beginning table are grouped and processed in the same way, as if the Having clause was not present.
❸   The Having clause eliminates rows from the result table.

Task

For all the employees who will attend two or more lunches, list the number of lunches each employee will attend. Identify each employee by their Employee Id, First Name, and Last Name.

Oracle & Access SQL

```
select employee_id, first_name, last_name,
       count(lunch_date)
from figure6_18
group by employee_id, first_name, last_name
having count(lunch_date) > 1 ❶
order by employee_id;
```

Beginning view (Figure 6-18 view) ❷

```
EMPLOYEE                          LUNCH
      ID FIRST_NAME LAST_NAME     DATE
-------- ---------- ----------    ----------
     201 SUSAN      BROWN         16-NOV-98
     201 SUSAN      BROWN         25-NOV-98
     201 SUSAN      BROWN         04-DEC-98
     202 JIM        KERN          16-NOV-98
     203 MARTHA     WOODS         16-NOV-98
     203 MARTHA     WOODS         04-DEC-98
     204 ELLEN      OWENS         25-NOV-98
     205 HENRY      PERKINS       25-NOV-98
     205 HENRY      PERKINS       04-DEC-98
     206 CAROL      ROSE          16-NOV-98
     207 DAN        SMITH         16-NOV-98
     207 DAN        SMITH         25-NOV-98
     208 FRED       CAMPBELL      25-NOV-98
     208 FRED       CAMPBELL      04-DEC-98
     209 PAULA      JACOBS        (null)
     210 NANCY      HOFFMAN       16-NOV-98
     210 NANCY      HOFFMAN       04-DEC-98
```

Result table ❸

```
EMPLOYEE
      ID FIRST_NAME LAST_NAME   COUNT(LUNCH_DATE)
-------- ---------- ----------  -----------------
     201 SUSAN      BROWN                       3
     203 MARTHA     WOODS                       2
     205 HENRY      PERKINS                     2
     207 DAN        SMITH                       2
     208 FRED       CAMPBELL                    2
     210 NANCY      HOFFMAN                     2
```

Figure 6-19   The Having clause

Occasions when a Where clause and a Having clause can do the same thing

Both the Where clause and the Having clause place conditions on the data that eliminate some data from the result table. The Where clause eliminates individual rows of data from the beginning table—and so also from the result. The Having clause eliminates groups of data from the result table after a column function has summarized them.

Figure 6-20 shows a Having clause that does not involve a column function. So it can be replaced with a Where clause. The condition is the same whether it is written in one clause or the other. The result table is exactly the same.

Writing the condition in the Where clause is usually preferred because it requires less processing. Hence, it is faster and costs less. The unneeded data is eliminated earlier in the processing, so the process can be more efficient.

In theory, this should not make a difference. People should specify only the result. The database should determine the most efficient way to obtain the result. However, optimizers are not always perfect, and no reason justifies pushing this principle to its limit.

A condition in the Having clause that does not involve a column function can always be relocated to a Where clause.

Figure 6-20
❶   This shows the condition limiting the data written in the Having clause.
❷   This shows the same condition written in the Where clause.

Task

For each Manager Id between 201 and 203, show the number of employees the manager supervises.

Oracle & Access SQL—using a Having clause

```
select manager_id,
       count(*)
from l_employees
group by manager_id
having manager_id between 201 and 203;  ❶
```

Oracle & Access SQL—getting the same result more efficiently, using a Where clause

```
select manager_id,
       count(*)
from l_employees
where manager_id between 201 and 203 ❷
group by manager_id;
```

Beginning table (L_employees)

EMPLOYEE ID	FIRST_NAME	LAST_NAME	DEPT CODE	HIRE_DATE	CREDIT LIMIT	PHONE NUMBER	MANAGER ID
201	SUSAN	BROWN	EXE	01-JUN-92	$30.00	3484	(null)
202	JIM	KERN	SAL	15-AUG-95	$25.00	8722	201
203	MARTHA	WOODS	SHP	01-FEB-97	$25.00	7591	201
204	ELLEN	OWENS	SAL	01-JUL-96	$15.00	6830	202
205	HENRY	PERKINS	SAL	01-MAR-98	$25.00	5286	202
206	CAROL	ROSE	ACT	15-OCT-97	$15.00	3829	201
207	DAN	SMITH	SHP	01-DEC-96	$25.00	2259	203
208	FRED	CAMPBELL	SHP	01-APR-97	$25.00	1752	203
209	PAULA	JACOBS	MKT	17-MAR-98	$15.00	3357	201
210	NANCY	HOFFMAN	SAL	15-FEB-96	$25.00	2974	203

Result table—both Select statements give the same result

MANAGER ID	COUNT(*)
201	4
202	2
203	3

Figure 6-20   Using DISTINCT more than once

Solutions to Some Problems

Counting the number of nulls in a column

How can you count the number of nulls in a column? This goal may seem to be a problem because the column function Count ignores nulls.

Figure 6-21 shows the technique. The Where clause limits the rows to the ones we want to count. The Count(*) function counts them.

Sometimes we are mostly interested in knowing whether a column contains any nulls at all. We are less interested in getting the exact count.

Task

Find the number of nulls in the Manager_id column of the Employees table.

Beginning table (L_Employees table)

```
EMPLOYEE                         DEPT               CREDIT PHONE   MANAGER
      ID FIRST_NAME LAST_NAME    CODE HIRE_DATE     LIMIT  NUMBER       ID
-------- ---------- ----------   ---- ----------    ------ ------  -------
     201 SUSAN      BROWN        EXE  01-JUN-92     $30.00 3484    (null)
     202 JIM        KERN         SAL  15-AUG-95     $25.00 8722       201
     203 MARTHA     WOODS        SHP  01-FEB-97     $25.00 7591       201
     204 ELLEN      OWENS        SAL  01-JUL-96     $15.00 6830       202
     205 HENRY      PERKINS      SAL  01-MAR-98     $25.00 5286       202
     206 CAROL      ROSE         ACT  15-OCT-97     $15.00 3829       201
     207 DAN        SMITH        SHP  01-DEC-96     $25.00 2259       203
     208 FRED       CAMPBELL     SHP  01-APR-97     $25.00 1752       203
     209 PAULA      JACOBS       MKT  17-MAR-98     $15.00 3357       201
     210 NANCY      HOFFMAN      SAL  15-FEB-96     $25.00 2974       203
```

Oracle & Access SQL

```
select count(*) as number_of_nulls
from l_employees
where manager_id is null;
```

Result table

```
NUMBER_OF_NULLS
---------------
              1
```

Figure 6-21   Counting the number of nulls in a column

Using DISTINCT more than once

Some SQL products allow you to use the word "Distinct" only once within a Select statement, even if it is within different column functions. Oracle does not have this restriction. This figure shows how to work around this restriction if you encounter it.

Access never allows the word "Distinct" within column functions. So, it does not have exactly this problem. Figure 6-9 shows the type of workaround required in Access.

Figure 6-20 shows a Select statement that counts the number of distinct values in two different columns. Some SQL products are not able to handle this within a single Select statement. They require that each Select statement can use the word "Distinct" only once.

In this example, two steps are needed to work around this restriction. The first step counts the number of different values in the Department Code column and it saves the result in a table. The second step counts the number of different values in the Credit Limits column and save the result in a table.

The third step displays both these results.

There are several restrictions that apply to any Select statement that summarizes data. I have not discussed the details of all these restrictions. But, these restrictions only apply if you are trying to do all the summarization within a single Select statement.

The example in figure 6-20 illustrates a process that can get around any of these restrictions. All you need to do is to use a series of Select statements and divide the process into a series of smaller and simpler steps.

Task

Show an example of a Select statement that contains Distinct in two separate places. Show that this works in Oracle. Show the workaround that may be needed in some other SQL products, which allow only one Distinct to be used in a Select statement.

Beginning table (L_employees table)

```
EMPLOYEE                        DEPT            CREDIT PHONE  MANAGER
      ID FIRST_NAME LAST_NAME  CODE HIRE_DATE    LIMIT NUMBER     ID
-------- ---------- ---------- ---- ----------  ------- ------ -------
     201 SUSAN      BROWN      EXE  01-JUN-92   $30.00 3484   (null)
     202 JIM        KERN       SAL  15-AUG-95   $25.00 8722      201
     203 MARTHA     WOODS      SHP  01-FEB-97   $25.00 7591      201
     204 ELLEN      OWENS      SAL  01-JUL-96   $15.00 6830      202
     205 HENRY      PERKINS    SAL  01-MAR-98   $25.00 5286      202
     206 CAROL      ROSE       ACT  15-OCT-97   $15.00 3829      201
     207 DAN        SMITH      SHP  01-DEC-96   $25.00 2259      203
     208 FRED       CAMPBELL   SHP  01-APR-97   $25.00 1752      203
     209 PAULA      JACOBS     MKT  17-MAR-98   $15.00 3357      201
     210 NANCY      HOFFMAN    SAL  15-FEB-96   $25.00 2974      203
```

Oracle SQL

```
select count(distinct dept_code) as number_of_dept_codes,
       count(distinct credit_limit) as number_of_credit_limits
from l_employees;
```

Some other SQL—step 1

```
create table temp_1 as
select count(distinct dept_code) as number_of_dept_codes
from l_employees;
```

Some other SQL—step 2

```
create table temp_2 as
select count(distinct credit_limit) as number_of_credit_limits
from l_employees;
```

Some other SQL: - step 3

```
select number_of_dept_codes, number_of_credit_limits
from temp_1, temp_2;
```

Result table

```
NUMBER_OF_DEPT_CODES NUMBER_OF_CREDIT_LIMITS
-------------------- -----------------------
                   5                       3
```

Figure 6-22   Using Distinct more than once

Summary

In this chapter, you learned how to summarize the data in a table using the column functions. You also learned how to control the level of summarization using the Group By and Having clauses. When data is summarized, it is always important to determine how the nulls are being handled.

In the next chapter, we will discuss joins—obtaining data from several tables at once. Up to now, we have primarily gotten the data from a single table or view. The exception is that we used lookup tables to find the meanings of codes. Also, the views could have been constructed for us by the professional programming staff. So, these views might be based on several tables behind the scenes, without our having to know about it.

Why did we discuss reporting from a single table in such detail? There are two reasons. One reason is that in some companies, this is what the end-users (people who are not professional computer programmers) are supposed to be able to do for themselves. Reporting from a single table, in theory at least, is supposed to be the "easy" part of using SQL. That leaves many people wondering why it does not seem easy to them when they use it. I wanted to provide the information they had not been told.

The second reason is that you need to know this material if you are actually going to use SQL products to perform real tasks. You need to know about datatypes, formats, functions, the properties of nulls, that computers are very sensitive about punctuation, that error messages are often incorrect or misleading, that summarized data should not be mixed with non-summarized data, and how to divide a complex process into several simple steps. Now that you know these things, I can go on to discuss the more "advanced" features of SQL.

Exercises

1. Goal: Show all the ways of summarizing a column of data in SQL. That is, show what all the column functions can do.

1A. Show the sum and average of the credit limits in the employees table of the lunches database.

Solution
Oracle & Access SQL

```
select sum(credit_limit),
       avg(credit_limit)
from l_employees;
```

1B. On the credit limit column use all the following column functions:
 Maximum
 Minimum
 Count(*)
 Count(credit limit)
 Count(distinct credit limit)—Access needs to do this one separately
 Sum
 Average
 Standard Deviation
 Variance
Make sure you understand all of the results. (Except you might not understand the last two statistical functions.) What is your opinion on how well, or poorly, these summaries give a picture of the data in the table?

1C. Do the same as 1B, but use the Hire Date column. The last four column functions cannot be applied to the hire date. Why?

2. Goal: Find the exceptions in the data. We will continue to explore this idea more in the next few chapters. When you have data that almost fits into a pattern, find the exceptions, the parts that do not fit in. On the level on management styles, this is similar to "Management by Exception" rather than "Management by handling all the details."

2A. The table EX6_2A contains the numbers between 1 and 100in a column called "N." However, some of the numbers occur several times in the table. Find all the numbers that occur more than once and find out how many times they occur. List them in numerical order.

After doing this, create a new copy of the table that contains each value only once and gets rid of all the duplicate values.

Solution - part 1:
Oracle & Access SQL

```
select n,
       count(n)
from ex6_2a
group by n
having count(n) > 1
order by n;
```

Solution - part 2

Oracle SQL	Access SQL
```create table no_duplicates as select distinct * from ex6_2a;```	```select distinct * into no_duplicates from ex6_2a;```

2B. Table EX6_2B contains the first and last names of people who will receive some material by mail. A few people have put their name on the list several times. Find the names that have been entered more than once.

Then create a new list where the duplicates have been eliminated.

3. Goal: Summarize data that groups dates together. The data in the table may contain specific dates and times. You want to summarize it by week, month, or year.

(Technique. One way to do this is to add a new column of data to the table, which names the months or years you want to use to group the data. There are other techniques that work also, but this one is the most reliable.)

3A. From the L_lunches table, find how many lunches will b served in each month.

Solution:
Step 1. Define the new column with a text datatype, not a date datatype. We do not want to group the data on the date and time—the granularity of this is too fine.

Oracle SQL   Access SQL

```
alter table l_lunches              alter table l_lunches
add grouping_col     varchar2(15); add column grouping_col    text(15);
```

Step 2. Put data in the new column. Again , this is text data, not SQL dates. The date format used here will make it easy to put the dates in order in step 4.

Oracle SQL

```
update l_lunches
    set grouping_col = to_char(lunch_date, 'yyyy-mm');
```

Access SQL

```
update l_lunches
    set grouping_col = format(lunch_date, 'yyyy-mm');
```

Step 3. Look at the table you have created. Is the data grouped correctly?

Oracle & Access SQL

```
select *
from l_lunches
order by grouping_col;
```

Step 4. Summarize the data to produce the requested report.

Oracle & Access SQL

```
select grouping_col as lunch_month,
         count(*) as number_of_lunches
from l_lunches
group by grouping_col
order by grouping_col;
```

3B. From the employees table of the lunches database, find the number of employees hired in each year.

4. Use the L_Lunches table. Count the number of lunches each employee will attend. (Notice that employee 209 is not attending any lunches.)

5. Use the L_Lunches table. Count the number of lunches each employee will attend during each month. (In relation to problem 4, this is sometimes called "Data Mining.")

6. Use the L_Lunch_Items table. Count the number of servings of each food. A food is identified by the Supplier_id and the Product_code. Pay attention to the quantity of each order.

Chapter 7

Inner Joins

So far, you have obtained data mostly from one table or view. In this chapter, you will learn to write queries using data from many tables.

Introduction to Joins

A join combines the data from two or more tables. The result of this is a single table, which is often quite large. Then the techniques you have learned in previous chapters are use to extract a small amount of data from this large table.

A query can use data from several tables

Often several different tables are used together in a Select statement. This approach is necessary when the data you need does not all reside in one table or view. The process has two steps. First, the separate tables are combined into a single table. Then the Select statement operates upon this table using any of the techniques we have employed so far.

Figure 7-1 shows these two steps. In the first step, four separate tables of data are combined together to form a single table. This table can be very large. It may contain several copies of the four beginning tables in different permutations and combinations. One row of any of the beginning tables can be matched with many combinations of rows from the other tables.

In the second step, a report is extracted from the single table that combines all the data. It gathers a few of the rows and a few of the columns of the table. It applies row functions and column functions to them. In short, it can use any of the techniques you have used in the previous chapters.

The single table that combines all the data may exist only in theory. It may never be formed physically within the computer, either in memory or on the disk. It may be too large for the computer to handle at any moment in time. However, the final report that is produced must be the same, *as if* this table was formed. The computer is allowed to take shortcuts in the process, as long as the shortcut does not affect the result.

The two steps shown here may be coded in SQL as a single Select statement. Or each step may be a separate Select statement. Or each step may be coded using several Select statements. You have many different ways to write the SQL statements, but the process, fundamentally, is always the same one shown in Figure 7-1.

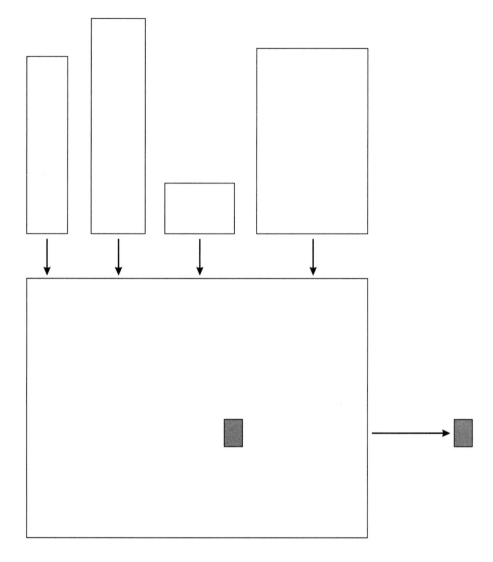

Figure 7-1   A query can use data from several tables

The best approach is to join two tables at a time

You can combine several tables at one time, as shown in Figure 7-1. However, this process often becomes difficult to control. It is prone to errors and it can become so complex that other people will have difficulty understanding it.

Often, the best thing to do is to combine the beginning tables two at a time. The first step of this process combines two of the tables. Then each of the steps after that adds one additional table.

Figure 7-2 shows this process with four beginning tables. This diagram shows the way the SQL code can be written. Each step in the diagram is a separate SQL statement. This process is written as a series of three SQL statements. Each statement creates a table or view. Usually, creating views is more efficient.

Step 1 combines tables 1 and 2. This can be coded as one Select statement and saved as a view.

Step 2 combines the result of step 1 with table 3. This can also be coded as a Select statement and saved as a view.

Step 3 combines the result of step 2 with table 4. The view this creates combines the data from all four of the beginning tables. Together, the three steps of this process are the first step of Figure 7-1.

To understand joins of several tables, you need to understand them only when two tables are being combined. The presentation in this chapter and in Chapter 8 is focused on joining two tables at a time.

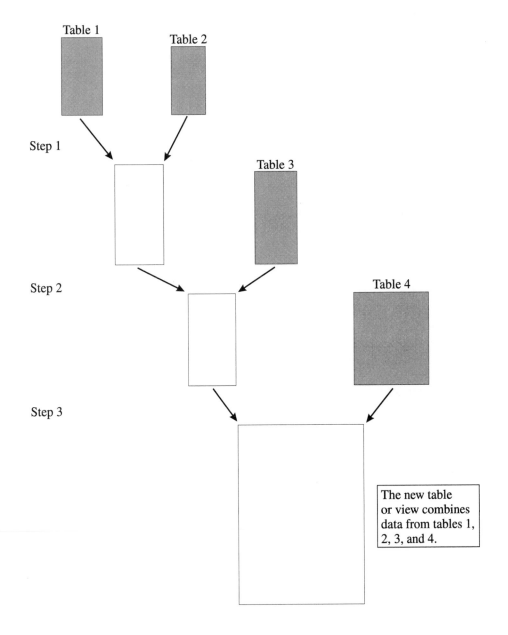

Figure 7-2   The best approach is to join two tables at a time

Inner Joins of Two Tables

The most common way to combine two tables is with an inner join. This chapter discusses the inner join in detail. Chapter 8 discusses the three types of outer joins.

A one-to-one relationship

Figure 7-3 shows a model case of combining two tables with an inner join. This shows the technique that is always used, but avoids any of the complexities. You will learn the complexities later. For now, just focus on this simple example.

Rows from one table are matched with rows from the other table. No hidden links are between the two tables. The data in the tables determines how to combine the rows. One column is chosen from each table. When these columns have the same value, the rows are combined.

In Figure 7-3, the "F_num" column is chosen from the Fruits table, and the "C_num" column is chosen from the Colors table. These are sometimes called the "matching columns." A row of the Fruits table is matched with a row of the Colors table when the matching columns have the same value. The apple is matched with red because both the matching columns contain a 1.

In this example, each row of the Fruits table matches with one and only one row of the Colors table, and vice versa (each row of the Colors table matches with one and only one row of the Fruits table). This matchup is called a "one-to-one relationship" between the two tables. It is a special condition that can occur only when both tables have the same number of rows.

The data in the chosen columns is what creates this relationship. The tables are seemingly being "zipped together" by the values of the data in the matching columns.

Figure 7-3

❶   The Select clause lists all the columns from both beginning tables. Columns from the Fruits table are preceded with "A" and columns from the Colors table are preceded with "B." A dot (period) is between the "A" or "B" and the name of the column.

❷   The From clause lists both the beginning tables. It assigns the short name, "A," to the Fruits table. The "A" is called a "table alias." It functions as a short name. The From clause also assigns the table alias, "B," to the Colors table.

The usual practice is to use a single letter for a table alias, because it makes the SQL code easier to read. However, a table alias is allowed to be much longer.

Note that a space is between the name of the table and the table alias. A comma is between the names of the two tables.

❸   The Where clause specifies the "join condition." Here, the join condition is that the two designated columns must have the same value.

❹   The Order By clause is not required for the join. However, it sorts the rows of the result table into a particular order, which makes the result easier to read.

Task

Join the Fruits table and the Colors table with an inner join. Match the F_num column of the Fruits table with the C_num column of the Colors table. Combine a row of the Fruits table with a row of the Colors table when the values in these matching columns are equal.

Because of the data in the beginning tables, this action creates a one-to-one relationship between the two beginning tables.

Oracle & Access SQL

```
select a.fruit, ❶
       a.f_num,
       b.c_num,
       b.color
from fig703_fruits a, ❷
     fig703_colors b
where a.f_num = b.c_num ❸
order by a.fruit; ❹
```

Beginning tables
Fig703_fruits table   Fig703_colors table

FRUIT	F_NUM		C_NUM	COLOR
APPLE	1		1	RED
BANANA	2		2	YELLOW
CHERRY	3		3	RED
GRAPE	4		4	PURPLE
ORANGE	5		5	ORANGE

Result table

FRUIT	F_NUM	C_NUM	COLOR
APPLE	1	1	RED
BANANA	2	2	YELLOW
CHERRY	3	3	RED
GRAPE	4	4	PURPLE
ORANGE	5	5	ORANGE

Figure 7-3   A one-to-one relationship

A many-to-one relationship

Figure 7-4 uses the same principles as Figure 7-3 to combine rows from one table with rows from the other table. However, a strawberry has now been added to the Fruits table.

The row of the strawberry has a 1 in the F_num column. This matches with the 1 in the C_num column for the color red. The result shows that a red apple and a red strawberry exist. So two rows of the Fruits table are matched with a single row of the Colors table.

In effect, the row "1-red" is duplicated within the result table. It occurs two times in the result table, even though it occurs only once in the beginning tables.

Another red is within the Colors table, the row "3-red." This shows that the Colors table can contain more than one row with the same color. Sometime you have a reason for keeping things separate this way—perhaps it is a different shade of red. If not, the "3-red" row could be removed from the Colors table and the F_num column for the cherry could be changed to 1.

This example is a "many-to-one relationship" between the two tables. Each fruit is matched with only one color. However, some colors are matched with more than one fruit.

Figure 7-4

❶   This code is the same as in Figure 7-3.

❷   This code does not assign column aliases in the From clause. Instead of writing "A" or "B," the full name of the table is written before the name of each column.

Task

Join the Fruits table and the Colors table with an inner join. Use the same specification as Figure 7-3. The data here creates a many-to-one relationship.

Oracle & Access SQL ❶

```
select a.fruit,
       a.f_num,
       b.c_num,
       b.color
from fig704_fruits a,
     fig704_colors b
where a.f_num = b.c_num
order by a.fruit;
```

Oracle & Access SQL—alternative code ❷

```
select fig704_fruits.fruit,
       fig704_fruits.f_num,
       fig704_colors.c_num,
       fig704_colors.color
from fig704_fruits,
     fig704_colors
where fig704_fruits.f_num = fig704_colors.c_num
order by fig704_fruits.fruit;
```

Beginning tables
Fig704_fruits table   Fig704_colors table

FRUIT	F_NUM
APPLE	1
BANANA	2
CHERRY	3
GRAPE	4
ORANGE	5
STRAWBERRY	1

C_NUM	COLOR
1	RED
2	YELLOW
3	RED
4	PURPLE
5	ORANGE

Result table

FRUIT	F_NUM	C_NUM	COLOR
APPLE	1	1	RED
BANANA	2	2	YELLOW
CHERRY	3	3	RED
GRAPE	4	4	PURPLE
ORANGE	5	5	ORANGE
STRAWBERRY	1	1	RED

Figure 7-4   A many-to-one relationship

A one-to-many relationship

Figure 7-5 shows an example of a one-to-many relationship. Here, two colors have a 1 in the matching column, red and green. The result table shows that the apple row is matched with both colors, giving a red apple and a green apple.

This is the reverse of Figure 7-5. Inner joins are symmetric. The principles work the same way regardless of the order of the tables.

Figure 7-5

❶   This is the same SQL code used in Figures 7-3 and 7-4, except for the names of the tables and the layout of the statement.

❷   This is another way to write the SQL code. In this code, no table aliases of "A" or "B" are assigned in the From clause. Also, in all the other clauses, the column names are not preceded by a table alias or a table name.

The SQL code is easier for people to understand and modify when the name of each column is preceded with a table alias or a table name. So that style of coding is highly recommended. However, the computer does not require it.

The column names within a table must be unique. A table cannot have two columns with the same name. However, two columns can have the same name if they occur in different tables.

In a Select statement, if a column name occurs in only one of the tables listed in the From clause, then the computer can figure out which table it is in and you do not need to specify the name of the table. However, if a column name is used in two or more of the tables listed in the From clause, then you must specify which of the columns you mean. To do so, you must include the table name or table alias with the column name, writing:

        Table_name.Column_name
or
        Table_alias.Column_name

The computer requires identification of the table only when two or more tables contain columns with the same names.

Task

Join the Fruits table and the Colors table with an inner join. Use the same specification as in Figure 7-4. The data here creates a one-to-many relationship.

Oracle & Access SQL ❶

```
select a.fruit, a.f_num,
       b.c_num, b.color
from fig705_fruits a,
     fig705_colors b
where a.f_num = b.c_num
order by a.fruit;
```

Oracle & Access SQL—another way to write the code ❷

```
select fruit, f_num,
       c_num, color
from fig705_fruits,
     fig705_colors
where f_num = c_num
order by fruit;
```

Beginning tables
Fig705_fruits table

FRUIT	F_NUM
APPLE	1
BANANA	2
CHERRY	3
GRAPE	4
ORANGE	5

Fig705_colors table

C_NUM	COLOR
1	RED
1	GREEN
2	YELLOW
3	RED
4	PURPLE
5	ORANGE

Result table

FRUIT	F_NUM	C_NUM	COLOR
APPLE	1	1	RED
APPLE	1	1	GREEN
BANANA	2	2	YELLOW
CHERRY	3	3	RED
GRAPE	4	4	PURPLE
ORANGE	5	5	ORANGE

Figure 7-5   A one-to-many relationship

A many-to-many relationship

Figure 7-6 shows a many-to-many relationship between the tables. Here, two fruits have a 1 in the matching column, an apple and a strawberry. Also, two colors have a 1 in the matching column, red and green.

The result table shows all the possible combinations and permutations of these matches. You see a red apple, a green apple, a red strawberry, and a green strawberry.

If 10 fruits and 10 colors all matched, then 100 rows would be in the result table. You can see that the result table can easily get very large.

Some people are critical of many-to-many relationships. They prefer to have a database designed so that no many-to-many relationships occur. This design can always be done, and I discuss it further in Chapter 12.

Task

Join the fruits table and the colors table with an inner join.

Oracle & Access SQL

```
select a.fruit,
       a.f_num,
       b.c_num,
       b.color
from fig706_fruits a,
     fig706_colors b
where a.f_num = b.c_num
order by a.fruit;
```

Beginning tables
Fig706_fruits table

FRUIT	F_NUM
APPLE	1
BANANA	2
CHERRY	3
GRAPE	4
ORANGE	5
STRAWBERRY	1

Fig706_colors table

C_NUM	COLOR
1	RED
1	GREEN
2	YELLOW
3	RED
4	PURPLE
4	GREEN
5	ORANGE

Result table

FRUIT	F_NUM	C_NUM	COLOR
APPLE	1	1	RED
APPLE	1	1	GREEN
BANANA	2	2	YELLOW
CHERRY	3	3	RED
GRAPE	4	4	PURPLE
GRAPE	4	4	GREEN
ORANGE	5	5	ORANGE
STRAWBERRY	1	1	RED
STRAWBERRY	1	1	GREEN

Figure 7-6   A many-to-many relationship

Dropping unmatched rows

Figure 7-7 shows that rows are deleted if they do not have a matching row in the other table. They do not appear in the result table. This situation occurs whether the rows are in the first table or the second table.

The only rows in the result tables are ones that have a matching row in the other table. That outcome is somewhat like having a party that is for couples only. This feature distinguishes an inner join. Outer joins provide an alternative and restore some of the dropped rows to the result. Chapter 8 discusses outer joins.

The inner join applies a strict interpretation to the join condition. To meet this condition, you must have a pair of rows, one from each of the beginning tables. When the join condition is applied to the matching columns of this pair of rows, the join condition statement must be true. Only then is the pair admitted to the result table.

With an inner join, many rows from the beginning tables can be dropped. Information in the beginning tables can be lost. You receive no warning when this occurs.

Task

Join the fruits table and the colors table with an inner join. The data in Figure 7-7 show that rows in beginning tables may not appear at all in the result table.

Oracle & Access SQL

```
select a.fruit,
       a.f_num,
       b.c_num,
       b.color
from fig707_fruits a,
     fig707_colors b
where a.f_num = b.c_num
order by a.fruit;
```

Beginning tables
Fig707_fruits table   ### Fig707_colors table

FRUIT	F_NUM
APPLE	1
BANANA	2
CHERRY	3
GRAPE	4
ORANGE	5
STRAWBERRY	1

C_NUM	COLOR
1	RED
2	YELLOW
1	GREEN
6	WHITE

Result table

FRUIT	F_NUM	C_NUM	COLOR
APPLE	1	1	RED
APPLE	1	1	GREEN
BANANA	2	2	YELLOW
STRAWBERRY	1	1	RED
STRAWBERRY	1	1	GREEN

Figure 7-7   Unmatched rows are dropped

Dropping rows with a null in the matching column

Figure 7-8 shows a detail of Figure 7-9. If the matching column of a row contains a null, then it cannot satisfy any join condition. So an inner join will always drop it.

In Figure 7-8, the kiwi has a null in the matching column. The color brown also has a null in the matching column. The join condition says that the values in the two matching columns must be equal before a pair of rows can be combined in the result table.

However, a null is an unknown value, and the two nulls are not considered to be equal. So both these rows are dropped from the result table.

Task

Join the fruits table and the colors table with an inner join.

Oracle & Access SQL

```
select a.fruit,
       a.f_num,
       b.c_num,
       b.color
from fig708_fruits a,
     fig708_colors b
where a.f_num = b.c_num
order by a.fruit;
```

Beginning tables
Fig708_fruits table   ### Fig708_colors table

FRUIT	F_NUM		C_NUM	COLOR
APPLE	1		1	RED
BANANA	2		2	YELLOW
CHERRY	3		3	RED
GRAPE	4		4	PURPLE
ORANGE	5		5	ORANGE
KIWI	(null)		(null)	BROWN

Result table

FRUIT	F_NUM	C_NUM	COLOR
APPLE	1	1	RED
BANANA	2	2	YELLOW
CHERRY	3	3	RED
GRAPE	4	4	PURPLE
ORANGE	5	5	ORANGE

Figure 7-8   Rows with a null in the matching column are dropped

Variations of the Join Condition

The previous examples all used a join condition that used just one matching column from each table and required the two matching columns to have the same value. This section shows examples of many other types of join conditions. These are all inner joins.

Using two or more matching columns

Figure 7-9 shows an example of a join condition that uses two matching columns from each table. This contrasts with the previous figures, which used a single column from each table to form the inner join. The same principle shown here can be used to join tables on any number of columns.

Here, a color is matched with a fruit only when both sets of matching columns have the same values.

Fruits.F_num_1 = Colors.C_num_1

and

Fruits.F_num_2 = Colors.C_num_2

The first rows of each table are matched, giving a red apple, because the first column of each table has the value 1 and the second column of each table has the value 5. However, the first row of the Fruits table does not match with the second row of the Colors table. That is, no yellow apple exists, because the second columns of these table have different values—the Fruits table has the value 5 and the Colors table has the value 6.

Figure 7-9

❶   All the columns are listed from both tables. The term "join" is used in two contexts. When we talk about joining tables in general terms, all the columns from both tables are listed. In Figure 7-1, this is the first step that combines the tables.

When we talk about joining tables to get some particular information, often only some of the columns are listed. In Figure 7-1, this is a combination of the two steps—combining the tables and selecting some columns from the combination.

❷   The join condition is written in the Where clause. Here, two conditions have an "And" between them. These are the same conditions written above, but using table aliases (assigned in the From clause) instead of table names.

❸   The Order By clause is not really part of the join. It is included here to make the result table easier to read.

Task

Join the fruits table and the colors table with an inner join that matches rows when the first two columns of each table are equal.

Oracle & Access SQL

```
select a.f_num_1, ❶
       a.f_num_2,
       a.fruit,
       b.c_num_1,
       b.c_num_2,
       b.color
from fig709_fruits a,
     fig709_colors b
where a.f_num_1 = b.c_num_1 ❷
  and a.f_num_2 = b.c_num_2
order by a.fruit; ❸
```

Beginning tables
Fig709_fruits table   Fig709_colors table

F_NUM_1	F_NUM_2	FRUIT	C_NUM_1	C_NUM_2	COLOR
1	5	APPLE	1	5	RED
1	6	BANANA	1	6	YELLOW
2	5	CHERRY	2	5	RED
2	6	GRAPE	2	6	PURPLE
2	7	ORANGE	2	7	ORANGE

Result table

F_NUM_1	F_NUM_2	FRUIT	C_NUM_1	C_NUM_2	COLOR
1	5	APPLE	1	5	RED
1	6	BANANA	1	6	YELLOW
2	5	CHERRY	2	5	RED
2	6	GRAPE	2	6	PURPLE
2	7	ORANGE	2	7	ORANGE

Figure 7-9   Using two or more matching columns

Using Between to match on a range of values

Figure 7-10 shows an example of using the Between condition in a join, rather than a condition of Equality. Three columns are involved in this join condition. The value in one column must lie between the values in the other two.

In this example, test scores between 90 and 100 get an A, those between 80 and 89 get a B, etc. The grade ranges must not overlap.

Figure 7-10

❶   Only three columns are listed in the Select clause. This is a "join" in the application sense of the word. If we wanted to "join" the tables using a more general sense of the word, we would need to list all the columns of both tables.

❷   The join condition is written in the Where clause. Note that this condition uses "Between." The test score is placed *between* the beginning score and the ending score.

❸   The Order By clause makes the result table easier to read. It is not part of the join.

Task

Assign grades to students by placing their individual test scores within one of the grading ranges.

Oracle & Access SQL

```
select a.student_name,  ❶
       a.test_score,
       b.letter_grade
from fig710_student_scores a,
     fig710_grade_ranges b
where a.test_score between b.beginning_score and b.ending_score  ❷
order by a.student_name;  ❸
```

Beginning tables
Fig710_student_scores table   Fig710_grade_ranges table

STUDENT_NAME	TEST_SCORE
CATHY	85
FRED	60
JOHN	95
MEG	92

BEGINNING SCORE	ENDING SCORE	LETTER GRADE
90	100	A
80	89	B
70	79	C
60	69	D
0	59	F

Result table

STUDENT_NAME	TEST_SCORE	LETTER_GRADE
CATHY	85	B
FRED	60	D
JOHN	95	A
MEG	92	A

Figure 7-10   Using Between to match on a range of values

Using Greater Than in the join condition

Figure 7-11 is an example of using a Greater Than condition in a join, rather than an Equality condition or a Between condition. Variations of this type of join can use:

> Less than
> Less than or equal
> Greater than or equal

In this example, each row of one table is usually paired with many rows of the other table. For example, the row 6 from the Bigger Numbers table is matched with rows 1 to 5 from the Smaller Numbers table.

Figure 7-11
❶   All the columns are listed from both tables.
❷   The Where clause contains the join condition. This condition says that one column "is greater than" another column.
❸   The Order By clause makes the result table easier to read.

Task

Join each Bigger Number with all the Smaller Numbers that are less than it.

Oracle & Access SQL

```
select a.*,  ❶
       b.*
from fig711_bigger_numbers a,
     fig711_smaller_numbers b
where a.larger_number > b.smaller_number  ❷
order by a.larger_number,  ❸
         b.smaller_number;
```

Beginning tables
Fig711_bigger_numbers table   Fig711_smaller_numbers table

LARGER_NUMBER	WORD		SMALLER_NUMBER	WORD
1	ONE		1	ONE
2	TWO		2	TWO
3	THREE		3	THREE
4	FOUR		4	FOUR
5	FIVE		5	FIVE
6	SIX		6	SIX

Result table

LARGER_NUMBER	WORD	SMALLER_NUMBER	WORD
2	TWO	1	ONE
3	THREE	1	ONE
3	THREE	2	TWO
4	FOUR	1	ONE
4	FOUR	2	TWO
4	FOUR	3	THREE
5	FIVE	1	ONE
5	FIVE	2	TWO
5	FIVE	3	THREE
5	FIVE	4	FOUR
6	SIX	1	ONE
6	SIX	2	TWO
6	SIX	3	THREE
6	SIX	4	FOUR
6	SIX	5	FIVE

Figure 7-11   Using Greater Than in the join condition

Inner Joins of Three or More Tables

So far, we have discussed joining two tables together. This section shows how to extend this to join three or more tables. You can take two approaches to writing the Select statement, in order to do this. One way joins all the tables with one Select statement. The other way joins the tables together two at a time in a series of Select statements, as shown in Figure 7-2.

Joining three tables with one Select statement

Figure 7-12 shows how to join three tables in one Select statement. Each of the tables in Figure 7-12 contains a number and the English word for the number. We want to join the tables with an inner join. The matching columns are the first columns of the tables, the number columns. The join condition is that the matching columns have equal values.

In this example, we also place an additional condition on the result. We require that the number be less than 7. The purpose of this is to show how additional conditions are handled within the SQL statement.

Since we are using an inner join, rows are dropped unless a matching row is in each of the tables. This causes the first table to drop rows 1 and 2, the second table to drop rows 2 and 8, and the third table to drop rows 8 and 9.

The Select statement

❶   The Select clause in this example lists all the columns of each of the tables. Notice that this uses dot notation. The table alias must precede the asterisk. Here, "A.*" means "list all the columns of the table 'A,' which is the Fig712_first table."

❷   The From clause lists all three tables and gives each table an alias. This gets the data from all the tables. Commas must be between the name of the tables.

❸   The Where clause has two separate parts—the join conditions and additional conditions. The first two conditions in this Where clause are the join conditions. These always involve at least two tables, because these conditions relate one table to another table. Since three tables exist, you must have at least two join conditions—one less than the number of tables. One join condition can relate two of the tables. The second join condition relates the third table to the other combination of the other two tables.

❹   The second part of the Where clause contains any additional conditions you want to require. Any condition that involves only one table is an additional condition. However, additional conditions can involve many tables. You can have many of these additional conditions. The join conditions and the additional conditions can be mixed together. However, the code is easier to understand if they are separated.

❺   The Order By clause is used here to put the rows of the result table in some particular order. Without this clause, the computer can put them in any order it chooses, which sometimes seems like random order.

Task

Join three tables with an inner join. Join rows when the first columns are equal. Add an additional condition that the value in the joined columns be less than 7. Write the SQL as a single Select statement.

Joining all the tables in one Select statement

Oracle & Access SQL

```
select a.*, ❶
       b.*,
       c.*
from fig712_first a, ❷
     fig712_second b,
     fig712_third c
where a.first_number = b.second_number ❸
 and a.first_number = c.third_number
 and a.first_number < 7 ❹
order by a.first_number; ❺
```

Beginning tables

Fig712_first table	**Fig712_second table**	**Fig712_third table**

FIRST   FIRST
NUMBER WORD
------ ----------
  1 ONE
  2 TWO
  3 THREE
  4 FOUR
  5 FIVE
  6 SIX
  7 SEVEN
	SECOND SECOND
	NUMBER WORD
	------ --------------
	  2 TWO
	  3 THREE
	  4 FOUR
	  5 FIVE
	  6 SIX
	  7 SEVEN
	  8 EIGHT
		THIRD THIRD
		NUMBER WORD
		------ ----------
		  3 THREE
		  4 FOUR
		  5 FIVE
		  6 SIX
		  7 SEVEN
		  8 EIGHT
		  9 NINE

Result table

FIRST FIRST NUMBER WORD		SECOND SECOND NUMBER WORD		THIRD THIRD NUMBER WORD	
---------	--------------	---------	---------------	---------	--------
3	THREE	3	THREE	3	THREE
4	FOUR	4	FOUR	4	FOUR
5	FIVE	5	FIVE	5	FIVE
6	SIX	6	SIX	6	SIX

Figure 7-12   Joining three tables with one Select statement

Joining three tables with a series of steps

Figure 7-13 shows a different coding technique to join three tables. The problem is the same as in Figure 7-12. This technique joins two tables together in each step. The idea is explained in Figure 7-2.

The advantage of using this coding technique is that each step is more focused and is a single logical unit. This makes the code easier to read and understand. It demonstrates greater control and is less prone to errors. If any errors occur, they are easier to debug and to fix.

Figure 7-13

❶ Step 1 creates a view that joins two of the tables. The Where clause for this step is simpler and easier to understand than in the previous SQL code. It consists only of the join condition(s) that relates the two tables.

❷ Step 2 creates a view that joins the third table to the other two tables. This refers to the view created in step 1. Again, the Where clause contains only the join condition(s) needed to relate the tables.

In this coding technique, other steps would be added if you had more tables to join. Each step would add one additional table. All these steps perform only the join. They do not contain additional conditions in the Where clause, a Group By clause, a Having clause, or an Order By clause.

❸ The last step creates a report from the join of all the tables. It can use all the techniques you learned in the previous chapters—row functions, column functions, additional conditions in the Where clause, a Group By clause, a Having clause, and an Order By clause.

Joining all the tables in one Select statement—from Figure 7-12

Oracle & Access SQL

```
select a.*,
       b.*,
       c.*
from fig712_first a,
     fig712_second b,
     fig712_third c
where a.first_number = b.second_number
  and a.first_number = c.third_number
  and a.first_number < 7
order by a.first_number;
```

Task

Rewrite the SQL from Figure 7-12 to use a series of steps that joins two tables at a time.

Joining two tables at a time using a series of steps

Step 1—join two of the tables ❶
Oracle SQL   Access SQL

```
create view step_1 as
select a.*,
       b.*
from fig712_first a,
     fig712_second b
where a.first_number =
      b.second_number;
```

(Enter the query in the SQL window)

```
select a.*,
       b.*
from fig712_first a,
     fig712_second b
where a.first_number =
      b.second_number;
```

(Save this query and name it "Step_1")

Step 2—join the third table to the other two ❷
Oracle SQL   Access SQL

```
create view step_2 as
select a.*,
       b.*
from step_1 a,
     fig712_third b
where a.first_number =
b.third_number;
```

(Enter the query in the SQL window)

```
select a.*,
       b.*
from step_1 a,
     fig712_third b
where a.first_number =
b.third_number;
```

(Save this query and name it "Step_2")

Step 3—apply all other logic ❸
Oracle & Access SQL

```
select *
from step_2
where first_number < 7
order by first_number;
```

Figure 7-13   Joining three tables with a series of steps

The New Syntax for an Inner Join

So far, we have been writing the join condition in the Where clause. The new SQL standard, SQL-92, also allows the join condition to be written in the From clause. The syntax is slightly different. Access supports this new syntax; Oracle will support it in the future, but does not support it yet.

Writing the join condition in the From clause

Figure 7-14 shows two ways of writing the join of the Fruits table with the Colors table. The older syntax was explained in Figure 7-3, and you have used it until now. This older syntax is still valid, and will remain valid in the future.

The newer syntax writes the join condition in an On clause within the From clause, instead of putting it in the Where clause. This allows the Where clause to be focused on the rows of data we want to use for the final report. It does not need to also handle the join conditions.

Two other differences exist in the newer syntax. No comma appears after the "A," which is the table alias for the first table. Instead of this comma, the words "inner join" are placed between the two tables.

Again, this newer syntax is supported by Access, but not by Oracle.

Figure 7-14

❶   The older syntax is valid in both Oracle and Access.

❷   The From clause lists the tables and assigns aliases (short names) to the tables. A comma is between the names of the tables.

❸   The join condition is written in the Where clause.

❹   The newer syntax is valid in Access, but not in Oracle. Oracle does plan to support it in the future.

❺   The From clause specifies that this is an inner join, in addition to listing the tables and assigning the aliases. No comma appears between the names of the tables.

❻   The join condition is written within the From clause. The word "On" precedes the join condition.

Task

Show the syntax for joining two tables in the From clause. Join the fruits table and the colors table as we have done before.

Oracle & Access SQL—older syntax ❶

```
select a.fruit, a.f_num,
       b.c_num, b.color
from fig703_fruits a, ❷
     fig703_colors b
where a.f_num = b.c_num ❸
order by a.fruit;
```

Oracle SQL

(This syntax is not currently supported.)

Access SQL—newer syntax ❹

```
select a.fruit, a.f_num,
       b.c_num, b.color
from fig703_fruits a ❺
     inner join fig703_colors b
     on a.f_num = b.c_num ❻
order by a.fruit;
```

Beginning tables

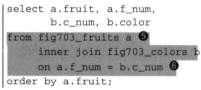

Fig703_Fruits : Table	
Fruit	**F_num**
▶ Apple	1
Banana	2
Cherry	3
Grape	4
Orange	5
*	0

Record: ⏮ ◀ 1 ▶ ⏭ ▶

Fig703_Colors : Table	
C_Num	**Color**
▶ 1	Red
2	Yellow
3	Red
4	Purple
5	Orange
*	0

Record: ⏮ ◀ 1 ▶ ⏭ ▶

Result table

Query1 : Select Query			
fruit	**f_num**	**c_num**	**color**
▶ Apple	1	1	Red
Banana	2	2	Yellow
Cherry	3	3	Red
Grape	4	4	Purple
Orange	5	5	Orange
*			

Record: ⏮ ◀ 1 ▶ ⏭ ▶* of 5

Figure 7-14   Writing the join condition in the From clause

Joining three tables with the new syntax in one Select statement

Figure 7-15 shows how to join three tables in one Select statement using the new syntax. This is the same problem as in Figure 7-12, except that here the join is written in the From clause instead of in the Where clause.

When tables are joined in the From clause, only two tables at a time are joined. In this example, the first table and the second table are joined together. This join is put in parentheses. Then the third table can be added to the join. So this From clause contains two joins, one embedded within the other.

If you have more than three tables, this process is repeated. The From clause shown here would be placed in another set of parentheses. Then another table could be added to the join.

You can contrast this with Figure 7-12. Using the older syntax, all the tables were joined in a single step.

Figure 7-15

❶   First, two tables are joined in the From clause. This is enclosed in parentheses.

❷   Then the third table is joined to the join created in ¶.

❸   Conditions that limit the data are written in the Where clause. However, the join conditions are no longer written in this clause.

❹   The Order By clause makes the result table easier to read.

Task

Perform the same task as in Figure 7-12. Join the three tables with an inner join. Do not include rows when the number is greater than 7.

Oracle SQL	**Access SQL**
(The new syntax is not yet supported.)	

```
select a.*,
       b.*,
       c.*
from (fig712_first a ❶
      inner join fig712_second b
      on a.first_number = b.second_number)
        inner join fig712_third c ❷
        on a.first_number = c.third_number
where a.first_number < 7 ❸
order by a.first_number; ❹
```

Beginning tables

Fig712_First : Table

First_Number	First_Word
1	One
2	Two
3	Three
4	Four
5	Five
6	Six
7	Seven
0	

Record: 1

Fig712_Second : Table

Second_Numb	Secord_Word
2	Two
3	Three
4	Four
5	Five
6	Six
7	Seven
8	Eight
0	

Record: 1

Fig712_Third : Table

Third_Number	Third_Word
3	Three
4	Four
5	Five
6	Six
7	Seven
8	Eight
9	Nine
0	

Record: 1

Result table

Query1 : Select Query

First_Number	First_Word	Second_Numb	Secord_Word	Third_Number	Third_Word
3	Three	3	Three	3	Three
4	Four	4	Four	4	Four
5	Five	5	Five	5	Five
6	Six	6	Six	6	Six

Record: 1 of 4

Figure 7-15   Joining three tables with the new syntax in one Select statement

Joining three tables with the new syntax in a series of steps

Figure 7-16 is similar to Figure 7-13, except that it uses the new syntax for the join. The tables are joined two at a time in a series of steps. It is also similar to Figure 7-15, except that the SQL is written as a series of steps instead of one single step.

In fact, Figures 7-12, 7-13, 7-15, and 7-16 all solve the same problem. But they use different methods to solve it. These are shown in the following diagram.

	One SQL statement	SQL has a series of steps
Older syntax	Figure 7-12	Figure 7-13
Newer syntax	Figure 7-15	Figure 7-16

Figure 7-16
❶   Step 1 joins the first two tables and saves the result as a view, which Access calls a saved query.

❷   Step 2 joins the third table to the other two tables. The first two steps do the join of the tables and nothing else.

❸   All the remaining logic is done after the joins are complete.

Joining all the tables in one Select statement— from Figure 7-15

Oracle SQL

(The new syntax is not yet sup-ported.)

Access SQL

```
select a.*,
       b.*,
       c.*
from (fig712_first a
     inner join fig712_second b
     on a.first_number = b.second_number)
     inner join fig712_third c
     on a.first_number = c.third_number
where a.first_number < 7
order by a.first_number;
```

Joining two tables at a time using a series of steps

Step 1—join two of the tables ❶
Oracle SQL   Access SQL

(This syntax is not supported.)	(Enter this query into the SQL window.)

```
select a.*,
       b.*
from fig712_first a
     inner join fig712_second b
     on a.first_number = b.second_number;
```

(Save this query. Name it "Step_1")

Step 2—join the third table to the other two ❷
Oracle SQL   Access SQL

(This syntax is not supported.)	(Enter this query into the SQL window.)

```
select a.*,
       b.*
from step_1 a
     inner join fig712_third b
     on a.first_number = b.third_number;
```

(Save this query. Name it "Step_2")

Step 3—apply all the other logic ❸
Oracle & Access SQL

John: Want to make this a heading 3? Christa
```
select * from step_2
where first_number < 7
order by first_number;
```

Figure 7-16 Joining three tables with the new syntax in a series of steps

Other Issues

Finally, I have a few other topics to discuss about inner joins. First, inner joins are symmetric. Second, you have standard ways to join tables. These are created when the database is designed. Views can also be created with these standard joins. This possibility enables people to work with a database more easily, since the joins are already done.

Inner joins are symmetric—the order in which the tables are joined does not matter

Suppose that you have two tables, A and B. The information in

A inner join B

is the same as the information in

B inner join A

They have identical rows, and the data values in the columns are identical. The only difference is the order of the columns. The first inner join has the columns of table A first. The second inner join has the columns of table B first. This difference does not affect the information in the table, so the tables are considered to be equal. This can be written

A inner join B = B inner join A

In mathematical terms, this means that the inner join is commutative.

A similar statement can be made about an inner join of three or more tables:

(A inner join B) inner join C = A inner join (B inner join C)

In mathematical terms, this means that the inner join is associative.

All this information may seem obvious and hardly worth saying. However, we are preparing to discuss outer joins. For two types of outer joins, these properties are *not* true.

$$A \times B = B \times A$$

$$A \times (B \times C) = (A \times B) \times C$$

where
    A, B, C are tables
    x is an inner join

Figure 7-17   Inner joins are symmetric

Some tables should always be joined to other tables in one particular way

Most tables are designed to be joined in a particular way to other tables in the database. The way one table relates to another table is determined by the initial design of the database. Certain columns of one table must be matched with particular columns of the other table. Data is entered into these columns based on the assumption that the join will be done in the specified way.

Figure 7-18 shows an example of this. The Foods table and the Lunch Items table are designed to be joined with two matching columns:

> Column 1 of the Foods table matches with
> Column 3 of the Lunch Items table

and

> Column 2 of the Foods table matches with
> Column 4 of the Lunch Items table

The first set of matching columns is named "Supplier_id." The second set of matching columns is named "Product_code." So the condition above can also be written:

> Foods.Supplier_id = Lunch_items.Supplier_id

and

> Foods.Product_code = Lunch_items.Product_code

You can join the tables using only one of these conditions or using some other condition. SQL can join the tables in any manner you specify. However, the "meaning" of the data would be changed.

The first row of the Lunch Items table in Figure 7-18 is intended to mean that lunch 2 includes two sandwiches. It gets this meaning when the tables are joined on both the Supplier Id and Product Code columns.

However, suppose that you joined the tables only on the Supplier Id and did not include the Product Code. Then the first row of the Lunch Items table would mean that lunch 2 includes two fresh salads, two soups, and two sandwiches—two of all the items supplied by supplier ASP.

Two methods to show the matching columns

Database designers often use the names of the columns to indicate how the tables should be joined. Two different naming conventions are often used.

In one method, the matching columns are given identical names. To join any two tables, you must match all the columns from those tables that have identical names. This is the method used in the Lunches database.

In the other method, the matching columns are given names that are very similar but not identical. Usually, each column name is unique throughout the entire database. Two different columns never have identical names. The advantage of this fact is that the name of the table can be inferred from the name of the column. So you never need to write the table name and a dot before the column name. The column name itself is sufficient.

Task

Show how to join the Foods table with the Lunch Items table. Show that this join should always use two columns—the Suppliers Id column and the Product code column.

Oracle & Access SQL

```
select b.lunch_id,
       a.description as food_item,
       a.price as unit_price,
       b.quantity,
       a.price * b.quantity as total_price
from l_foods a,
     l_lunch_items b
where a.supplier_id = b.supplier_id
and a.product_code = b.product_code
 and b.lunch_id = 2;
```

Beginning table 1 (L_foods table)

```
SUPPLIER PRODUCT   MENU                                        PRICE
ID       CODE      ITEM DESCRIPTION              PRICE INCREASE
-------- -------  ------- --------------------  -------- --------
ASP      FS          1 FRESH SALAD              $2.00    $0.25
ASP      SP          2 SOUP OF THE DAY          $1.50   (null)
ASP      SW          3 SANDWICH                 $3.50    $0.40
CBC      GS          4 GRILLED STEAK            $6.00    $0.70
CBC      HB          5 HAMBURGER                $2.50    $0.30
FRV      BR          6 BROCCOLI                 $1.00    $0.05
FRV      FF          7 FRENCH FRIES             $1.50   (null)
JBR      AS          8 SODA                     $1.25    $0.25
JBR      VR          9 COFFEE                   $0.85    $0.15
VSB      AS         10 DESSERT                  $3.00    $0.50
```

Beginning table 2 (L_lunch_items table—where lunch_id = 2)

```
                      SUPPLIER PRODUCT
 LUNCH_ID ITEM_NUMBER ID       CODE    QUANTITY
 -------- ----------- -------- ------- ---------
        2           1 ASP      SW             2
        2           2 FRV      FF             1
        2           3 JBR      VR             2
        2           4 VSB      AS             1
```

Result table

```
LUNCH_ID FOOD_ITEM            UNIT_PRICE QUANTITY TOTAL_PRICE
-------- -------------------- ---------- -------- -----------
       2 SANDWICH                 $3.50         2      $7.00
       2 FRENCH FRIES             $1.50         1      $1.50
       2 COFFEE                    $.85         2      $1.70
       2 DESSERT                  $3.00         1      $3.00
```

Figure 7-18   Some tables should always be joined to other tables in one particular way

A view can standardize the way tables are joined

A view can be used to standardize the method for joining together two or more tables. Once this view is created, most users of the database will use it in their queries instead of using the tables directly. In effect, this makes the database appear as if it is one large table. By using this technique, most people using the database will never need to write SQL code to join the tables, because it will already be written for them.

Of course, you do not need to join all the tables in a single view. You can create several views that have different amounts of information in them. Sometimes you do so for the convenience of the people using the database, or sometimes to make the database perform more efficiently, since using a join of all the table can be inefficient when some parts of the information are not needed.

Figure 7-20 shows this technique. It creates a view called "all_lunches" that joins all the tables of the lunches database.

Task

Create a view that joins all the tables of the lunches database.

Oracle SQL

```
create view all_lunches as
select a.*,
       b.department_name,
       c.lunch_id,
       c.lunch_date,
       d.supplier_id,
       d.product_code,
       d.quantity,
       e.description,
       e.price,
       e.price_increase,
       f.supplier_name
from l_employees a,
     l_departments b,
     l_lunches c,
     l_lunch_items d,
     l_foods e,
     l_suppliers f
where a.dept_code = b.dept_code
 and a.employee_id = c.employee_id
 and c.lunch_id = d.lunch_id
 and d.supplier_id = e.supplier_id
 and d.product_code =
        e.product_code
 and d.supplier_id = f.supplier_id;
```

Access SQL

(Enter this query in the SQL window.)

```
select a.*,
       b.department_name,
       c.lunch_id,
       c.lunch_date,
       d.supplier_id,
       d.product_code,
       d.quantity,
       e.description,
       e.price,
       e.price_increase,
       f.supplier_name
from l_employees a,
     l_departments b,
     l_lunches c,
     l_lunch_items d,
     l_foods e,
     l_suppliers f
where a.dept_code = b.dept_code
 and a.employee_id = c.employee_id
 and c.lunch_id = d.lunch_id
 and d.supplier_id = e.supplier_id
 and d.product_code =
        e.product_code
 and d.supplier_id = f.supplier_id;
```

(Save this query. Name it "All_Lunches.")

Figure 7-19   A view can standardize the way tables are joined (part 1 of 2)

Part 2 of Figure 7-19 shows a query that uses the All Lunches view, which you created on the previous page. This query does not require any joins. The view has already done all of the joins. The query is written as if all the data in the Lunches database was in a single table.

Then the same query is written again, without using the All Lunches view. The data is obtained directly from the tables of the Lunches database. The tables are joined together within From and Where clauses of the query.

Figure 7-19, part 2

❶   Here, the From clause refers to the All Lunches view, which combines all the data from the Lunches database.

❷   Here, the From clause refers directly to the tables of the Lunches database. This fact causes the query to be more complex.

Task

Write a query using the All Lunches view. Write the same query without using this view—getting the data directly from the tables of the Lunches database.

Oracle & Access SQL

Getting data from the All Lunches view	Getting data directly from the tables of the Lunches database
| ```
select employee_id,
       first_name,
       last_name,
       credit_limit,
       sum(price * quantity)
          as total_price
from all_lunches ❶
group by employee_id,
         first_name,
         last_name,
         credit_limit
order by employee_id;
``` | ```
select a.employee_id,
       a.first_name,
       a.last_name,
       a.credit_limit,
       sum(d.price * c.quantity)
          as total_price
from l_employees a, ❷
     l_lunches b,
     l_lunch_items c,
     l_foods d
where a.employee_id =
             b.employee_id
and b.lunch_id = c.lunch_id
and c.supplier_id = d.supplier_id
and c.product_code =
             d.product_code
group by a.employee_id,
         a.first_name,
         a.last_name,
         a.credit_limit
order by a.employee_id;
``` |

Result table

```
EMPLOYEE                         CREDIT
      ID FIRST_NAME LAST_NAME     LIMIT  TOTAL_PRICE
-------- ---------- ----------   ------- -----------
     201 SUSAN      BROWN        $30.00      $30.05
     202 JIM        KERN         $25.00      $13.20
     203 MARTHA     WOODS        $25.00      $25.30
     204 ELLEN      OWENS        $15.00      $12.70
     205 HENRY      PERKINS      $25.00      $24.35
     206 CAROL      ROSE         $15.00      $13.70
     207 DAN        SMITH        $25.00      $24.75
     208 FRED       CAMPBELL     $25.00      $23.10
     210 NANCY      HOFFMAN      $25.00      $25.55
```

Figure 7-19   A view can standardize the way tables are joined (part 2 of 2)

Sometimes tables can be joined to each other in several different ways

Usually the designers of a database decide how the tables should be joined with each other. This decision establishes a relationship between the tables, and the data is entered with this relationship in mind. The relationship is built into the design of the database, and it might seem to be unchangeable.

However, relational databases are intended for use in ad-hoc reporting. That is, they are intended to help you respond to new situations and create reports that have never been thought of before. You might want to see what effect a new law would have on your business. Or you might want to respond to a change in the currency exchange rates.

To support ad-hoc reporting, relational databases allow you to join tables together in many different ways, even in ways the database designers never considered. Naturally, you must be very careful when you do this type of join. You much check it carefully to be sure that you know what you are getting.

Figure 7-20 is a lighthearted example to remind you that sometimes two tables can be joined together in several different ways. We all know that boys and girls find lots of reasons to join with each other.

In this example, the boys table and the girls table can be joined in two different ways. A girl and a boy can be joined because they go to the same school. Or they can be joined because they are interested in the same things. Each of these joins gives a different result table.

Task

Show an example of tables that can be joined in several different ways.

Beginning tables
Fig720_boys tableFig720_girls table

```
NAME      SCHOOL            INTEREST     NAME      SCHOOL            INTEREST
-------   ---------------   ---------    -------   ---------------   ---------
BOB       INDIANA U         HIKING       ALICE     UC BERKELEY       MUSIC
GREG      U OF MIAMI        MOVIES       CAROL     U OF ILLINOIS     BIKING
JOHN      UC BERKELEY       YOGA         NANCY     U OF MIAMI        YOGA
MIKE      NYU               MUSIC        PAULA     U OF KENTUCKY     MOVIES
```

Oracle & Access SQL—joining the tables on school

```
select b.*, g.*
from fig720_boys b,
     fig720_girls g
where b.school = g.school;
```

Result table—matched on school

```
NAME      SCHOOL            INTEREST     NAME      SCHOOL            INTEREST
-------   ---------------   ----------   -------   ---------------   ----------
GREG      U OF MIAMI        MOVIES       NANCY     U OF MIAMI        YOGA
JOHN      UC BERKELEY       YOGA         ALICE     UC BERKELEY       MUSIC
```

Oracle & Access SQL—joining the tables on interest

```
select b.*, g.*
from fig720_boys b,
     fig720_girls g
where b.interest = g.interest;
```

Result table—matched on interest

```
NAME      SCHOOL            INTEREST     NAME      SCHOOL            INTEREST
-------   ---------------   ----------   -------   ---------------   ----------
GREG      U OF MIAMI        MOVIES       PAULA     U OF KENTUCKY     MOVIES
MIKE      NYU               MUSIC        ALICE     UC BERKELEY       MUSIC
JOHN      UC BERKELEY       YOGA         NANCY     U OF MIAMI        YOGA
```

Figure 7-20   Sometimes tables can be joined in several different ways

Summary

In this chapter, you learned how to use the information in several tables within a Select statement or series of Select statements. You learned the characteristics of inner joins:

- They contain all the combinations of rows that satisfy the join condition.
- They drop rows that do not have a match in every table.

You saw examples of several types of inner joins—ones based on equality, ones based on Between, and ones based on Greater Than. You saw how to join several tables together at one time and how to join them in a series of steps. You learned the syntax to write the join condition in the Where clause, and also how to write it in the From clause.

In Chapter 2, I discussed how to use a lookup table to find the meanings of coded fields. The technique I used there was an inner join. By the term "lookup table," I meant a table that contains the meanings of all the codes in a column of some table. This list of codes should be complete. If any code is missing, and an inner join is used to determine the meanings of the codes, then ant row that uses a missing code is automatically deleted from the result.

To ensure that this does not cause a problem, a relationship between the columns can be set up by the database designers. This relationship is called "Referential Integrity." It is used primarily as a rule to regulate and validate the data that can be entered into a column of a table—to restrict the values entered into a column so that only valid codes can be entered. When Referential Integrity is enforced, you can be sure that no rows of data will be dropped if you use an inner join to find the meanings of the codes in that column.

Exercises

1. Goal: Join two tables. List some of the columns and some of the rows. Apply row functions when needed.

1A. From the Lunches database, list the names of the people who are attending each lunch. Show this information in the formats:

Name:	Perkins, Mary	first column
Lunch date:	Monday, October 12, 1998	second column

Sort this by the last name of the employee.

Solution
Oracle SQL

```
select (rtrim(a.last_name) || ', ' || rtrim(first_name)) as full_name,
       to_char(b.lunch_date, 'day, month dd, yyyy') as lunch_reservation
from l_employees a,
     l_lunches b
where a.employee_id = b.employee_id
order by last_name;
```

Access SQL

```
select (rtrim(a.last_name) & ', ' & rtrim(first_name)) as full_name,
       format(b.lunch_date, 'ddd, mmmmm dd, yyyy') as lunch_reservation
from l_employees a,
     l_lunches b
where a.employee_id = b.employee_id
order by last_name;
```

1B. For each type of food in the Foods table, list:

    the full name of the supplier
    the description of the food
    the price plus the price increase, call this the "Total_price"

Where the price increase is null, assume that ten cents will be added to the price. Sort this information by the total price.

2. Goal: Join three or more tables. Summarize the data using a column function.

2A. For each lunch date, list the total quantity of each food needed for that lunch. List the columns:

> lunch date, in a format like : Mon, Oct 12, 1998
> food description
> full name of the supplier
> total quantity
> total price with the price increase and null being $0.10.

Sort this information by the lunch date and the food description.

Solution

Oracle SQL (You can adjust this code to run in Access)

```
First, I will join the tables. I will get only the columns needed in
this exercise. I will do this join as a series of steps.


create view step_1 as
select a.lunch_date,
       b.supplier_id,
       b.product_code,
       b.quantity
from l_lunches a,
     l_lunch_items b
where a.lunch_id = b.lunch_id;


create view step_2 as
select a.*,
       b.description,
       b.price,
       b.price_increase
from step_1 a,
     l_foods b
where a.supplier_id = b.supplier_id
  and a.product_code = b.product_code;


create view step_3 as
select a.*,
       b.supplier_name
from step_2 a,
     l_suppliers b
where a.supplier_id = b.supplier_id;
```

```
Next, I look at what I have created to check it.


select *
from step_3;


Then, I summarize the data.
(Note: I need to group by the supplier name because it is not a summa-
rized item. Alternatively, I could have used MAX or MIN with the sup-
plier name in the Select clause and taken it out of the Group By
clause.)


column lunch_date format a16;
column total_quantity heading "TOTAL|QUANTITY";
column total_price format $99.99 heading "TOTAL|PRICE";

select to_char(lunch_date, 'dy, mon dd, yyyy') as "lunch date",
       description as "food item",
       supplier_name as supplier,
       sum(quantity) as total_quantity,
       sum(price + nvl(price_increase,0.10) * quantity) as total_price
from step_3
group by lunch_date,
         description,
         supplier_name
order by lunch_date,
         description;
```

2B. Summarize the report in exercise 2A. Combine all the lunches together and do not list the lunch date. This will list the foods eaten in all the lunches with the total quantity and the total price.

2C. Modify the report in 2B to provide detail by department and omit the name of the supplier. That is, group the data on department and food. List the columns:

> full name of the department
> food description
> total quantity for all the lunches
> total price (price plus the price increase) for all the lunches

3. Goal: Use an inner join to find the intersection of two sets.

3A. Tables EX7_3A and EX7_3B contain lists of numbers. Find the numbers that are on both lists.

Solution.
Oracle & Access SQL

```
select a.n
from ex7_3a a,
       ex7_3b b
where a.n = b.n
order by n;
```

3B. Find the numbers that are in both the tables EX7_3A and EX7_3C.

3C. Find the numbers that are on all three lists, EX7_3A, EX7_3B, and EX7_3C.

4. Goal: Find the difference between two sets. That is, find all the items in one set that are not in the other set.
(Hint: this uses a subquery)

4A. Find all the numbers in EX7_3A that are not in EX7_3B.

Solution.
Oracle & Access SQL

```
select n
from ex7_3a
where not n in (select n
                from ex7_3b);

Note: The first "select n" refers to the column n in the table ex7_3a.
The second "select n" refers the column n in the table ex7_3b.
```

4B. Find all the numbers in EX7_3A that are not in EX7_3C.

4C. Find all the numbers in EX7_3A that are not in EX7_3B and are also not in EX7_3C.

5. Goal: Create the union of two sets.

5A. Create a table that contains all the numbers from both tables EX7_3A and EX7_3B.

Solution
Oracle SQL (You can adjust this code to run in Access)

```
create table temp_1 as
select n
from ex7_3a;


insert into temp_1
select n
from ex7_3b;


create table the_union as
select distinct n
from temp_1;
```

5B. create a table that has all the numbers from the three tables EX7_3A, EX7_3B, and EX7_3C.

6. Goal: Prepare for the discussion of outer joins in the next chapter.

6A. List the two tables TWOS and THREES. Then create the inner join of these tables. Notice that many of the rows are dropped. Also find the union of these two tables using the techniques of the exercises above.

Chapter 8

Outer Joins and Unions

Outer Joins

Inner joins often drop some of the rows of the beginning tables. A row is dropped if just one table in the join does not have a matching row. If you want to keep these unmatched rows, instead of dropping them, you must use an outer join.

Outer joins are derived from inner joins

An outer join is derived from an inner join by adding back some of the rows that the inner join dropped from the beginning tables. Of the three types of outer joins, each type adds back a different set of rows. However, all three types of outer joins begin by forming the inner join.

Most of the discussion of outer joins will be based on two tables named "Twos" and "Threes." The Twos table contains a column of numbers, which consists of all the multiples of two up to twenty with the addition of one null. This table also contains a column of words that describe the numbers and the null.

The Threes table is similar, except that it contains the multiples of three up to twenty. The joins will be done on the columns of numbers. The columns of words are there to show that the tables have columns other than the ones used in the joins. Often, many such columns exist.

In both tables, the number column contains a null. The word column for that row does not contain a null. It contains a word with four letters, which are N, U, L, and L. These are meant to be a description of what is in the number column.

The inner join of these tables contains three rows—6, 12, and 18. All the other rows of the beginning tables are dropped from the result table.

Rows that are dropped from the inner join
Twos table   Threes table

NUMBER_2	WORD_2	NUMBER_3	WORD_3
2	TWO	3	THREE
4	FOUR	9	NINE
8	EIGHT	15	FIFTEEN
10	TEN	(null)	NULL
14	FOURTEEN		
16	SIXTEEN		
20	TWENTY		
(null)	NULL		

Task

Show the inner join of the Twos table and the Threes table. Manually construct a list of the rows that are dropped from the result table.

Oracle & Access SQL

```
select a.*,
       b.*
from twos a,
     threes b
where a.number_2 = b.number_3
order by a.number_2;
```

Beginning tables
Twos table   ## Threes table

```
NUMBER_2 WORD_2                  NUMBER_3 WORD_3
-------- --------------         -------- ---------------
       2 TWO                            3 THREE
       4 FOUR                           6 SIX
       6 SIX                            9 NINE
       8 EIGHT                         12 TWELVE
      10 TEN                           15 FIFTEEN
      12 TWELVE                        18 EIGHTEEN
      14 FOURTEEN        (null)        NULL
      16 SIXTEEN
      18 EIGHTEEN
      20 TWENTY
(null)    NULL
```

Result table

```
NUMBER_2 WORD_2              NUMBER_3 WORD_3
-------- --------------      -------- --------------
       6 SIX                        6 SIX
      12 TWELVE                     12 TWELVE
      18 EIGHTEEN                   18 EIGHTEEN
```

Figure 8-1   Outer joins are derived from inner joins

The three types of outer joins

Three types of outer joins occur—the left outer join, the right outer join, and the full outer join. They all begin with the inner join, and then they add back some of the rows that have been dropped.

The left outer join adds back all the rows that are dropped from the first table. Nulls are placed in the columns that come from the Threes table. For instance, the row "2-two" is added back to the result table. The columns for the matching row of the Threes table, Number_3 and Word_3, are set to null.

The right outer join adds back all the rows that are dropped from the second table. In all the rows that are added back, the columns for the matching rows of the Twos table are set to null.

The full outer join adds back all the rows dropped from both tables.

Beginning tables
Twos table   ## Threes table

NUMBER_2	WORD_2
2	TWO
4	FOUR
6	SIX
8	EIGHT
10	TEN
12	TWELVE
14	FOURTEEN
16	SIXTEEN
18	EIGHTEEN
20	TWENTY
(null)	NULL

NUMBER_3	WORD_3
3	THREE
6	SIX
9	NINE
12	TWELVE
15	FIFTEEN
18	EIGHTEEN
(null)	NULL

Inner join

NUMBER_2	WORD_2	NUMBER_3	WORD_3
6	SIX	6	SIX
12	TWELVE	12	TWELVE
18	EIGHTEEN	18	EIGHTEEN

Task

For the Twos table and the Threes table, show the results of the three types of outer joins.

Left outer join—has all the rows from the first table

```
NUMBER_2 WORD_2             NUMBER_3 WORD_3
-------- ---------------    -------- ---------------
       2 TWO                 (null)   (null)
       4 FOUR                (null)   (null)
       6 SIX                      6  SIX
       8 EIGHT               (null)   (null)
      10 TEN                 (null)   (null)
      12 TWELVE                  12  TWELVE
      14 FOURTEEN            (null)   (null)
      16 SIXTEEN             (null)   (null)
      18 EIGHTEEN                18  EIGHTEEN
      20 TWENTY              (null)   (null)
 (null)  NULL                (null)   (null)
```

Right outer join—has all the rows from the second table

```
NUMBER_2 WORD_2             NUMBER_3 WORD_3
-------- ---------------    -------- ---------------
 (null)  (null)                   3  THREE
       6 SIX                      6  SIX
 (null)  (null)                   9  NINE
      12 TWELVE                  12  TWELVE
 (null)  (null)                  15  FIFTEEN
      18 EIGHTEEN                18  EIGHTEEN
 (null)  (null)              (null)   NULL
```

Full outer join—has all the rows from both tables

```
NUMBER_2 WORD_2             NUMBER_3 WORD_3
-------- ---------------    -------- ---------------
       2 TWO                 (null)   (null)
 (null)  (null)                   3  THREE
       4 FOUR                (null)   (null)
       6 SIX                      6  SIX
       8 EIGHT               (null)   (null)
 (null)  (null)                   9  NINE
      10 TEN                 (null)   (null)
      12 TWELVE                  12  TWELVE
      14 FOURTEEN            (null)   (null)
 (null)  (null)                  15  FIFTEEN
      16 SIXTEEN             (null)   (null)
      18 EIGHTEEN                18  EIGHTEEN
      20 TWENTY              (null)   (null)
 (null)  NULL                (null)   (null)
 (null)  (null)              (null)   NULL
```

Figure 8-2   The three types of outer joins

The left outer join

Both Oracle and Access can produce a left outer join. The result tables are exactly the same. However, they write the SQL code in different ways.

Oracle uses the older syntax for writing joins. It places the join condition in the Where clause. Access uses the new syntax for writing joins, which it does in the From clause.

The syntax that Access uses is from the newest SQL standard, SQL-92. Probably, within a few years, Oracle will support this syntax in addition to its present syntax.

A left outer join keeps all the rows from the first table, but has from the second table only the rows that match with a row from the first table.

In Figure 8-3, the rows of the result table are sorted on the Number column from the first table, in order to put them in a logical order. In Oracle, the null is sorted at the end of the table. In Access, it is sorted at the beginning.

The Order By clause in this example is not needed to join the two tables together. If you are creating a view to join the tables, you will omit this clause. It is used here to display the rows of the result in a logical order.

Figure 8-3 shows only the process of joining the tables. You can also include other logic in a Select statement that performs a left outer join. This includes all the other constructs you have studied:

Row functions, expressions, and column functions in the Select clause
Additional conditions in the Where clause
A Group By clause
A Having clause
An Order By clause

Figure 8-3

❶ In Oracle, the join condition is written in the Where clause. A plus sign in parentheses, "(+)," is written to the right of the join condition. This specifies a left outer join. When several clauses are in the join condition, the plus sign must be written to the right of each of them.

Putting the plus sign on the right may not seem to make sense in order to write a left outer join. One way to think about this order is that the plus sign is written on the side where the nulls are added to the incomplete rows that are added back.

❷ The Order By clause puts the rows in a logical order. It is not required in a left outer join.

❸ In Access, "left outer join" is written in the From clause. This specifies a left outer join. The word "outer" is optional, so you can also write "left join" here.

❹ In Access, the join condition is written in the On sub-clause of the From clause.

Task

Show the syntax to write a left outer join in Oracle and in Access.

Oracle SQL

```
select a.*,
       b.*
from twos a,
     threes b
where a.number_2 = b.number_3 (+) ❶
order by a.number_2; ❷
```

Access SQL

```
select a.*,
       b.*
from twos a
  left outer join threes b ❸
  on a.number_2 = b.number_3 ❹
order by a.number_2;
```

Beginning tables
Twos table

Threes table

NUMBER_2	WORD_2
2	TWO
4	FOUR
6	SIX
8	EIGHT
10	TEN
12	TWELVE
14	FOURTEEN
16	SIXTEEN
18	EIGHTEEN
20	TWENTY
(null)	NULL

NUMBER_3	WORD_3
3	THREE
6	SIX
9	NINE
12	TWELVE
15	FIFTEEN
18	EIGHTEEN
(null)	NULL

Result table—left outer join

NUMBER_2	WORD_2	NUMBER_3	WORD_3
2	TWO	(null)	(null)
4	FOUR	(null)	(null)
6	SIX	6	SIX
8	EIGHT	(null)	(null)
10	TEN	(null)	(null)
12	TWELVE	12	TWELVE
14	FOURTEEN	(null)	(null)
16	SIXTEEN	(null)	(null)
18	EIGHTEEN	18	EIGHTEEN
20	TWENTY	(null)	(null)
(null)	NULL	(null)	(null)

Figure 8-3   The left outer join

The right outer join

The right outer join is similar to the left outer join, except that it is the reverse. The rows dropped from the second table are added back instead of the rows from the first table.

The syntax is also similar. The difference between the syntax for Oracle and Access is the same for both the left and right outer joins.

Figure 8-4

❶   In Oracle, the join condition is written in the Where clause. A plus sign in parentheses, "(+)," is written to the left of the join condition. This specifies a right outer join. When several clauses are in the join condition, the plus sign must be written to the left of each of them.

❷   The Order By clause puts the rows in a logical order. It is not required in a right outer join.

❸   In Access, "right outer join" is written in the From clause. This specifies a right outer join. The word "outer" is optional, so you can also write "right join" here.

❹   In Access, the join condition is written in the On sub-clause of the From clause.

Task

Show the syntax to write a right outer join in Oracle and in Access.

Oracle SQL

```
select a.*,
       b.*
from twos a,
     threes b
where a.number_2 (+) = b.number_3  ❶
order by b.number_3;  ❷
```

Access SQL

```
select a.*,
       b.*
from twos a
     right outer join threes b  ❸
     on a.number_2 = b.number_3  ❹
order by b.number_3;
```

Beginning tables
Twos table

Threes table

NUMBER_2	WORD_2
2	TWO
4	FOUR
6	SIX
8	EIGHT
10	TEN
12	TWELVE
14	FOURTEEN
16	SIXTEEN
18	EIGHTEEN
20	TWENTY
(null)	NULL

NUMBER_3	WORD_3
3	THREE
6	SIX
9	NINE
12	TWELVE
15	FIFTEEN
18	EIGHTEEN
(null)	NULL

Result table—right outer join

NUMBER_2	WORD_2	NUMBER_3	WORD_3
(null)	(null)	3	THREE
6	SIX	6	SIX
(null)	(null)	9	NINE
12	TWELVE	12	TWELVE
(null)	(null)	15	FIFTEEN
18	EIGHTEEN	18	EIGHTEEN
(null)	(null)	(null)	NULL

Figure 8-4   The right outer join

The full outer join

The full outer join adds back all the rows dropped from both tables by the inner join. It keeps all the rows from both tables and makes as many matches as the data and the join condition allow.

Some SQL products have direct support for the full outer join. However, Oracle and Access do not support it directly. If you want to use a full outer join, you have to construct it.

You can create a full outer join by writing a union of the left outer join and the right outer join. We will discuss these unions in "An introduction to unions," next in this chapter. For now, you can think of them as a way to combine a left outer join and a right outer join.

The SQL may look complicated, but it is only:

> left outer join
> union
> right outer join

The order of the left and right outer joins does not matter and can be reversed. So the full outer join can also be written:

> right outer join
> union
> left outer join

Additional logic and clauses can be put into the Select statements, such as Where conditions, Group By clauses, and Having clauses. Use of an Order By clause, however, requires a few special considerations that I discuss later in this chapter.

Beginning tables
Twos table   Threes table

NUMBER_2	WORD_2	NUMBER_3	WORD_3
2	TWO	3	THREE
4	FOUR	6	SIX
6	SIX	9	NINE
8	EIGHT	12	TWELVE
10	TEN	15	FIFTEEN
12	TWELVE	18	EIGHTEEN
14	FOURTEEN	(null)	NULL
16	SIXTEEN		
18	EIGHTEEN		
20	TWENTY		
(null)	NULL		

Task

Show the syntax to write a full outer join in Oracle and in Access.

Oracle SQL

```
select a.*,
       b.*
from twos a,
     threes b
where a.number_2 = b.number_3 (+)
union
select c.*,
       d.*
from twos c,
     threes d
where c.number_2 (+) = d.number_3;
```

Access SQL

```
select a.*,
       b.*
from twos a
     left outer join threes b
     on a.number_2 = b.number_3
union
select c.*,
       d.*
from twos c
     right outer join threes d
     on c.number_2 = d.number_3;
```

SQL—products with direct support for the full outer join

```
select a.*,
       b.*
from twos a
     full outer join threes b
     on a.number_2 = b.number_3;
```

Result table—full outer join

NUMBER_2	WORD_2	NUMBER_3	WORD_3
2	TWO	(null)	(null)
(null)	(null)	3	THREE
4	FOUR	(null)	(null)
6	SIX	6	SIX
8	EIGHT	(null)	(null)
(null)	(null)	9	NINE
10	TEN	(null)	(null)
12	TWELVE	12	TWELVE
14	FOURTEEN	(null)	(null)
(null)	(null)	15	FIFTEEN
16	SIXTEEN	(null)	(null)
18	EIGHTEEN	18	EIGHTEEN
20	TWENTY	(null)	(null)
(null)	NULL	(null)	(null)
(null)	(null)	(null)	NULL

Figure 8-5   The full outer join

An introduction to unions

A "union" of two tables adds the rows of one table to the other table. The two beginning tables are combined to form a single table. The rows of the two tables must be identical, or nearly identical in structure, so that they can all fit together within the framework of one table. This requirement means that they must have the same number of columns and that the datatypes of these columns must be in the same order. Otherwise, a union cannot be formed.

Duplicate rows are eliminated from a union. If two rows have the same values in every column, the union will keep only one of them and will drop the other one. This action is taken whether both rows come from the same table or whether they come from different tables.

The "union" of tables in the theory of relational databases corresponds closely to the way a union of sets is defined in mathematics. This reason is why the duplicate rows are eliminated.

You have formed a union of two tables before, in the exercises. The method used there was to insert the rows from one table into the other table and then to use Select Distinct to eliminate the duplicate rows.

When a union is written within SQL code, Select statements stand for the two tables. So the word "union" is placed between two Select statements.

In the case of a full outer join, the union is placed between the Select statements for the left outer join and the right outer join. These two tables always have the same number of columns, and the datatypes of those columns are always in the same order. Hence, this union can always be formed.

Another way to form a union

Step 1
```
insert into B
      select *
      from A;
```

Step 2
```
create table C as
      select distinct *
      from B;
```

The Process of Forming a Union

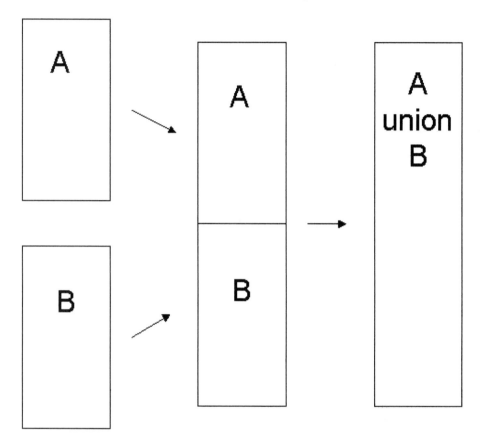

Oracle & Access SQL

```
select *
from A
union
select *
from B;
```

Figure 8-6 An introduction to unions

An example of a union of two tables with matching columns

Figure 8-7 shows an example of a union. The two tables have the same structure. That is, they both have three columns, and the datatypes of these columns are:

numeric
text
date/time

in that order. These are the three main types of columns that are used in relational databases. This example shows that they can all be used in a union.

The result table contains all the rows from both beginning tables. We can call these rows 1 through 7. Rows 1 and 2 come only from the first beginning table. Rows 6 and 7 come only from the second beginning table. Rows 3, 4, and 5 come from both beginning tables; however, only a single copy of these rows is kept in the result table, because the duplicate copies of rows are eliminated.

The SQL code contains two Select statements with the word "union" between them. In Figure 8-7, these Select statements are very simple, but they can be any of the Select statements you have studied and they can use any of the clauses of the Select statement, except the Order By clause.

Look at the column headings of the result table. The first Select statement sets them. The column headings of the first beginning table are used, unless a column alias is assigned. The column alias in this example is "Text_1."

The Order By clause is the last line, and it is placed after the second Select statement. Even a union of three or more tables can have only one Order By clause, and it must be the last line of the union. This clause sorts all the rows of the union into a designated order.

The Order By clause can refer to a column in several different ways. The ones used the most are:

Order By Number_1   Uses the column name from the first Select statement.

Order By Text_1   Uses a column alias from the first Select statement.

Order by 1   Uses the numeric position of the column within the union.

Figure 8-7

❶   The first Select statement lists three columns. It determines the heading for the columns. It cannot have an Order By clause.

❷   The word "Union" is placed between the two Select statements.

❸   The second Select statement must have the same number of columns as the first Select statement, and the datatypes of the matching columns must be compatible.

❹   The Order By clause is placed at the end of the union.

Task

Show an example of a Select statement that uses a union.

Oracle & Access SQL

```
select a.number_1, ❶
       a.word_1 as text_1,
       a.date_1
from fig807_first a
union ❷
select b.number_2,❸
       b.word_2,
       b.date_2
from fig807_second b
order by number_1; ❹
```

Beginning tables
Fig807_first table   Fig807_second table

NUMBER_1	WORD_1	DATE_1
--		
1	ONE	01-DEC-98
2	TWO	02-DEC-98
3	THREE	03-DEC-98
4	FOUR	04-DEC-98
5	FIVE	05-DEC-98

NUMBER_2	WORD_2	DATE_2
--		
3	THREE	03-DEC-98
4	FOUR	04-DEC-98
5	FIVE	05-DEC-98
6	SIX	06-DEC-98
7	SEVEN	07-DEC-98

Result table

NUMBER_1	TEXT_1	DATE_1
1	ONE	01-DEC-98
2	TWO	02-DEC-98
3	THREE	03-DEC-98
4	FOUR	04-DEC-98
5	FIVE	05-DEC-98
6	SIX	06-DEC-98
7	SEVEN	07-DEC-98

Figure 8-7   An example of a union of two tables with matching columns

A full outer join in sorted order

Figure 8-8 shows a full outer join of the Twos table with the Threes table. The rows of the result table are sorted into their logical order.

The difficulty in sorting the rows this way is that they should be sorted on two columns, Number_2 and Number_3. Sometimes one of these columns contains a null. Then the other column contains the value to use in sorting the rows. Sometimes both columns contain the same value.

The solution in Oracle is to use the NVL ("null value") function:

$$NVL(a.number\_2, b.number\_3) = a.number\_2 \quad \text{if a.number\_2 is not null}$$
$$= b.number\_3 \quad \text{if a.number\_2 is null}$$

This function must be defined as a column of the union, so it must be included in both the first and second Select clauses. It is given a column alias, "sort_order," and that column alias is used in the Order By clause.

The solution in Access is similar. The NZ function is used instead of the NVL function. However, one additional trick is used here. The result of the NZ function is multiplied by one.

Without this trick, the rows are put in the order:

   null, null, 10, 12, 14, 15, 16, 18, 2, 20, 3, 4, 6, 8, 9

The reason is that the NZ function produces text output instead of numeric output. So the numbers are sorted as strings of text characters. In Access, the nulls come first in the sort order.

Multiplying by one changes the text into numbers. It invokes automatic datatype conversion. Another way to invoke this is to use the CINT function. Then the rows are sorted by their numeric order:

   null, null, 2, 3, 4, 6, 8, 9, 10, 12, 14, 15, 16, 18, 20

Figure 8-8

❶   The first Select statement is a left outer join. It includes all the columns of both tables and an additional column to determine the sort order.

❷   The Null Value function, NVL, is used in Oracle to determine the sort order. This is equal to the Number_2 column, except if that column contains a null. Then it is equal to the Number_3 column. The column alias "Sort_order" is given to this column.

❸   Here is the Union, which is used to form the full outer join.

❹   The second select statement is the right outer join.

❺   The NVL function to create the Sort_order column must be included in the second Select statement.

❻   The full outer join, which is formed with a union, is sorted by the Sort_order column.

❼   In Access, the NZ function is multiplied by one to give it a numeric datatype.

Task

Create a full outer join of the Twos table and the Threes table. Sort the rows in numeric order.

Oracle SQL

```
select a.*, b.*, ❶
       nvl(a.number_2,b.number_3) as sort_order ❷
from twos a, threes b
where a.number_2 = b.number_3 (+)
union ❸
select c.*, d.*, ❹
       nvl(c.number_2,d.number_3) ❺
from twos c, threes d
where c.number_2 (+) = d.number_3
order by sort_order; ❻
```

Access SQL

```
select a.*, b.*,
       nz(a.number_2,b.number_3) * 1 as sort_order ❼
from twos a left outer join threes b
     on a.number_2 = b.number_3
union
select c.*, d.*,
       nz(c.number_2,d.number_3) * 1
from twos c right outer join threes d
     on c.number_2 = d.number_3
order by sort_order;
```

Result table

NUMBER_2	WORD_2	NUMBER_3	WORD_3	SORT_ORDER
2	TWO	(null)	(null)	2
(null)	(null)	3	THREE	3
4	FOUR	(null)	(null)	4
6	SIX	6	SIX	6
8	EIGHT	(null)	(null)	8
(null)	(null)	9	NINE	9
10	TEN	(null)	(null)	10
12	TWELVE	12	TWELVE	12
14	FOURTEEN	(null)	(null)	14
(null)	(null)	15	FIFTEEN	15
16	SIXTEEN	(null)	(null)	16
18	EIGHTEEN	18	EIGHTEEN	18
20	TWENTY	(null)	(null)	20
(null)	NULL	(null)	(null)	(null)
(null)	(null)	(null)	NULL	(null)

Figure 8-8 A full outer join in sorted order

The symmetry of full outer joins

The full outer join is symmetric, meaning that in a full outer join, the order in which the tables are joined does not matter. The tables may be joined in any order at all; the result will always be the same. The order of the columns may differ, but no significance is placed on this order.

The inner join has this same property. When you can limit your joins to inner joins and full outer joins, you do not need to be concerned with the order in which the tables are joined.

However, a left outer join and a right outer join are not symmetric. They operate differently on the first table from the way they do on the second table. In practice, this difference means that when you use a right outer join or a left outer join, you will need to be very concerned about the order of the tables and the order in which the joins are performed.

Readers who do not like mathematics can skip the rest of this discussion and turn the page at this point.

Mathematics expresses the symmetry by showing that the inner join is commutative and associative. For this discussion, A, B, and C are tables, any tables.

The commutative rule says that when two tables are being joined together, which one is first and which one is second does not matter. More formally,

A full outer join B = B full outer join A

which is similar to

A inner join B = B inner join A

The associative rule says that when three tables are being joined together, which two are joined together first does not matter (see Figure 8-9). More formally,

(A full outer join B) full outer join C =
A full outer join (B full outer join C)

which is similar to

(A inner join B) inner join C = A inner join (B inner join C)

A x B = B x A

(A x B) x C = A x (B x C)

where A, B, and C are tables
x is a full outer join

Figure 8-9   The symmetry of full outer joins

Unions

A union of tables combines the rows of all the tables together. For this to make sense, the rows of the tables must all have the same structure. Unions were introduced when I discussed the full outer join earlier in this chapter. Here, they are discussed in more detail.

The difference between a union and a join

A union and a join are similar in that they are both ways of combining two tables to form another table. But they do this combining in very different ways. First, the geometry is different.

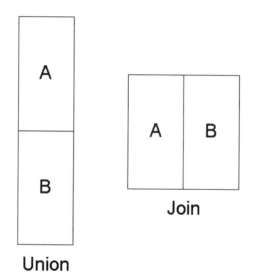

In a union, the rows of one table must fit into the other table. The number of columns in the result table is the same as the number in the beginning tables. No new columns are added. The structure of each row in the result table is the same as in the beginning tables. Here, :the structure of a row" means the sequence of the datatypes of the columns.

In a join, the rows of one table may be very different from the rows of the other table. The result table contains columns from both the first and second tables. It may contain all the columns of the first table, with the new addition of all the columns of the second table. An outer join has the same structure as an inner join, but it may have more rows.

In a union, the maximum number of rows is the SUM of the number of rows of the two tables. In a join, the maximum number of rows is the PRODUCT of them.

Task

Show an example of the difference between a union and a join.

Oracle & Access SQL—for a union

```
select * from fig807_first
union
select * from fig807_second
order by number_1;
```

Beginning tables

Fig807_first table   Fig807_second table

NUMBER_1	WORD_1	DATE_1		NUMBER_2	WORD_2	DATE_2
1	ONE	01-DEC-98		3	THREE	03-DEC-98
2	TWO	02-DEC-98		4	FOUR	04-DEC-98
3	THREE	03-DEC-98		5	FIVE	05-DEC-98
4	FOUR	04-DEC-98		6	SIX	06-DEC-98
5	FIVE	05-DEC-98		7	SEVEN	07-DEC-98

Result table—showing a union

NUMBER_1	WORD_1	DATE_1
1	ONE	01-DEC-98
2	TWO	02-DEC-98
3	THREE	03-DEC-98
4	FOUR	04-DEC-98
5	FIVE	05-DEC-98
6	SIX	06-DEC-98
7	SEVEN	07-DEC-98

Oracle & Access SQL—for an inner join

```
select a.*, b,*
from fig807_first a,
     fig807_second b
where a.number_1 = b.number_2
order by a.number_1;
```

Result table—showing an inner join

NUMBER_1	WORD_1	DATE_1	NUMBER_2	WORD_2	DATE_2
3	THREE	03-DEC-98	3	THREE	03-DEC-98
4	FOUR	04-DEC-98	4	FOUR	04-DEC-98
5	FIVE	05-DEC-98	5	FIVE	05-DEC-98

Figure 8-10   The difference between a union and a join

Union all

"Union All" is another way to combine tables. It is very similar to a union. The only difference is that duplicate rows are not eliminated. In some situations, you may want to keep all the duplicate rows.

However, in most situations, you will not want any duplicate rows. If you are sure that you can never have any duplicate rows, then you may want to use Union All instead of using Union. The reason for doing this is that it makes the processing more efficient for the computer, because it does not need to try to eliminate duplicate rows.

In Figure 8-11, the Union All has two identical rows numbered "3." The Union has only one of these rows. Except for duplicate rows, the result tables of the Union and the Union All are the same.

Beginning tables
Fig807_first table   Fig807_second table

NUMBER_1	WORD_1	DATE_1	NUMBER_2	WORD_2	DATE_2
1	ONE	01-DEC-98	3	THREE	03-DEC-98
2	TWO	02-DEC-98	4	FOUR	04-DEC-98
3	THREE	03-DEC-98	5	FIVE	05-DEC-98
4	FOUR	04-DEC-98	6	SIX	06-DEC-98
5	FIVE	05-DEC-98	7	SEVEN	07-DEC-98

Task

Show how Union All differs from a Union.

Oracle & Access SQL—for a Union

```
select number_1, word_1, date_1
from fig807_first
union
select *
from fig807_second
order by number_1;
```

Result table—showing a Union

```
NUMBER_1 WORD_1            DATE_1
-------- ---------------   ---------
       1 ONE               01-DEC-98
       2 TWO               02-DEC-98
       3 THREE             03-DEC-98
       4 FOUR              04-DEC-98
       5 FIVE              05-DEC-98
       6 SIX               06-DEC-98
       7 SEVEN             07-DEC-98
```

Oracle & Access SQL—for a Union All

```
select number_1, word_1, date_1
from fig807_first
union all
select *
from fig807_second
order by number_1;
```

Result table—showing a Union All

```
NUMBER_1 WORD_1            DATE_1
-------- ---------------   ---------
       1 ONE               01-DEC-98
       2 TWO               02-DEC-98
       3 THREE             03-DEC-98
       3 THREE             03-DEC-98
       4 FOUR              04-DEC-98
       4 FOUR              04-DEC-98
       5 FIVE              05-DEC-98
       5 FIVE              05-DEC-98
       6 SIX               06-DEC-98
       7 SEVEN             07-DEC-98
```

Figure 8-11   Union all

Using a literal in a union to identify the source of the data

Figure 8-12 shows a union of two tables that uses a literal to identify the source of each row of data. Here, a "literal" means a constant value that is enclosed in quotation marks. Oracle requires single quotes, rather than double quotes.

When a literal is used in a Select clause, it creates a column in the result table. This column contains the same value for every row. You are allowed to use a literal in the Select clause of any query. However, usually, doing so does not make sense.

In a union, each Select clause can use a different literal. The identifies the source of each row within the result table.

In a way, this process interferes with the elimination of duplicate rows. The rows of one table are never duplicates of the rows from another table. If the data comes from different tables, then the literals are different.

Figure 8-12 shows that two copies exist of rows 3, 4, and 5. Without the literal, these rows are duplicates. With the literal, they are distinct. In fact, these rows now have distinct meanings. One row says that row 3 occurs in the first table. The other row 3 says that it occurs in the second table.

In Figure 8-12, the second literal is slightly longer than the first. This fact does not cause a problem. SQL automatically adjusts the length of the column to the longer length.

Figure 8-12

❶   The first Select statement lists the rows from the first table. It attaches a literal to each of these rows.

❷   The literal is text placed within quotation marks. A column alias gives this column a name. Every row of the first table will have the same value in this new column.

❸   The union is essential; it combines the rows into a single result table.

❹   The second Select statement lists the rows from the second table. It attaches a different literal to each of these rows.

❺   This is the text that is added to each row of the second table.

Task

Show an example of a Select statement that uses a union with literals that identify the source of each row.

Oracle & Access SQL

```
select number_1, ❶
     word_1,
     date_1,
     'data from the first table' as source_of_the_data ❷
from fig807_first
union ❸
select number_2, ❹
     word_2,
     date_2,
     'data from the second table' ❺
from fig807_second
order by number_1;
```

Beginning tables
Fig807_first table   Fig807_second table

NUMBER_1	WORD_1	DATE_1	NUMBER_2	WORD_2	DATE_2
1	ONE	01-DEC-98	3	THREE	03-DEC-98
2	TWO	02-DEC-98	4	FOUR	04-DEC-98
3	THREE	03-DEC-98	5	FIVE	05-DEC-98
4	FOUR	04-DEC-98	6	SIX	06-DEC-98
5	FIVE	05-DEC-98	7	SEVEN	07-DEC-98

Result table

NUMBER_1	WORD_1	DATE_1	SOURCE_OF_THE_DATA
1	ONE	01-DEC-98	DATA FROM THE FIRST TABLE
2	TWO	02-DEC-98	DATA FROM THE FIRST TABLE
3	THREE	03-DEC-98	DATA FROM THE FIRST TABLE
3	THREE	03-DEC-98	DATA FROM THE SECOND TABLE
4	FOUR	04-DEC-98	DATA FROM THE FIRST TABLE
4	FOUR	04-DEC-98	DATA FROM THE SECOND TABLE
5	FIVE	05-DEC-98	DATA FROM THE FIRST TABLE
5	FIVE	05-DEC-98	DATA FROM THE SECOND TABLE
6	SIX	06-DEC-98	DATA FROM THE SECOND TABLE
7	SEVEN	07-DEC-98	DATA FROM THE SECOND TABLE

Figure 8-12   Using a literal in a union to identify the source of the data

Automatic datatype conversion in a union

In a union, the datatypes of matching columns must be "compatible," but they do not need to be exactly the same. They may differ in length, for example. Three separate categories of columns exist:

> Numbers
> Text
> Dates

Matching columns must match in these categories.

All kinds of numeric columns are compatible with each other. Different types of numbers are automatically converted into the same datatype. SQL converts integers, floating point numbers, and decimal numbers, to make them all the same datatype.

All kinds of text columns are compatible with each other. Different types of text columns are automatically converted into the same datatype. Fixed-length text, variable-length text, and text of different lengths can all be made compatible.

Only one datatype is available for dates and times. So all date and time columns have identical datatypes, even though their formatting may differ.

Figure 8-13 shows an example of this automatic datatype conversion using Oracle. Access works in a similar way.

Oracle datatypes of beginning tables

```
SQL> describe fig813_first
 Name                                Null?    Type
 ----------------------------------- -------- ----
 NUMBER_N7                                    NUMBER(7)
 TEXT_T7                                      VARCHAR2(7)

SQL> describe fig813_second
 Name                                Null?    Type
 ----------------------------------- -------- ----
 NUMBER_N2                                    NUMBER(2)
 TEXT_T2                                      VARCHAR2(2)
```

Oracle datatypes of result table

```
SQL> describe fig813_union
 Name                                Null?    Type
 ----------------------------------- -------- ----
 NUMBER_N7                                    NUMBER
 TEXT_T7                                      VARCHAR2(7)
```

Task

Show an example of automatic datatype conversion taking place in a union.

Oracle SQL

```
create view fig813_union as
select number_n7 as number_col,
        text_t7 as text_column
from fig813_first
union
select number_n2,
        text_t2
from fig813_second;

column text_column format a11;
select * from fig813_union;
```

Access SQL

(enter the query in the SQL window)

```
select number_n7 as number_col,
            text_t7 as text_column
from fig813_first
union
select number_n2,
            text_t2
from fig813_second;
```

(save the query. Name it "fig813_union.")

```
select * from fig813_union;
```

Beginning tables
Fig813_first tableFig813_second table

```
NUMBER_N7 TEXT_T7
--------- -------
  1111111 AAAAAAA
  2222222 BBBBBBB
  3333333 CCCCCCC
  4444444 DDDDDDD
  5555555 EEEEEEE
```

```
NUMBER_N2 TEXT_T2
--------- -------
       33 CC
       44 DD
       55 EE
       66 FF
       77 GG
```

Result table

```
NUMBER_COL TEXT_COLUMN
---------- -----------
        33 CC
        44 DD
        55 EE
        66 FF
        77 GG
   1111111 AAAAAAA
   2222222 BBBBBBB
   3333333 CCCCCCC
   4444444 DDDDDDD
   5555555 EEEEEEE
```

Datatypes of the columns in Oracle

Column of the result table	Data from the beginning tables		Result table
	fig813_first	**fig813_second**	
number column	number(7)	number(2)	number(24)
text column	varchar2(7)	varchar2(2)	varchar2(7)

Figure 8-13   Automatic datatype conversion in a union

Using datatype conversion functions in a union

Figure 8-14 shows a union that explicitly uses a datatype conversion function, rather than relying on automatic datatype conversion. Here, numeric data is changed into text data so that it can be combined in the union with other text data.

The TO_CHAR function in Oracle changes numeric data and date/time data into text data. Using this function, all types of data can be changed into text. So all types of data can be combined within a union.

This example begins to modify the statement, "a union can combine two tables only if they have the same number of columns and if the datatypes of the corresponding columns are compatible." This may be true on the most detailed level. However, it is not true on a more general level of handling information.

This example suggests that all datatypes can be changed into text. So all types of columns can be combined in a union. If the datatypes are not compatible, they can be made to be compatible. One method to do so is to convert them into text.

Datatypes of beginning tables in Oracle

```
SQL> describe fig813_first
    Name                             Null?    Type
    ------------------------------   -------- ----
    NUMBER_N7                                 NUMBER(7)
    TEXT_T7                                   VARCHAR2(7)

SQL> describe fig813_second
    Name                             Null?    Type
    ------------------------------   -------- ----
    NUMBER_N2                                 NUMBER(2)
    TEXT_T2                                   VARCHAR2(2)
```

Datatypes of result table in Oracle

```
SQL> describe fig814_union
    Name                             Null?    Type
    ------------------------------   -------- ----
    FIRST_COLUMN                              VARCHAR2(40)
    SECOND_COLUMN                             VARCHAR2(40)
```

Datatypes of the columns in Oracle

Column of the result table	Data from the beginning tables		Result table
	Fig813_first	**Fig813_second**	
first column	number(7)	varchar2(2)	varchar2(40)
second column	varchar2(7)	number(2)	varchar2(40)

Task

Show how to use datatype conversion functions in a union.

Converting the numbers to text
Oracle SQL

```
create view fig814_union as
select to_char(number_n7)
                 as first_column,
       text_t7 as second_column
from fig813_first
union
select text_t2,
       to_char(number_n2)
from fig813_second;

select * from fig814_union;
```

(enter the query in the SQL window)

```
select Cstr(number_n7) as
first_column,
       text_t7 as second_column
from fig813_first
union
select text_t2,
       Cstr(number_n2)
from fig813_second;
```

(Save the query. Name it "fig814_union.")

```
select * from fig814_union;
```

Beginning tables
Fig813_first tableFig813_second table

NUMBER_N7	TEXT_T7
1111111	AAAAAAA
2222222	BBBBBBB
3333333	CCCCCCC
4444444	DDDDDDD
5555555	EEEEEEE

NUMBER_N2	TEXT_T2
33	CC
44	DD
55	EE
66	FF
77	GG

Result table

FIRST_COLUMN	SECOND_COLUMN
1111111	AAAAAAA
2222222	BBBBBBB
3333333	CCCCCCC
4444444	DDDDDDD
5555555	EEEEEEE
CC	33
DD	44
EE	55
FF	66
GG	77

Figure 8-14   Using datatype conversion functions in a union

A union of two tables with different numbers and types of columns

When two tables have different numbers of columns, you can still combine them in a union. Figure 8-15 shows two methods to do this combination. One method drops the extra columns that do not have a matching column in the other table. The other method matches the extra column with a column of nulls or some other constant value.

The result tables show that the elimination of duplicate rows works differently for these two methods. The result table for method 1 contains one row with a 3 in the first column. Method 2 contains two such rows.

For method 2, the SQL code is slightly different for Access from what it is for Oracle. Access allows you to code 'null' in a date/time column. This is the way that nulls are supposed to work. Oracle requires the null to be converted into date/time format using the TO_DATE function.

The point of Figures 8-14 and 8-15 is to show that you can combine any two tables with a union. They do not have to have the same number of columns. The datatypes of the columns do not have to match. However, when you create a union, you want to make sure that the data in each column has a consistent meaning.

Method 1: drop the columns that do not match
Oracle & Access SQL

```
select a.number_col,
       a.text_col
from fig815_first a
union
select b.number_col,
       b.text_col
from fig815_second b;
```

Result table 1

```
NUMBER_COL TEXT_COL
---------- --------
   1111111 AAAAAAA
   2222222 BBBBBBB
   3333333 CCCCCCC
   4444444 DDDDDDD
   5555555 EEEEEEE
   6666666 FFFFFFF
   7777777 GGGGGGG
```

Task

Show how to form a union of two tables that have different numbers of columns.

Method 2: put nulls in the column that is missing

Oracle SQL	Access SQL

```
select a.number_col, a.text_col,
      a.date_col
from fig815_first a
union
select b.number_col, b.text_col,
      to_date(null)
from fig815_second b;
```

```
select a.number_col, a.text_col,
      a.date_col
from fig815_first a
union
select b.number_col, b.text_col,
      null
from fig815_second b;
```

Beginning tables

Fig815_first table	Fig815_second table

```
NUMBER_COL TEXT_COL DATE_COL
---------- -------- ---------
   1111111 AAAAAAA  01-DEC-98
   2222222 BBBBBBB  02-DEC-98
   3333333 CCCCCCC  03-DEC-98
   4444444 DDDDDDD  04-DEC-98
   5555555 EEEEEEE  05-DEC-98
```

```
NUMBER_COL TEXT_COL
---------- --------
   3333333 CCCCCCC
   4444444 DDDDDDD
   5555555 EEEEEEE
   6666666 FFFFFFF
   7777777 GGGGGGG
```

Result table 2

```
NUMBER_COL TEXT_COL DATE_COL
---------- -------- ---------
   1111111 AAAAAAA  01-DEC-98
   2222222 BBBBBBB  02-DEC-98
   3333333 CCCCCCC  03-DEC-98
   3333333 CCCCCCC  (null)
   4444444 DDDDDDD  04-DEC-98
   4444444 DDDDDDD  (null)
   5555555 EEEEEEE  05-DEC-98
   5555555 EEEEEEE  (null)
   6666666 FFFFFFF  (null)
   7777777 GGGGGGG  (null)
```

Figure 8-15   A union of two tables with different numbers and types of columns

Applications of Unions (Divide and Conquer)

Determining whether two tables are equal

When two tables have the same number of columns and rows, they may appear to be identical. But perhaps one of the cells has a different value in one table from what is in the other. How can you check on this possibility?

One way is to form the union of the two tables. If they are identical, the union will have the same number of rows as the beginning tables. All the rows of the second table will be eliminated as duplicates. If they are not identical, the union will have more rows.

Beginning table 2 (Fig816_foods table)

SUPPLIER ID	PRODUCT CODE	MENU ITEM	DESCRIPTION	PRICE	PRICE INCREASE
ASP	FS	1	FRESH SALAD	$2.00	$0.25
ASP	SP	2	SOUP OF THE DAY	$1.50	(null)
ASP	SW	3	SANDWICH	$3.50	$0.40
CBC	GS	4	GRILLED STEAK	$6.00	$0.70
CBC	HB	5	HAMBURGER	$2.50	$0.30
FRV	BR	6	BROCCOLI	$1.00	$0.05
FRV	FF	7	FRENCH FRIES	$1.50	(null)
JBR	AS	8	SODA	$1.25	$0.25
JBR	VR	9	COFFEE	$0.85	$0.15
VSB	AS	10	DESSERT	$3.00	$0.50

Task

Test whether the two beginning tables are identical.

Step 1
Oracle SQL

```
create view fig816_union as
select * from l_foods
union
select * from fig816_foods;
```

Access SQL

(Enter the query in the SQL window)

```
select * from l_foods
union
select * from fig816_foods;
```

(Save the query. Name it "fig816_union.")

Oracle & Access SQL—step 2

```
select count(*) from l_foods;
select count(*) from fig816_foods;
select count(*) from fig816_union;
```

Beginning table 1 (L_foods table)

```
SUPPLIER PRODUCT   MENU                                      PRICE
ID       CODE      ITEM DESCRIPTION              PRICE INCREASE
-------- -------   ------- -------------------- -------- --------
ASP      FS           1 FRESH SALAD              $2.00    $0.25
ASP      SP           2 SOUP OF THE DAY          $1.50  (null)
ASP      SW           3 SANDWICH                 $3.50    $0.40
CBC      GS           4 GRILLED STEAK            $6.00    $0.70
CBC      HB           5 HAMBURGER                $2.50    $0.30
FRV      BR           6 BROCCOLI                 $1.00    $0.05
FRV      FF           7 FRENCH FRIES             $1.50  (null)
JBR      AS           8 SODA                     $1.25    $0.25
JBR      VR           9 COFFEE                   $0.85    $0.15
VSB      AS          10 DESSERT                  $3.00    $0.50
```

Result tables

```
COUNT(*)
---------
       10
```

Conclusion

The tables are identical.

Figure 8-16   Determining whether two tables are equal

Attaching messages for warnings and errors

Figure 8-17 shows how to attach messages to rows of data. This technique is useful for checking the data for errors and adding error messages. Any kind of information can be added, such as flagging exceptional data.

This technique uses a separate Select statement and a Where clause to divide the rows of data into groups that receive each message. One group exists for all the rows that get no message at all. Then the union is formed from all of these groups.

Task

List the foods and their prices. Add the message: "This item costs more than $2.00" to the foods that cost more than $2.00. List the foods in alphabetical order.

Oracle & Access SQL

```
select description,
       price,
       'this item costs more than $2.00' as message
from l_foods
where price > 2.00
union
select description,
       price,
       ' '
from l_foods
where not (price > 2.00)
order by description;
```

Beginning table (L_Foods table)

```
SUPPLIER PRODUCT  MENU                                   PRICE
ID       CODE     ITEM DESCRIPTION          PRICE INCREASE
-------- -------  ----- -------------------- -------- --------
ASP      FS         1 FRESH SALAD            $2.00    $0.25
ASP      SP         2 SOUP OF THE DAY        $1.50    (null)
ASP      SW         3 SANDWICH               $3.50    $0.40
CBC      GS         4 GRILLED STEAK          $6.00    $0.70
CBC      HB         5 HAMBURGER              $2.50    $0.30
FRV      BR         6 BROCCOLI               $1.00    $0.05
FRV      FF         7 FRENCH FRIES           $1.50    (null)
JBR      AS         8 SODA                   $1.25    $0.25
JBR      VR         9 COFFEE                 $0.85    $0.15
VSB      AS        10 DESSERT                $3.00    $0.50
```

Result table

```
DESCRIPTION                       PRICE MESSAGE
------------------------------    -------- -----------------------------
BROCCOLI                          $1.00
COFFEE                            $0.85
DESSERT                           $3.00 THIS ITEM COSTS MORE THAN $2.00
FRENCH FRIES                      $1.50
FRESH SALAD                       $2.00
GRILLED STEAK                     $6.00 THIS ITEM COSTS MORE THAN $2.00
HAMBURGER                         $2.50 THIS ITEM COSTS MORE THAN $2.00
SANDWICH                          $3.50 THIS ITEM COSTS MORE THAN $2.00
SODA                              $1.25
SOUP OF THE DAY                   $1.50
```

Figure 8-17   Attaching messages for warnings and errors

Overriding several rows of data in a table

Figure 8-18 shows how to override several rows of data in a table. You might want to do this when you are sharing a large table of data with several other people and you want to change the data in a few of the rows for your own purposes, without affecting the data that other people are using.

If you own the table and you are the only person using it, then to make the changes directly to the table itself is easier. Also, if the table is small, then to make a copy of it and make changes to your personal copy is easier.

The technique shown here makes a separate table containing only the rows of data you want to change. Then you change these rows to create a table of overrides. Last, you create a view that contains all the rows of the original table but that replaces the ones you have changed with your overrides.

Task

On the menu of lunch foods, substitute carrots for broccoli, and mashed potatoes for french fries.

Step 1: create a table of overrides
Oracle and Access SQL

```
create table foods_overrides as
select a.*
from l_foods a
where (a.supplier_id = 'frv' and a.product_code = 'br')
  or (a.supplier_id = 'frv' and a.product_code = 'ff');

update foods_overrides
  set description = 'carrots'
where description = 'broccoli';

update foods_overrides
  set description = 'mashed potatoes'
where description = 'french fries';
```

Table of overrides

SUPPLIER ID	PRODUCT CODE	MENU ITEM	DESCRIPTION	PRICE	PRICE INCREASE
FRV	FF	7	MASHED POTATOES	$1.50	(null)
FRV	BR	6	CARROTS	$1.00	$0.05

Figure 8-18   Overriding several rows of data in a table (part 1)

Beginning table (L_foods table)

```
SUPPLIER PRODUCT   MENU                                       PRICE
ID       CODE      ITEM DESCRIPTION              PRICE INCREASE
-------- -------   ------- -------------------- -------- --------
ASP      FS           1 FRESH SALAD              $2.00    $0.25
ASP      SP           2 SOUP OF THE DAY          $1.50   (null)
ASP      SW           3 SANDWICH                 $3.50    $0.40
CBC      GS           4 GRILLED STEAK            $6.00    $0.70
CBC      HB           5 HAMBURGER                $2.50    $0.30
FRV      BR           6 BROCCOLI                 $1.00    $0.05
FRV      FF           7 FRENCH FRIES             $1.50   (null)
JBR      AS           8 SODA                     $1.25    $0.25
JBR      VR           9 COFFEE                   $0.85    $0.15
VSB      AS          10 DESSERT                  $3.00    $0.50
```

Step 2: create a view combining the overrides and other data
Oracle SQL

```
create view foods_with_overrides as
select a.*
from l_foods a
where (a.supplier_id || a.product_code) not in
      (select (b.supplier_id || b.product_code)
        from foods_overrides b)
union
select c.*
from foods_overrides c;
```

Access SQL

(Enter the query in the SQL window.)

```
select a.*
from l_foods a
where (a.supplier_id & a.product_code) not in
      (select (b.supplier_id & b.product_code)
        from foods_overrides b)
union
select c.*
from foods_overrides c;
```

(Save the query. Name it "foods_with_overrides.")

Result table

SUPPLIER ID	PRODUCT CODE	MENU ITEM	DESCRIPTION	PRICE	PRICE INCREASE
ASP	FS	1	FRESH SALAD	$2.00	$0.25
ASP	SP	2	SOUP OF THE DAY	$1.50	(null)
ASP	SW	3	SANDWICH	$3.50	$0.40
CBC	GS	4	GRILLED STEAK	$6.00	$0.70
CBC	HB	5	HAMBURGER	$2.50	$0.30
FRV	BR	6	CARROTS	$1.00	$0.05
FRV	FF	7	MASHED POTATOES	$1.50	(null)
JBR	AS	8	SODA	$1.25	$0.25
JBR	VR	9	COFFEE	$0.85	$0.15
VSB	AS	10	DESSERT	$3.00	$0.50

Figure 8-18   Overriding several rows of data in a table (part 2)

Dividing data into different columns

Figure 8-19 shows how to divide one column of data into two or more columns. This technique can be useful in making some types of data stand out or in sorting the data into several categories. In an accounting application, you might want to put the expenses of each quarter into a separate column.

The technique is similar to the ones we have used before. Several Select statements divide the data in the beginning table into separate groups. This division is done in the Where clauses of the Select statements.

Then the data is listed in the desired column, and blanks are placed in all the other columns. A union puts all these pieces back together.

Beginning table (L_employees)

EMPLOYEE ID	FIRST_NAME	LAST_NAME	DEPT CODE	HIRE_DATE	CREDIT LIMIT	PHONE NUMBER	MANAGER ID
201	SUSAN	BROWN	EXE	01-JUN-92	$30.00	3484	(null)
202	JIM	KERN	SAL	15-AUG-95	$25.00	8722	201
203	MARTHA	WOODS	SHP	01-FEB-97	$25.00	7591	201
204	ELLEN	OWENS	SAL	01-JUL-96	$15.00	6830	202
205	HENRY	PERKINS	SAL	01-MAR-98	$25.00	5286	202
206	CAROL	ROSE	ACT	15-OCT-97	$15.00	3829	201
207	DAN	SMITH	SHP	01-DEC-96	$25.00	2259	203
208	FRED	CAMPBELL	SHP	01-APR-97	$25.00	1752	203
209	PAULA	JACOBS	MKT	17-MAR-98	$15.00	3357	201
210	NANCY	HOFFMAN	SAL	15-FEB-96	$25.00	2974	203

Task

mns, placing data in a column according to its meaning. List the names and department codes of all the employees. Put the department codes in one column for the sales and shipping departments. Put all the other department codes in a different column.

Oracle column formats

```
column sales_and_shipping format a10 heading 'SALES AND|SHIPPING'
column other_departments format a12 heading 'OTHER|DEPARTMENTS'
```

Oracle & Access SQL

```
select employee_id, first_name, last_name,
    dept_code as sales_and_shipping,
    '      ' as other_departments
from l_employees
where dept_code in ('shp', 'sal')
union
select employee_id, first_name, last_name,
    '      ',
    dept_code
from l_employees
where not (dept_code in ('shp', 'sal'))
order by employee_id;
```

Result table

```
EMPLOYEE                         SALES AND  OTHER
      ID FIRST_NAME  LAST_NAME   SHIPPING   DEPARTMENTS
-------- ----------  ----------  ---------- ------------
     201 SUSAN       BROWN                  EXE
     202 JIM         KERN        SAL
     203 MARTHA      WOODS       SHP
     204 ELLEN       OWENS       SAL
     205 HENRY       PERKINS     SAL
     206 CAROL       ROSE                   ACT
     207 DAN         SMITH       SHP
     208 FRED        CAMPBELL    SHP
     209 PAULA       JACOBS                 MKT
     210 NANCY       HOFFMAN     SAL
```

Figure 8-19   Dividing data into different columns

Applying two functions to different parts of the data

Figure 8-20 shows how to apply several different calculations to different parts of the data. First, use Select statements with Where clauses to divide the rows into groups. Make a separate group for each calculation and perform the calculations. Then use a union to combine all the groups together again.

Task

Show how to make two different calculations, depending on the data in a row. Increase the prices of all foods costing more than $2.00 by 5%. Increase the prices of all other foods by 10%.

Oracle column formatting

```
column new_price format $90.99
```

Oracle & Access SQL

```
select description,
     price + (price * .05) as new_price
from l_foods
where price > 2.00
union
select description,
     price + (price * .10)
from l_foods
where price <= 2.00
order by description;
```

Beginning table (L_Foods table)

SUPPLIER ID	PRODUCT CODE	MENU ITEM	DESCRIPTION	PRICE	PRICE INCREASE
ASP	FS	1	FRESH SALAD	$2.00	$0.25
ASP	SP	2	SOUP OF THE DAY	$1.50	(null)
ASP	SW	3	SANDWICH	$3.50	$0.40
CBC	GS	4	GRILLED STEAK	$6.00	$0.70
CBC	HB	5	HAMBURGER	$2.50	$0.30
FRV	BR	6	BROCCOLI	$1.00	$0.05
FRV	FF	7	FRENCH FRIES	$1.50	(null)
JBR	AS	8	SODA	$1.25	$0.25
JBR	VR	9	COFFEE	$0.85	$0.15
VSB	AS	10	DESSERT	$3.00	$0.50

Result table

DESCRIPTION	NEW_PRICE
BROCCOLI	$1.10
COFFEE	$0.94
DESSERT	$3.15
FRENCH FRIES	$1.65
FRESH SALAD	$2.20
GRILLED STEAK	$6.30
HAMBURGER	$2.63
SANDWICH	$3.68
SODA	$1.38
SOUP OF THE DAY	$1.65

Figure 8-20   Applying two functions to different parts of the data

Set Intersection and Set Difference in Oracle

Oracle has created extensions to standard SQL that provide direct support to finding the intersection and difference of two tables. The exercises of Chapter 7 showed how to perform these operations in standard SQL. However, the Oracle extensions make it much easier.

Set Intersection

- Set Intersection shows the rows that occur in both tables (see Figure 8-21).
- Set Intersection is an Oracle extension to standard SQL.
- The same result can be achieved using standard SQL.

Task

Show how to use Set Intersection.

Method 1
Oracle SQL

```
select number_1,
       word_1,
       date_1
from fig807_first
intersect
select number_2,
       word_2,
       date_2
from fig807_second
order by number_1;
```

Access SQL

(Access does not support this method.)

Method 2
Oracle & Access & Standard SQL

```
select a.number_1,
       a.word_1,
       a.date_1
from fig807_first a,
     fig807_second b
where a.number_1 = b.number_2
 and a.word_1 = b.word_2
 and a.date_1 = b.date_2
order by number_1;
```

Beginning tables
Fig807_first tableFig807_second table

NUMBER_1	WORD_1	DATE_1	NUMBER_2	WORD_2	DATE_2
1	ONE	01-DEC-98	3	THREE	03-DEC-98
2	TWO	02-DEC-98	4	FOUR	04-DEC-98
3	THREE	03-DEC-98	5	FIVE	05-DEC-98
4	FOUR	04-DEC-98	6	SIX	06-DEC-98
5	FIVE	05-DEC-98	7	SEVEN	07-DEC-98

Result table

NUMBER_1	WORD_1	DATE_1
3	THREE	03-DEC-98
4	FOUR	04-DEC-98
5	FIVE	05-DEC-98

Figure 8-21   Set Intersection

Set Difference

- Set Difference shows all the rows that occur in the first table, but not in the second table (see Figure 8-22).
- Set Difference, as Oracle has implemented it, is a one-sided operation. It shows the rows from the first table that do not occur in the second table. But it does not show the rows from the second table that do not occur in the first table.
- Minus (Set Difference) is an Oracle extension to standard SQL.
- The same result can be achieved using standard SQL, but it is more difficult to code. I will show this when I discuss subqueries.

Task

Show how to use Set Difference in Oracle.

Part 1—rows in the first table, but not in the second one

Oracle SQL   Access SQL

`select * from fig807_first`
`minus`
`select * from fig807_second;`
	(Access does not support this method.)

Beginning tables
Fig807_first tableFig807_second table

```
NUMBER_1 WORD_1           DATE_1        NUMBER_2 WORD_2           DATE_2
-------- --------------- ---------     -------- --------------- ---------
       1 ONE             01-DEC-98            3 THREE           03-DEC-98
       2 TWO             02-DEC-98            4 FOUR            04-DEC-98
       3 THREE           03-DEC-98            5 FIVE            05-DEC-98
       4 FOUR            04-DEC-98            6 SIX             06-DEC-98
       5 FIVE            05-DEC-98            7 SEVEN           07-DEC-98
```

Result table

```
NUMBER_1 WORD_1           DATE_1
-------- --------------- ---------
       1 ONE             01-DEC-98
       2 TWO             02-DEC-98
```

Part 2—rows in the second table, but not in the first one

Oracle SQL   Access SQL

`select * from fig807_second`
`minus`
`select * from fig807_first;`
	(Access does not support this method.)

Result table

```
NUMBER_2 WORD_2           DATE_2
-------- --------------- ---------
       6 SIX             06-DEC-98
       7 SEVEN           07-DEC-98
```

Figure 8-22   Set Difference

Summary

In this chapter, you learned the three types of outer joins:

> Left outer join
> Right outer join
> Full outer join

They all begin with an inner join and add back some of the rows that were deleted from it. The Left Outer Join adds back all the rows dropped from the first table in the From clause. The Right Outer Join adds back all the rows that were dropped from the second table. The Full Outer Join adds back all the rows hat were dropped from both tables.

You saw that the syntax to write an outer join differs from one product to another, even though all these products agree completely on the definitions of the outer joins.

You also learned about unions and some of the ways they can be applied. The idea of a union is very simple. But, the ways it can be applied are ver powerful. Unfortunately, many of the graphical (GUI) tools that generate SQL do not support unions. This is one of their major failings.

In many SQL products, Unions are not yet an "industrial strength" operation. In particular, their Order By clause may be weak. If you are writing a Union query with an Order By clause, you may have to try several variations of the Order By clause before you find one that works.

It almost always works if you refer to the columns of the result table by their numerical order, such as:

> Order By 2, 4, 7

Other variations which sometimes work and sometimes do not are:

Referring to a column by its name without a table alias, such as:

> Order By Last_name.

Referring to a column by its name with a table alias, such as:

> Order By A.Last_name.

Referring to a column by a column alias assigned in the Select clause, such as:

> Select Last_Name as Lname
> ....
> Order By Lname.

Exercises

1. Goal: Find rows that are not matched. (They are dropped from an inner join.)

1A. Find out if there are any foods that have not been ordered.

Solution.
Oracle SQL

```
There are many ways to solve this. Here is one way.
This method uses an outer join. It keeps all the foods, even the ones
that have not been ordered. Then it looks for the nulls an outer join
uses to complete unmatched rows.

select a.supplier_id,
        a.product_code,
        a.description
from l_foods a,
        l_lunch_items b
where a.supplier_id = b.supplier_id (+)
    and a.product_code = b.product_code (+)
    and b.supplier_id is null;
```

Access SQL

```
select a.supplier_id,
        a.product_code,
        a.description
from l_foods a
        left outer join l_lunch_items b
        on a.supplier_id = b.supplier_id
        and a.product_code = b.product_code
where b.supplier_id is null;
```

1B. Are there any employees who are not attending any of the lunches? If so, who are they?

1C. List the suppliers that are not supplying any food on the current menu.

2. Goal: When using COUNT, show unmatched data with zeros.

2A. For each food, count the number of lunches that have ordered it. Show a zero for unordered foods. For this problem, do not consider the quantity of each food that is ordered.

Solution:
Oracle SQL

The technique here is:
1. Form the outer join. (Unmatched rows will be completed with nulls in the second table - for instance in the b.supplier_id column. This column is only null for unmatched rows, it has a non-null value for all matched rows.)
2. Group the outer join so all the rows for each food are together.
3. Count on a column that contains nulls for unmatched foods. The COUNT(column) function will show zero for unmatched rows.
(Note: Do not use COUNT(*). It will show a one for unmatched rows.
Try it. Do you understand why?)

```
select a.description,
          count(b.supplier_id)
from l_foods a,
        l_lunch_items b
where a.supplier_id = b.supplier_id (+)
   and a.product_code = b.product_code (+)
group by a.description;
```

Access SQL

```
select a.description,
          count(b.supplier_id)
from l_foods a
        left outer join l_lunch_items b
        on a.supplier_id = b.supplier_id
        and a.product_code = b.product_code
group by a.description;
```

2B. Count the number of lunches each employee will attend. If an employee is not attending any of the lunches, list their name with a zero.

2C. Count the number of foods supplied by each supplier.

2D. Count the number of servings for each food.
(Hint: Same as 2A, except add up the quantities instead of counting the lunches. Use SUM(b.quantity) instead of COUNT(b.supplier_id).)

3. Goal: Show all the types of joins. Also, show a union. Use the table Ten_fruits and Ten_colors or, even better, make up your own tables to show this.

3A. Show the right outer join of the Ten_fruits and the Ten_colors tables. Explain a detail that shows this is a right outer join.

Solution:
Oracle SQL

```
First, look at the tables.

select * from ten_fruits;
select * from ten_colors;

select a.fruit,
          a.f_num,
          b.c_num,
          b.color
from ten_fruits a,
        ten_colors b
where a.f_num (+) = b.c_num;

This is a right outer join because it lists the color "black" even
though there is no black fruit.
```

Access SQL

```
select a.fruit,
          a.f_num,
          b.c_num,
          b.color
from ten_fruits a
        right outer join ten_colors b
          on a.f_num (+) = b.c_num;
```

3B. Do the same and show all the types of join and the union:
> inner join
> left outer join
> right outer join
> full outer join
> union

Use the join condition: f_num = c_num

3C. Form the full outer join with the join condition: f_num = c_num.
Also form a full outer join with the join condition   fruit = color.
How do the result tables compare to each other? What is similar? What is different?

4. Goal: Find numbers that are duplicated or missing from a list of numbers.

4A. Table Ex8_4A contains a list of the multiples of 11 up to 880. Except a few numbers occur more than once and a few numbers are missing. Find all the exceptions.

Solution

Step 1. Create a view that has all the number we are interested in.

Oracle SQL	Access SQL
```create view temp_1 as select 11 * n as n from numbers_0_to_99 where 11 * n <= 880;```	```select 11 * a.n as n from numbers_0_to_99 a where 11 * a.n <= 880;``` (Save this query. Name it "temp_1")

Step 2. Then use an outer join and look for the nulls to find the missing values.

Oracle SQL	Access SQL
```select a.n from temp_1 a, ex8_4a b where a.n = b.n (+) and b.n is null;```	```select a.n from temp_1 a left outer join ex8_4a b on a.n = b.n where b.n is null;```

Step 3. Use the Count function to look for duplicate values. You can show thee missing values with zeros at the same time.

Oracle SQL	Access SQL
```select a.n, count(b.n) from temp_1 a, ex8_4a b where a.n = b.n (+) group by a.n having not (count(b.n) = 1) order by a.n;```	```select a.n, count(b.n) from temp_1 a left outer join ex8_4a b on a.n = b.n group by a.n having not (count(b.n) = 1) order by a.n;```

4B. The table Ex8_4b contains a series of dates. A few date are missing and a few are duplicated. Find all these exceptions.

5. Goal: Find out if two tables are identical.

5A. See figures 8-16 and 8-22.

5B. See if the table Ex8_5 is identical to L_lunch_items. If they are different, find the differences.

6. Goal: Override some data

6A. See figure 8-18.

6B. Create the following overrides to the L_employees table:

Change the name of Ellen Owens to Ellen Smith.

Change the phone number for Paula Jacobs to 7492.

Use a view with these overrides to list the names and phone numbers of all the employees.

Chapter 9

Self joins, Cross Joins, and Subqueries

Self Joins

A self join is any inner or outer join in which a table is joined with itself. Many database designers consider self joins to be confusing and unintuitive. Most databases are designed so that self joins are rarely needed for everyday tasks. However, using a self join can provide information that cannot be obtained in any other way.

Why join a table with itself?

To join a table with itself does not seem to make sense

Joining a table with itself does not seem to make sense. Usually we think about tables on an information level; a table contains information about a certain subject. For instance, the Customers table contains information about the customers.

When we work on a problem, one of the first things we need to do is decide what tables are needed. To make this decision, we think about the tables as containing certain kinds of information.

Joining a table with itself doesn't give you any more information. Therefore, it does not seem to make sense.

Why it does make sense

All databases, Oracle and Access included, process one row of a table at a time. You can access all the columns within a row, but only within one row. If the information you need is contained in several different rows of the table, then you need to join the table with itself.

If T is a table, then

$$T \; inner \, join \; T$$

allows you to access two rows at a time. To access three rows at a time, you need to use

$$T \; inner \, join \; T \; inner \, join \; T$$

and so on. To join every row of a table with every other row, you just need to leave out the Where clause.

You need to have only one copy of the table

Only one copy of the table needs to be stored on the disk. If you are using a view instead of a table, you need to have the view defined only once. The database will act "as if" you have many separate copies of the table or view. This is all done automatically for you in the computer memory.

Task

Show an example of joining a table with itself.

Oracle & Access SQL

```
select a.col_1,
       a.col_2,
       b.col_1,
       b.col_2
from fig901 a,
     fig901 b;
```

Beginning table (Fig901 table)

```
COL_1          COL_2
---------- ---------
A                  1
B                  2
C                  3
D                  4
```

Result table

```
COL_1          COL_2 COL_1          COL_2
---------- --------- ---------- ---------
A                  1 A                  1
B                  2 A                  1
C                  3 A                  1
D                  4 A                  1
A                  1 B                  2
B                  2 B                  2
C                  3 B                  2
D                  4 B                  2
A                  1 C                  3
B                  2 C                  3
C                  3 C                  3
D                  4 C                  3
A                  1 D                  4
B                  2 D                  4
C                  3 D                  4
D                  4 D                  4
```

- The result table contains every pair of rows from the beginning table.

Figure 9-1 Why join a table with itself

An example of a self join

Figure 9-2 shows an example of a self join. We want to list information about the employee and the manager on the same row of a report. The problem is that the information about the manager is in a different row from the information about the employee. So we need to use two different rows of the table at the same time. We might picture the situation like this:

Employee_id	Name	Phone	Manager_id	
XXXXX	XXXXX	XXXXX	◯	employee information
◯←	XXXXX	XXXXX		manager information

Changing this to a picture where the table is joined to another copy of itself, we have:

Employee Information				Manager Information			
Employee Id	Name	Phone	Manager Id	Employee Id	Name	Phone	Manager Id
XXXXX	XXXXX	XXXXX	◯→◯		XXXXX	XXXXX	

In SQL, the Employees table is joined to itself. The first copy is given the table alias "EMP," meaning that employee information is taken from this copy of the table. The second copy is given the table alias "BOSS," meaning that manager information is taken from this copy of the table.

The pictures above shows why the join condition is:

emp.manager_id = boss.employee_id

A left outer join is used because the top manager does not have a boss, and we want to keep her in this listing.

The computer needs only one copy of the table stored on the disk. It will create the result as if it has two copies of the table.

Task

From the Employees table, list the employee id, last name, and phone number of each employee with the name and phone number of his/her manager. Include a row for the top person, who does not have a manager. Sort the rows by employee id.

Oracle column formats

```
column manager_name format a12
column manager_phone format a13
```

Oracle & Access SQL

```
select emp.employee_id, emp.last_name, emp.phone_number,
     boss.last_name as manager_name,
     boss.phone_number as manager_phone
from l_employees emp,
     l_employees boss
where emp.manager_id = boss.employee_id (+)
order by emp.employee_id;
```

Beginning table (L_Employees table)

EMPLOYEE ID	FIRST_NAME	LAST_NAME	DEPT CODE	HIRE_DATE	CREDIT LIMIT	PHONE NUMBER	MANAGER ID
201	SUSAN	BROWN	EXE	01-JUN-92	$30.00	3484	(null)
202	JIM	KERN	SAL	15-AUG-95	$25.00	8722	201
203	MARTHA	WOODS	SHP	01-FEB-97	$25.00	7591	201
204	ELLEN	OWENS	SAL	01-JUL-96	$15.00	6830	202
205	HENRY	PERKINS	SAL	01-MAR-98	$25.00	5286	202
206	CAROL	ROSE	ACT	15-OCT-97	$15.00	3829	201
207	DAN	SMITH	SHP	01-DEC-96	$25.00	2259	203
208	FRED	CAMPBELL	SHP	01-APR-97	$25.00	1752	203
209	PAULA	JACOBS	MKT	17-MAR-98	$15.00	3357	201
210	NANCY	HOFFMAN	SAL	15-FEB-96	$25.00	2974	203

Result table

EMPLOYEE ID	LAST_NAME	PHONE NUMBER	MANAGER_NAME	MANAGER_PHONE
201	BROWN	3484	(null)	(null)
202	KERN	8722	BROWN	3484
203	WOODS	7591	BROWN	3484
204	OWENS	6830	KERN	8722
205	PERKINS	5286	KERN	8722
206	ROSE	3829	BROWN	3484
207	SMITH	2259	WOODS	7591
208	CAMPBELL	1752	WOODS	7591
209	JACOBS	3357	BROWN	3484
210	HOFFMAN	2974	WOODS	7591

Figure 9-2   An example of a self join

Generating the numbers from 0 to 99

Figure 9-3 shows how to create a table containing all the numbers from 0 to 99. First, you create a table of all the digits, all the numbers from 0 to 9. Then you join this table with itself to create the numbers from 0 to 99.

You have already been using these tables. The database for each chapter of this book creates them for you. Here, you will see how to create them for yourself, so you can use them with other databases.

In the first step, a table is created to contain all the digits. Oracle and Access must use their own datatypes, "number" for Oracle and "short" for Access. Otherwise, the SQL is the same. At this point, the table contains no data.

In the second step, the data is put into the table. You have only ten records, so this is easy to do. The SQL is exactly the same in Oracle and Access.

In the third step, this table of digits is used to create a new table containing the numbers from 0 to 99. The table, "numbers_0_to 9," is joined with itself, without any join condition. You can see this self join in the From clause, which lists the table twice. The first copy of the table is given the alias "A," and the second copy is given the alias "B." The result of this join is every combination of two digits.

The Select clause turns each combination of two digits into a single, two-digit number. It multiplies one of the digits by ten and adds the other digit; for example:

two digits: 3   and   4

become one number: $(3 * 10) + 4 = 30 + 4 = 34$

This much of the third step is the same in both Oracle and Access. However, they differ in their techniques to save these results in a table. To do so, Oracle uses a "Create table" clause before the Select clause, and Access uses an "Into" clause after the Select statement.

Task

Create a table with all the numbers from 0 to 99. First, create a table of the numbers from 0 to 9. Then join it with itself.

Step 1—create a table to contain all 10 digits
Oracle SQL   Access SQL

```
create table numbers_0_to_9      create table numbers_0_to_9
(digit    number(1));            (digit    short);
```

Step 2—put the data in the table
Oracle & Access SQL

```
insert into numbers_0_to_9 values (0);
insert into numbers_0_to_9 values (1);
insert into numbers_0_to_9 values (2);
insert into numbers_0_to_9 values (3);
insert into numbers_0_to_9 values (4);
insert into numbers_0_to_9 values (5);
insert into numbers_0_to_9 values (6);
insert into numbers_0_to_9 values (7);
insert into numbers_0_to_9 values (8);
insert into numbers_0_to_9 values (9);
```

Step 3—create a table of numbers from 0 to 99
Oracle SQL   Access SQL

```
create table numbers_0_to_99 as   select ((a.digit * 10) + b.digit) as n
select ((a.digit * 10) + b.digit) as n   into numbers_0_to_99
from numbers_0_to_9 a,            from numbers_0_to_9 a,
    numbers_0_to_9 b;                 numbers_0_to_9 b;
```

Result table

```
          N
---------
          0
          1
etc
         99
```

Figure 9-3   Generating the numbers from 0 to 99

Generating the numbers from 1 to 10,000

Figure 9-4 shows how to generate the numbers from 1 to 10,000. Using this technique, you can generate as many numbers as you want. If you generate more than you have disk space to save in a table, you can save them in a view.

Step 1 creates the table that will contain the numbers. The method used here defines the datatypes of the columns. The datatypes can be chosen to fit the data that will be placed in the table. This step can reduce the amount of disk space required by the table.

Step 2 puts the data into the table. Here, the table of digits is joined to itself several times. This action generates the numbers from 0 to 9999. By adding one to every number, you get the numbers from 1 to 10,000.

Step 3 displays the table. Be sure to include the Order by clause. Otherwise, the rows may be displayed in any order—probably one that you do not expect.

Task

Create a table with all the numbers from 1 to 10,000. To control the datatype, define the table first and then put data into it.

Step 1—define the table
Oracle SQL   Access SQL

```
create table numbers_1_to_10000      create table numbers_1_to_10000
(n  number(5));                      (n  short);
```

Step 2—put the data in the table
Oracle & Access SQL

```
insert into numbers_1_to_10000 (n)
select (a.digit * 1000) + (b.digit * 100) + (c.digit * 10)
+ d.digit + 1
from numbers_0_to_9 a,
     numbers_0_to_9 b,
     numbers_0_to_9 c,
     numbers_0_to_9 d;
```

Step 3—display the table
Oracle & Access SQL

```
select n
from numbers_1_to_10000
order by n;
```

Result table

```
        N
---------
        1
        2
        3
etc
     9997
     9998
     9999
    10000
```

Figure 9-4   Generating the numbers from 1 to 10,000

Numbering the lines of a report in Oracle and Access

Sometimes you have a report and all the lines of the report are sorted in a particular order. You may want to number these lines in the order they appear in the report. To do this, you can create a new column in the report that contains the line numbers.

Both Oracle and Access have special features to help you do this. However, these features work differently.

The Access method

The Access method is very easy:

1. Create a new table that contains the report. (Use the Into clause.)
2. Use "Design" to add a new column to this table with the datatype "AutoNumber." This will assign the numbers automatically.

The Oracle method

Oracle has a feature called "Rownum" that can be used to number the rows of the report. "Rownum" can be added to the Select clause, and it assigns sequential numbers to the rows. Unfortunately, it assigns these numbers as the data is retrieved, *before* the Order By clause sorts the rows.

This chronology can put the line numbers in the wrong order. However, you do have a way to work around this problem:

1. Create a view containing the report. Replace the Order By clause with a Group By clause. A view cannot contain an Order By clause, so it must be omitted. Replacing it with a Group By clause is a trick that relies on the way Oracle works internally. Oracle will sort the rows on the Group By clause before Rownum assigns the row numbers.

2. Because of the Group By clause, all the columns in the Select clause must be grouped data. Column functions must be applied to any columns not listed in the Group By clause, and a column alias should be assigned. In Figure 9-5, the column

    description
becomes
    min(description) as description

3. List the view and put "rownum" in the Select clause.

Task

You have a Select statement that creates a report in Oracle. All the lines of the report are sorted in a particular order. You want to number the lines of this report sequentially, beginning with the number one.

Beginning Select statement

```
select price,
       description
from l_foods
where price > 1.75
order by price;
```

Beginning report

```
   PRICE DESCRIPTION
------- --------------------
  $2.00 FRESH SALAD
  $2.50 HAMBURGER
  $3.00 DESSERT
  $3.50 SANDWICH
  $6.00 GRILLED STEAK
```

Oracle SQL—step 1   ## Access SQL

`create view temp_1 as`
`select price,`
`       min(description) as description`
`from l_foods`
`where price > 1.75`
`group by price;`
	(Access has a much easier way to do this. Add a column with the datatype "AutoNumber.")

Oracle SQL—step 2

```
select rownum as line_number,
       a.*
from temp_1 a
order by a.price;
```

Result table

```
LINE_NUMBER    PRICE DESCRIPTION
-----------  -------- ------------------------
          1    $2.00 FRESH SALAD
          2    $2.50 HAMBURGER
          3    $3.00 DESSERT
          4    $3.50 SANDWICH
          5    $6.00 GRILLED STEAK
```

Figure 9-5   Numbering the lines of a report in Oracle and Access

Numbering the lines of a report in standard SQL

Figure 9-6 shows how to number the lines in standard SQL, without using "Rownum" or "AutoNumber." This technique, consisting of four steps, uses a self join to generate the numbers:

Step 1. Create a view containing all the rows and columns of the original report. Add any columns used in the Order By clause that are not shown in the Select clause. The Order By clause must be omitted when you create a view.

This step separates the logic of the original report from the logic that creates the line numbers and keeps these two things from interacting with each other. The view created in this step, like all views and tables, keeps the rows in no particular order.

Step 2. Create a view containing only the columns used in the Order By clause of the beginning Select statement. These columns are used to sort the original report. Each row of the original report corresponds to exactly one row of this view.

Step 3. Add the line numbers to the view from Step 2. Create the line numbers by joining the view from Step 2 with itself. For each row of Step 2, count the number of rows that precede it or are equal to it. This action will give the line numbers beginning with one.

This step joins the view created in Step 2 with itself. It matches each line (alias A) of the report with all the lines (alias B) that precede it, and also matches each line with itself. Then for each line (A) of the report, it counts the number of lines (B) matched with it. This action creates the line number you want.

The Group By clause expresses "for each line (A)" in the previous paragraph. Each line (A) of the original report gets its own line number, so each line (A) forms its own group.

Step 4 is the last step. It combines the line numbers created in Step 3 with the lines of the original report. Since it is a Select statement, not a Create View, it can use the Order By clause of the beginning Select statement.

Task

Show how to number the lines of a report in standard SQL, when "Rownum" and "AutoNumber" are not available. This technique uses a self join. The beginning table and result table are the same as Figure 9-5.

Beginning Select statement

```
select price,
       description
from 1_foods
where price > 1.75
order by price;
```

Standard SQL—step 1

```
create view temp_1 as
select price,
       description
from 1_foods
where price > 1.75;
```

Standard SQL—step 2

```
create view temp_2 as
select price
from temp_1;
```

Standard SQL—step 3

```
create view temp_3 as
select count(b.price) as line_number,
       a.price
from temp_2 a,
     temp_2 b
where b.price <= a.price
group by a.price;
```

Standard SQL—step 4

```
select b.line_number,
       a.*
from temp_1 a,
   temp_3 b
where a.price = b.price
order by a.price;
```

Figure 9-6   Numbering the lines of a report in standard SQL

Numbering the lines of each group

Figure 9-7 shows how to number the lines of each group of a report. The line numbers begin again whenever the group changes.

Steps 1 and 2 number all the lines of the report sequentially, using the method of Figure 9-5.

Step 3 finds the minimum line number for each group of lunches. This is the same as the beginning line number for each group.

Step 4 adjusts the line numbers created in Step 2 by subtracting the beginning line number of each group from all the members of that group. Then you add one to all these line numbers, if you want each group to start with one.

The procedure is similar in Access, although a few details are different. Steps 1 and 2 are done using "AutoNumber." Step 3 saves the Select statement using the GUI, instead of using "Create View." The idea is the same—adjust the line numbers by subtracting the starting line number of each group.

Task

You have a Select statement that creates a report in which the rows are organized in groups. You want to number the lines separately within each group. In this example, you want to number the lunches separately for each lunch date.

Beginning Select statement

```
select a.lunch_date,
       b.first_name,
       b.last_name
from l_lunches a,
     l_employees b
where a.employee_id = b.employee_id
order by a.lunch_date,
         b.last_name;
```

Goal
Beginning report   The new column to create

LUNCH DATE	FIRST_NAME	LAST_NAME	LINE_NUMBER
16-NOV-98	SUSAN	BROWN	1
16-NOV-98	NANCY	HOFFMAN	2
16-NOV-98	JIM	KERN	3
16-NOV-98	CAROL	ROSE	4
16-NOV-98	DAN	SMITH	5
16-NOV-98	MARTHA	WOODS	6
25-NOV-98	SUSAN	BROWN	1
25-NOV-98	FRED	CAMPBELL	2
25-NOV-98	ELLEN	OWENS	3
25-NOV-98	HENRY	PERKINS	4
25-NOV-98	DAN	SMITH	5
04-DEC-98	SUSAN	BROWN	1
04-DEC-98	FRED	CAMPBELL	2
04-DEC-98	NANCY	HOFFMAN	3
04-DEC-98	HENRY	PERKINS	4
04-DEC-98	MARTHA	WOODS	5

Figure 9-7   Numbering the lines of each group (part 1 of 2)

Beginning Select statement

```
select a.lunch_date,
       b.first_name, b.last_name
from l_lunches a,
     l_employees b
where a.employee_id = b.employee_id
order by a.lunch_date,
         b.last_name;
```

Step 1—prepare to number all the lines
Oracle SQL   Access SQL

```
create view temp_1 as
select a.lunch_date,
       min(b.first_name) as first_name,
       b.last_name
from l_lunches a,
     l_employees b
where a.employee_id = b.employee_id
group by a.lunch_date,
         b.last_name;
```

(Access has a much easier way to do this. Add a new column with the datatype "AutoNumber.")

Step 2—use "rownum" to number all the lines
Oracle SQL

```
create view temp_2 as
select rownum as line_number,
       a.lunch_date,
       a.first_name, a.last_name
from temp_1 a;
```

Result table—step 2

```
            LUNCH
LINE_NUMBER DATE        FIRST_NAME LAST_NAME
----------- ----------  ---------- ----------
          1 16-NOV-98   SUSAN      BROWN
          2 16-NOV-98   NANCY      HOFFMAN
          3 16-NOV-98   JIM        KERN
          4 16-NOV-98   CAROL      ROSE
          5 16-NOV-98   DAN        SMITH
          6 16-NOV-98   MARTHA     WOODS
          7 25-NOV-98   SUSAN      BROWN
          8 25-NOV-98   FRED       CAMPBELL
          9 25-NOV-98   ELLEN      OWENS
         10 25-NOV-98   HENRY      PERKINS
         11 25-NOV-98   DAN        SMITH
         12 04-DEC-98   SUSAN      BROWN
         13 04-DEC-98   FRED       CAMPBELL
         14 04-DEC-98   NANCY      HOFFMAN
         15 04-DEC-98   HENRY      PERKINS
         16 04-DEC-98   MARTHA     WOODS
```

Step 3—find the minimum line number for each group
Oracle SQL

```
create view temp_3 as
select lunch_date,
       min(line_number) as beginning_line_number
from temp_2
group by lunch_date;
```

Result table—step 3

```
LUNCH
DATE      BEGINNING_LINE_NUMBER
--------- ---------------------
16-NOV-98                     1
25-NOV-98                     7
04-DEC-98                    12
```

Step 4—adjust the line numbers
Oracle & Access SQL

```
select (a.line_number - b.beginning_line_number + 1) as line_number,
       a.lunch_date,
       a.first_name, a.last_name
from temp_2 a,
     temp_3 b
where a.lunch_date = b.lunch_date
order by a.lunch_date, a.last_name;
```

Result table—step 4

```
            LUNCH
LINE_NUMBER DATE      FIRST_NAME LAST_NAME
----------- --------- ---------- ----------
          1 16-NOV-98 SUSAN      BROWN
          2 16-NOV-98 NANCY      HOFFMAN
          3 16-NOV-98 JIM        KERN
          4 16-NOV-98 CAROL      ROSE
          5 16-NOV-98 DAN        SMITH
          6 16-NOV-98 MARTHA     WOODS
          1 25-NOV-98 SUSAN      BROWN
          2 25-NOV-98 FRED       CAMPBELL
          3 25-NOV-98 ELLEN      OWENS
          4 25-NOV-98 HENRY      PERKINS
          5 25-NOV-98 DAN        SMITH
          1 04-DEC-98 SUSAN      BROWN
          2 04-DEC-98 FRED       CAMPBELL
          3 04-DEC-98 NANCY      HOFFMAN
          4 04-DEC-98 HENRY      PERKINS
          5 04-DEC-98 MARTHA     WOODS
```

Figure 9-7   Numbering the lines of each group (part 2 of 2)

Cross Joins

You need to understand cross joins, because they provide the foundation for both inner and outer joins The properties of inner joins are derived from the properties of cross products.

Cross products are a very powerful tool for some tasks, but they should be used with care because they can use up a large amount of any computer's resources.

What is a cross join?

Figure 9-8 shows an example of a "cross join." Cross joins are also called "cross products" and "Cartesian products." A cross join matches every row of the first table with every row from the second table. Cross joins often generate a lot of data. They should be used infrequently and with care. You have already used a cross join. You used it to generate a series of numbers.

Cross joins are important to understand for several reasons:

1.   The exact definition of an inner join is based on them.
2.   The properties of an inner join come from the properties of a cross join.
3.   It is important to avoid using them unintentionally.
4.   They can indicate that an error has occurred.

The number of columns and rows in a cross join are:

    Columns in cross join = Sum of the number of columns in the tables. (Add)
    Rows in cross join = Product of the number of rows in the tables. (Multiply)

Task

Show an example of a cross join.

Oracle & Access SQL

```
select a.*,
       b.*
from fig908_first a,
     fig908_second b;
```

Beginning tables
Fig908_first table   Fig908_second table

FCOL_1	FCOL_2
1	A
2	B
3	C
4	D

SCOL_1	SCOL_2	SCOL_3
95	VV	08-AUG-95
96	WW	09-SEP-96
97	XX	10-OCT-97
98	YY	11-NOV-98
99	ZZ	12-DEC-99

Result table

FCOL_1	FCOL_2	SCOL_1	SCOL_2	SCOL_3
1	A	95	VV	08-AUG-95
2	B	95	VV	08-AUG-95
3	C	95	VV	08-AUG-95
4	D	95	VV	08-AUG-95
1	A	96	WW	09-SEP-96
2	B	96	WW	09-SEP-96
3	C	96	WW	09-SEP-96
4	D	96	WW	09-SEP-96
1	A	97	XX	10-OCT-97
2	B	97	XX	10-OCT-97
3	C	97	XX	10-OCT-97
4	D	97	XX	10-OCT-97
1	A	98	YY	11-NOV-98
2	B	98	YY	11-NOV-98
3	C	98	YY	11-NOV-98
4	D	98	YY	11-NOV-98
1	A	99	ZZ	12-DEC-99
2	B	99	ZZ	12-DEC-99
3	C	99	ZZ	12-DEC-99
4	D	99	ZZ	12-DEC-99

Figure 9-8   What is a cross join?

Inner joins are derived from cross joins

Task

Show all the steps to create an inner join from a cross join:
1. A cross join is formed from the tables.
2. The join condition is evaluated for every row of the cross join.
3. The result table consists only of the rows for which the join condition is true.

Beginning tables
Fig909_fruits table   Fig909_colors table

FRUIT	F_NUM
APPLE	1
BANANA	2
STRAWBERRY	1
GRAPE	4
KIWI	(null)

C_NUM	COLOR
1	RED
2	YELLOW
1	GREEN
5	WHITE
(null)	BROWN

Oracle & Access SQL—inner join

```
select a.*, b.*
from fig909_fruits a,
     fig909_colors b
where a.f_num = b.c_num;
```

Step 1—form the cross product of the two tables

FRUIT	F_NUM	C_NUM	COLOR
APPLE	1	1	RED
APPLE	1	1	GREEN
APPLE	1	2	YELLOW
APPLE	1	5	WHITE
APPLE	1	(null)	BROWN
BANANA	2	1	RED
BANANA	2	1	GREEN
BANANA	2	2	YELLOW
BANANA	2	5	WHITE
BANANA	2	(null)	BROWN
GRAPE	4	1	RED
GRAPE	4	1	GREEN
GRAPE	4	2	YELLOW
GRAPE	4	5	WHITE
GRAPE	4	(null)	BROWN
KIWI	(null)	1	RED
KIWI	(null)	1	GREEN
KIWI	(null)	2	YELLOW
KIWI	(null)	5	WHITE
KIWI	(null)	(null)	BROWN
STRAWBERRY	1	1	RED
STRAWBERRY	1	1	GREEN
STRAWBERRY	1	2	YELLOW
STRAWBERRY	1	5	WHITE
STRAWBERRY	1	(null)	BROWN

Step 2—evaluate the join condition in each row of the cross join

Assign an evaluation to each row, one of these three: True, False, or Unknown.
Here, the join condition is: f_num = c_num.

```
FRUIT            F_NUM       C_NUM COLOR       EVALUATION
----------   ---------   --------- ----------  ----------
APPLE                1           1 GREEN       TRUE
APPLE                1           1 RED         TRUE
APPLE                1           2 YELLOW      FALSE
APPLE                1           5 WHITE       FALSE
APPLE                1  (null)     BROWN       UNKNOWN
BANANA               2           1 GREEN       FALSE
BANANA               2           1 RED         FALSE
BANANA               2           2 YELLOW      TRUE
BANANA               2           5 WHITE       FALSE
BANANA               2  (null)     BROWN       UNKNOWN
GRAPE                4           1 GREEN       FALSE
GRAPE                4           1 RED         FALSE
GRAPE                4           2 YELLOW      FALSE
GRAPE                4           5 WHITE       FALSE
GRAPE                4  (null)     BROWN       UNKNOWN
KIWI        (null)               1 GREEN       UNKNOWN
KIWI        (null)               1 RED         UNKNOWN
KIWI        (null)               2 YELLOW      UNKNOWN
KIWI        (null)               5 WHITE       UNKNOWN
KIWI        (null)      (null)     BROWN       UNKNOWN
STRAWBERRY           1           1 GREEN       TRUE
STRAWBERRY           1           1 RED         TRUE
STRAWBERRY           1           2 YELLOW      FALSE
STRAWBERRY           1           5 WHITE       FALSE
STRAWBERRY           1  (null)     BROWN       UNKNOWN
```

Step 3—keep only the rows that evaluate as true.

```
FRUIT            F_NUM       C_NUM COLOR       EVALUATION
----------   ---------   --------- ----------  ----------
APPLE                1           1 RED         TRUE
APPLE                1           1 GREEN       TRUE
BANANA               2           2 YELLOW      TRUE
STRAWBERRY           1           1 RED         TRUE
STRAWBERRY           1           1 GREEN       TRUE
```

Step 4—remove the evaluation (this is the inner join)

```
FRUIT            F_NUM       C_NUM COLOR
----------   ---------   --------- ----------
APPLE                1           1 RED
APPLE                1           1 GREEN
BANANA               2           2 YELLOW
STRAWBERRY           1           1 RED
STRAWBERRY           1           1 GREEN
```

Figure 9-9   Inner joins are derived from cross joins

The properties of an inner and outer join are derived from the properties of a cross join

Many of the properties of an inner join come from the properties of a cross join. Figure 9-10 shows some examples.

Properties of an inner join

• The join contains all valid combinations of rows. Each row of one table can match with many rows of the other table.

• Rows are dropped from the join if no matching row is in the other table.

• Rows are dropped from the join if any of the matching column(s) contains a null.

• Inner joins are symmetric. The order in which the tables are joined does not matter.

Outer joins

Outer joins are formed in a two-step process:

1. First, the inner join is formed.

2. Then the rows dropped from one or both of the beginning tables are added back into the result table.

Figure 9-10   The properties of an inner and outer join are derived from
the properties of a cross join

An error in the join condition can appear as a cross join

One frequent type of error that occurs in SQL is to omit one of the join conditions within the Where clause. The result resembles a cross join. You may see the data you expected repeated many times.

If you were expecting to have 100 rows in the result, you may find that you have 2000, with each of the rows you wanted repeated 20 times.

If this result occurs, do not panic. Just examine your Where clause carefully to be sure that it contains all the conditions it needs. Sometimes you may not be sure whether a condition is needed or not. It may seem redundant and unnecessary. Putting unneeded conditions in the Where clause may cause more processing to occur, but at least the results are accurate. Putting too few conditions in the Where clause can produce the wrong results.

So when in doubt, add extra conditions to the Where clause.

As you write SQL, you should pay attention to the size of your tables and know approximately how much data to expect. If your results do not meet your expectations, you will need to search for possible coding errors.

Notes

- The incorrect SQL has left out one of the join conditions. The Where clause does not contain the condition that the product codes must match.

- The effect here is subtle because the tables are not very large and the data does not cause a dramatic change.

- You might suspect that the incorrect report has an error by noticing that the supplier id repeats the same supplier several times and does so for several suppliers.

- You could confirm your suspicions by checking the number of items in lunch 2. Since this lunch contains four items, you could be certain that the report is incorrect.

Task

Correct SQL

```
select a.lunch_id, b.supplier_id,
       b.product_code, b.description,
       b.price, a.quantity
from l_lunch_items a,
     l_foods b
where a.supplier_id = b.supplier_id
and a.product_code = b.product_code
 and a.lunch_id = 2;
```

Correct report

```
         SUPPLIER PRODUCT
LUNCH_ID ID       CODE    DESCRIPTION           PRICE  QUANTITY
-------- -------- ------- --------------------- ------ ---------
       2 ASP      SW      SANDWICH              $3.50         2
       2 FRV      FF      FRENCH FRIES          $1.50         1
       2 JBR      VR      COFFEE                $0.85         2
       2 VSB      AS      DESSERT               $3.00         1
```

Incorrect SQL

```
select a.lunch_id, b.supplier_id,
       b.product_code, b.description,
       b.price, a.quantity
from l_lunch_items a,
     l_foods b
where a.supplier_id = b.supplier_id
 and a.lunch_id = 2;
```

Incorrect report

```
         SUPPLIER PRODUCT
LUNCH_ID ID       CODE    DESCRIPTION           PRICE  QUANTITY
-------- -------- ------- --------------------- ------ ---------
       2 ASP      FS      FRESH SALAD           $2.00         2
       2 ASP      SP      SOUP OF THE DAY       $1.50         2
       2 ASP      SW      SANDWICH              $3.50         2
       2 FRV      BR      BROCCOLI              $1.00         1
       2 FRV      FF      FRENCH FRIES          $1.50         1
       2 JBR      AS      SODA                  $1.25         2
       2 JBR      VR      COFFEE                $0.85         2
       2 VSB      AS      DESSERT               $3.00         1
```

Figure 9-11   An error in the join condition can appear as a cross join

Subqueries

A Select statement that is embedded within another Select statement is called a "subquery." Several variations on this idea exist. This section discusses them.

Introduction to subqueries

Figure 9-12 shows an example of a subquery, which is highlighted in the SQL code. In this example, the subquery is evaluated first:

```
select avg(b.price)
from l_foods;
```

The result is $2.31. Next, this value is substituted in the outer query:

```
select a.description,
       a.price
from l_foods a
where a.price < 2.31
order by a.description;
```

Then the outer query is evaluated, producing the result table.

In this case, the subquery acted like a variable in the Where clause.

Historical perspective

When the SQL language was first created, people thought that subqueries would be the most important feature of the language. One style of coding SQL makes extensive use of subqueries; this style can be found in older code, and some people write code this way. However, this style has now fallen out of favor.

It has largely been replaced by a style that prefers to use joins, when offered a choice. Three reasons justify this change. One reason is that the processing of joins has become much more efficient. Originally, subqueries were expected to always process much more quickly than joins. But many improvements have been made to make joins more efficient. So now, joins are often just as efficient as subqueries. Sometimes a join is more efficient than a subquery.

The second reason is that outer joins have now become a standard part of the language. The early SQL standards, SQL-86 and SQL-89, did not include outer joins. Subqueries were used to write outer joins. But now, most products support outer joins and they are included in the SQL-92 standard.

The third reason is that code written with many subqueries is difficult to understand and maintain. Code written with joins is often easier to understand and modify when changes are needed. Other people can also work with the code more easily.

Task

Show an example of a subquery. List the foods that cost less than the average price of the items on the menu. List the prices of these foods and sort the foods in ascending order.

Oracle & Access SQL

```
select a.description,
       a.price
from l_foods a
where a.price < (select avg(b.price)
                 from l_foods b)
order by a.description;
```

Beginning table

SUPPLIER ID	PRODUCT CODE	MENU ITEM	DESCRIPTION	PRICE	PRICE INCREASE
ASP	FS	1	FRESH SALAD	$2.00	$0.25
ASP	SP	2	SOUP OF THE DAY	$1.50	(null)
ASP	SW	3	SANDWICH	$3.50	$0.40
CBC	GS	4	GRILLED STEAK	$6.00	$0.70
CBC	HB	5	HAMBURGER	$2.50	$0.30
FRV	BR	6	BROCCOLI	$1.00	$0.05
FRV	FF	7	FRENCH FRIES	$1.50	(null)
JBR	AS	8	SODA	$1.25	$0.25
JBR	VR	9	COFFEE	$0.85	$0.15
VSB	AS	10	DESSERT	$3.00	$0.50

Result table

DESCRIPTION	PRICE
BROCCOLI	$1.00
COFFEE	$0.85
FRENCH FRIES	$1.50
FRESH SALAD	$2.00
SODA	$1.25
SOUP OF THE DAY	$1.50

Figure 9-12   Introduction to subqueries

Subqueries that result in a list of values

Figure 9-13 shows subqueries that result in a list of values. This list is used with the following conditions:

- IN
- NOT IN

Figure 9-13

❶ The result of this subquery is the list (3, 6, 9, 12, 15, 18, null). When this list is substituted in the main query, the Select statement is:

```
select number_2,
       word_2
from twos
where number_2 in (3, 6, 9, 12, 15, 18, null);
```

❷ The result of this subquery is the list (3, 6, 9, 12, 15, 18). The null has been removed because the NOT IN condition is used—see Figure 9-15. When this list is substituted in the main query, the Select statement is:

```
select number_2,
       word_2
from twos
where number_2 not in (3, 6, 9, 12, 15, 18);
```

Example 1—using the IN condition
Oracle & Access SQL

```
select number_2,
       word_2
from twos
where number_2 in (select number_3 ❶
                   from threes);
```

Result table

```
NUMBER_2 WORD_2
-------- ---------------
       6 SIX
      12 TWELVE
      18 EIGHTEEN
```

Task

Show a subquery that results in a list of values.

Example 2—using the NOT IN condition
Oracle & Access SQL

```
select number_2,
       word_2
from twos
where number_2 not in (select number_3 ❷
                       from threes
                       where number_3 is not null);
```

Beginning tables
Twos table   Threes table

```
                              NUMBER_3 WORD_3
  NUMBER_2 WORD_2             -------- ------------
 -------- ------------               3 THREE
        2 TWO                        6 SIX
        4 FOUR                       9 NINE
        6 SIX                       12 TWELVE
        8 EIGHT                     15 FIFTEEN
       10 TEN                       18 EIGHTEEN
       12 TWELVE             (null)    NULL
       14 FOURTEEN
       16 SIXTEEN
       18 EIGHTEEN
       20 TWENTY
 (null)    NULL
```

Result table

```
NUMBER_2 WORD_2
-------- ------------
       2 TWO
       4 FOUR
       8 EIGHT
      10 TEN
      14 FOURTEEN
      16 SIXTEEN
      20 TWENTY
```

Figure 9-13   Subqueries that result in a list of values

Subqueries that result in a single value

Figure 9-14 shows subqueries that result in a single value. Often a column function is used to ensure that the result can be only a single value. They can be used only in these two clauses:

- Where clause
- Having clause

They can be used with the following:

- = (equal)
- <> (not equal)
- < (less than) or > (greater than)
- IN
- NOT IN

Figure 9-14

❶   This subquery results in the value 18. When this value is substituted in the main query, the Select statement is

```
select number_2,
       word_2
from twos
where number_2 = 18;
```

❷   This subquery results in the value 18.

Example 1—using the EQUAL condition
Oracle & Access SQL

```
select number_2,
       word_2
from twos
where number_2 = (select max(number_3) ❶
                  from threes);
```

Result table

```
NUMBER_2 WORD_2
--------- ---------------
      18 EIGHTEEN
```

Task

Show a subquery that results in a single value.

Example 2—using the NOT EQUAL condition
Oracle & Access SQL

```
select number_2,
       word_2
from twos
where number_2 <> (select max(number_3)  ❷
                   from threes);
```

Beginning tables
Twos table   ## Threes table

```
                                  NUMBER_3 WORD_3
  NUMBER_2 WORD_2                  -------- ------------
--------- ------------                   3 THREE
        2 TWO                            6 SIX
        4 FOUR                           9 NINE
        6 SIX                           12 TWELVE
        8 EIGHT                         15 FIFTEEN
       10 TEN                           18 EIGHTEEN
       12 TWELVE                 (null)    NULL
       14 FOURTEEN
       16 SIXTEEN
       18 EIGHTEEN
       20 TWENTY
(null)     NULL
```

Result table

```
NUMBER_2 WORD_2
--------- ------------
        2 TWO
        4 FOUR
        6 SIX
        8 EIGHT
       10 TEN
       12 TWELVE
       14 FOURTEEN
       16 SIXTEEN
       20 TWENTY
```

Figure 9-14   Subqueries that result in a single value

Avoiding NOT IN with nulls

Figure 9-15 shows that no rows are selected when

- The result of a subquery is a list that includes a null.
- The list is used with a NOT IN condition

This makes sense because a null is an unknown value. We cannot say that rows are definitely not in a list, when the list contains an unknown value.

On the other hand, the IN condition ignores the null.

Figure 9-15

❶ This subquery results in the list (3, 6, 9, 12, 18, null). The "null" in this list does not cause a problem when it is used with an IN condition.

❷ This subquery results in the list (3, 6, 9, 12, 18, null). The "null" in this list causes a major problem when it is used with a NOT IN condition. The query does not run; it produces an error message.

❸ This subquery results in the list (3, 6, 9, 12, 18). The Where condition in the subquery removes the "null." This list works with a NOT IN condition.

Example 1—the IN condition is not affected by nulls
Oracle & Access SQL

```
select number_2,
       word_2
from twos
where number_2 in (select number_3 ❶
                   from threes);
```

Result table

```
NUMBER_2 WORD_2
--------- --------------
       6 SIX
      12 TWELVE
      18 EIGHTEEN
```

Task

Show what happens when the result of a subquery is a list that includes a null.

Example 2—the NOT IN condition does not work with nulls
Oracle & Access SQL

```
select number_2,
       word_2
from twos
where number_2 not in (select number_3 ❷
                       from threes);
```

Beginning tables
Twos table   Threes table

```
                              NUMBER_3 WORD_3
  NUMBER_2 WORD_2             --------- -----------
--------- -----------               3 THREE
        2 TWO                        6 SIX
        4 FOUR                       9 NINE
        6 SIX                       12 TWELVE
        8 EIGHT                     15 FIFTEEN
       10 TEN                       18 EIGHTEEN
       12 TWELVE              (null)    NULL
       14 FOURTEEN
       16 SIXTEEN
       18 EIGHTEEN
       20 TWENTY
(null)     NULL
```

Result message

"no rows selected"

Example 3—how to use the NOT IN condition with nulls
Oracle & Access SQL

```
select number_2,
       word_2
from twos
where number_2 in (select number_3 ❸
                   from threes
                   where number_3 is not null);
```

Result table

```
NUMBER_2 WORD_2
--------- -------------
        6 SIX
       12 TWELVE
       18 EIGHTEEN
```

Figure 9-15   Avoiding NOT IN with nulls

Many subqueries can also be written with a join

Figure 9-16 shows that some subqueries can also be written as joins. Actually, *many* subqueries can be written as joins. Which way to write the code is your decision. Most shops prefer that you use joins.

If you have a query that takes a long time to run, you might try shifting from a join to a subquery or vice versa. Sometimes this can make a dramatic difference.

Task

Show a subquery and a join that produce the same result table.

A query written with a subquery
Oracle & Access SQL

```
select number_2,
       word_2
from twos
where number_2 in (select number_3
                   from threes);
```

The same query written with a join
Oracle & Access SQL

```
select a.number_2,
       a.word_2
from twos a,
     threes b
where a.number_2 = b.number_3;
```

Beginning tables
Twos table   Threes table

```
                                 NUMBER_3 WORD_3
   NUMBER_2 WORD_2               --------- ------------
---------- ------------                 3 THREE
         2 TWO                          6 SIX
         4 FOUR                         9 NINE
         6 SIX                         12 TWELVE
         8 EIGHT                       15 FIFTEEN
        10 TEN                         18 EIGHTEEN
        12 TWELVE              (null)    NULL
        14 FOURTEEN
        16 SIXTEEN
        18 EIGHTEEN
        20 TWENTY
(null)     NULL
```

Result table

```
NUMBER_2 WORD_2
--------- --------------
        6 SIX
       12 TWELVE
       18 EIGHTEEN
```

Figure 9-16   Many subqueries can also be written with a join

Finding the differences between two tables

Figure 9-17 shows how to find the differences between two tables. This method uses a subquery, which removes all the rows that are identical in the two tables, so that only the different rows remain.

You have two queries. The first query shows the rows of the first table that are not present in the second table. The second query is almost the same, but the roles of the two tables are reversed. It shows the rows of the second table that are not present in the first table.

Since the two queries are almost the same, I explain only the first one. The Select clause lists all the columns of the first table. This is what you want to see—the entire row that has a difference in at least one column.

The only trick here is in the Where clause. A "Not In" condition is used to find the rows of the first table that do not match exactly with any row from the second table. However, the "Not In" condition is oriented to comparing single values with one another.

To get the "Not In" condition to compare two entire rows, you need to turn the rows into single values. This is accomplished

Rows in the original table, but not in the modified table
Oracle SQL

```
select a.number_2,
       a.word_2
from twos a
where (number_2 || a.word_2) not in (select (b.number_2 || b.word_2)
                                      from twos_modified b);
```

Access SQL

```
select a.number_2,
       a.word_2
from twos a
where (number_2 & a.word_2) not in (select (b.number_2 & b.word_2)
                                     from twos_modified b);
```

Result table

```
NUMBER_2 WORD_2
--------- ---------------
       8 EIGHT
      20 TWENTY
```

Task

Show how to find the differences between two tables using a subquery.

Rows in the modified table, but not in the original table
Oracle SQL

```
select a.number_2,
       a.word_2
from twos_modified a
where (number_2 || a.word_2) not in (select (b.number_2 || b.word_2)
                                     from twos b);
```

Access SQL

```
select a.number_2,
       a.word_2
from twos_modified a
where (number_2 & a.word_2) not in (select (b.number_2 & b.word_2)
                                    from twos b);
```

Beginning tables

| Twos table | | Twos_modified table | |

NUMBER_2	WORD_2	NUMBER_2	WORD_2
2	TWO	2	TWO
4	FOUR	4	FOUR
6	SIX	6	SIX
8	EIGHT	8	HUIT
10	TEN	10	TEN
12	TWELVE	12	TWELVE
14	FOURTEEN	14	FOURTEEN
16	SIXTEEN	16	SIXTEEN
18	EIGHTEEN	18	EIGHTEEN
20	TWENTY	21	TWENTY
(null)	NULL	(null)	NULL

Result table

NUMBER_2	WORD_2
8	HUIT
21	TWENTY

Figure 9-17   Finding the differences between two tables

Summary

In this chapter, you learned to use a self join. A self join is used where you need to combine the information from several different rows of the beginning table to create a single row of the result table.

You only need to have one copy of a table physically stored on the disk drive. The computer will act as if you have several copies of the table. Each virtual copy of the table must be given a separate table alias.

A cross join matches every row of one table with every row of another table. It shows every possible combination of rows from the two tables. A cross join between two small tables can be useful to enumerate every possibility when you are doing an analysis. Performing a cross join between two large tables should almost always be avoided.

The definitions of an inner and outer joins are derived from the cross join. Understanding a cross join can help you understand the details of these other joins.

Subqueries occur when one Select statement is embedded within another one. They were used extensively in the early days of SQL, before the processing of joins became efficient. Now they are used much less. The SQL language still contains many complex features to support subqueries, even though these features are rarely used anymore. Many subqueries can also be written as joins and that is usually a better way to write them.

The most useful types of subquery are the ones where the inner join results in a single value or in a list of values. This result, in a way, functions as a variable within the outer Select statement. The data in the database determine the value of this variable. Unfortunately, the SQL-89 standard restricts the number of places where such a variable (a subselect) can be used.

In these types of queries, the inner Select statement can be evaluated first, independent from the outer Select statement. These are called "non-correlated subqueries." After the inner Select statement is evaluated, the result replaces the inner Select statement within the outer Select statement—this is where the idea of a "variable" comes in. Finally, the outer Select statement is evaluated.

There is another type of subquery, called a "correlated" subquery. Here the inner Select statement contains a reference to the outer Select statement. This creates a situation where both Select statements must be evaluated together—a rather complex process. Correlated subqueries were used mostly to create outer joins, before most SQL products had direct support for them. Today, most correlated subqueries can be replaced with another Select statement that uses a join or an outer join.

Subqueries can sometimes be useful when you are working with a query that will be run frequently and you want to make it as efficient as possible. Sometimes a query will run more quickly when it is written as a subquery. Sometimes it will run more quickly when it is written as a join. Often, you will need to try both methods and measure the processing time. In theory, the optimizer should find the most efficient way to process a query no matter how you write it. Optimizers are getting fairly good at doing this. However, most optimizers today still do not compare processing a query as a join with processing it as a subquery.

Exercises

1. Goal: add a column of line numbers to a report.

1A. Add a column of line numbers to the report created by the SQL statement

Problem

```
select a.lunch_id, c.supplier_name, a.product_code, a.quantity
from l_lunch_items a,
        l_foods b,
        l_suppliers c
where a.supplier_id = b.supplier_id
   and a.product_code = b.product_code
   and b.supplier_id = c.supplier_id
order by a.lunch_id, c.supplier_name, a.product_code, a.quantity;
```

Solution
Oracle SQL

```
-- step 1
create or replace view temp_1 as
select a.lunch_id, c.supplier_name, a.product_code, a.quantity
from l_lunch_items a,
        l_foods b,
        l_suppliers c
where a. supplier_id = b.supplier_id
   and a.product_code = b.product_code
   and b.supplier_id = c.supplier_id
group by a.lunch_id, c.supplier_name, a.product_code, a.quantity;

-- step 2
create or replace view temp_2 as
select rownum as line_number, a.*
from temp_1 a;
```

Access solution

Step 1. Save the results as a table.

```
select a.lunch_id, c.supplier_name, a.product_code, a.quantity
into temp_1
from l_lunch_items a,
         l_foods b,
         l_suppliers c
where a. supplier_id = b.supplier_id
   and a.product_code = b.product_code
   and b.supplier_id = c.supplier_id
order by a.lunch_id, c.supplier_name, a.product_code, a.quantity;
```

Step 2. Add a column of line numbers.

```
alter table temp_1
add column line_num  counter;
```

1B. List all the employees. Give their full name, first name, and last name. Sort this by the last name. Create a column of line numbers for this report.

2. Goal: When the rows of a table are ordered in a particular way (This is done by the data in the table- not by the database itself.). , determine information about the sequence of the rows.

You can do this by joining the table with itself, and joining each line to the one that comes after it. The join condition here is

a.line_number + 1 = b.line_number

2A. Table Ex9_2 contains a log of the sales made by a store. This table already contains line numbers. Here is the table

```
LINE_NUMBER SALE_DATE
----------- ---------
          1 03-MAR-99
          2 05-MAR-99
          3 01-MAR-99
          4 08-MAR-99
          5 10-MAR-99
```

Write SQL to to find the dates that have been entered out of sequence.

Solution.
Oracle & Access SQL—look for the exceptions to the rule

```
select a.*, b.*
from ex9_2 a,
     ex9_2 b
where a.line_number + 1 = b.line_number
  and a.sale_date > b.sale_date;
```

2B. Determine if there are any gaps in the way the lunches have been numbered. (A gap might be created if a person signed up for a lunch and then cancelled.) Use the L_lunches table.

2C. Determine if the employees have been entered in employee_number sequence for each lunch in the L_lunches table.

3. Generate a calendar for yourself. Begin on your the day you were born and list all the days you plan to live. If you are not sure how long you will live, make the calendar cover 120 years (about 40,000 days).

4.Goal: Generate all the prime numbers less than 1000. Add a column of sequential numbers to number all the primes sequentially.

Solution
Step 1. List all the prime numbers.

Oracle SQL	Access SQL

``
create table numbers_0_to_999 as
select 100 * a.digit
         + 10 * b.digit
         + c.digit as n
from numbers_0_to_9 a,
       numbers_0_to_9 b,
       numbers_0_to_9 c;
``
	``
	select 100 * a.digit
	         + 10 * b.digit
	         + c.digit as n
	into numbers_0_to_999
	from numbers_0_to_9 a,
	       numbers_0_to_9 b,
	       numbers_0_to_9 c;
	``

``
select a.n as prime_number
from numbers_0_to_999 a,
       numbers_0_to_999 b
where a.n > 1
   and b.n > 1
   and b.n <= a.n
   and mod(a.n, b.n) = 0
group by a.n
having count(b.n) = 1
order by a.n;
``
	``
	select a.n as prime_number
	from numbers_0_to_999 a,
	       numbers_0_to_999 b
	where a.n > 1
	   and b.n > 1
	   and b.n <= a.n
	   and a.n mod b.n = 0
	group by a.n
	having count(b.n) = 1
	order by a.n;
	``

Step 2. Add a column of sequential numbers to the list of primes.

Oracle SQL	Access SQL

``
create or replace view prime_1 as
select a.n as prime_number
from numbers_0_to_999 a,
       numbers_0_to_999 b
where a.n > 1
   and b.n > 1
   and b.n <= a.n
   and mod(a.n, b.n) = 0
group by a.n
having count(b.n) = 1;
``
	``
	select a.n as prime_number
	into prime_table
	from numbers_0_to_999 a,
	       numbers_0_to_999 b
	where a.n > 1
	   and b.n > 1
	   and b.n <= a.n
	   and a.n mod b.n = 0
	group by a.n
	having count(b.n) = 1;
	``

``` create table prime_2 as select rownum as seq_num, a.prime_number from prime_1 a; ```	``` alter table prime_table add column seq_num counter; ```

4B. Create a list of numbers or dates. Add a column of sequence numbers to them.

5. Determine if any employee is working for a manager who was hired after they were.

6. Of all the people who order desert with their lunch, how many of them also order coffee?

Chapter 10

Advanced Queries

The Decode and IIF functions

Sometimes people say that the Decode function in Oracle introduces "If-Then-Else" logic into SQL. The examples in this section show what they mean by this statement. They imply that this makes SQL more powerful and capable of doing new things.

Actually, everything that can be done using this function can also be done using a Union. No new capabilities are added. However, the Decode function does make the SQL statements easier to write.

In Access, the Immediate If (IIF) function can do everything that the Decode function can do. In fact, it can do a little bit more.

The Decode function in Oracle

The Decode function is an extension to standard SQL, which Oracle has added. It performs a series of tests to determine whether the value in a column is equal to one of a few specific values. It then places a new value in the column, based on which value is matched. If it does not find any match, it also places a new value in the column.

Again, this function is based on a series of tests for an "equal" condition. It can also test for a "less than" or "greater than" condition by using a trick with the "Sign" function. An "in" or "between" condition can be coded as a combination of these tests. However, a "like" condition cannot be used.

Oracle syntax
DECODE (tested_value, if_1, then_1, if_2, then_2, if_3, then_3, . . . , else)

where
        tested_value = a column of a table or a function of the columns of a row.

If tested_value equals "if_1," then the Decode function equals "then_1."
If tested_value equals "if_2," then the Decode function equals "then_2."
If tested_value equals "if_3," then the Decode function equals "then_3."
And so on.
If tested_value is not equal to any of the "if" values, then the Decode function equals the last value, in the "else" position.

The "if," "then," or "else" may be:
        a literal (of any datatype)
        a null
        a column
        a row function, using one or several columns in a single row

Task

Show an example using the Decode function in Oracle. Substitute carrots for broccoli in the menu of lunch foods.

Oracle SQL

```
-- Override a value in one column.
select decode(description,
       'broccoli', 'carrots',
       description) as new_menu,
       price
from l_foods;
```

Beginning table (L_Foods table)

SUPPLIER ID	PRODUCT CODE	MENU ITEM	DESCRIPTION	PRICE	PRICE INCREASE
ASP	FS	1	FRESH SALAD	$2.00	$0.25
ASP	SP	2	SOUP OF THE DAY	$1.50	(null)
ASP	SW	3	SANDWICH	$3.50	$0.40
CBC	GS	4	GRILLED STEAK	$6.00	$0.70
CBC	HB	5	HAMBURGER	$2.50	$0.30
FRV	BR	6	BROCCOLI	$1.00	$0.05
FRV	FF	7	FRENCH FRIES	$1.50	(null)
JBR	AS	8	SODA	$1.25	$0.25
JBR	VR	9	COFFEE	$0.85	$0.15
VSB	AS	10	DESSERT	$3.00	$0.50

Result table

NEW_MENU	PRICE
FRESH SALAD	$2.00
SOUP OF THE DAY	$1.50
SANDWICH	$3.50
GRILLED STEAK	$6.00
HAMBURGER	$2.50
CARROTS	$1.00
FRENCH FRIES	$1.50
SODA	$1.25
COFFEE	$0.85
DESSERT	$3.00

The Decode function changes the value in a single column, not in an entire row. To change several columns, a separate Decode function must be written for each column.

Figure 10-1   The Decode function in Oracle

The Immediate If (IIF) function in Access

The Immediate If (IIF) function is used to create an "If-Then-Else" condition in Access. This is an extension to standard SQL, which Access has added. It tests a statement to determine whether it is true or false. It assigns one value to the function if the statement is true. It assigns a different value if the statement is false.

The condition used in the test can be any SQL condition, including:

Equal
Less than
Greater than
In
Between
Like
Is null

The IIF function handles nulls with the "is null" condition. This is more precise than the Decode function, which handles nulls with the "equal to" condition.

Access syntax:

IIF(true_or_false_expression, true_value, false_value)

where
"true_or_false_expression" is any expression resulting in a value of True or False

In Access,
"False" is the value 0
"True" is any other value ("-1" is often used)

If "true_or_false_expression" is True, then the IIF function equals true_value
If "true_or_false_expression" is False, then the IIF function equals false_value
If "true_or_false_expression" is Unknown, then the IIF function equals false_value

Task

Show an example of an SQL statement using the IIF function. Substitute carrots for broccoli in the menu of lunch foods.

Access SQL

```
select iif (description='broccoli',
            'Carrots',
            description) as new_menu,
      price
from l_foods;
```

Beginning table (L_Foods table)

	Supplier_id	Product_code	Menu_item	Description	Price	Price_increase
▶	Asp	Fs	1	Fresh Salad	$2.00	$0.25
	Asp	Sp	2	Soup of the Day	$1.50	
	Asp	Sw	3	Sandwich	$3.50	$0.40
	Cbc	Gs	4	Grilled steak	$6.00	$0.70
	Cbc	Hb	5	Hamburger	$2.50	$0.30
	Frv	Br	6	Broccoli	$1.00	$0.05
	Frv	Ff	7	French Fries	$1.50	
	Jbr	As	8	Soda	$1.25	$0.25
	Jbr	Vr	9	Coffee	$0.85	$0.15
	Vsb	As	10	Dessert	$3.00	$0.50
*			0		$0.00	$0.00

Record: I◄ ◄ 1 ► ►I ►* of 10

Result table

	new_menu	price
▶	Fresh Salad	$2.00
	Soup of the Day	$1.50
	Sandwich	$3.50
	Grilled steak	$6.00
	Hamburger	$2.50
	Carrots	$1.00
	French Fries	$1.50
	Soda	$1.25
	Coffee	$0.85
	Dessert	$3.00
*		$0.00

Record: I◄ ◄ 1 ►

Figure 10-2   The Immediate If (IIF) function in Access

Attaching messages to rows

Figure 10-4 shows how to attach messages to rows of data. The messages can be used to convey information, to give warnings, or to show errors. I present three different methods of doing so. You can compare them to see how they contrast with each other. The union works in both Oracle and Access.

Figure 10-4

❶   This Select statement attaches a message to some of the rows from the beginning table.

❷   This Select statement lists all the rows to which no message is attached.

❸   This column is needed to match the message column. It puts a blank space in the message column.

❹   In Oracle, the Sign function allows Decode to cover a range of values, rather than just a few specific values. This is a trick. The Sign function is +1 for all positive numbers. It is -1 for all negative numbers. Otherwise, it is 0. In this example, it creates a +1 when the price is more that $3.00, a 0 when the price is equal to $3.00, and a –1 when the price is less than $3.00.

❺   In Access, the statement "price > 3.00" is much clearer and easier to understand.

Oracle & Access SQL—using a union

```
select description, ❶
          price,
          'this item costs more than three dollars' as message
from l_foods
where price > 3.00
union
select description, ❷
          price,
          ' ' ❸
from l_foods
where not (price > 3.00);
```

Beginning table (L_Foods table)

SUPPLIER ID	PRODUCT CODE	MENU ITEM	DESCRIPTION	PRICE	PRICE INCREASE
ASP	FS	1	FRESH SALAD	$2.00	$0.25
ASP	SP	2	SOUP OF THE DAY	$1.50	(null)
ASP	SW	3	SANDWICH	$3.50	$0.40
CBC	GS	4	GRILLED STEAK	$6.00	$0.70
CBC	HB	5	HAMBURGER	$2.50	$0.30
FRV	BR	6	BROCCOLI	$1.00	$0.05
FRV	FF	7	FRENCH FRIES	$1.50	(null)
JBR	AS	8	SODA	$1.25	$0.25
JBR	VR	9	COFFEE	$0.85	$0.15
VSB	AS	10	DESSERT	$3.00	$0.50

Task

List all the food items and mark the ones that cost more than three dollars.

Oracle SQL—using Decode

```
select description,
       price,
       decode (sign(price - 3.00), ❹
              +1, 'this item costs more than three dol-
lars',
               0, '   ',
              -1, '   ',
              null) as message
from l_foods;
```

Access SQL—using IIF

```
select description,
       price,
       iif (price > 3.00, ❺
            'this item costs more than three dollars',
            '   ') as message
from l_foods;
```

Result table

```
DESCRIPTION          PRICE  MESSAGE
-------------------  ------ ----------------------------------------
FRESH SALAD          $2.00
SOUP OF THE DAY      $1.50
SANDWICH             $3.50  THIS ITEM COSTS MORE THAN THREE DOLLARS
GRILLED STEAK        $6.00  THIS ITEM COSTS MORE THAN THREE DOLLARS
HAMBURGER            $2.50
BROCCOLI             $1.00
FRENCH FRIES         $1.50
SODA                 $1.25
COFFEE               $0.85
DESSERT              $3.00
```

Figure 10-3   Attaching messages to rows

Overriding several rows of a table

In Chapter 8, you saw how to override the values in several rows of a table using a union. Here is another way to do the same thing using the Decode and IIF functions. For this purpose, the Decode function works better than the IIf function, because you do not have to embed one level within another.

Figure 10-4

❶   In Oracle, the Decode function can change several values in one statement. Here, "broccoli" is changed to "carrots" and "french fries" is changed to "mashed pota-toes"—all easily formatted within a single statement.

❷   This Decode statement changes the value in the Price column. However, note that it is not testing the Price column in order to determine which values to change. Instead, it tests the Description column. This test enables it to change the price of a specific item, rather than change all prices of $1.00 to $1.30.

To be even more specific about which rows are changed, you could use the primary key of the table. For a compound primary key, such as this table has, you would need to concatenate all the columns of the primary key—(supplier_id || product_code).

❸   A column alias, "Price," is required here to give a name to the column formed by the Decode function. In Oracle, this column alias can be the same as a name of one of the columns of the beginning table.

❹   In Access, changing two or more rows requires embedding one IIF statement within another. To change ten rows would require nesting ten IIf statements within each other—not a recommended practice.

❺   Access gets confused if the word "Price" is used twice on this line—once refer-ring to a column of the beginning table and once as a column alias. To avoid this confu-sion, the table name is added to the first reference, giving "L_foods.price." Another method is to change the column alias from "Price" to "Price_2."

Beginning table (L_Foods table)

SUPPLIER ID	PRODUCT CODE	MENU ITEM	DESCRIPTION	PRICE	PRICE INCREASE
ASP	FS	1	FRESH SALAD	$2.00	$0.25
ASP	SP	2	SOUP OF THE DAY	$1.50	(null)
ASP	SW	3	SANDWICH	$3.50	$0.40
CBC	GS	4	GRILLED STEAK	$6.00	$0.70
CBC	HB	5	HAMBURGER	$2.50	$0.30
FRV	BR	6	BROCCOLI	$1.00	$0.05
FRV	FF	7	FRENCH FRIES	$1.50	(null)
JBR	AS	8	SODA	$1.25	$0.25
JBR	VR	9	COFFEE	$0.85	$0.15
VSB	AS	10	DESSERT	$3.00	$0.50

Task

On the menu of lunch foods, substitute carrots for broccoli, and mashed potatoes for french fries. Change the price of the carrots to $1.30and the price of the mashed potatoes to $1.40.

Oracle SQL—using Decode

```
select decode (description, ❶
            'broccoli', 'carrots',
            'french fries', 'mashed potatoes',
            description) as new_menu,
        decode (description, ❷
            'broccoli', 1.30,
            'french fries', 1.40,
            price) as price ❸
from l_foods;
```

Access SQL—using IIF

```
select iif (description='broccoli', 'Carrots', ❹
        iif (description='french fries', 'mashed pota-
toes',
            description)) as new_menu,
    iif (description = 'broccoli', 1.30,
        iif (description = 'french fries', 1.40,
            l_foods.price) as price ❺
from l_foods;
```

Result table

```
NEW_MENU                PRICE
--------------------  --------
FRESH SALAD             $2.00
SOUP OF THE DAY         $1.50
SANDWICH                $3.50
GRILLED STEAK           $6.00
HAMBURGER               $2.50
CARROTS                 $1.30
MASHED POTATOES         $1.50
SODA                    $1.25
COFFEE                  $0.85
DESSERT                 $3.00
```

Figure 10-4   Overriding several rows of a table

Dividing data into different columns

In Chapter 8, you saw how to divide information into separate columns by using a union. Figure 10-6 shows how to do it by using the Decode and IIF functions. For this application, the IIF function produces much better code than the Decode function.

Figure 10-5

❶   In Access, this column alias must be enclosed in square brackets because it contains spaces. Also, note that Access does not allow a period to be used within a column alias. So "$2" must be used instead of "$2.00."

❷   The Sign function is used with Decode to indicate a range of values. See Figure 10-3.

❸   In Oracle, this column alias must be enclosed in double quotes because it contains spaces. Note that Oracle allows a period to be used with a column alias.

❹   Here, one Decode statement must be embedded within another.

❺   Note that "TO_NUMBER(NULL)" is needed to determine the datatype of this column. The datatype of the first value sets the datatype of the Decode function. If the first value is a null, then Text is the default datatype.

Access SQL—using IIF

```
select description,
        iif (price <= 1.00,
             price,
             null) as [$1 and under], ❶
        iif (price between 1.01 and 2.00,
             price,
             null) as [$1 to $2],
        iif (price >= 2.01,
             price,
             null) as [$2 and up]
from l_foods;
```

Beginning table (L_Foods table)

SUPPLIER ID	PRODUCT CODE	MENU ITEM	DESCRIPTION	PRICE	PRICE INCREASE
ASP	FS	1	FRESH SALAD	$2.00	$0.25
ASP	SP	2	SOUP OF THE DAY	$1.50	(null)
ASP	SW	3	SANDWICH	$3.50	$0.40
CBC	GS	4	GRILLED STEAK	$6.00	$0.70
CBC	HB	5	HAMBURGER	$2.50	$0.30
FRV	BR	6	BROCCOLI	$1.00	$0.05
FRV	FF	7	FRENCH FRIES	$1.50	(null)
JBR	AS	8	SODA	$1.25	$0.25
JBR	VR	9	COFFEE	$0.85	$0.15
VSB	AS	10	DESSERT	$3.00	$0.50

Task

List the prices of the foods in three columns—$0.01 to $1.00, $1.01 to $2.00, $2.01 and up.

Oracle column formats

```
set null '   '
column '$1.00 and under' format $0.99
column '$1.01 to $2.00' format $9.99
column '$2.01 and up' format $99.99
```

Oracle SQL—using Decode

```
select description,
        decode (sign(1.00 - price), ❷
            +1, price,
             0, price,
            -1, null,
            null) as "$1.00 and under", ❸
        decode (sign(2.00 - price),
            +1, decode (sign (1.00 - price), ❹
                                +1, to_number(null), ❺
                                 0, null,
                                -1,price),
             0, price,
            -1, null,
            null) as "$1.01 to $2.00",
        decode (sign(2.00 - price),
            +1, to_number(null),
             0, price,
            -1, price,
            null) as "$2.01 and up"
from l_foods;
```

Result table

```
DESCRIPTION          $1.00 AND UNDER $1.01 TO $2.00 $2.01 AND UP
-------------------- --------------- -------------- ------------
FRESH SALAD                           $2.00
SOUP OF THE DAY                       $1.50
SANDWICH                                             $3.50
GRILLED STEAK                                        $6.00
HAMBURGER                                            $2.50
BROCCOLI              $1.00
FRENCH FRIES                          $1.50
SODA                                  $1.25
COFFEE               $0.85
DESSERT                                              $3.00
```

Figure 10-5   Dividing data into different columns

Applying two functions to different parts of the data

Figure 10-6 shows how to apply one function to some of the rows of a table and apply a different function to the other rows. Here, both the Decode and IIF functions produce code that is easy to read and understand. However, if three or more functions were to be applied, then these functions would need to be embedded several levels deep. This embedding would quickly become difficult code.

The union works in both Oracle and Access. Coding three or more functions with a union would make the code longer, but would not make its structure more complex.

Figure 10-6

❶   In Oracle, this formats the New Price column. It puts in a dollar sign, limits the number to two decimal places, and adds a zero before the decimal point for items that cost less than $1.00.

Oracle & Access SQL—using a union

```
select description,
       price + (price * .05) as new_price
from l_foods
where price >= 2.00
union
select description,
       price + (price * .10)
from l_foods
where price < 2.00;
```

Beginning table (L_Foods table)

SUPPLIER ID	PRODUCT CODE	MENU ITEM	DESCRIPTION	PRICE	PRICE INCREASE
ASP	FS	1	FRESH SALAD	$2.00	$0.25
ASP	SP	2	SOUP OF THE DAY	$1.50	(null)
ASP	SW	3	SANDWICH	$3.50	$0.40
CBC	GS	4	GRILLED STEAK	$6.00	$0.70
CBC	HB	5	HAMBURGER	$2.50	$0.30
FRV	BR	6	BROCCOLI	$1.00	$0.05
FRV	FF	7	FRENCH FRIES	$1.50	(null)
JBR	AS	8	SODA	$1.25	$0.25
JBR	VR	9	COFFEE	$0.85	$0.15
VSB	AS	10	DESSERT	$3.00	$0.50

Task

Increase the price of all foods costing more than $2.00 by 5%. Increase the price of all other foods by 10%.

Oracle column formats

```
column new_price format $90.99 ❶
```

Oracle SQL—using Decode

```
select description,
       decode (sign(2.00 - price),
                        +1, price + (price * .10),
                         0, price + (price * .10),
                        -1, price + (price * .05),
                       null) as new_price
from l_foods;
```

Access SQL—using IIF

```
select description,
      iif(price >= 2.00,
          price + (price * .05),
          price + (price * .10)) as new_price
from l_foods
order by description;
```

Result table

```
DESCRIPTION           NEW_PRICE
-------------------- ---------
FRESH SALAD              $2.20
SOUP OF THE DAY          $1.65
SANDWICH                 $3.68
GRILLED STEAK            $6.30
HAMBURGER                $2.63
BROCCOLI                 $1.10
FRENCH FRIES             $1.65
SODA                     $1.38
COFFEE                   $0.94
DESSERT                  $3.15
```

Figure 10-6   Applying two functions to different parts of the data

Using the environment in which SQL runs

SQL by itself has some limitations. This fact is not surprising—SQL was developed to be a language to handle large amounts of data. It was never intended to be able to do everything. But in fact, it can do so much that people are sometimes astonished to find its limitations. The environment in which SQL runs can handle most of these limitations.

One limitation is that standard SQL contains no variables. A user cannot enter parameters and have them entered automatically into a query. To modify a query, the user must edit the code directly. Parameter queries fix this limitation.

Another limitation involves summarization. You can always list a set of details, or their subtotals, or their final total. But SQL does not provide any way to combine this information into a single report. Creating reports that include all this information is usually left to the SQL environment.

Parameter queries in Oracle

Figure 10-7

❶   Sets the SQL Plus environment to accept variables.

❷   Sets the ampersand (&) to designate variables.

❸   Sets the environment to show when variable values are used and what values are assigned to them.

❹   The Prompt command writes a message to the user.

❺   The Accept command asks the user to enter a value for a parameter. "Number" indicates the datatype of the parameter. Note that the name of the variable, "Employee_num," does not begin with an ampersand.

❻   Here the variable is used within SQL code. The name of the variable must be preceded with an ampersand.

Task

Write a procedure in Oracle that will ask for an Employee Id number. After the user enters this number, the procedure finds the information about that employee in the L_employee table.

Oracle Environment—SQL Plus

set scan on ❶
set define on ❷
set verify on ❸

prompt 'Enter the a valid Employee Id number' ❹
accept employee_num number prompt 'Employee Id number > ' ❺

Oracle SQL

select *
from l_employees
where employee_id = &employee_num; ❻

Procedure to run this code

1. The code above cannot be run from the SQL> prompt. It must be saved in a file.
2. At the SQL> prompt, enter:
        START followed by the name of the file

Prompt for information

```
'Enter the a valid Employee Id number'
Employee Id number >  201
```

Result

```
old   3: where employee_id = &employee_num
new   3: WHERE EMPLOYEE_ID =        201

EMPLOYEE                          DEPT                   CREDIT PHONE  MANAGER
      ID FIRST_NAME LAST_NAME  CODE HIRE_DATE      LIMIT NUMBER      ID
-------- ---------- ---------- ---- ---------- ------- ------ -------
     201 SUSAN      BROWN       EXE  01-JUN-92  $30.00 3484   (null)
```

Figure 10-7   Parameter queries in Oracle

Parameter queries in Access

Access automatically prompts you for a value of any variable it does not recognize. It is tuned to prompt you for parameter values. You may have encountered this situation already. If you misspell the name of a column, it prompts you to enter a value for that column. Usually, that action is not what you want. This discrepancy creates some strange error messages.

But when you want to create a parameter query in Access, it is easy to do. Access is always ready to accept parameters.

Figure 10-8

❶   The text within the square brackets indicates a single parameter. The actual text is used to prompt for the information. This technique will work even without the square brackets, as long as the text contains no spaces. For instance:

Access SQL

```
select *
from L_Employees
where employee_id = Enter_an_Employee_Id_number;
```

Task

Write a procedure in Access that will ask for an Employee Id number. After the user enters this number, the procedure finds the information about that employee in the L_employee table.

Access SQL

```
select *
from L_Employees
where employee_id= [Enter an Employee Id number]; ➊
```

Prompt for information

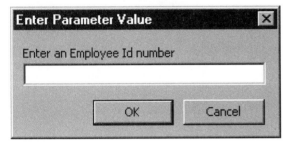

Result

	Employee_id	First_name	Last_name	Dept_code	Hire_date	Credit_limit	Phone_number	Manager_id
▶	201	Susan	Brown	Exe	06-01-1992	$30.00	3484	
*	0					$0.00		0

Record: |◄ ◄ | 1 | ► ►I ►* | of 1

Figure 10-8   Parameter queries in Access

Reporting details, subtotals, and grand totals in Oracle

Oracle uses the SQL Plus environment to create subtotals and grand totals for reports. Two distinct levels of software are working together here. The SQL level lists the detail data and puts it in the correct sort order. The SQL Plus environment adds blank lines to group the data within the report. It also adds subtotals for each group and a grand total at the end of the report. SQL Plus uses two commands to do so—"Breaks" and "Computes."

Figure 10-9

❶ ❷ This clears any Break or Compute commands that have previously been issued in the SQL Plus environment.

❸   This command sets the width of the Description column to 15 characters.

❹   The Break command adds a blank line when a change occurs in the Employee Id. It also triggers the Compute commands at this time and at the end of the report.

❺   This Compute command creates the subtotals that are written when the Employee Id changes.

❻   This Compute command creates the grand total for the report.

Oracle Environment—SQL Plus

```
clear breaks ❶
clear computes ❷

column description a15 ❸

break on employee_id skip 1 on report ❹
compute sum of price on employee_id ❺
compute sum of price on report ❻
```

Oracle SQL

```
select employee_id,
       first_name,
       lunch_date,
       description,
       quantity,
       (price * quantity) as price
from all_lunches
order by lunch_date, employee_id;
```

Report with subtotals and a grand total

```
EMPLOYEE            LUNCH
      ID FIRST_NAME DATE       DESCRIPTION           QUANTITY     PRICE
-------- ---------- ---------- -------------------- ---------  --------
     201 SUSAN      16-NOV-98  FRESH SALAD                 1     $2.00
         SUSAN      16-NOV-98  SANDWICH                    2     $7.00
         SUSAN      16-NOV-98  COFFEE                      2     $1.70
********                                                        --------
sum                                                             $10.70

     202 JIM        16-NOV-98  SANDWICH                    2     $7.00
         JIM        16-NOV-98  FRENCH FRIES                1     $1.50
         JIM        16-NOV-98  COFFEE                      2     $1.70
         JIM        16-NOV-98  DESSERT                     1     $3.00
********                                                        --------
sum                                                             $13.20

     203 MARTHA     16-NOV-98  FRESH SALAD                 1     $2.00
         MARTHA     16-NOV-98  GRILLED STEAK               1     $6.00
         MARTHA     16-NOV-98  FRENCH FRIES                1     $1.50
         MARTHA     16-NOV-98  COFFEE                      1     $0.85
         MARTHA     16-NOV-98  SODA                        1     $1.25
********                                                        --------
sum                                                             $11.60


     205 HENRY      04-DEC-98  FRESH SALAD                 1     $2.00
         HENRY      04-DEC-98  SOUP OF THE DAY             1     $1.50
         HENRY      04-DEC-98  GRILLED STEAK               1     $6.00
         HENRY      04-DEC-98  FRENCH FRIES                1     $1.50
         HENRY      04-DEC-98  SODA                        1     $1.25
********                                                        --------
sum                                                             $12.25

     208 FRED       04-DEC-98  FRESH SALAD                 1     $2.00
         FRED       04-DEC-98  GRILLED STEAK               1     $6.00
         FRED       04-DEC-98  COFFEE                      1     $0.85
         FRED       04-DEC-98  SODA                        1     $1.25
         FRED       04-DEC-98  FRENCH FRIES                1     $1.50
********                                                        --------
sum                                                             $11.60

     210 NANCY      04-DEC-98  SOUP OF THE DAY             1     $1.50
         NANCY      04-DEC-98  GRILLED STEAK               1     $6.00
         NANCY      04-DEC-98  COFFEE                      2     $1.70
         NANCY      04-DEC-98  DESSERT                     1     $3.00
********                                                        --------
sum                                                             $12.20


                                                               --------
sum                                                            $192.70
```

Figure 10-9   Reporting details, subtotals, and grand totals in Oracle

Reporting details, subtotals, and grand totals in Access

Access uses the Report Tab to create reports with details, subtotals, and grand totals. The first step is to use the Report Wizard to get a report that is close to the one you want. Then, you need to refine it to get exactly the report you want. I will only show you the Report Wizard part here, so the report will be only an approximation of what I want it to be. To finish it, I would have to add further refinements.

Within the Report Wizard, I choose to base the report on the "All_lunches" query, which is a saved query (also called a view.) This is where the SQL part meets the report features part. As in Oracle, the SQL part provides the detail. The report features part provides the subtotals and the grand totals.

The Report Wizard is supposed to be intuitive and easy to use. Generally, it is. However, since it is based on lots of graphics, it can be difficult to remember exactly what you have done or show it to other people. It is also easy to get lost in the process, not know where you are, and not have control over what is occurring. You have much more control with written code.

Here are the steps of the Report Wizard and the way the screen looks after each step.

Step 1. Press the REPORTS Tab.

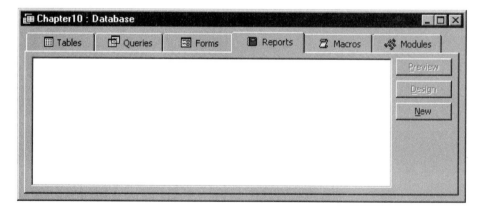

Step 2. Press the NEW button.

Step 3. Choose the REPORT WIZARD and enter "All_lunches" as the source of the data. Press the OK button.

Figure 10-10   Reporting details, subtotals, and grand totals in Access (part 1 of 5)

Step 4. Choose the columns for the report in the order you want them to appear on the report. I choose:

> Employee_id
> Lunch_date
> First_name
> Description
> Quantity
> Total_price

Report Wizard

Which fields do you want on your report?

You can choose from more than one table or query.

Tables/Queries:

Query: All_lunches

Available Fields:

department_name
lunch_id
supplier_id
product_code
description
price
price_increase
supplier_name

Selected Fields:

Employee_id
lunch_date
First_name
quantity
total_price

Cancel   < Back   Next >   Finish

Step 5. Press the NEXT button.

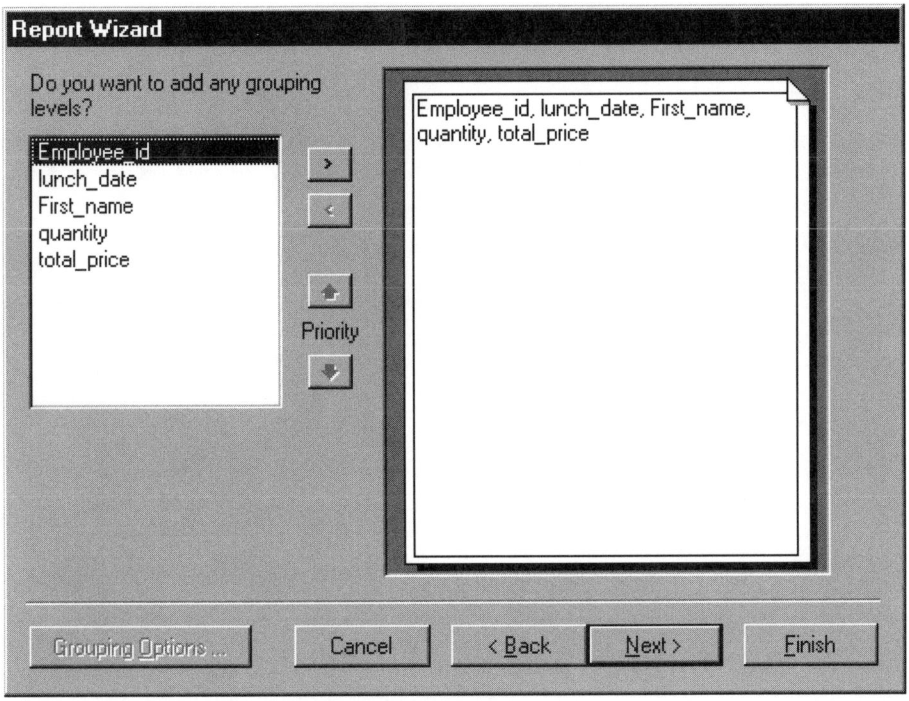

Figure 10-10 Reporting details, subtotals, and grand totals in Access (part 2 of 5)

Step 6. Choose the grouping levels for the report. Access will place them as the left-most columns of the report. I choose:

> Lunch_date
> Employee_id

Step 7. Press the NEXT button.

Step 8. Choose the fields for summary information. I choose Lunch_date.

Figure 10-10   Reporting details, subtotals, and grand totals in Access
(part 3 of 5)

Step 9. Press the SUMMARY OPTIONS button.

Step 10. Choose the summary functions. I choose to check the SUM box for Total_price.

Step 11. Press the OK button.

Step 12. Press the NEXT button.

Figure 10-10   Reporting details, subtotals, and grand totals in Access
(part 4 of 5)

Step 13. Press the NEXT button.

Step 14. I choose CORPORATE and press the NEXT button.

lunch_date by Month	*Employee_id*	*lunch_date*	*First_nam*	*quantity*	*total_price*
November 1998					
	201				
		11-16-1998	Susan	2	$7.00
		11-16-1998	Susan	2	$1.70
		11-16-1998	Susan	1	$2.00
		11-25-1998	Susan	1	$6.00
		11-25-1998	Susan	1	$2.00
		11-25-1998	Susan	1	$1.25
	Summary for 'Employee_id' = 201 (6 detail records)				
	Sum				19.95
	202				
		11-16-1998	Jim	2	$1.70
		11-16-1998	Jim	1	$1.50

Page: 1

Figure 10-10 Reporting details, subtotals, and grand totals in Access (part 5 of 5)

Spreadsheet reports

Reports that are like spreadsheets have one index column that goes across the page, instead of having all the index columns go down the page. Access calls these reports "cross-tab queries."

Of course, these reports are not spreadsheets. They do not have any active parts. They are reports, and that is all they are. Sometimes these reports are loaded into actual spreadsheets, such as Excel or Lotus 1-2-3. But, right now, I will just focus on the reports.

These reports can be much easier to read than a report that only goes down the page. But before I show you how to produce these reports, I want you to see an example of the difference between these two formats.

Database format and spreadsheet format

Suppose we have a table with two columns in the primary key. The spreadsheet format lists one of these columns horizontally and one vertically. The database format lists both of them vertically. Figure 10-11 shows an example of this using the alphabet:

Task

Show the difference between the database format for data and the spreadsheet format.

Database format

R_key	C_key	Letter
R1	C1	A
R1	C2	B
R1	C3	C
R1	C4	D
R2	C1	E
R2	C2	F
R2	C3	G
R2	C4	H
R3	C1	I
R3	C2	J
R3	C3	K
R3	C4	L
R4	C1	M
R4	C2	N
R4	C3	O
R4	C4	P
R5	C1	Q
R5	C2	R
R5	C3	S
R5	C4	T
R6	C1	U
R6	C2	V
R6	C3	W
R6	C4	X
R7	C1	Y
R7	C2	Z

Spreadsheet format

	C1	C2	C3	C4
R1	A	B	C	D
R2	E	F	G	H
R3	I	J	K	L
R4	M	N	O	P
R5	Q	R	S	T
R6	U	V	W	X
R7	Y	Z		

Figure 10-11   Database format and spreadsheet format

Creating a spreadsheet report in Oracle

This SQL code is a little tricky, so I want to explain it in two parts. The SQL only requires one single step, however it is too tricky to explain all at once.

In the first part of the explanation, all the letters are sorted into the correct columns. However, the number of rows is the same as the database format. This leaves a lot of extra "white space" on the report.

Part 1

To see how the letters get put in the correct columns, consider the first Decode function in the Select clause:

```
decode (c_key, 'c1', letter, '   ') as c1,
```

This Decode function creates a column on the report named "C1," which is one of the values of the C_KEY column.

For most rows of the result table, this column contains a space. The only exception is when the C_key column of the beginning table contains the value "C1." In that case, the value of the Letter column of the beginning table is placed in this column.

The same goes for all the other Decode functions. Note that you have to write a separate Decode function for every one of the possible values of the C_key column.

In general, you pick one column to go across the page. Then every possible value in that column must be coded as a separate Decode function. That may seem like a lot of work and sometimes it can be. But usually, the Decode function is coded once and then it is pasted as many times as it is needed. For each value in the column, a substitutions of that value is placed in one of the Decode statements. Essentially, the "C1" gets replace by "C2" on the next line, and by "C3" after that, and so on until all the possible values in the column have been used.

This is a good start. The columns are correct, but we need to reduce the number of rows. The only way to do this is to make this a summary report. We want the summary report to have more than one row, so we will need to group the rows together.

Task

Create a spreadsheet report from the alphabet table in Oracle using the Decode function.

In Oracle, we can use the Decode function to create a report in spreadsheet format. This is a little tricky, so we will do it two parts.

Part 1

Oracle SQL

```
select r_key,
       decode(c_key, 'c1', letter, ' ') as c1,
       decode(c_key, 'c2', letter, ' ') as c2,
       decode(c_key, 'c3', letter, ' ') as c3,
       decode(c_key, 'c4', letter, ' ') as c4
from alphabet_table
order by r_key;
```

Result table

R_KEY	C1	C2	C3	C4
R1	A			
R1		B		
R1			C	
R1				D
R2	E			
R2		F		
R2			G	
R2				H
R3	I			
R3		J		
R3			K	
R3				L
R4	M			
R4		N		
R4			O	
R4				P
R5	Q			
R5		R		
R5			S	
R5				T
R6	U			
R6		V		
R6			W	
R6				X
R7	Y			
R7		Z		

Figure 10-12   Creating a spreadsheet report in Oracle (part 1 of 2)

Part 2

Part 2 makes two additional changes to the SQL code. It adds a Group By clause shown in ❷ to summarize the result table. It summarizes the data, grouping it on the R_key column. The result of this is that there will be only a single row for each possible value of the R_key column. That is what we wanted to have.

But now it seems we have a slight problem. Remember, we cannot summarized data with data that is not summarized. Now the first column, R_key, is summarized data because it is listed in the Group By column. However, the other columns, the Decode functions, are not summarized. So, the query will not run.

To solve this problem, we add the MAX function to each Decode function, as in ❶. This summarizes all the values in the column to give the maximum value for each group. For instance,

```
R_KEY C1 C2 C3 C4
----- -- -- -- --
R1    A
R1       B
R1          C
R1             D
```

is turned into

```
R_KEY C1 C2 C3 C4
----- -- -- -- --
R1    A  B  C  D
```

because all the values in the C1 column, "A" and three spaces, are summarized to give the maximum value, which is "A." The same holds for all the other columns.

Part 2

Oracle SQL

```
-- create a spreadsheet report.
select r_key,
     max(decode(c_key, 'c1', letter, ' ')) as c1, ❶
     max(decode(c_key, 'c2', letter, ' ')) as c2,
     max(decode(c_key, 'c3', letter, ' ')) as c3,
     max(decode(c_key, 'c4', letter, ' ')) as c4
from alphabet_table
group by r_key ❷
order by r_key;
```

Result table

```
R_KEY C1 C2 C3 C4
----- -- -- -- --
R1    A  B  C  D
R2    E  F  G  H
R3    I  J  K  L
R4    M  N  O  P
R5    Q  R  S  T
R6    U  V  W  X
R7    Y  Z
```

Figure 10-12   Creating a spreadsheet report in Oracle (part 2 of 2)

Creating a spreadsheet report in Access

In Access, a spreadsheet report is called a "crosstab query." Access added two new clauses to the Select statement to support crosstab queries. These are extensions to standard SQL. They are "Transform" and "Pivot." Since these are not standard SQL, I will not explain them here. You can read about them in the Help files within Access.

Access has a wizard, called the "Crosstab Query Wizard" that can help you use these new clauses and create spreadsheet reports. You can use the wizard, then modify the SQL code if you desire.

Figure 10-13

❶   This "Transform" clause has the value "Max(Letter)." This is closely related to the Oracle SQL in figure 10-13. The summarization function MAX occurs in both places. And it is the maximum based on the value of the Letter column.

❷   The Select clause here does not account for the "extra columns" that will be spread across the page.

❸   This Group By clause is the same as the Oracle SQL in figure 10-12.

❹   The "Pivot" clause names the column that will be spread horizontally across the page.

Task

Create a spreadsheet report from the alphabet table using Access.

Access SQL

```
transform max(Letter) ❶
select r_key ❷
from alphabet_table
group by r_key ❸
pivot c_key; ❹
```

Result table

r_key	C1	C2	C3	C4
R1	A	B	C	D
R2	E	F	G	H
R3	I	J	K	L
R4	M	N	O	P
R5	Q	R	S	T
R6	U	V	W	X
R7	Y	Z		

Query1 : Crosstab Query

Record: ◄◄ ◄ 1 ► ►► ►* of 7

Figure 10-13   Creating a spreadsheet report in Access

Creating a spreadsheet report in Access using the IIF function

The purpose here is to show the similarity between the Decode function in Oracle and the IIF function in Access. You can compare this Access SQL code with the Oracle SQL in figure 10-12. They are very similar.

However, the best method to use in Access is the method in figure 10-13.

Task

Create a spreadsheet report from the alphabet table using the IIF function in Access.

Access SQL

```
select r_key,
     max(iif(c_key = 'c1', letter, ' ')) as c1,
     max(iif(c_key = 'c2', letter, ' ')) as c2,
     max(iif(c_key = 'c3', letter, ' ')) as c3,
     max(iif(c_key = 'c4', letter, ' ')) as c4
from alphabet_table
group by r_key
order by r_key;
```

Result table

r_key	c1	c2	c3	c4
R1	A	B	C	D
R2	E	F	G	H
R3	I	J	K	L
R4	M	N	O	P
R5	Q	R	S	T
R6	U	V	W	X
R7	Y	Z		

Record: 1 of 7

Figure 10-14   Creating a spreadsheet report in Access using the IIF function

Creating a spreadsheet report using a union

The Decode function and IIF function are not available in many SQL products. They are not a part of Standard SQL. How can you create a spreadsheet report without these functions or one like them?

It requires a little more work to write the SQL code, but it can be done using a Union. A view is created for each column of the spreadsheet. Each of these views also contains the index columns that will be displayed vertically down the page. As a final step, these views are pasted together with an outer join matching the columns that are displayed vertically down the page.

In this example, the outer join is shown in the Oracle format. There is no point in showing this example in Access format, because this coding technique is not usually used in either Oracle or Access. The techniques for Oracle and Access were shown in the previous figures. This shows the code that must be used with some other SQL products. With any product, you must use the syntax for the outer join that is used in that product.

Task

Create a spreadsheet report from the alphabet table using standard SQL.

Standard SQL
Step 1—Create a view for each column of the spreadsheet

```
create view column_c1 as
select r_key,
       letter
from alphabet_table
where c_key = 'c1';
```

Step 2

```
create view column_c2 as
select r_key,
       letter
from alphabet_table
where c_key = 'c2';
```

Step 3

```
create view column_c3 as
select r_key,
       letter
from alphabet_table
where c_key = 'c3';
```

Step 4

```
create view column_c4 as
select r_key,
       letter
from alphabet_table
where c_key = 'c4';
```

Step 5—Glue the separate columns together to create a spreadsheet report.

```
-- Standard SQL.
-- With outer joins in Oracle format.
-- Without the Decode or IIF functions.
--
-- Oracle SQLplus: set null format
set null ' '
--
```

—SQL

```
select a.r_key,
       a.letter as c1,
       b.letter as c2,
       c.letter as c3,
       d.letter as c4
from column_c1 a,
     column_c2 b,
     column_c3 c,
     column_c4 d
where a.r_key = b.r_key (+)
  and a.r_key = c.r_key (+)
  and a.r_key = d.r_key (+)
order by a.r_key;
```

Result table

```
R_KEY C1 C2 C3 C4
----- -- -- -- --
R1    A  B  C  D
R2    E  F  G  H
R3    I  J  K  L
R4    M  N  O  P
R5    Q  R  S  T
R6    U  V  W  X
R7    Y  Z
```

Figure 10-15   Creating a spreadsheet report using a union

Graphing one column against another

You can create many variations on a spreadsheet report. This figure shows one of them. Here data points are plotted using an X. One index column goes down the page. Another index column goes across the page. An X is placed where there is a data point relating the two columns. This creates a type of graph.

Notice that the result table does not show employee 209. That is because this employee is not attending any of the lunches and is not accounted for in the Lunches table. On the next page, I will correct this omission using an outer join with the Employees table, which does account for all the employees.

Beginning table (L_Lunches table)

LUNCH_ID	LUNCH DATE	EMPLOYEE ID
1	16-NOV-98	201
2	16-NOV-98	202
3	16-NOV-98	203
4	16-NOV-98	207
5	16-NOV-98	206
6	16-NOV-98	210
7	25-NOV-98	201
8	25-NOV-98	205
9	25-NOV-98	204
10	25-NOV-98	207
11	25-NOV-98	208
12	04-DEC-98	201
13	04-DEC-98	203
14	04-DEC-98	205
15	04-DEC-98	210
16	04-DEC-98	208

Task

From the Lunches table, plot the employees who attended each lunch. List the Employee Ids down the page and list the lunches across the page. Use an X to mark when an employee is attending a lunch.

Oracle column formats

```
column lunch_1 format a9
column lunch_2 format a9
column lunch_3 format a9
```

Oracle SQL

```
create view temp_1 as
select employee_id,
    max(decode(lunch_date, '16-nov-98', 'x', ' ')) as lunch_1,
    max(decode(lunch_date, '25-nov-98', 'x', ' ')) as lunch_2,
    max(decode(lunch_date, '04-dec-98', 'x', ' ')) as lunch_3
from l_lunches
group by employee_id;
```

Result table

```
EMPLOYEE
      ID LUNCH_1    LUNCH_2    LUNCH_3
-------- ---------- ---------- ----------
     201 X          X          X
     202 X
     203 X                     X
     204            X
     205            X          X
     206 X
     207 X          X
     208            X          X
     210 X                     X
```

Figure 10-16   Graphing one column against another (part 1 of 2)

Now we can correct the omission in the graph on the previous page and we can label the graph. The labels show the names of the employees and the dates of the lunches. The technique here adds the information from the Employees table to the graph.

Figure 10-16 (part 2)

❶   We outer join will create nulls. This command displays the nulls as blanks. Another method to do this would be to use the NVL function of each of the affected columns. For instance:

```
NVL (b.lunch_1, '   ')
```

But that method requires using the NVL function on several columns. This method is easier.

❷   These three commands set the column heading for the report. They label the dates of the lunches.

❸   The Employee Id column must get its data from the Employees table. The other table does have all the employees. This also applies to the two columns for the First Nmae and the Last Name.

❹   The columns that mark the lunches must come from the table created on the previous page. The Employees table does not have this information.

❺   The From clause must list both the Employees table and the graph created on the previous page. The purpose of this query is to combine the information from these two sources.

❻   The information must be combined with an outer join, since only the Employees table can list all the employees.

❼   In the result table, the missing employee is now shown.

Task

Add all the missing employees to the graph create on the previous page. Modify that graph to show all the employees. Also add labels to the graph to show the names of the employees and the dates of the lunches.

Oracle Environment command

```
set null '   '; ❶
column lunch_1 heading 'Lunch 1|Nov 16'; ❷
column lunch_2 heading 'Lunch 2|Nov 25';
column lunch_3 heading 'Lunch 3|Dec 4';
```

Oracle SQL

```
select a.employee_id, ❸
       a.first_name,
       a.last_name,
       b.lunch_1, ❹
       b.lunch_2,
       b.lunch_3
from l_employees a, ❺
     temp_1 b
where a.employee_id = b.employee_id (+); ❻
```

Result table

EMPLOYEE ID	FIRST_NAME	LAST_NAME	Lunch 1 Nov 16	Lunch 2 Nov 25	Lunch 3 Dec 4	
201	SUSAN	BROWN	X	X	X	
202	JIM	KERN	X			
203	MARTHA	WOODS	X		X	
204	ELLEN	OWENS		X		
205	HENRY	PERKINS		X	X	
206	CAROL	ROSE	X			
207	DAN	SMITH	X	X		
208	FRED	CAMPBELL		X	X	
209	PAULA	JACOBS				❼
210	NANCY	HOFFMAN	X		X	

Figure 10-16   Graphing one column against another (part 2 of 2)

Summary

In this chapter, you learned how to use the Decode and IIF functions. They can add if-then-else logic to queries. Sometimes, they can be used to make the code easier to write and to read. At other times, they can become too complex. Oracle and Access use a very different syntax, sometimes one is better than the other. But in other situations, the other syntax is better.

You also learned about parameter queries. These can add variables to the SQL code.

Having SQL work with another layer of software solved the problem of mixing summarized data with non-summarized data. The SQL layer provided all the details. The other software layer put spaces between the groups, calculated subtotals and grand totals.

According to the original design, that is an example of the way SQL is supposed to work. The idea was to make a division between the "information layer" of software and the "presentation layer." SQL was designed to handle the details and supply the information where and when it was needed. That is difficult enough. It is enough for one layer of the software to do.

Another layer of software would format the reports, number the pages, make the headings look nicer, print it on a special type of paper, and take care of all the other details to present the information well. This "division of labor" was intended to eliminate many errors in programs, make them more reliable, and easier to modify.

This is fine, so long as there is a clear distinction between the information and the presentation of that information. Spreadsheet reports show that this distinction is not always so clear. Sometimes the details do not speak for themselves. Sometimes information needs to be shown in a condensed format for people to grasp it and handle it easily.

Congratulations. You have now learned SQL and you can apply your knowledge to Oracle and Access and over 100 other products as well. You have seen their similarities and some of their differences. You may not need to use this knowledge right away, but in the next few years, you may find it is a good skill to have.

Index

Z

LICENSE AGREEMENT AND LIMITED WARRANTY

READ THE FOLLOWING TERMS AND CONDITIONS CAREFULLY BEFORE OPENING THIS SOFTWARE MEDIA PACKAGE. THIS LEGAL DOCUMENT IS AN AGREEMENT BETWEEN YOU AND PRENTICE-HALL, INC. (THE "COMPANY"). BY OPENING THIS SEALED SOFTWARE MEDIA PACKAGE, YOU ARE AGREEING TO BE BOUND BY THESE TERMS AND CONDITIONS. IF YOU DO NOT AGREE WITH THESE TERMS AND CONDITIONS, DO NOT OPEN THE SOFTWARE MEDIA PACKAGE. PROMPTLY RETURN THE UNOPENED SOFTWARE MEDIA PACKAGE AND ALL ACCOMPANYING ITEMS TO THE PLACE YOU OBTAINED THEM FOR A FULL REFUND OF ANY SUMS YOU HAVE PAID.

1. **GRANT OF LICENSE:** In consideration of your payment of the license fee, which is part of the price you paid for this product, and your agreement to abide by the terms and conditions of this Agreement, the Company grants to you a nonexclusive right to use and display the copy of the enclosed software program (hereinafter the "SOFTWARE") on a single computer (i.e., with a single CPU) at a single location so long as you comply with the terms of this Agreement. The Company reserves all rights not expressly granted to you under this Agreement.

2. **OWNERSHIP OF SOFTWARE:** You own only the magnetic or physical media (the enclosed SOFTWARE) on which the SOFTWARE is recorded or fixed, but the Company retains all the rights, title, and ownership to the SOFTWARE recorded on the original SOFTWARE copy(ies) and all subsequent copies of the SOFTWARE, regardless of the form or media on which the original or other copies may exist. This license is not a sale of the original SOFTWARE or any copy to you.

3. **COPY RESTRICTIONS:** This SOFTWARE and the accompanying printed materials and user manual (the "Documentation") are the subject of copyright. You may not copy the Documentation or the SOFTWARE, except that you may make a single copy of the SOFTWARE for backup or archival purposes only. You may be held legally responsible for any copying or copyright infringement which is caused or encouraged by your failure to abide by the terms of this restriction.

4. **USE RESTRICTIONS:** You may not network the SOFTWARE or otherwise use it on more than one computer or computer terminal at the same time. You may physically transfer the SOFTWARE from one computer to another provided that the SOFTWARE is used on only one computer at a time. You may not distribute copies of the SOFTWARE or Documentation to others. You may not reverse engineer, disassemble, decompile, modify, adapt, translate, or create derivative works based on the SOFTWARE or the Documentation without the prior written consent of the Company.

5. **TRANSFER RESTRICTIONS:** The enclosed SOFTWARE is licensed only to you and may not be transferred to any one else without the prior written consent of the Company. Any unauthorized transfer of the SOFTWARE shall result in the immediate termination of this Agreement.

6. **TERMINATION:** This license is effective until terminated. This license will terminate automatically without notice from the Company and become null and void if you fail to comply with any provisions or limitations of this license. Upon termination, you shall destroy the Documentation and all copies of the SOFTWARE. All provisions of this Agreement as to warranties, limitation of liability, remedies or damages, and our ownership rights shall survive termination.

7. **MISCELLANEOUS:** This Agreement shall be construed in accordance with the laws of the United States of America and the State of New York and shall benefit the Company, its affiliates, and assignees.

8. **LIMITED WARRANTY AND DISCLAIMER OF WARRANTY:** The Company warrants that the SOFTWARE, when properly used in accordance with the Documentation, will operate in substantial conformity with the description of the SOFTWARE set forth in the Documentation. The Company does not warrant that the SOFTWARE will meet your requirements or that the operation of the SOFTWARE will be uninterrupted or error-free. The Company warrants that the

media on which the SOFTWARE is delivered shall be free from defects in materials and workmanship under normal use for a period of thirty (30) days from the date of your purchase. Your only remedy and the Company's only obligation under these limited warranties is, at the Company's option, return of the warranted item for a refund of any amounts paid by you or replacement of the item. Any replacement of SOFTWARE or media under the warranties shall not extend the original warranty period. The limited warranty set forth above shall not apply to any SOFTWARE which the Company determines in good faith has been subject to misuse, neglect, improper installation, repair, alteration, or damage by you. EXCEPT FOR THE EXPRESSED WARRANTIES SET FORTH ABOVE, THE COMPANY DISCLAIMS ALL WARRANTIES, EXPRESS OR IMPLIED, INCLUDING WITHOUT LIMITATION, THE IMPLIED WARRANTIES OF MERCHANTABILITY AND FITNESS FOR A PARTICULAR PURPOSE. EXCEPT FOR THE EXPRESS WARRANTY SET FORTH ABOVE, THE COMPANY DOES NOT WARRANT, GUARANTEE, OR MAKE ANY REPRESENTATION REGARDING THE USE OR THE RESULTS OF THE USE OF THE SOFTWARE IN TERMS OF ITS CORRECTNESS, ACCURACY, RELIABILITY, CURRENTNESS, OR OTHERWISE.

IN NO EVENT, SHALL THE COMPANY OR ITS EMPLOYEES, AGENTS, SUPPLIERS, OR CONTRACTORS BE LIABLE FOR ANY INCIDENTAL, INDIRECT, SPECIAL, OR CONSEQUENTIAL DAMAGES ARISING OUT OF OR IN CONNECTION WITH THE LICENSE GRANTED UNDER THIS AGREEMENT, OR FOR LOSS OF USE, LOSS OF DATA, LOSS OF INCOME OR PROFIT, OR OTHER LOSSES, SUSTAINED AS A RESULT OF INJURY TO ANY PERSON, OR LOSS OF OR DAMAGE TO PROPERTY, OR CLAIMS OF THIRD PARTIES, EVEN IF THE COMPANY OR AN AUTHORIZED REPRESENTATIVE OF THE COMPANY HAS BEEN ADVISED OF THE POSSIBILITY OF SUCH DAMAGES. IN NO EVENT SHALL LIABILITY OF THE COMPANY FOR DAMAGES WITH RESPECT TO THE SOFTWARE EXCEED THE AMOUNTS ACTUALLY PAID BY YOU, IF ANY, FOR THE SOFTWARE.

SOME JURISDICTIONS DO NOT ALLOW THE LIMITATION OF IMPLIED WARRANTIES OR LIABILITY FOR INCIDENTAL, INDIRECT, SPECIAL, OR CONSEQUENTIAL DAMAGES, SO THE ABOVE LIMITATIONS MAY NOT ALWAYS APPLY. THE WARRANTIES IN THIS AGREEMENT GIVE YOU SPECIFIC LEGAL RIGHTS AND YOU MAY ALSO HAVE OTHER RIGHTS WHICH VARY IN ACCORDANCE WITH LOCAL LAW.

ACKNOWLEDGMENT

YOU ACKNOWLEDGE THAT YOU HAVE READ THIS AGREEMENT, UNDERSTAND IT, AND AGREE TO BE BOUND BY ITS TERMS AND CONDITIONS. YOU ALSO AGREE THAT THIS AGREEMENT IS THE COMPLETE AND EXCLUSIVE STATEMENT OF THE AGREEMENT BETWEEN YOU AND THE COMPANY AND SUPERSEDES ALL PROPOSALS OR PRIOR AGREEMENTS, ORAL, OR WRITTEN, AND ANY OTHER COMMUNICATIONS BETWEEN YOU AND THE COMPANY OR ANY REPRESENTATIVE OF THE COMPANY RELATING TO THE SUBJECT MATTER OF THIS AGREEMENT.

Should you have any questions concerning this Agreement or if you wish to contact the Company for any reason, please contact in writing at the address below.

Robin Short
Prentice Hall PTR
One Lake Street
Upper Saddle River, New Jersey 07458

How to Use the CD-ROM

The CD-ROM contains all the tables of data used in this book. There is a separate file for each chapter. All the data is available in both Oracle and Access formats.

The Oracle files are scripts that need to be run in the SQL Plus environment. Instructions to start this environment are at the end of chapter one. Each script cleans the userid, creates the tables you will need for that chapter, and sets up a standard working environment. You should use one of these scripts every time you start to use Oracle because the environmental settings last for only one session. As soon as you exit Oracle, the environmental settings are gone. For example, to run the script for chapter two, you enter the command:

```
START    Z:\ORACLE\CHAPTER2.SQL
```

Substitute the letter assigned to your CD-ROM drive for the letter Z in this command. The command can be entered in upper or lower case letters. After you run the script, you should reset the buffer width to 300 from the Options pull-down menu. If it is already set to 300, then reset it to 301.

The Access databases are ready to be used. However, you must copy them onto your disk drive, so that you have read/write access to them. You should create a new directory for these databases. Then you can use Explorer to drag a file, such as:

```
Z:\Access 97\Chapter2.mdb
```

to the directory you created.

Before you open the database, you must reset the "Read-only" property. To do this:

Use Explorer
Right-click on the file on your hard drive, such as "Chapter2.mdb"
Choose Properties
Uncheck the Read-only box
Press the OK button

Now the database is ready for you to use. You can open it from within Access or you can double-click on it from Explorer.

Note: This CD-ROM is not compatible with Windows 3.1.

Technical Support

Prentice Hall does not offer technical support for this software. However, if there is a problem with the media, you may obtain a replacement copy by emailing us with your problem at:
discexchange@phptr.com